Transfigurations

Transfigurations

Violence, Death and Masculinity in American Cinema

Asbjørn Grønstad

AMSTERDAM UNIVERSITY PRESS

Front cover illustration: Still from the movie AMERICAN PSYCHO (2000), starring Christian Bale

Cover design: Kok Korpershoek, Amsterdam
Lay-out: JAPES, Amsterdam

ISBN   978 90 8964 010 9 (paperback)
ISBN   978 90 8964 030 7 (hardcover)
NUR   674

Contents

Acknowledgments

Academic work rarely takes place in a void, and over the course of the research-ing and writing of this text I have incurred many debts to a number of institu-tions and individuals. The Faculty of Arts, University of Bergen, made this re-search possible by providing me first with a two-month research grant (1997-1998) to write a thesis proposal, and then with a four-year stipend (1999-2002) to write the dissertation that became the basis of this book. I also wish to thank the Fulbright Foundation for a grant that enabled me to spend the 1998-1999 academic year at the University of Wisconsin-Madison's excellent research facil-ities; the Norway-America Association and the Norwegian Research Council, whose grants facilitated subsequent visits to Madison; the L. Meltzers Høyskolefond for numerous grants which allowed me to present material from the dissertation at various international conferences; the Department of Com-munication Arts, University of Wisconsin-Madison, for assisting me in every way during my many sojourns there; and last but not least, the English Depart-ment, for always being so cooperative and accommodating. Thanks are also due to the Wisconsin Center for Film and Theater Research; UW-M's Memorial Library; and, above all, the University Library in Bergen, whose staff members have been immensely perseverant in putting up with my seemingly never-end-ing loan requests. A second thank you to the Norwegian Research Council for generously providing me with a publication grant for this project.

Several friends and colleagues have at various stages contributed valuable commentary to parts of the manuscript. My warmest thanks go to Ruben Moi, Øyvind Vågnes, Øyunn Hestetun, Orm Øverland, Charles Armstrong, Lene Jo-hannesen, Anne Holden Rønning, Andrew Kennedy, Randi Koppen, Janne Sti-gen Drangsholt, and Michael Prince for their input. For their helpful sugges-tions I am also grateful to the many scholars I have met at conferences in Europe and in the United States, particularly the participants at the conferences "Nordic Film Theory at the Turn of the Millenium" in Copenhagen in December 1999 and the "East-West American Studies Conference" held at the Johann Wolfgang Goethe-Universität in Frankfurt in May 2001.

My work has also benefited from conversations with David Bordwell, Per Persson, Panayiota Mini, Eija Niskanen, Erik Hedling, Torben Grodal, and Adriana Neagu. I also owe special thanks to Nick Browne and Anne Jerslev for their careful reading of the manuscript and for articulating their criticism so elegantly and constructively during my doctoral defense in December 2003. I am also grateful to my co-advisor Peter Larsen for his productive observations and incisive insights.

Since I joined the Department of Information Science and Media Studies in 2005, I have much enjoyed its convivial environment and the many stimulating discussions with my friends and colleagues there.

I would also like to thank Thomas Elsaesser for his judicious reading of the manuscript and for suggesting alterations to it that proved to be composition-ally significant. I am greatly indebted to my editor at Amsterdam University Press and to its staff – Jaap Wagenaar, Jeroen Sondervan, Marieke Soons, Anniek Meinders, Randy Lemaire, and Magdalena Hernas – for their excellent work and efficiency. Kristian Jensen also deserves thanks for making the indices for me.

A very special thank you goes to Željka Švrljuga, mentor, colleague and friend, for her unflinching encouragement, boundless patience, and inestimable guidance.

Finally, my deepest thanks go to my friends and family, my parents Liv-Tor-unn og John Grønstad for their constant support and encouragement, and my dear Stephanie and Sunniva, for making the days radiant.

Some segments of this book have been previously published in abridged or slightly different versions. Chapter 4 has been published as "Mean Streets: Death and Disfiguration in Hawks's *Scarface*," in *Nordic Journal of English Studies*, 2.2 (2003). Chapter 7 has appeared as "As I Lay Dying: Violence and Subjectivity in Tarantino's *Reservoir Dogs*," in Karen Patrick Knutsen, Elin Nesje, and Eva Lambertsson Bjørk, eds. *Modi Operandi*. Høgskolen i Østfold, 2003, and a version of chapter 8 has been published as "One-Dimensional Men: *Fight Club* and the Poetics of the Body," in *Film Criticism* 28.1 (2003). I thank the anonymous referees for helpful suggestions and the editors for the permission to reuse the material.

Prolegomenon

Please note:
This exhibition contains extremely graphic and violent images, which may offend
some viewers
Poster outside the Porter Butts Gallery, Memorial Union

One day during one of my field trips to the University of Wisconsin-Madison, I went to the Memorial Union's Porter Butts Gallery to see an exhibition called "Representations of Violence: Art of the Sierra Leonean Civil War." Consisting overwhelmingly of atrocious images, the works on display – nearly all of which were by young Sierra Leonean artists – transmitted a Boschian sense of horror whose lingering impression did not cease to repulse the spectator. Moses Silma's "Kamajors Attack on Koribondo" (2001) and "The Bo-Freetown Highway Ambush" (2002), and Ayo Peters's "January 6, 1999 Invasion" (1999) rendered in a fashion suggestive of comic-book graphics the mutilation and torture of civilian Leonean men, women, and children by the Revolutionary United Front (RUF). At that stage of my book project I had already interrogated and abandoned, examined and rejected a number of theories on the topic of both actual and artistic forms of violence, though my sole emphasis throughout has been on the latter. So, could it be that the caveat at the gallery's entrance, quoted epigraphically at the top of this page, was also intended for someone who in a moment that in retrospect seems oddly foolhardy had decided to research a subject as elusive and recalcitrant as screen violence? Was I among the viewers offended by this exhibition's images? The pictures appalled me more than anything I can recall having seen, except for perhaps the first twenty minutes of Gaspar Noé's IRRÉVERSIBLE (2002).

But for all the unpleasantness of my gallery tour I found the encounter strangely rewarding, not necessarily in and of itself, but because of its experiential adjacency to the viewing of another work of art that had captured my attention only days before. This was Carlos Saura's metafictional musical TANGO (1998), a sumptuous yet minimalist homage to the gracefulness of the Argentinean dance. I was particularly drawn to a sequence near the end, where the filmmaker within the film stages a theatrical, expressionistic ballet that references the misdeeds of Jorge Rafael Videla's dictatorship in a coloramic choreography whose preternatural movements seemed to truncate the space between violence and art. I was reminded of the popular belief that the sequences of steps that evolved into the tango allegedly were a derivation of the knife-wielding postural violence of the patrons of the brothels and bars of late 19th-century Buenos Aires.[1] If the balletic convulsions of BONNIE AND CLYDE (1967) and THE WILD BUNCH (1969) could be described as dances of death by proxy, the tango ballet that was the climax of Saura's film was a far more literal, yet at the same time no less figural dance of death. Somehow I sensed a connection, an amorphous similarity, between the Saurian performance and those of Arthur Penn and Sam Peckinpah. I also read that, according to Paula Ponga (153), Videla's henchmen would play loud tango music as they tortured their victims. Pondering what increasingly appeared to be the indissolubility of poetics and cruelty in Saura's narrative, I became aware of the emblematic expediency of the tango as a metaphor for the enigmatically intertwined phenomena of aesthetics and violence, imagination and destruction, desire and revulsion, narrative and spectacle, ethics and form. Here was a sequence of film that sublimated these contradictions, that not only made violence aesthetic but the aesthetic violent. I can think of no more apposite term for this numinous process than transfiguration.

Enraptured by the film yet repelled by the exhibition, the peculiar incongruity of my response to these two artifacts elicited further questions. I began to re-contemplate *Representations of Violence*. Armed with a notebook, a pencil, a laptop, and finally even a camera, I revisited the gallery for a second and then a third time. The more I scrutinized the pictures the less I came to like them. I was furthermore struck by a tacit inconsistency in the gallery's contextualization of these images and their historical background. The Sierra Leonean civil war that lasted throughout the 1990s had claimed fifty thousand lives, and the expressed purposes of both the artists and the curators were evidently to document the terrors of this violence and to commemorate its victims. Posted by the gallery's entry was the exhibitors' message which announced that their intention was to "raise awareness and encourage empathy" with the afflicted. If the objective of this exposition is at the core epistemological and ethical, which I do not for a moment query, why is it introduced by such a direct, extra-textual address to the prospective viewers, one that no doubt will deter scores of patrons from attending the exhibition? How can you raise awareness if nobody is present? The first and third time I went, both on late Saturday mornings, I was the only visitor in the gallery; the second time there were two other visitors beside myself. Each time I went I stayed for close to an hour. When I left the third time, I took the poster down; an irresponsible indulgence and an act of public vandalism, perhaps, but the absence of any such commentary would anneal the integrity of the curators' intentions. Though I remain fully aware not only of the social convention but of the legal incentive of appending such a word of warning to works of art that may be controversial, the practice tends to overlook the imperative to be seen by a viewer that every ethical image requires. What the text that I so promptly removed unfortunately neglected is that one cannot *not* be offended by these images; in fact, in their capacity to offend the audience lies the affirmation of the moral value of the artworks. The caveat, therefore, should have said something along the lines of "[t]his exhibition contains extremely graphic and violent images, which nevertheless may not offend some viewers." Am I being frivolous? I do not think so. Considering the realities of the events that these images are the memory of, I believe it would be deeply unethical not to have the audacity to be offended, if only for a little while.

Irrespective of their medial and generic differences, the *Representations of Violence* exhibition and the Saura film share with all other narratives of violence a metatextual awareness of the problems that attend their own readings. They not only invite interrogation but request that the viewers, in turn, interrogate their own methods for relating to the texts. I am certainly not proposing that the subject of fictional violence has a special purchase on this process, but in a time when, as Murray Krieger (208) pointed out not long ago, aesthetic texts seem to affect us less and less and reading has increasingly become a matter of Pavlovian appropriations of hegemonic theory, we may need offensive artists like Noé, Michael Haneke, or David Fincher to shatter the lull. Examining the pictures in the Porter Butts Gallery did little to abrogate my suspicion of the interpretive assumptions and approaches that I refer to as fallacies in the first part of this text. I wondered what new insights could possibly be had from an empirical cataloguing of the heinous acts of torture that recur in the photographs; I then wondered if and how one could claim that mainstream movie mayhem should be treated any differently. Aristotelianism, moreover, seemed even more parochial than I had long suspected it to be in terms of its explanatory riches in the field of violence. In the face of images such as Michael P. Silma's OPERATION NO VIRGIN (1999), the time-honored concepts of pity and fear, purgation and purification represented not so much a theory of viewer response as a perversion, an insult to the work of theory itself. I thought of the grand mythological rationalizations of violence by scholars such as Richard Slotkin and René Girard and how they had always appeared to labor to make the materiality and contextuality of violence into something abstract and universal. Then there remain what for me are the most salient questions, which orbit around the unwieldy but interlaced problems of aesthetics, mimesis, fictionality, form, and ethics, to name a few. When they write about violence, some film critics become easily enamored of the notion of aestheticization, a terminological decoy which, like the social scientist's conscientious classification of types of violence,[2] does much to vitiate the quality of our reflection on narrative violence. While it is not difficult to imagine scenes from TANGO being praised for their "aestheticization" of violence, few would have the inappropriate temerity to invoke that same term with reference to the paintings in the Memorial Union Gallery. I shall leave the implications of this discrepancy to my discussion of the aesthetic fallacy in chapter one.

Finally, the Sierra Leone exhibition signals in its very title what is perhaps the overriding theoretical concern in the pages to follow, the validity of the notion of the mimetic for the analysis and comprehension of violent images. Mediated through discursive means that are both narrative, figural and political, violence itself becomes interpretive – Ronald Bogue and Marcel Cornis-Pope (6) have suggested –, and therefore cannot be representational, at least not purely so. If the ensuing argument contributes to a keener awareness of the plasticity of aesthetic violence, a key purpose shall be fulfilled.

Introduction: Film Violence as Figurality

This book explores the figuration of screen violence, as well as its historical and institutional contexts,[1] in a number of metaviolent films both celebrated and vilified, and attempts thereby to forge a new understanding of a phenomenon whose defining feature seems to be perpetually elusive. As *Transfigurations* grapples with a series of issues that at times may seem only tenuously interrelated, I shall here take the liberty to summarize and pinpoint its major preoccupation. The objective is to re-establish an awareness of the transtextual opacity of film fiction, an awareness long occluded both by theoretical fallacies and by the petrification of our acquired ways of seeing. Films that narrate violence have provided me with a method by which to pursue this examination, though other textual taxonomies would doubtlessly also have been valuable. The attraction of using screen violence in a critique of the mimetic is in part rhetorical (the desire to show that processes of textualization determine even the immediacy of spectacle, that "strongest possible expression of certain themes" that is corporeal destruction (Stein 40)), in part thematic (the conceptual proximity of violence and death to the notion of mimesis and writing in an extended sense). Questions regarding representation seem to accrue to the subject of violence more acutely than they do to other matters. Black, for instance, notes that "[n]owhere has the blurring of fiction and reality occasioned more confusion and controversy than in the media's depiction of violence" (Black 111). The act of violence in the cinema is an event that, like Barthes's punctum, pierces the viewer. In the sense that violence often punctures, or punctuates, the image (consider the slicing of the nostril in CHINATOWN, or the shooting of the bank clerk in BONNIE AND CLYDE), it also seems to pierce the process of narration itself, marking it off as a special instance of signification.

More than any other subject, violence italicizes the figurality of film form and discloses its artificiality. For the audience there is more at stake when it comes to the depiction of violence; they demand signs of its fictionality, and on the fringes of their desire there is a discernment of the fundamental separateness of aesthetic form from everyday experience. Because it so obdurately intercepts the experience of aesthetic pleasure, violence is also constitutive of a moment of ethical intervention in the flow of reading or viewing. More than perhaps any other textual event, violence makes us aware of our own act of watching. And no less importantly, violent images tend to produce autopoeticity, metafigural statements that make the modes of the amimetic palpable.

As is so often the case, the identification of the inaugural moment of a theoretical inquiry seems to be the recognition of a deficiency; from negativity emerge gestures of epistemic contestation. My limning of the trends and approaches that have influenced critical work in the area of screen violence evolves as a response to that lack, or insufficiency, that is integral to all of them. Whether empirical or mythological, the fallacies discussed below are hampered by what I would term a pre-textual consciousness. Impeded by their understanding of the image as a screen rather than a figuration, they never really discern film's filmicity. To remain oblivious to the opacity of the image is also to be unaware of its persistent textuality. This is how a social scientist sees only violence where she should have seen *filmic* violence, and though her agendas vary, the Aristotelianist, the aesthetic, the mythologist and the mimeticist follow suit. Rather than recapitulate the specific problems that beleaguer each individual approach, I want instead to address what may be shown to be their shared, collective fallacy – their unstated, unreflective subscription to a defunct notion of representation that is untenable even with reference to a putatively realist medium such as film.[2] Russell (220) has suggested that "[a]ny critique of violence must first come to terms with the techniques of realist representation that the media exploits," but far more urgently, a critique of violence must start from the realization that representationality in film fiction is actually the problem.[3] Because films are *not* transparent, they cannot imitate.

What should be acknowledged, then, is the inadequacy of considering "violence" as a critical object without the support of some kind of theory of visuality, viewing, and film aesthetics. As it turns out, ruminations on the interconnectedness of text and theory, visuality and writing, or reading and interpretation are legion, though there is a sense in which the panoply of reflections on these relations demands to be refracted through a coherent lens. The chiasmus of *theory film* (as a counterpart rather than as an opposition to film theory) provides us with a metadiscursive concept that condenses a host of inter-related ideas that all seem to converge in the perception that aesthetic texts themselves may be constitutive of theoretical thought.

The key theoretical idioms that nourish my argument throughout – narrathanatography, the *amimetic*, the tropological, *transtextuality*, and poethics – are all somehow attached to the notion of *figural cinema/figural violence*.[4] There are two important issues that crystallize in the notion of the figural. First, visual forms may be *autopoetical*, or capable of producing new concepts on a par with, but nevertheless different from, linguistic concepts.[5] In short, images may engender thought (fig. 1), or in fact be a mode of thought (an idea the elaboration of which forms the substance of Gilles Deleuze's two cinema books).[6] The other issue that the figural addresses is the reciprocal relation between the theoretical text and the aesthetic work. In symbolic terms, the indeterminate quality of the figural dispels the logocentric crust whose function it is to keep the language of theory uncontaminated by the visuality of the filmic text (or the reverse, if one is so inclined). The figural is the promise of having theory and film transform each other in the same reading.

Fig. 1. "'Whatever else it may be, cinema is primarily a thinking practice, a singular form of thought'" (Casarino 148). Mario Suarez, the filmmaker in Saura's Tango, *contemplates a segment from Lucas Demare's 1955 film* Mercado de abasto. *Reproduction from DVD set.*

The turn to figurality, which substantiates another significant phase in the exploration of a new poetics of visual culture, promises both a sublation of logocentrism that goes beyond deconstruction and a new semiotic epistemology founded in the image. But this is of course at the same time the beginning of another set of thorny questions, because, even though one has attributed the faculty of thought to pictures,[7] it remains open to discussion *how* they think and, furthermore, how we write about the way they think. For the notion of the theory film to make any sense, however, one must be prepared to dispose of the routine manners in which one conceptualizes theory itself, since films do not normally evince the kind of logic where arguments follow upon an initial proposition and so on. For this reason, it may be that the pursuit of the figural leads us into not only post-semiotic but even post-hermeneutic landscapes of interpretation. Designed to fill the semiotic vacancies of linguistic speech, cinema

comes to theory from the allegorical. Boris Eikhenbaum once referred to film as
"a special system of allegory" (28),[8] and transtextuality – or transcinematicity –
is a vital manifestation of what may be grasped as a visual tropology. Most
films refer to other texts, thereby already adding to that "intractable opacity of
the visible" that is the work of the figural (Rodowick, *Reading the Figural* 6).
Thus, a provisional answer to the question of how film might generate this visual discourse of the figural and of the metapictorial would be that we can ap-
preciate how films "think" and "do" theory by starting with an analysis of how
they rework quotations and tropes. As will later become apparent, my reading
of the film texts will to a certain extent foreground their calorific allusiveness.

But we should be cautious not to forget that the image is not only a cartogra-
phy of quotations; that is, the image is not just an object or something seen but
is at the same time something which sees, a gaze. An image is at once a sight
and a process of seeing, a position that immediately re-positions itself. One implication of this strange redoubling is that the (inter)textual object framed can
never really be considered apart from the spatial and rhetorical positionality of
the glance of which it is a trace. By investigating the possibility of a different
type of vision "capable of seeing something other than what is given to be
seen" (Silverman 227), Kaja Silverman's THRESHOLD OF THE VISIBLE WORLD fur-
nishes my argument with a theoretical passageway between the idea of a tropology of cinema and the claim that film (and film violence in particular) is a
way of seeing amimetically. What I mean to suggest is that Eikhenbaum's "special system of allegory," going beyond even the transtextual, is recuperative of a
theoretical imagination which does not so much reflect the world as re-consti-
tute it.

Aesthetic figurations, which is to say the figural, unveil the sedulous, material
density of the image. To scrape away its ostensible layers is unfeasible; there is
nothing, no other world, beyond its ocular thickness. A film image, Bellour (24)
helpfully reminds us, is a sign situated "half-way between the semi-transpar-
ency of written titles and dialogue and the more or less complete opacity of
music and noise." That the history of mainstream filmmaking has persistently
staged the occlusion of the image's opacity does not detract from its resiliently
material being. Trope and allegory at its disposal, film is the transfiguration of
physical reality. As Eikhenbaum (9) points out, art merely uses the phenomenal
world as pretext and material, "to which it gives an unexpected interpretation
or a new arrangement in some blatantly deformed or 'grotesque' aspect." Mimesis, and our received ideas of representation defined by it, is incommensurate
with the allegorical. No art is *really* mimetic (film perhaps least of all); Paul de
Man (*Resistance*10) suggests that mimesis in fact is only "one trope among
others," one that is as susceptible to historical variability as texts themselves
(Hansen 196). By re-thinking mimesis as a trope, de Man thereby does not see it

as an effect but as a feature of signification. To characterize any given film as mimetic, accordingly, would simply be to emphasize the formal dominance of that particular trope over others. The work of Harmony Korine, for instance, may in this sense of the word be more "mimetic" than that of Joel Coen.

Where Rodowick posits the figural as the epitome of a neoaesthetic logic of signification, I propose to append the prefix *trans* to denote the process which brings together the allegorical (self)-theorizing of cinematic ideation with the poetic ritualization of violence, death and aberrant forms of masculinity. Johannes H. Birringer pictures the transfigurative as a "search for pure forms which can transcend the objective, concrete world and all *representational ballast* that suggests and reminds us of the very contingency and impermanence of this world" (140, emphasis added).[9] Transfiguration is the general principle which subsumes the amimetic and the allegorical, thus permitting the utterance of violence as aesthetic form.

Due to its conceptual contiguity with mortality, violence is the privileged conveyor of film's figural opacity. Stewart holds that filmic death "often finds itself figured as the moment when textuality erupts from beneath mimesis" (*Between* 152). Another way of putting this would be to claim that the "representation" of death and violence is what makes us most easily aware of the amimetic ontology of film fiction. Why this is the case has to do with the inaccessibility of the phenomena in question:

> Just as the literary death scene tends both to evince and ultimately to characterize death in figurative terms – as the moment when all subjective representation turns metaphoric, there being no worldly referents left for mimetic report – so film tends not just to render but to *define* death in specifically cinematic (hence metatextual) terms. (Stewart, *Between* 164, emphasis in original)

Before becoming a metaphor proper, violence is thus already an allegory of the impermissibility of straightforward, transparent readings. Though Stewart's involvement is with aesthetic death, not violence, his inference seems no less apposite for the figurative function of the latter. As a matter of fact, his thesis is vaguely redolent of Joel Black's assertion in *The Aesthetics of Murder* (1991) that "[l]iterary narratives or films that describe murder in a manner that evokes an aesthetic response in the reader or viewer are actually metafictions – works of art about art" (40).

My readings of selected films by Hawks, Kubrick, Peckinpah, Tarantino, and Fincher will attempt to illuminate how the transfigural works to parlay violence into a theorization of film form, narrative temporality, death, masculinity and ethics. The transitions between these readings are deliberately loose, and I prefer to look upon them as separate, self-contained excursions – or "essayistic forays," to borrow a phrase from Mitchell (Wiesenthal and Bucknell 5) – which tap into and try to tease out the distinctive kind of theoretical discourse that violent films embody. Hawks's mise en scène at the beginning of SCARFACE parlays this principle of opacity that I will labor to expound in what follows. As I note in my chapter on the film, Hawks infuses his images with a sense of abstraction, a tendency most fully realized in the scene in which Camonte slays Costillo. Favoring contour over texture, Hawks films the killing through a window panel, thus adding an extra screen interpose between the camera and the event. With realism dissipating before our eyes, the anatomy of the configuration imparts an incomparably apt visualization of the theoretical premise that the screen is never innocent, and always non-transparent. Hawks's metapictorial image at once instantiates a visual counterpart to Riffaterre's distinctive understanding of subtext as "texts within the text that are neither subplots nor themes but diegetic pieces whose sole function is to be vehicles of symbolism" (*Fictional Truth* xvii). SCARFACE's subtext, in this respect, is classical cinema's repression of the violated body; in THE WILD BUNCH, it is the theorization of an ethics of looking, embodied in the image of the children in the Starbuck sequence who watch in gleeful horror at the carnage wrought by the bunch and Harrigan's bounty hunters.

There is another dimension to the theory of the amimetic that I have not yet paid proper attention to, that is its repercussions for a pedagogy of the visual. A concept such as opacity is not merely a contribution to a specialized discourse on the ontology of filmicity – though I do not deny that there is a measure of that too feeding into my argument – it also serves a less abstrusely philosophical end in its insinuation of a different hermeneutics of viewing. One does not need to be a follower of the likes of Debord or Baudrillard to recognize the degree to which the relation between the world and its image has largely become inverted. Not only does the materiality of fiction not represent what we still tend to refer to as the real, which I would maintain it has never done anyway, but that fiction, or textuality, is increasingly imposing its aesthetic regime on the site of the everyday. The work of modern writers and filmmakers, Black writes, has subverted "the classical idea of mimesis ... to the point where being and appearance, ethics and aesthetics, are no longer distinguishable, but have become virtual simulacra of each other" (*Aesthetics* 16).[10] A decade later, in *The Reality Effect* (2002), he proposes, without even a hint of sensationalism, that the new media and recording techniques have transformed reality itself, which has shrunk to "anything that is filmable" (8). If Black's postulation that the only thing left unreal is the unseen is correct (*Reality Effect* 10), his directive that "[m]ore than ever, film audiences are in need ... of a code of cinematic literacy that will allow them to maintain a healthy skepticism in the face of ever more spectacular effects" appears more than timely (19). A theory of filmic non-transparency may offer at least a conceptual foundation for a visual ethics of suspicion that can insure and sustain a vigorous critique of the environment of postreality.

Once the amimetic nature of cinematic fiction has been established as a theoretical prolegomenon for an inquiry into the discourse and aesthetics of violence, space has been cleared for a reflection on the features and modes of the amimetic. I have come to the conclusion that the tradition of seeing (or reading) mimetologically can best be replaced by a method of seeing tropologically. By tropology I not only mean a system of more or less fixed visual metaphors, but also more broadly a set of formal conventions, a uniquely cinematic texture, even a particular way of looking that is opposed to the duplication or repetition of what already is. The impulse or attitude which produces this particular way of looking is what I would call transfigurative. As James Elkins has suggested, seeing is a dual process which changes not only the nature of what is seen, Heisenberg-style, but also the one who does the seeing (*Object* 12). In thinking through the implications of this argument and in questioning its underlying assumptions, I trust that the reader will recall T.E. Hulme's aphoristic but instructive reminder that if fiction "did really resemble life, it would be interminable, dreary" (58). I am certainly willing to accept the criticism that the deconstruction of the mimetic has been undertaken many times before, but what I will go along with less easily is the redundancy of the effort. There is still little evidence to suggest that even sophisticated viewers have stopped seeing through films, that they have become aware of the opacity of the image. Knowing this lends a sense of purpose to a continued critique of the mimetic fallacy.

Rather than approaching the tropology of film violence as something that can be decoded, or translated, into the semantic fixities of conventional interpretive practice, I have endeavored to foreground the extent to which the movements of filmic figuration represent an ongoing activity, a methodology of seeing, which does not posit a transitive, teleological object or address. In other words, the tropes of violence are not necessarily regarded as a relation between meaning and sign, tenor and vehicle, but as a metarhetorical gesture that probes the existential conditions of the text itself. More often than not, I have found that the violence in the films addresses the ineluctable problem of mortality in relation to both character and narrative. Organicist theories have usually tended to view narrative progression in terms of growth and consummation, but as a process, narration may also be found to cede to pressures of deterioration. Whether tragic or not, closure implies a cessation of the act of storytelling, and insofar as this act is felt to be pleasurable, every narrative ending is imbued with a sense of loss as well as an admittance of the imminence of death. Cinema, Stewart writes, partakes in "the encorpsing of the scopic object" (*Between* 154), an assertion exquisitely reminiscent of Jean Cocteau's remark in ORPHÉE (1949), that cinema "films death at work." The trope of violence, I would argue, renders film's narrathanatographic accent perceptible. "Presentations of death," Gunzenhäuser suggests, "create particular problems of authorization; therefore, cultural discourses on death are carefully controlled" (75). We may construe narratives of violence as an allegorization of the culture's and the subject's conflicted relations to that temporality, "no longer backed by presence," which is death (Stewart, *Between* 153).

Apart from the cinematicization of death, what unites the texts that I have discussed in part III is their denaturalization of masculinity, which is generally revealed to be a matter either of a set of abstract moralities, as in Peckinpah, or perpetual trauma, as in Fincher. Infantile in SCARFACE, submissive in THE KILLING, impotent in BONNIE AND CLYDE, suicidal in THE WILD BUNCH, unprofessional in RESERVOIR DOGS, and psychotic in FIGHT CLUB, the protagonists in these six films sublimate Silverman's view that mortality may afford "a possible avenue of escape from the psychic, sexual, and political givens of a classic masculinity" (*Male Subjectivity* 270). This escape, if that is what it is, is facilitated by transfigurations at the site of the body. Though on the one hand, to read the body as a "text" has long since become a cliché of humanities scholarship, it is on the other hand – and as Cynthia Marshall has shown (4) – difficult even to conceive of the concept of violence without also taking into account its object. In this respect, Browne has usefully adumbrated an interpretive strategy for making sense of the troping of the body in American film:

> 'Film violence' and its corresponding modes of filmic representation are cultural constructions that encode historically changing versions of metaphors of the human body. The body of the hero has passed through the stage of the organic (first the idealized body of the classical cinema, then to the vulnerable, wounded body of Vietnam-era dramaturgy) and has emerged as the mechanico-cybernetic postmodern body. ("Aesthetics" 1: 551)

Though I believe we ought to proceed with great caution in hypothesizing a before-and-after-postmodernism view of cinematic corporeality (BLADE RUNNER and THE MATRIX aside, there is a vital parallel strain of hyper-organicist violence in contemporary Hollywood cinema, as evidenced in films like CASINO (Scorsese 1995), FIGHT CLUB and Christopher McQuarrie's Peckinpahesque THE WAY OF THE GUN (2000)), Browne's overall claim that violence can be seen as a kind of metaphorical *cinécriture* that encapsulates historically circumscribed ways of thinking about the body is a viable position. Violence is also a means by which to explore the choreography of the body in terms of poetic movement, a suggestion which Faure has made explicit by comparing the violence in BONNIE AND CLYDE and THE WILD BUNCH to Maya Deren's experimental film from 1948, *Meditation on Violence* (65).

My concern with screen violence was impelled by what I take to be a set of ill-conceived but stupendously obstinate methods for thinking and writing about violence in art in general and in the cinema in particular. It seemed crucial that these approaches be appraised before moving on to a distinctly different form of theorizing screen violence. This is the subject of the first part of the book, which is by nature metacritical. Comprising two separate chapters, the following section delves more rigorously into the problem of aesthetics and mimesis first brought up in the introduction, an investigation which precedes a chapter on what I refer to as *narrathanatograph* – the preoccupation with and the narration of death and the body so central to a cinema of violence. The final part of the book continues the process of theorizing the ideas developed throughout, but alters the hermeneutic perspective in the sense that it is now individual film texts that occupy the theoretical locus. I choose to approach the films not as objects of analysis in the conventional sense but as potential theories, the features of which my reading intends to elicit.

1
Screen Violence: Five Fallacies

We need to ask more subtle questions about textual violence,
about its provenance and purpose as well as its form and extent.
Cynthia Marshall

Violence, as William Pechter has remarked, is "the staple diet of the American film" (83). Incorporated into a variety of filmic forms, violence has a bearing on most genres and historical periods. From THE GREAT TRAIN ROBBERY (Edwin Porter 1903), in which violent conflict propels what is often identified as the first movie narrative, to GANGS OF NEW YORK (Martin Scorsese 2002), "fashions in narrating violence" have changed in accordance with the stylistic, technological and cultural evolution of the medium (Miller 89). Most of the time, however, film violence is dismissed as mere exploitation. Despite the fact that, like eroticism, violence represents "one of cinema's fundamental obsessions from the beginning" (Atkins 5), it is only on rare occasions that it warrants critical salutation. While theoretical reflection on the phenomenon of violence has been unduly neglected, discussions in the mass media and among the public have been rampantly on the increase. Because of this relative silence on the part of aesthetically oriented film and media studies, both the research and the discourse on film violence have been monopolized by social scientists and psychologists, on the one hand, and by the populist media, on the other. The paradox, of course, is that violence in fiction is firmly rooted in the domain of aesthetics and textual studies. Humanities scholars, however, have nearly relinquished the subject altogether. What is needed, therefore, is an approach to violence that may complement, as well as provide an alternative to, social science research. Thomas Munro understood this well when in an article on art and violence published in 1969, the year of THE WILD BUNCH's initial release, he announced that he would "like to see aestheticians take a more active lead, as individuals and through their institutions, in studying the good and bad effects of art on a large and systematic scale. The problem is closely related to that of aesthetic value" ("Art and Violence" 320). However, by continuing to privilege quantification over interpretation in the study of textual violence, Fraser's almost thirty-year-old complaint that violence in the arts is an intellectual terra incognita has remained sadly relevant (2).

There are three main traditions of research on screen violence: studies that pertain to censorship issues and social regulations of the medium, cultural and ideological studies (examinations of individual films and directors, and of mythological frameworks that underpin audiovisual violence), and representational and epistemological studies (theories of gender, genre and spectatorship) (Slocum, "Violence" 5-19). Endeavors in the field have been scattershot, and they have failed to achieve a sustained multidisciplinary quality. W.J.T. Mitchell notes that there exists "a conspicuous lack of interdisciplinary theoretical reflection across the numerous domains of violence and representation" ("Representation" 3: 44), whereas Hent de Vries and Samuel Weber propose that in order to better illuminate the problem of violence, it must be tackled in a "distinctly transdisciplinary manner" (2).[1]

In the following chapters, I intend to show that earlier work on cinema violence may usefully be reconceptualized according to a set of methodological and thematic procedures that epitomize ways of thinking about and attending to this particular subject matter. Not all of them are scholarly approaches in any systematic sense, nor are they sufficiently systematic to be called theories. They can, however, be made to congeal into reasonably consistent perspectives of film and violence. What characterizes these tendencies is their mode of analysis and explanation – the frameworks within which the knowledge of screen violence is pursued and negotiated – and these protocols of comprehension can sometimes be found to contain tacit evaluations as well as even skeletal definitions of the subject in question. Whether empirical or mimetic, the proposed approaches tend to be doctrinaire in nature, apprehending screen violence as a problem to be solved rather than as a text to be interpreted in all its miscellaneous contexts. In expounding the axiomatic tenets of each of these approaches, the ensuing chapters intend to metatheoretically abet a holistic mapping of a multifaceted research area. With respect to methodology, these five orientations in unequal degrees represent the adversarial "other" to the theory of figurality presented in the introduction. As epistemic regimes, these approaches tend to be formulas for stagnation.

Empiricism

Far from being mindless, violence is usually
the cutting edge of ideas and ideologies.
John Fraser

Various kinds of empirical studies form the hegemonic school of research on film and television violence. Though internally diverse, what unites these approaches is their shared basis in either the social sciences or in psychology, their emphasis on quantifiable evidence, their concern with the potentially undesirable effects of screen violence on the audience (children and adolescents in particular), their affiliation with politically instituted research initiatives, their reductive use of primary texts and the concomitant refusal to engage with films holistically, the artificiality of their experimental conditions, their frequently moralistic and censorial overtones, their vast underestimation of the viewer,[2] and, finally, their notorious inconclusiveness.[3]

What can be referred to as the *Effects Tradition* in research on violence and imitation dates back to at least the late 19th century and people like Delos Wilcox, Frederick Peterson, Frances Fenton, and Gabriel de Tarde.[4] Uniformly behavioristic in method, studies in this tradition revolve around "the psychology of suggestion" (Murdock 79) and the potentially harmful effects exposure to newspapers may instill in the gullible reader. Graham Murdock criticizes this approach for what he perceives to be its "single-minded search for simple, direct links between stimulus and response," something which represents the trademark of "an unbroken line of banal science that succeeds in its own terms only because it fails to acknowledge that the making and taking of meaning in everyday life is never as straightforward as it first appears" (83). Such procedural shortcomings have since continued to impede the legitimacy of effects-based surveys.

The Payne Fund Studies (PFS) of the 1930s were the first consistent attempt to apply sociological methods to chart the influence that the medium of film might exert on the viewers.[5] A parameter for the methods of the PFS was what in retrospect has been referred to as the "magic bullet theory," a supposition that the mass media had instantaneous and invariable effects on everyone who was subjected to media information. The conclusions confirmed the concern of critics and parents that the movies were a negative influence on Depression-era American youth. For the next seventy years the methodology and assumptions originating in the PFS would remain dominant in the field of screen violence.[6] Prince explains that the social scientists' monopolization of research on violence supervenes from the neglect of humanities scholars to embrace empirical approaches ("Graphic" 19). Perhaps more by circumstance than by determination, the refusal of cinema scholars to participate in an empirical agenda had the serious consequence of leaving the study of film violence almost exclusively to social scientists. The numerous problems that tax quantitative methodologies aside, the relative absence of critical and theoretical work on screen violence from a humanist's point of view has left the topic epistemologically disadvantaged.

In his preface to *The Content of Motion Pictures* (1935), Edgar Dale advocates a closer scrutiny of the film medium in order to "set up adequate forms of social control" (ix).[7] His call to action, based on an alertness to the potential influence of the movies on the "American public mind" (ix), is symptomatic of the conti-

nuing affiliation of social science research initiatives on the topic of violence
with political campaigns and social reform. The PFS is just an early instance.
More recent examples would be the publications of the National Commission
on the Causes and Prevention of Violence (NCCPV) (1969), the Second Report
to the Surgeon General (SRSG) (1982), the project "Cultural Indicators" and The
Annenberg School for Communication at the University of Pennsylvania,[8] and
UNESCO's program "International Clearinghouse on Children and Violence on
the Screen," established by the Nordic Information Centre for Media and Communication Research in 1997.[9] Bushman and Anderson's survey article "Media
Violence and the American Public," published in *American Psychologist* in 2001,
updates past findings in the field while displaying the same inimical bias that
encumbers this particular tradition as a whole. Below I shall identify two specific sources of difficulty that impinge upon the empiricist framework; one rhetorical, and the other methodological.

Shortly after the publication of the PFS, one of its own participants, Mortimer
J. Adler, launched a fierce critique of some of the studies as part of his *Art and
Prudence* (1937). What particularly enraged Adler was the tacit value judgments
that underwrote the brand of social science embraced by several members of the
PFS. A deep-seated suspicion of art and entertainment seems to have been the
impetus behind the large-scale research projects Adler was involved in. Incidentally, the concern with the disruptive consequences of viewing motion pictures
rehabilitates the widely known misgivings of illustrious pundits like Plato and
Tolstoy about the possible moral corruption that may result from exposure to
works of art and imitation.[10] This suspicion, on which acts of moralizing and
censorship are regularly attendant, divulges the fear of "art's infecting the real
world with its own (possibly false) patterns and values" (Nesbet 22). It is this
failure to disentangle preconception from procedure that constitutes one of the
most deleterious flaws integral to empiricist discourses on violence and visual
art. Though it must be granted that no academic point of view can pretend to
circumvent the inescapability of interest or influence, a distinction between dog-
matic adherence and metacritical self-examination still remains in force. Criticism, Berel Lang suggests, "comes finally to a point where taste rules," but "it
need hardly … begin there" (45).

From the early efforts of the PFS, to Fredric Wertham's caution against the
violent content of comic books in his *Seduction of the Innocent* (1954), the research
conducted by the NCCPV, and Michael Medved's book-length diatribe *Hollywood vs. America* (1992), empirical approaches have consistently tended to conflate scholarship and policy. Unlike non-empirical investigations, the fields of
psychology and social science have acquired a luster of objectivity in which to
couch a rhetoric of cultural value. These endeavors attempt not only to establish
a link between fictional violence and social behavior and attitudes, but also to

pass ideological and aesthetic judgment on certain kinds of texts. Medved's text provides abundant evidence of this pairing of an empirical perspective with a moral-political rhetoric. His thesis is that contemporary Hollywood cinema has alienated its audience by manufacturing uncommonly transgressive films that violate the sensibilities of the viewer:

> Between 1965 and 1969 the values of the entertainment industry changed, and audiences fled from theaters in horror and disgust. Those disillusioned moviegoers have stayed away to this day – and they will remain estranged until the industry returns to a more positive and populist approach to entertaining its audiences (279).

Implicated in this argument is a not too subtly disguised aesthetic preference – Frank Capra over Stone, for instance – which at once connects Medved's study to the much-touted subject of the culture wars.[11]

Because this ideological impulse appears so endemic to the inquiries on screen violence undertaken by psychologists and social scientists, it is difficult to consider the pitfalls of empiricism without taking into account the sociology of censorship and aesthetic judgment. In 1969, Arthur M. Schlesinger, Jr. published *The Crisis of Confidence*, in which he problematizes the notion of censorship: "Authentic artistic merit and purpose should never be censored. But prefabricated trash can properly be subject to control. Who is to decide which is which? Expert testimony would seem the best answer" (31). A question still left unresolved, however, is whose expert testimony should be brought to bear on the issue. As Richard Maltby has pointed out, the logic of censorship was typically grounded in subjectivist notions of taste and quality in Britain in the 1960s, whereas in the United States film censoring was largely based on quantifiable forms of evidence ("Disgusting" 110). One of Maltby's conclusions seems to be that "where an art of excess was a form of social criticism, an entertainment of excess was a form of cultural debasement" (111). Since the implications of the issues that Schlesinger, Jr. and Maltby raise are so wide-ranging, I shall pursue some of them in more detail in chapter three.

The methodological difficulty which besets empirical research on film violence is perhaps more fundamental than the problem outlined above and involves the absence of the realization that fictionalized violence is not a quantifiable phenomenon to begin with. By isolating violent film segments, by ignoring contextual information, and by placing subjects in viewing situations that are highly controlled, empirical and sociological approaches reveal a disheartening illiteracy as regards the architectonics of cinematic perception. A mere enumeration and classification of the different types of violent action found in a fictional text – be it a Tom and Jerry cartoon or a Tarantino movie – are on the whole insignificant for an adequate understanding of screen violence.[12] As Martin Barker has made clear, the futility of key aspects of quantitatively oriented studies becomes palpable in the failure to indicate an awareness of the ontological basis from which an understanding of violence may be derived: "There simply isn't a 'thing' called 'violence in the media' that either could or couldn't 'cause' social violence. There is nothing to be researched. That being so, it means that 70 years of research have poured hundreds of millions of dollars and pounds down the drain of meaningless questions" (10). What should be resisted, Barker writes, is the preposterous tendency "to think that 'violence' can be abstracted from the hugely different contexts of meaning and use in which it occurs" (10).[13] This charge is reminiscent of a suggestion André Glucksmann makes in *Violence on the Screen* (1971):

> when we analyse the meaning of a scene in Shakespeare or in Joyce, we are careful to put it back in its context, in its place in the play, in the totality of the author's work, even in the dramatic art of the period and the rules of composition then current; the same method could be used to grasp the specific meaning of violence in westerns (52).

Before we can begin to draw conclusions with respect to the phenomenon of screen violence, we must first become familiar with the forms, structures, and, above all, figures of film aesthetics. To the extent that these are knowable, we need to found the claims we make on the actual material conditions that configure cinematic segments into coherent narratives.

The problems inherent in quantificational methodologies have also been critically assessed by social scientists themselves. In a foreword to a study by Pablo Gonzáles Casanova, Adam Schaff presents this diagnosis:

> the principal weakness of present-day empirical research in the social sciences consists in the domination of quantitative methods, combined with a far-reaching, if not complete, disregard of the qualitative aspect of the problems involved. ... before we proceed to measure a phenomenon we must know *what* is to be measured, and that accordingly a qualitative analysis is the foundation of the quantitative one (ix-x).[14]

In spite of the benefits that this procedure promises, psychological and social science studies of media violence have been slow to acknowledge the crucial value of textual analysis. The empiricist refrains from engaging with film on multiple levels even when the need to resort to a qualitative methodology seems ineludible. A case in point is Medved's assertion that "the distinctions [between the film violence of the 1930s and that of today] are so obvious and so fundamental that they serve to define two very different forms of entertainment" (185). Rather than seeking to explain this discrepancy in the context of aesthetic, cultural and perceptual changes, Medved instead chooses to focus on the extent to which contemporary film violence indicates a moral decline. The gap between these two approaches is the sliding from an analytical to a normative point of view.

Since the "effects tradition," as Barker says, "reduces films to stimulus-response mechanisms, without history or meaning" (11), its relationship to the films is itself one of violence. By decontextualizing individual shots and segments, quantificational studies violate its unity and formal integrity. In the final instance this irreverence also extends to the viewers, who in the social scientist's laboratory become "twitching semiconductors without prior expectations, understandings or skills" (Barker 11). Dolf Zillmann, among others, has called attention to the essential appeal of fictional violence as a "salient form of entertainment," an appeal often overlooked by social scientists (182). Even more seriously, their naive conception of the viewer is impossibly asynchronous with recent research on film and cognition.[15] An exception here is Annette Hill's investigation of how viewers experience extreme forms of screen violence. Her book *Shocking Entertainment* argues that the discussion of violence must be reconsidered in terms of a focus on emotional rather than behavioral effects. Although her study does not reflect a sensitivity to film style or aesthetics, it offers a productive account of how spectators cognitively and emotionally interact with movie violence. Hill's procedure is premised on the evident but often under-reported observations that the viewing event is a social activity, that the viewer is an active participant in the process, and that watching violent movies is a popular and self-conscious decision (1).

In order to be able to understand the nature of the interaction between viewers and film violence, Hill organized extensive in-depth discussion sessions with selected participants over a six-month period. The interviewees were divided into what she calls "self-contained focus groups," and her method was to collect data from the group interaction. With Hill as an auditor, the groups discussed specific topics involving personal experiences with movie violence. From an analysis of the results, she was able to extrapolate the cognitive processes at work which, in turn, were used to affirm or contradict her general hypotheses. One of the factors Hill discovered was that viewers of film violence employ what she calls "portfolios of interpretation," a term which appears to be interchangeable with that of "mental schemata" that the first generation of cognitive film theorists employed. Hill's concept embodies cognitive strategies specific to the reception of violent film images. It operates on a more finely graded level than that of schemata. The portfolios of interpretation feature spectator activities such as the anticipation of violent scenes, building of character relationships, self-censoring and boundary-testing (4). Far from being a full-fledged taxonomy of cognitive processes at work in the viewing of film violence, it does afford a starting point from which more elaborate hypotheses may be formulated.

In attempting to understand why viewers choose to watch the selected films, Hill learned that factors such as media hype, peer pressure, advertising, individual preference for certain directors or actors, and personal experience were vital motivations (19). The act of viewing violence is a conscious process, and the spectators exhibit a considerable degree of awareness of conditions such as the social circumstance (being part of the theatre collective) and motivation (i.e., reasons for choosing this type of films). They are also highly sensitive to their own physical and emotional responses – feelings like fear, anger, excitement and disgust. This leads Hill to conclude that there is no one singular reaction to watching violent films (27). More accurately, the viewer's response appears to be a complex composite, where several physiological, emotional and cognitive impressions intertwine.

Hill's survey of audience response to violent movies establishes a number of results which tend to contradict the assumptions that inform empirical approaches. These include the apprehension that one function of violent movies is to test the audience's threshold and that watching violence is an essentially social activity. Moreover, viewers maintain an unambiguous distinction between real violence, which unequivocally is considered "raw and brutal," and fictional violence, which is considered entertaining. Within the province of the cinema, viewers can actively explore the issue of violence within the safety of fiction, and they typically proceed to do so by testing boundaries, by self-censoring undesirable content, and by imaginatively hypothesizing the wider effects and contexts of violence.

Aristotelianism

> *When I cleanse myself, I shall kill evil.*
> Kazimir Malevich

Vastly influential in literary criticism, Aristotle's concepts of pity and fear have ignited numerous scholarly debates. It may therefore seem redundant to revisit the subject of *catharsis*, but since its relevance for the topic of screen violence is undisputed, it cannot be ignored. Those who subscribe to a theory of catharsis hold that the experience of watching fictional violence can be emotionally and morally beneficial, since it contributes to a purging of destructive impulses in the viewer. This is in some ways an instrumental theory of simulated violence, one in which the experience of spectacle provides an aesthetic means to a moral end. Fictional violence acts as a safety valve which mollifies whatever violent impulses the viewer may possess. By necessity, the appeal to catharsis is also a renunciation of the copycat argument implicit in much of the research of the "effects" tradition.

The meaning of the term catharsis is by no means unequivocal in the *Poetics*, where it is only mentioned once and in a context which falters in defining it.[16] Despite Aristotle's cryptic explication, one can extrapolate from it a particular theoretical logic, if not a full-fledged philosophy. Among the most commonly accepted interpretations is that of purification, where catharsis designates the process in which whatever is unsound in the tragic deed is expunged.[17] Within the world of the *Poetics*, a concrete manifestation of impurity would be the knowingly intentional murder of a close relative. An example of a non-cognizant intention would be to murder someone who was a close kin, but without being aware of this relationship. The latter describes the scenario in which Oedipus, unaware of the identity of his victim, kills his father. While the first example would be an impure act, the second is "pure" in Aristotle's sense. However, the purity of the action must be affirmed, and the catharsis would therefore be the authentication of this purity. In the *Nicomachean Ethics*, Aristotle suggests that the repentance of the perpetrator may be taken as a catalyst for the process of purification (80). Importantly, it is this aspect that conditions the emotions of pity (eleos) and fear (phobos) that are so central to the substantiation of the catharsis effect.

The theory of catharsis has long since extended into discussions of violence on the screen, where it has invited both opposition and support. While some reviewers and film artists endorse the idea,[18] it also has its advocates among film scholars. For Doug McKinney – who wrote one of the first monographs on Peckinpah's cinema –catharsis is a means by which to approach the violence (129), and more recently Bernard Dukore has undertaken an Aristotelian reading of the function of the carnage in THE WILD BUNCH (96). Similarly, Vivian C. Sobchack seems to ratify a purificational view of film violence: "Our films are trying to make us feel secure about violence and death as much as it is possible; they are allowing us to purge our fear, to find safety in what appears to be knowledge of the unknown. To know violence is to be temporarily safe from the fear of it" ("Violent Dance" 117).[19] These views notwithstanding, the theory of catharsis seems to have more detractors than adherents. Prince has repeatedly rejected the relevance of the catharsis theory for film, arguing that the effects of cinema are unlike those of the theater:

> The amplification of viewer shock, horror, nausea ... achieved through such tools of cinema as montage editing, loud music, or gory prosthetic effects, is unrelated to the emotions and reactions Aristotle described. ... To use his notion of catharsis in connection with cinema violence, as Peckinpah did, is a misapplication of the term (*Savage Cinema* 111).

Elsewhere, Prince dismisses the possibility of catharsis in film altogether ("Graphic" 1). In an article on the (un)attractiveness of screen violence, Clark McCauley also questions the applicability of the notion of catharsis. First, McCauley believes that a theory of purgation will not work if there is nothing to be purged to begin with. Second, he challenges the assumption that exposure to cathartic drama functions to decrease rather than augment aggressiveness in the viewers. Third, McCauley wonders why dramatized violence would actually lead to purgation in the first place (147).

Although Prince and McCauley are not necessarily mistaken in their general negation of theories of catharsis, their reasons for rejecting them may be called into question. A problematic aspect of Prince's renunciation of Aristotle's hypothesis in relation to cinema is the belief that only violence that takes place off-stage is capable of producing catharsis. When the violence is made explicit, as in film, Prince argues that the experience becomes non-cathartic (*Savage Cinema* 110). That is, graphic violence evokes mere aggression rather than pity and fear. However, the fact that violent action in the Greek theater took place off-stage is a convention of the medium which precedes Aristotle's theory of the tragic. The argument concerning pity, fear and catharsis in the *Poetics* inevitably had to draw on the artistic forms and practices available at the time. It is therefore not entirely legitimate to claim that a qualification of the catharsis effect is that violence be implied rather than shown, invisible rather than graphic. If violent acts were shown on-stage, they would not be nearly as affective as the heightened realism with which violence is represented in the cinema. The distinction between on-stage and off-stage violence in the theater may not be particularly salient, since even on-stage acts would be graphically euphemistic in comparison to those of the cinema.[20] Consequently, the unavailability of cinematic representation at the point of the formulation of the Aristotelian notion of catharsis suggests that the theory is not necessarily irrelevant for the type of violence portrayed in film. Prince's delimitation of the catharsis effect to Greek theater is thus unconvincing. Although Prince holds that "[t]here seems to be no essential reason for assuming that Aristotle's concept would necessarily generalize to a medium that can use its elements of style to graphically portray and enhance explicit violence" (*Savage Cinema* 110), it is difficult to repudiate the relevance of catharsis for film. Prince's emphasis on the theatrical performance as the principal medium of catharsis also excludes violent representations in literary fiction from having this function. Thus, he seems to dismiss a whole interpretative tradition which has accorded violence and other transgressive acts in fiction a socially redemptive function in their potential for emotional purification.

The extent to which McCauley misunderstands the catharsis theory, furthermore, is evidenced in his comparison of three documentary films – one showing the dissection of a monkey's brain, the other a slaughterhouse incident and the third facial surgery – on the one hand, to violent horror films on the other. Aristotle's concept, McCauley inveighs, "does not suggest why the three disgusting films are unappealing" (153). However, what McCauley seems to be unaware of is that Aristotle's conception of catharsis cannot be considered in isolation from his general theory of tragic composition. Much of the *Poetics* can be read as an explanation of the crucial place of cathartic release in the spectator's experience of a tragedy. Aristotle's markedly prescriptive delineation of the most successful narrative structure is not an end in itself; that is, the particular structure that he champions has been selected as a compositional paragon because it is judged to be the one best equipped to produce the desired effects of pity and fear in an audience. His conception of aesthetics, therefore, is strongly functionalistic. Effect is primary, structure secondary. In light of this state of affairs, it makes little sense to even discuss catharsis apart from Aristotle's specific musings on the structure of tragedy. One would be hard pressed to identify the required components of tragic structure, such as complication, resolution, recognition, and reversal, in the kind of documentary films that McCauley uses as examples. Without these elements of plot structure, there can be no pity and fear and, in turn, no purgation. The notion of catharsis is inextricably linked to these functions.

Part of the problem of determining if and how catharsis might still be a useful notion for the comprehension of film violence is related to the viewer-text dialectic. The tendency to confuse the protagonists' emotions with those of the audience testifies to this conundrum, as does the uncertainty with regard to the locus of the cathartic itself, which may at once refer to a narrative function, a textual effect, and a spectatorial mode of response. In order to arrive at a more precise understanding of these relations, one must turn to examine what is essentially accomplished through the experience of catharsis. The meaning of the terms purification and purging is clear enough; they may imply anything from a literal cleansing, or disinfecting, to a more abstract sense of removal or elimination. Moreover, the assumption that pity and fear may represent both the object and instrument of purification indicates that these emotions exist, perhaps latently, in the viewer independent of the text. Otherwise, the aesthetic project of first arousing, then exorcising these passions would not appear to be justifiable in the first place. Hence, the theory of catharsis presupposes the existence of a specifiable set of active emotions – particularly pity, fear, and anger – in the audience. Furthermore, the theory assumes that these emotions need an outlet through simulation if they are not to become potentially disruptive. If one accepts this premise – that pity and fear are the spectator's latent emotions which may manifest themselves at any time – the argument that tragic or violent action may help purge these emotions seems more plausible. In addition, the problem of placing relating pity and fear either in the text or in the perceiver is resolved, given that it is the fictional action which re-enacts the emotions of the audience by externalizing them in the form of a dramatic representation. The spectators in turn re-experience their own latent feelings of pity and fear, but in a simulated rather than actual fashion, and the text represents the means by which they can undertake this vicarious process. In the complex chain of actions and reactions which produce catharsis, the moment where it occurs in its most pure form may be in the transformation of the experience of pity and fear into pleasure.[21]

Catharsis as purgation accentuates its therapeutic aspect; the sequential dynamic of the experience is one where the emotions of the viewer develop from tension to release (crisis), to a calm pleasure. Incidentally, the movement resembles the general pattern of narrative construction, in which an initial state of balance is interrupted by some element which brings tension and disharmony. The further complication of the action is subsequently developed until it reaches a climax where the pressure is released by a crisis. Most classical narrative films exhibit this structure. But where theorists like Catherine Russell tend to argue that violent spectacle represents a debasement of the story (a narrative mortification)[22] – a desperate attempt to end narratives which cannot appropriately be resolved in any other way – it is also possible to see the escalated violence of a film like THE WILD BUNCH as a reinforcement of the crisis, and hence the catharsis effect, which ultimately provides the spectators' release in the end. In this latter sense, the violence may be found to enhance the structure of the narrative through its amplification of the crisis.

While Aristotle primarily saw catharsis as a religious and medical process, interpretations of it over the centuries have emphasized the moral and ethical dimension of the concept.[23] The medical orientation of Aristotle's original thesis may have some significance for the reception of film violence in an emotional-cognitive context, but the ethical and aesthetic meanings of his concept are more central to the current discussion. That catharsis made the experience of a tragedy moral and the audience wiser is a common belief held by both playwrights and critics like Corneille, Racine and Lessing. The assertion singles out the function of catharsis as the pivotal structure of the play, as the precondition for the ethical import of the fictional text. Notably, the conjunction of catharsis and ethics establishes a link between the textual transgressions and an emerging morality. The aesthetic significance of tragedy and drama is qualified by an ethical rationale which prescribes a holistic function to the cathartic experience. Hence, the encounter between text and perceiver should contain both an aesthetic and an ethical axis or, rather, the two elements should be inseparable.

The theory of catharsis implies that there is a therapeutic dimension to art; Rudolf Arnheim has said that "[b]y demonstrating what it can do for the distressed," he writes, "art reminds us what it is meant to do for everybody" (257).[24] This view need not be dismissed entirely, but the premises upon which

the cathartic argument is based are too crude and reductive. As emotional categories, or states, pity and fear are too monolithic. The viewer's experience of
film fiction and art in general is considerably more complex than the theory of
catharsis allows for.[25] Audiences come to the movies equipped with a range of
different emotions, among which pity and fear might not even be included. Secondly, although I do not support the claims of the "effects tradition," it has by
no means been established that violent artworks actually cleanse the viewer's
negative emotions, and it is even possible, in theory, that at least for some viewers, these emotions may actually be reinforced by fictional violence. The concept
of "art-as-therapy" suggests a broader reach than the theory of catharsis, but
only on a flagrantly speculative level does it explain the creation of, and immersion in, violent fictions. Furthermore, the notion of catharsis hardly contributes
to a problematization of the nature, meaning, context, and symbolic significance
of screen violence, as it merely accepts its presence in works of fiction and then
tries to ascribe to it a palliative function. Theories of purification also fail to discriminate between different forms and traditions of violence, preferring instead
to lump their diverse depictions together in the category of spectacle. Like the
empirical paradigm, writings which support themselves on theories of catharsis
reveal scant potential for elucidating the semiotic dimension of film violence.

The reductionism implied by Aristotelian theories that apprehend violent cinema as a pharmacy for the psyche should not distract us from the significance of
other functions of spectacle, functions which possess the potential for promot-
ing insight rather than purgation. Sergei Eisenstein's notion of conflictual montage and Antonin Artaud's Theatre of Cruelty represent two focal conceptuali-
zations of the value of shock and spectacle that avoid the impasse of the theories
of purification and catharsis. Paramount in Eisenstein's theory is the idea that
the moral or political engagement of the spectators can be activated most effi-
ciently through the preliminary perceptual stages of sensory shock and emotion.[26] Eisenstein saw film as a medium designed to arouse the spectators' emotions through shock in order to facilitate cognition, much like for Dziga Vertov
for whom the cinema could become a "cine-fist" capable of stirring the audience's feelings.[27] Thus, STRIKE (1925) features scenes of violence toward children, and in the Odessa steps sequence in THE BATTLESHIP POTEMKIN (1925)
one shot graphically shows an old woman being shot in the eye. The logical design behind this montage of cruelty was that the more explicit the images of
suffering, the more effective the audience's disgust with the victimizers. In this
respect, Eisenstein's working method and thesis depart from the traditional notion of catharsis. Although the intended sensory and emotional effects of his
montage seem cathartic, the Aristotelian conception is arguably too narrow to
encompass Eisenstein's overall agenda. While Aristotle is specifically concerned
with the emotions of pity and fear, Eisenstein wanted his films to engage a wide

range of spectator emotion. Moreover, Aristotle conceives of pity and fear as functional ends in themselves, whereas Eisenstein believes that emotional affectivity is mostly a means for serving the cognitive processing of the political statement of the film. His conception of the viewing process as a progressive activity which moves from raw perceptual shock to emotion and cognition represents a synthetic and highly didactic approach to cinema. In advocating the construction of knowledge through passion, Eisenstein rejected art that compartmentalized the different functions of his dialectical scheme: perceptual shock that failed to lead to emotion and cognition was nothing but cheap sensationalism; emotion and psychologizing cut off from social and political relations was the legacy of the despised bourgeois theater; and cognition without the accompanying sensory and emotional impact he assigned to the classroom. Therefore, the rhetoric of an aesthetic style which promoted new political ends necessitated the introduction of the kind of artistic and perceptual process theorized by Eisenstein. Like the theater of the Grand Guignol, or Artaud's theater of cruelty, the montage of attractions as cultivated in Eisenstein's 1920s films implies a sensuous, direct assault on the audience's sensibility. Since the cinematic attractions constitute the pivotal formal structure of Eisenstein's work, narrative and plot become secondary to the spectacle.

If Eisenstein's thesis suggests a blueprint for the use of shock and spectacle which escape the well-worn connotations of purification, Artaud's advocacy of a theatre of profound physicality complements his philosophy. In an unprecedented attack on modern drama, Artaud (57) disowns the notion of a theatre that fails to affect the public violently. Artaud wanted to replace the placidity of contemporary drama with a relentlessly confrontational art that "restore[d] an impassioned convulsive concept of life to theatre … a kind of severe mental purity" (81). His Theater of Cruelty was to be the vehicle for such a radical reinvention of stage art,[28] which, as William Blum has shown, also contains the model for a Cinema of Cruelty (26).[29] As a matter of fact, Blum identifies THE WILD BUNCH, with its "exaltation of brutality" (30), as the first film in which traces of an emergent cinematic cruelty manifest themselves: "In Artaudian terms, THE WILD BUNCH is only partially successful, but it offers encouraging evidence that the groundwork has been laid, and that cinema is a usable medium for the experience" (32).[30] Whether or not cinema has fulfilled the promise that is vaguely present in Peckinpah's film is an issue I shall return to in a later chapter, but Artaud's theory – especially when considered against the background of Eisenstein's aesthetic – offers a useful template for rethinking the purpose of spectacle and shock in cinema along the lines of reflection rather than purification.

Aestheticism

The work of art is beautiful to the degree to which it opposes
its own order to that of reality.
Herbert Marcuse

The aesthetic fallacy manifests itself as a desire instinctively and arbitrarily to make a distinction between commendable and prurient forms of violence. To the extent that any given film may be defined as a work of art, i.e. as an art film, its violence is generally accepted as an intrinsic component of the total artistic design.[31] In some cases the violence might even be complimented for its alleged neologisms, for its stylistic elegance, or at least for its degree of provocativeness. For instance, some reviewers found the violence in THE WILD BUNCH appropriate because it was appalling (Cook 176). But the aestheticist would claim that the violence in the mainstream film is devoid of artistic value and should therefore be censured. Taken to its extreme, this kind of reasoning would sanction a film of questionable morality as long as its violence is "artfully" composed, and reject a morally responsible film for its "inartistic" rendering of violence. The framing of violence within specific configurations of narrative and characterization seems thus to be directly related to the politics of moral sanctioning. Victoria Harbord, for instance, points out that violence is deemed acceptable in mainstream films – and even children's' films – as long as it takes place within a clearly defined moral setting that contains the protagonist-antagonist polarity. Her evidence implies that films which transgress this structure might also be accepted as long as they are not part of mainstream cinema (143). In 1992 and 1994, the Board of British Film Classification (BBFC) withheld the video releases of RESERVOIR DOGS and NATURAL BORN KILLERS respectively, while the far more violent MAN BITES DOG (Rémy Belvaux, André Bonzel and Benoît Poelvoorde 1992) remained uncensored. The first two features were classified as mainstream films with no clear-cut moral dichotomy, and as such they attracted a great deal of controversy upon their release. MAN BITES DOG – although similarly lacking the seemingly required ethos – escapes public censure because its exhibition is limited to the art-house circuit and thus is considered harmless to general audiences. Hence, we can note that compositional choices openly bear on the cultural reception of violent movies. Clyde R. Taylor maintains that a film like THE BIRTH OF A NATION "confronts us with the possibility of a work being powerfully persuasive, affecting, and aesthetically rewarding, while at the same time saturated with noxious conceits and ideas: beautiful yet evil" (120). To complicate matters further, the categorical distinction between art and entertainment can also be manipulated to support the reverse argument that mainstream, blockbuster violence is harmless because it has no artistic merits, and thus the much more (potentially) subversive art-film violence should be the ones banned from the screens. From A CLOCKWORK OR-ANGE to NATURAL BORN KILLERS, most of the films that have been deprecated by journalists, politicians and audiences alike have belonged to the latter group.

Regardless of the ways in which it may be exploited, the dichotomy of these two kinds of screen violence informs a relatively widespread approach to the subject. The trouble with the aestheticization-of-violence account is that film irrepressibly and by definition lays bare an aesthetic system; all fictional representations are *already* aestheticized. Furthermore, even if one could make a case for the existence of a level of super-aestheticization, the conditions for determining its existence would be highly arbitrary. How, for example, is it possible to claim that the violence in A CLOCKWORK ORANGE is aestheticized whereas that in STRAW DOGS is not?[32] If critics are compelled to marshal the concepts of aestheticization and stylization only when they are confronted with slow motion cinematography and rapid montage, it speaks volumes of their general alertness to the specificities of film form. There are different stylistic traditions and registers of aestheticization of film violence. Differences on the level of aesthetics are by nature qualitative, not quantitative, and as Charles Wolfe makes clear, the putative escalation of graphic imagery is attributable not to changes in intensity but to the evolution of aesthetic form (1: 518). There can never be a form-less representation of violence, and the customary recourse to the vacuous notion of aestheticization thus amounts to a theoretical cul de sac. Prince's assertion that the medium of film cannot help but aestheticize violence is symptomatic of this conundrum. The diverse techniques of cinematic fiction, Prince holds, function to transform every image into an aestheticized object: "Changing camera positions, controlled lighting, montage editing, music, and special effects create significant aesthetic pleasure and emotional distance for viewers, who can use these cues as a means of insulating themselves from the depicted violence" (28). Such a point of view is not tenable unless we grant cinema the special privilege of being inherently more aesthetically resourceful than the other arts.

In order to unveil the essence of the aesthetic fallacy, what first needs attending to is the premise that undergirds the film critic's deployment of the term aestheticization. When one enthusiastically remarks that a particular film skillfully aestheticizes violence – and when the skeptic incensed by the same film disapproves of it for that very reason – they are both implying that a process of beautification has occurred in the image. As a result of specific stylistic machinations, the segments that contain the violence have become more visually and viscerally attractive than all the segments that do not contain any violence. In this usage, the concept of aestheticization is isomorphous with the concept of beauty. As I have indicated above, however, film violence in any shape or form cannot be aestheticized (it is already aesthetic by definition), and *because* it cannot be aestheticized, the question of whether it is beautiful or not is rendered irrelevant.

It is the connotations of beauty of which aesthetic criticism has to divest itself before it meaningfully can begin to apprehend the complexities of different textual forms. As R.G. Collingwood has shown in *The Principles of Art* (1938), the association of the aesthetic with the beautiful is erroneous (38), and must be abandoned in order to achieve a more precise formulation of the aesthetic.[33] This is a crucial step for any theory of forms, but especially for one which also involves violence. Violent content in the audiovisual media is either extolled or condemned because of the perceived beauty of its composition. The various ways in which the violent scenes in, say, BONNIE AND CLYDE or HANA-BI (Takeshi Kitano 1997) are appropriated – i.e., as either "art" or "speculation" – all have a common basis in the interpretation of the depicted violence as expressing a kind of beauty. However, while some endorse the violence because it is presented in a beautifying manner, others condemn it for that very reason.[34] In the former case, the argument is that aesthetic value redeems (or overrides) ethical considerations; that which is beautiful is exempted from morality. It is beyond moral critique and cannot – due to an obscure leap of logic – be harmful. In the latter case, the putatively aestheticized depictions of violence are considered insidious because the imitation of repulsive acts in a beautifying formal register disguises the cruel reality of the content. The viewer is thus seduced into an illegitimate enjoyment of violence.

The propensity for defining the aesthetic narrowly as those aspects of artistic form which are beautiful is infelicitous for at least three reasons. Firstly, a conflation of the aesthetic with the beautiful only implies that every other formal constituent of the text must be defined negatively as non-aesthetic.[35] If we presuppose that there is an intimate link between the aesthetic and the artistic, moreover, all fictional texts which fail to manifest unequivocally beautiful forms do not qualify as aesthetic. I take the absurdity of the proposition to be self-evident. In an historical perspective, linking beauty with art is a relatively recent development. In Greek antiquity there was no connection between the two; nor was there a distinction between the practical arts, or crafts, and the fine arts (Collingwood 5).[36] For Plato, beauty was the immanent quality in an object or a phenomenon which impels us to desire it. While he associates the notion of the beautiful with the triad of eros, ethics and epistemology, his contemporaries also attributed a quality of beauty to certain artful objects like poetry and pottery. We habitually ascribe a sense of beauty indiscriminately to phenomena such as a painting, a building, a piece of furniture or a natural landscape. The idea of the sublimely beautiful cannot be limited to the realm of aesthetics; in fact, the concept is not even remotely useful in defining that which is specifically and exclusively artistic. Collingwood argues that:

> The words 'beauty', 'beautiful', as actually used, have no aesthetic implication. We speak of a beautiful painting or statue, but this only means an admirable or excellent one. Certainly the total phrase 'a beautiful statue' conveys an implication of aesthetic excellence, but the aesthetic part of this implication is conveyed not by the word 'beautiful' but by the word 'statue' (38).

Collingwood's argument, notably, locates the origin of the aesthetic function in the work itself, not in a quality of beauty assumed to belong a priori to the category of art. Consequently, an aesthetic text like a motion picture may or may not contain beauty; if it does, the quality inheres neither in the work nor in the viewer alone, but in the *dialectical transformation* of percept and perception. A violent film segment might be perceived as beautiful by some viewers due to their cognitive-emotional assessment of the text, and not to the aesthetic quality of the work. In his *Emotion and the Structure of Narrative Film*, Ed S. Tan expresses a similar view when he writes that beauty

> has often been used to describe the aesthetic emotion that flows from the formal characteristics of a work of art, as opposed to its contents. Here we will use the term *appreciation of the artefact* to refer to the motive that consists in finding enjoyment in formal film characteristics (34).[37]

The concept of beauty is thus attributed more to viewer psychology and the realm of emotion than to the text, which at the very most can be considered a catalyst for such emotional impressions.

A reader who can agree with this argument may object that it is not true that some films give us a strong sense of a highly self-conscious, stylish representation of violent impact that clearly is intended to be beautiful. An example may be the slow-motion deaths of the characters in Penn's and Peckinpah's films, which have inevitably received much negative criticism precisely because they have been interpreted as provocatively pretty. A reply to such a complaint would be that, again, the function of the beautiful lies not in the representation but in the active experience of it. One can conceive the production of screen violence as particular stylistic choices made from a range of formal options. Why a certain option is privileged at a given moment involves both textual and extra-textual factors such as available technical resources, narrative context, generic motivation, the nature of the material, directorial style, and censorship practice. It is by no means clear why we should attribute the notion of beauty to some of these choices and not to others. From a stylistic point of view, all technical options are equally valid as vehicles of artistic beauty, since the aesthetic function does not rely on the beautiful but on the formal qualities of the work.

Moreover, the representation of death in the cinema is always consequential, never trivial, and as such it is not at all surprising that the narrative moment of violent death is stylistically highlighted. The passage from movement to stasis which the process of dying embodies foregrounds the moment in which the signifying impulse is at its most intense. The activity of signification reaches a focused climax because the process of dying implies the cessation of the semiotic activity itself. Violence in fiction can be understood as posing a constant threat to narrational functionality, in that too much violence tends to suppress narrativity. Thus, the formal bracketing of violence as excessive in films like BONNIE AND CLYDE, THE WILD BUNCH, and HANA-BI must be regarded as a response to the threat of continuity that violence represents. What causes the italicization of violent action toward the end of Penn's and Peckinpah's films is a narrative effort to delay the termination of the story. That is, the text accentuates and extends the duration of the act of violence because it is unable to carry on with the story. The figuration of violent action diverges stylistically from the remaining text. This, however, does not imply an aestheticization but, rather, a formal bracketing of one of the most salient events in the narrative, dying.

Moreover, the couching of the aesthetic in terms of the beautiful involves contingencies of taste and value that are ultimately arbitrary and subjective. The standards which the critic calls upon when she decides that a textual aspect is either beautiful or repulsive are embedded in idiosyncratic, personal schemata which in turn are nested in large-scale cultural norms which to some extent can be described as relativistic. For David Hume, writing in 1757, the faculty of taste, however capricious, may be nurtured by the qualities of practice, comparison, and *"delicacy* of imagination" (216, emphasis in original). In part I of his *Critique of Judgement* (1790), Kant defines taste solely in terms of it being the instrument for "estimating the beautiful" (41). As such, taste is a capacity whose fundamental conditions *"cannot be other than subjective"* (41, emphasis in original). Despite the individual freedom of judgment that this position entails, Kant's aesthetic judgment avoids relativism by invoking the notion of subjective universality.[38] Nevertheless, his assumptions invite disputation, particularly the delimitation of a separate "aesthetic" faculty – one which lies beyond objective logic – as the agency of the judgment of taste. Postmodernist discourses have largely disqualified such as a rhetoric of universalization. Among contemporary thinkers, it is above all Pierre Bourdieu who has exposed the contextual embeddedness of the notion of taste, which, he writes,

> is an acquired disposition to 'differentiate' and 'appreciate' … to establish and mark differences by a process of distinction which is not (or not necessarily) a distinct knowledge … since it ensures recognition (in the ordinary sense) of the object without implying knowledge of the distinctive features which define it (*Distinction* 466).[39]

In the final instance, one cannot escape the fact that the appeal to beauty (in definitions of the aesthetic) is a covert gesture of subjective taste.[40] The origin of the aesthetics-as-beauty argument can be traced to the authoritative manifestations of a specific politics of taste. Underlying these politics are social and cultural conditions which facilitate and legitimize the appropriation of the mechanisms of differentiation that determine what artifacts may be called works of art.

Finally, the conflation of the beautiful and the aesthetic tends to alienate art and fiction from questions of morality and ethics in the sense that that which is considered beautiful is to be exempted from ethical evaluation. It should be clear that this issue is particularly significant in relation to a discussion of the forms and styles of film violence. Joshua Reynolds's dictum in *Discourses on Art* (1797) that beauty is the means by which art pursues its moral ends therefore appears anathema to a contemporary conceptualization of the nature and function of art. Modernism and postmodernism have to a large extent moved away from pleasurable art to generate works that are often discomforting, shocking and confrontational.[41] Movements such as Constructivism and Surrealism challenged the placid aura of Romanticist art. In music, the atonal pieces of composers like Schönberg, Webern and Boulez redefined the parameters of the medium, and in the 1960s Conceptual Art seemed to eradicate the boundaries between art and the commonplace, the beautiful and the reprehensible. In transcending the beautiful and the aestheticized, figurations of violence are perhaps closer to Julia Kristeva's reading of the sublime as the instant in which the abject "collapses" and changes into something else (210). Although less inadequate than the concept of beauty, that of the sublime from Longinus through Burke and Kant seems both too vague and too weathered to be overly useful for a theorization of the relation between poetics and violence.[42] Here, again, the term transfiguration is the more apposite.

As many of the most significant and innovative artworks in the 20th century have been concerned with forms and subjects which defy our received notions of beauty, some critics have come to regard what one may refer to as confrontational texts as inquisitive tracts that self-reflexively probe the conditions and limits of artistic practice. Black, for instance, hypothesizes that "the violence depicted in works of art ultimately seems directed against the idea of art itself, and should be seen as art's suicidal attempt to pass beyond its culturally conditioned self-image of falsity, and to achieve some transcendent or nihilistic – but, in any case, pre-aesthetic –'reality'" (*Aesthetics* 5). In his *Kant After Duchamp* (1996), Thierry de Duve counterposes the former's "classical aesthetic judgment" and the latter's "modern aesthetic judgment" to make tangible the gap that has arisen between conventional definitions of art and beauty, on the one hand, and post-romantic modes of representation and self-interrogation, on the other:

> a lot depends on whether one situates one's judgment within the accepted conventions of art, or whether those conventions are themselves at issue. The history of modernism and of avant-garde art tilts the balance toward the latter but settles the question of meaning only in those extreme cases where disgust has prompted first the rejection then the acceptance of the work. Indeed, every masterpiece of modern art – from Courbet's *Stonebreakers*, Flaubert's *Madame Bovary*, and Baudelaire's *Fleurs du mal* to Manet's *Olympia*, Picasso's *Demoiselles d'Avignon*, Stravinski's *Rites of Spring*, Joyce's *Ulysses*, and Duchamp's readymades – was first met with an outcry of indignation: 'this is not art!' In all these cases, 'this is not art' expresses a refusal to judge aesthetically; it means, 'this doesn't even deserve a judgment of taste' (303).

Arthur Danto declares that, with modernism, "the conditions of representation themselves become central, so that art in a way becomes its own subject" (*After the End* 7). In her much-anthologized article "The Pornographic Imagination," Susan Sontag notes that certain radical texts cannot be approached without raising the question of the ontology of literary art. Re-locating the source and substance of art from the empirically manifest work to the forms of consciousness from which it derives, Sontag claims that the continuous modification of the nature of the aesthetic in order to accommodate new forms of consciousness is a necessary function of the philosophy of art (44). Thus, there appears to exist a relation of mutual consolidation between, on the one hand, the kind of textual self-awareness that Black, de Duve and Danto identify in controversial artworks, and on the other, the cultivation in specific texts of formal qualities that are decidedly anti-beautiful (one of Sontag's examples is the work of Georges Bataille). Sontag further insists that "the human standard proper to ordinary life and conduct seems misplaced when applied to art" (44). The reinforcement of the "stature" of art in the first half of the 20th century is due to the assignment art has taken upon itself of venturing into "the frontiers of consciousness" (45). This development is perhaps most explicit within various avant-garde movements from 1910 until the outbreak of the Second World War.

For many Futurists, for instance, violence became attractive subject matter, and, as an aesthetic preoccupation, it was emblematic of the undermining of conventional attitudes toward art nurtured within the academies. In particular, the Futurists attacked the idea of the artistic enterprise as one limited to the realm of the beautiful. "Violence," Alison Sinclair explains, "was appropriated by the avant-garde as proper subject matter for art in company with other unconventional types of experience, such as technology, or even the ordinary" (79). Furthermore, Nesbet notes that "[i]t is not coincidental that the early Formalists, so concerned with the structure of the literary text, should also be intrigued by questions of violence" (48). If Sontag's thesis that the forms of consciousness provide the materials of art is to be taken seriously, this artistic gravitation toward the themes of violence, technology and the commonplace might be seen as indicative of a shift in aesthetic sensibility from the center to the margins of perception. In other words, the immersion in violence by some avant-garde artists is the expression of a form of consciousness not hitherto recognized as constituting a valid "material" basis for art making. Crucial to an understanding of this practice, however, is that its embrace of violence in both form and method does not necessarily imply an aestheticization of that subject matter. As a matter of fact, avant-garde conceptions of violence are often deprived of the elements one ordinarily associates with processes of aestheticization. Examining Goya's *Desastres de la guerra*, Picasso's *Guernica* and Wilfred Owen's war poem "The Show," Sinclair notes that "[l]ike Goya, Owen gives no alleviation to his inclusion of violence in poetry by making it overly aesthetic" (87). Reluctant to embellish their representations of violence, these texts employ formal strategies which promote a renunciation of the idea of the beautiful; neither the subject matter nor the stylistic rendering of it conform to what Sinclair calls the "academy-led attitudes which held that the world of the artistic should be restricted, and be more beautiful, than the world of the real" (79). Since the heterogeneous forms of consciousness are infinitely expansive, it follows that its aesthetic manifestations must be correspondingly unrestrained. In this context, violence, as a problematic but undeniable facet of consciousness, is a valid object of poetic transformation, although this does not mean that violence in artistic form is acknowledged as beautiful. Rather, it is the *concept* of the aesthetic that is transformed, not the fact of the violence itself.

As far as the depiction of violence is concerned, aspects of the avant-garde aesthetic may also be found in the cinema. The frequently discussed Odessa steps sequence in Eisenstein's POTEMKIN is one of the most famous episodes of extreme violence from the silent era. Fraser maintains that the scene is "especially shocking, because the image of the sabred face of the respectably dressed middle-aged gentlewoman comes at the end of an absolute anthology of violences [sic] to the normally sacrosanct, including cripples and babies" (80). Another notorious scene from roughly the same period is the infamous eye-slicing segment in Luis Buñuel and Salvador Dali's UN CHIEN ANDALOU (1929). Here the close-up image of a razor's cut across the eyeball is extraordinarily transgressive, since the object of violence represents the delicate instrument through which the perceiver has access to the image. The position of the viewer is one of unprecedented vulnerability; the violence to the filmed object is easily experienced as violence to the viewers themselves. For Fraser, the frontiers of transgression are approached in situations like the following: "The true mental daring and hardihood are those displayed when the artist simultaneously acknowledges the worth of what is being violated and yet presents unflinchingly its violation. And it *hurts* the reader or viewer to be involved in that process and to feel the broader implications of that violation" (116). This description is apt for many a depiction of violent actions both in the cinema and in literature.

By introducing the idea of the forms of consciousness as the materials of art, and by identifying the work of certain artistic movements of the first half of the 20th century as vital to the transformation of the definition of art, Sontag has presented us with a productive framework in which to consider and clarify the nature of film violence. Her thesis also indicates a first step toward a subtler assessment of the different functions that fictional displays of violence play, both within the textual diegesis and in the minds of the spectators. As Fraser suggests, violence is multi-functional: "The functions of violence are ... numerous – violence as release, violence as communication, violence as play, violence as self-affirmation, or self-defense, or self-discovery, violence as a flight from reality, violence as the truest sanity in a particular situation" (9). These two aspects – form (of consciousness) and function (of that form) – will be examined more closely in the chapters to follow.

Once the disturbingly tenacious relationship between aesthetics and beauty has been sundered, analyses less obscured by the vagaries of taste may forge a new awareness of the meaning of violent forms in film. However, a repudiation of the concept of beauty is a mere prolegomenon to the real problem of screen violence, which is not one of aestheticization but of aesthetics. Black proposes that once we understand the circumstances of the incorporation of the term aesthetics into the English language in the early 19th century, "we may begin to sense ... the extent to which our customary experience of murder and other forms of violence is primarily aesthetic, rather than moral, physical, natural" (*Aesthetics* 3). Derived from the Greek *aesthesis*, meaning "perceptible things," the English term was allegedly introduced by Thomas De Quincey in his 1827 essay "On Murder Considered as One of the Fine Arts" (Black, *Aesthetics* 2).[43] From its inception, then, the word aesthetics in English has somewhat morbidly been associated with acts of violence,[44] and it was not until much later in the 19th century that the designation became less controversial. With the rise of the aforementioned art movements like Futurism, the subject of violence renewed its connection to aesthetics. In her dissertation on violence in Russian and East German literature, Nesbet discerns that "philosophies of art and philosophies of violence have an uncanny tendency to intersect as cultures with filial ties to violence ... construct a new aesthetics" (vi). Revolutionary movements thus seem to conceive of the relation between aesthetics and violence in quite intimate terms.

It should be clear from the present discussion that, at least within the carto-graphies of 20th century art, it is hardly feasible to consider an aesthetics of violence without also considering the violence of aesthetics. As we shall see later, Peckinpah repeatedly emphasized his intention to make the viewers un-comfortable. If a film's ability to stimulate responses of displeasure can be taken as a measure of that film's ethical import, is that quality then a testament to an aesthetic impoverishment? Edgar Wind is an aesthetician who laments the di-minishing ability of art to move its audience. "We are much given to art," he writes, "but it touches us lightly, and that is why we can take so much of it, and so much of so many different kinds ... . Art is so well received because it has lost its sting" (7). Wind cites the Angry-Young-Men and Brecht as examples of artists who attempted to overcome this "atrophy of the receptive organs" (8). The problem with a confrontational aesthetic, however, is that its effect de-creases with repetition. Perhaps nowhere is this more readily witnessed than in the historiography of screen violence, and it can be debated whether post-Peck-inpah aesthetics of violence has been successful in inventing new forms in which the nature of violence can be analyzed and rethought. In the context of Wind's thesis, a film like THE WILD BUNCH may even be read as a protest state-ment which addresses not only the topic of violence but also the dispassionate and non-threatening element that John Bayley, in his foreword to Wind's book, claims defines contemporary art (xvi). It seems that Peckinpah's work attempts to remind us of the real teleology of art – or the teleology of real art – which Albert Camus believed should lead us "back to the origins of rebellion" (258).

If we discard the notion of beauty as a defining principle of art, what is left of the aesthetic? There is good reason to be skeptical about the possibility of ever being able to determine the nature of an eternal aesthetic essence, because, first of all, philosophies of art continue to change over time. Second, because there are crucial differences in the material basis of the various artistic media, it would be difficult to arrive at a common standard of aesthetic evaluation. A constructive theory of aesthetic specificity should be founded on principles that are inherent to the medium, that differentiate the work from non-aesthetic texts, and that cannot be reduced to the idiosyncrasies of taste. The criterion of beauty falls short on all of these accounts. It is not intrinsic to the work but to the con-sciousness of the beholder (factors that are inherent to the text would, for in-stance, be the use of deep focus in film or direct free style in prose fiction), it fails to discriminate between aesthetic and non-aesthetic texts, and it regularly comes down to a matter of subjective preference. In other words, the concept of beauty is useless as a measure of aesthetic specificity.

What should not be forgotten, however, is that there are at least two different uses of the term 'aesthetic,' of which only one is acceptable. The first of these, the transcendental, involves the tradition of comprehending art as a manifestation of essential beauty. I have already tried to expose some of the fundamental weaknesses of this argument. But the concept of aesthetics can also be used in a less specialized sense, which includes *form*, *style* and *structure*. A theory of aesthetics that is based on the features of composition is able to fulfill the criteria outlined above. Compositional form is inherent to the text itself, not in any standard outside it; the various manifestations of form productively differentiate aesthetic from non-aesthetic texts; and the identification of formal structures are able to eliminate the contingencies of taste. Once the fallacious association of screen violence with the aesthetic-as-beautiful has been cleared away, one is better prepared to explore the actual forms of violence in the cinema, which manifest themselves both narratively and stylistically. The former concerns the ways in which violent film segments might be analyzed in terms of a process of narration; that is, how the violence is temporally, spatially and causally constructed, and how it correlates with the global structure of the narrative. Stylistically, one needs to examine the compositional configurations of violence, how it exploits the resources of the medium, and how a particular stylistic option might be explained both in terms of the immediate local context, the wider generic context and ultimately the overarching historical context.

Mythologicism

> *No other narrative form is so replete with violence as myth.*
> James Jakób Liszka

Myth-oriented approaches to violence operate on a high level of abstraction, arguing that violence is foundational or in other ways essential to the logic of the mythologies we live by. Such theories are usually associated with the work of individual scholars, the most prominent of which are Girard and Slotkin, but a host of film and media theorists have also increasingly come to approach screen violence in terms of mythical elements like rebirth and sacrifice.[45] For Girard, an act of originary violence constitutes the core of all mythical formations, whereas for Slotkin, the mythology that most forcefully defines American history is one of *regeneration through violence*.[46] Other theorists also emphasize the intimate relation between violence and mythic narratives, among them James Jakób Liszka: "The violences [sic] that occur in myth generally play a strategic role in the narration. They usually occur at the interstices of three stages, in most cases effecting the transition from one to the other" (238). Inversely, as Sharrett has suggested, narratives of violence can be grasped as embodiments of a type of "mythic speech" which "conflate[s] nature with culture" (10).

Violent films such as THE WILD BUNCH and RESERVOIR DOGS, Sharrett proposes, are the products not so much of postmodern nihilism or even formal playfulness as of a long mythological tradition that has woven violence into the structure of narrativity itself; the cinematic reworking of crucial historical traumas like The Alamo, Custer's Last Stand, and Omaha Beach must be read as "sentimental valorizations of sacrificial violence" (416). Sharrett concludes that the regeneration mythos is a pragmatic narrative whose overall purpose is to justify or rationalize political discourse and action metaphysically. For Girard, Slotkin, Liszka and Sharrett myth and violence appear to be interdependent processes whose overarching forms suffuse a potentially infinite number of myth-based narratives.

Slotkin's seminal trilogy on the mythology of the frontier presents the concept of regeneration through violence as a virtually all-embracing theoretical model which builds on the rationale of violence in American culture.[47] On an even more general note, Girard proposes his theory of sacrifice in order to explain the structure and function of violence in human life. Both theories translate as grand narratives couched in the form of super-mythologies that provide a cognitive framework for the conceptualization of a wide range of cultural experiences that converge at the phenomenon of violence. However, these frameworks face bankruptcy in that their legitimacy as explanatory models is compromised by the deteriorating value of the notion of grand metanarratives. Slocum, for example, brings up the question of whether contemporary narratives of violence are still in any meaningful way related to an overarching mythology ("Violence" 22). Slotkin's regeneration thesis and Girard's theory of sacrifice may help illuminate the narrative structure of films such as THE SEARCHERS (John Ford 1956) and THE GODFATHER, but seem inapplicable to postmodernist films such as PULP FICTION, NATURAL BORN KILLERS and FIGHT CLUB. The reshuffling of temporality in Tarantino's films and the hyper-chaotic collage of forms in Stone's film are symptomatic of a certain confusion with respect to the viability of grand narratives in a post-mythological era. Aesthetic disorientation becomes indicative of a moral bewilderment.

According to Slotkin's analysis of what Richard Jewett and John Shelton Lawrence in a book of the same title have referred to as the *American monomyth*, the notion of regeneration through violence functions as a cultural metaphor capable of fashioning collective experience into a coherent and meaningful narrative:

> the first colonists saw in America an opportunity to regenerate their fortunes, their spirits and power of their church and nation; but the means to that regeneration ultimately became the means of violence, and the myth of regeneration through violence became the structuring metaphor of the American experience. (*Regeneration* 5)

Slotkin reveals the implicit transition in which the focal center of the myth slides from a conception of the land itself as regenerator to a suggestion of violence as the principal force of regeneration. The colonists' experience in the new world was shaped by the sum of their encounters with the wilderness, which also contained malevolent forces that continuously threatened the survival of the settlers. Thus, although the idea of America as a topographical entity was not linked to violence a priori, the potentially menacing forces contained within it, such as the vagaries of the climate, wild animals and the natives, transmuted the perception of the wilderness from empty territory to symbolic topos.[48] It is no longer the land itself but the various manifestations of resistance within it that come to be regarded as the means of regeneration. As Slotkin also contends, the early mythmakers conceived of the wilderness in terms of "demonic personification" (*Regeneration* 14), as a partially anthropomorphized antagonist that constituted, within the structure of the myth, an adversary for the narrative protagonist. The inevitable conflict that provides the motor of this narrative is one so fundamental that only violence can resolve it and renew the energies of the protagonist. The role of narrative is of capital importance in this respect. As Lyotard points out, narrative form validates not only the logic of the story told but also the social conditions upon which the criteria of its narration rest (20).

The narrative of regeneration through violence is a primitive myth both structurally and morally. On a surface level, myth represents a crude alternative to cultural disunity. The concept of violence as a ritualistic, and occasionally even sacred instrument of societal renewal is inherently problematic, but it is perhaps most useful as a kind of interpretive heuristic that assists a culture in making sense of the multiplicity of narratives – factual and fictional – that organize the world of that culture. That the notion of renewal is linked to violence is not surprising if one postulates an associative, quasi-organic connection between the two.[49] In a strictly biological perspective, decay and birth are interconnected. What is less clear in the context of the regeneration myth is why the process of disintegration necessarily has to be a violent one. Furthermore, how is the appropriation of an essentially biological model for the explanation of a cultural myth motivated? There is no evidence of a causal relationship between violence and regeneration; the link is tenuous and conventional at best.

The foundations for the regeneration-through-violence mythos were established by the literature of the northern American Puritan colonies of the 17th century. Slotkin stresses the position of their placement – on the frontier of a vast, uncharted wilderness – as a crucial motivation for the creation of the mythology. This predicament was complicated further by the historical context of the Puritans' experience:

> the colonists themselves doubted their own motives: were they going, as they said, to redeem the Satanic forest for Jesus, or were they self-seekers, degenerate in virtue? ...

As Puritans, they were convinced that the natural world was corrupt from its very roots, requiring total regeneration. ("Dreams and Genocide" 52)

The mythological tradition of American violence derives from this existential matrix, and the multiple narratives that ensue are inflections and variations of the basic tenets of this tradition.[50] These comprise ideas of renewal, conversion, purification, eschatology and sacrifice, and represent various emphases or sub-narratives within the overall mythology.[51] While regeneration is the common objective of all manifestations of this myth, the miscellaneous stories may stress different aspects of it. The genre of the captivity tales typically concerns rituals of initiation, conversion and purification,[52] and finds its modern counterpart in films such as THE SEARCHERS, THE UNFORGIVEN (John Huston 1960), THE MAN-CHURIAN CANDIDATE (John Frankenheimer 1962), THE DEER HUNTER (Michael Cimino 1978), and APOCALYPSE NOW (Coppola 1979). In American culture, Mary White Rowlandson's *The Soveraignty & Goodness of God... A Narrative of the Captivity and Restauration* (1682) seems to be the model for these later narratives, but, according to Black, the theme of "the hostage-turned-defector" is not uncommon in European literature either (*Aesthetics* 173). Examples are the narrative of the Trojan war, Goethe's *Faust* (in which the imprisoned Gretchen refuses to be liberated), and some of Angela Carter's short fiction like "Our Lady of the Massacre" (1979) (which takes its plot from Ford's THE SEARCHERS), and "Peter and the Wolf."

More significant than the captivity stories are the interpretations of the regeneration mythos in terms of eschatology and sacrifice. Sharrett claims that contemporary culture has inherited an "apocalyptic consciousness" from the Puritan era (Introduction 12). This millennialism has percolated down into some American film genres, notably the horror genre, which, since PSYCHO and THE BIRDS (Hitchcock 1963), has become a vehicle for both a critique and a reinforcement of various strands of apocalyptic beliefs. Moreover, no myth-narrative is intact without the presence of antagonists, who in the regeneration mythos are cast as sacrificial victims. The process of victimization, as Sharrett sees it, establishes the idea of the "Other" as a scapegoat indispensable to the construction of the "Self" "under millennial and apocalyptic narrative" ("Afterword" 424).[53] Sacrificial narratives such as the Last Stand are vital in giving form to this process. From the inception of the frontier myth as documented in Turner's essay, the Indians have served as the scapegoats.[54] "Turner's essay," Michael Bliss writes, "identifies Indians as scapegoats who are used to compensate not only for fear of barbarism but also for an entire host of vague anxieties" (*Justified Lives* 4).

The specifically American mythology that Slotkin explicates is also interpretable in the context of the large-scale mimetic scenario which Girard has described so extensively. There is a vital distinction, however, in the type of material the two theorists take as their object of study. In discussing prohibition and sacrifice, Girard is referring to religious practice in a sociological or anthropological sense. He is theorizing communal experience directly. Slotkin, on the other hand, believes the object under examination is the kind of myth for which concrete texts represent the prime vehicle: "myth-narratives rarely occur in pure form, but rather are contained, perhaps hidden, in 'ordinary' cultural phenomena like literary or journalistic narratives or in the stories people tell of themselves" ("Dreams of Genocide" 51). Insofar as Girard's theory reads as a narrative (but not necessarily a myth), it comes much closer to the "pure form" which Slotkin mentions. Both explore interrelated forms of social praxis, one through religious ritual, the other through a set of largely fictional texts.[55]

In "Mimesis and Violence," Girard describes the nature of violent sacrifice thus:

> Real or symbolic, sacrifice is primarily a collective action of the entire community, which purifies itself of its own disorder through the unanimous immolation of a victim, but this can happen only at the paroxysm of the ritual crisis. … Sacrifice is the resolution and conclusion of ritual because a collective murder or expulsion resolves the mimetic crisis that ritual mimics. What kind of mechanism can this be? Judging from the evidence, direct and indirect, this resolution must belong to the realm of what is commonly called a scapegoat effect (11).

In its structure, Girard's thesis is simple and assumes the form of a master narrative. Violence is recast as both a symbolic and a pragmatic solution to some sort of societal crisis. Conceptually speaking, such a crisis is related to moments during which constitutive differences in a given society are in a state of disintegration. Girard calls this phenomenon "a mimetic crisis" (11). Appropriation and acquisition represent modes of behavior that are unlikely to be imitated. If they were subject to imitation, the result would be that two individuals A and B – due to A's act of appropriating through imitation some element that B possesses – become rivals for that same object. Should the impulse to imitate appropriation turn reciprocal, mimetic rivalry and violence would be a probable outcome.[56] Girard proclaims that "violence is generated by this process [imitative rivalry]; or rather violence is the process itself when two or more partners try to prevent one another from appropriating the object they all desire through physical or other means" (9). The exact nature of this obscure object is not explicitly spelled out in this context (Girard's explication is too indeterminate to suggest anything concrete), although one would assume that the question of power is a significant vehicle for the constitution of that kind of desire which invites mimetic rivalry.

Girard discards the theories of aggression and scarcity of material necessities as originative causes of violence, and instead proposes his own idea of "appropriative mimicry" as the superior explanation. His account of the problem of violence is more abstract though perhaps also more convincing than the aggression theory – especially as propounded by someone like Robert Ardrey[57]- in that it overcomes the narrow referencing of violence to the domain of biological instincts. Girard holds that his theory of mimetic violence is able to heighten our sensitivity toward many different spheres within human culture, that of religion in particular. He draws on the cultural praxis of ritual in order to illustrate how the threat of mimetic rivalry might be contained and placated. For Girard, ritual can be understood as a "theatrical reenactment of a mimetic crisis in which the differences that constitute the society are dissolved" (11). This, in turn, represents a different mimetic conception which has as its principal function the deterrence of the potential crisis that Girard identifies as mimetic rivalry. The state of social undifferentiation – which may result from the death of a prominent member (Girard's example is the death of a sacred king) – represents the threat of a social breakdown, chaos or epidemic violence, which needs to be curtailed at any cost. The biblical scholar James G. Williams provides the following synopsis of the interrelation of mimetic desire, violence and differentiation:

> The truth of the human condition is the truth of a mimesis that both gives rise to and structures desire, the wish to acquire what the other has and is imagined to desire and of being what the other is. This leads inevitably to conflict and rivalry and will issue in violence unless averted or overcome by a differentiation process that requires that in the event of crisis, a victim can be found by 'chance' ... in order to regain the stable order of differences that supposedly reigned before the crisis began (239).

Upon the threat of disaster, the society responds by mimicking precisely that crisis with which it is faced, and which the ordinary mechanisms of prohibition fail to keep in check. As Girard notes, it is the provision of sacrifice that acts as mediator in the ritual process.[58] In this respect, he proposes the following equation: "Sacrifice stands in the same relationship to the ritual crisis that precedes it as the death or expulsion of the hero to the undifferentiated chaos that prevails at the beginning of many myths" ("Mimesis and Violence" 11). It is thus through the sacrificial performance that the disaster is mitigated; and ritual becomes a means of purgation.[59] Sacrifice requires a victim, and Girard designates the specific status of this victim in terms of what he calls a scapegoat:[60] "Instead of trying to roll back mimetic violence it [the community] tries to get rid of it by encouraging it and by bringing it to a climax that triggers the happy solution of ritual sacrifice with the help of a substitute victim" (13). The conflicting scenario which is evidenced here is one in which the act of sacrifice itself can be grasped as a metonymization of violence. That is, the sacrifice of the victim, the scapegoat, represents a symbolic circumscription of the act of violence which – through figurative displacement – reduces it to a necessary minimum. Hence, a threat of internal violence is restrained by the initiation of the scapegoating mechanism.

The notion of sacrificial violence may be brought to bear on a range of films. Kubrick's PATHS OF GLORY (1957) and Coppola's APOCALYPSE NOW, for example, both identify a sacrificial victim – a scapegoat – whose execution provides the main impetus for the narrative. In Kubrick's film, which is set during the First World War, three French soldiers are court-martialed and sentenced to death in order to set an example for the rest of their platoon. The context is a failed attempt to seize control of enemy territory. Upon realizing that his men are severely outnumbered, Colonel Dax orders the retreat of his troops, an unpopular decision among his superiors. To maintain order General Broulard orders the execution of three more or less randomly selected soldiers. In his analysis of the film, Alexander Walker stresses the scapegoat dimension of the execution: "We realize over the generals' breakfast that what Broulard decided was not to save the three scapegoats, but to add a fourth to them" (*Stanley Kubrick Directs* 117). Thus, a scapegoat mechanism may be attributed to more than one event in the film; the public execution of the three soldiers and General Mireau's demise. In APOCALYPSE NOW, Captain Willard, the film's character-narrator, is assigned to track down and "eliminate" Colonel Kurtz. Willard's killing of the deranged colonel takes on an overtly sacrificial dimension, not the least because the filmic depiction of the event is set up as a scene that crosscuts Willard's slaying of his victim with the slaughtering of a buffalo. The juxtaposition is unambiguously present to reinforce the ritualistic aspect. The slow and lengthy build-up to the violent climax underscores the ceremonial spirit of the killing; Willard takes his time to converse with and to study the colonel carefully prior to the assassination. There are, notwithstanding, certain contextual twists that make a strictly Girardian reading of these two instances problematic. In the Kubrick film, the execution of the soldiers is not related to any kind of ritual crisis. Because the environment of the story is one of excessive trench warfare, the effect of deterrence seems irrelevant. Violence is already omnipresent, and it does not make any immediate sense to arrange a ritual of sacrifice in which the potential horrors of escalated violence are fended off via an act of socially sanctioned symbolic purification. In a sense, this scenario is the inverse of what Girard stipulated. In APOCALYPSE NOW, Kurtz is a victim who complies with the sacrificial process, which, one could argue, undermines the mission because the execution actually comes across as a suicide rather than as the sacrifice of a scapegoat.

Does the cinema now provide the arena in which the contradictions of Slotkin's and Girard's mythologies are played out? In *The Political Unconscious* (1981), Frederic Jameson seems to indicate that culture cannot evade the influ-

ence of grand narratives, as these in effect form part of the conditions that gov-
err acts of textual production: "if interpretation in terms of expressive causality
or of allegorical master narratives remains a constant temptation, this is because
such master narratives have inscribed themselves in the texts as well as in our
thinking about them" (34). Myths may once have been both indispensable and
convincing as explanatory super-narratives, but, I would argue, that in the era
that Danto has dubbed "posthistorical" (*After the End* 2), they have become obsolete.[61] As for the cinema, a hyper-awareness of tradition as well as an ever
more rampant self-reflexivity have increasingly come to inhabit and command
the textual enterprise, and these tendencies challenge the routine reproduction
of master mythologies.

Furthermore, when mythology is applied as an interpretive shorthand for
textual analysis, it often courts reductionism. A work of fiction is never just a
rewriting of a grand narrative, but contains more – such as something that goes
beyond the perimeters of mythic speech. Thus, while I do not claim that all
textual analyses involving myth are fallacious, any use of myth alone in the
interpretation of fictional texts falls prey to the mythological fallacy. Film texts
embody contradictions and ambiguities; structures that resist any attempt at
homogenization. While myth simplifies, the *metaphoricity* of fiction complicates
and multiplies. Feature films harbor a potential for simultaneously critiquing
and glorifying violence, a paradox that epitomizes this ambivalence of signification which characterizes fiction. Film analyses within the parameters of myth
run the risk of being inopportunely formulaic, as the same interpretive structure
is repetitively superimposed onto each individual text. Finally, the real material
of film violence is the body, a concrete and conceptual entity that is beyond the
grasp of mythological exegesis.

Mimeticism

> *The reel is the allegory of the real.*
> Azade Seyhan

In an attempt to defend his film NATURAL BORN KILLERS against charges of exploitation, director Oliver Stone resorted to a very familiar rhetoric: "violence is
all around us; it's in nature, and it's in every one of us – .... I think this film deals
with the *idea* of violence" (in Pizzello 156, emphasis in original). Symptomatic
readings of movie violence tend to promote the theory that fiction is a reflection
of the society in which it was made. The artist cannot but portray the world "as
it is," and if movies are violent it is because society is violent. However irrefuta-

ble the claim may be, symptomatic readings can still be challenged on several accounts. What I refer to as the mimetic fallacy assumes a simplistic correlation between the non-fictional and the fictional.[62] It disregards the numerous complexities of imagination, convention and craft involved in a work of fiction, reducing the phenomenology of the text to a matter of mechanical recording. Second, it is highly unlikely that the amount of film violence the average viewer is exposed to is in any way proportionate to the violence he or she is exposed to outside of the movie theatre. It is possible that for the majority of viewers, violence is the subject furthest removed from their own experience. Hence, even if fiction *did* accurately reflect events and conditions in the external world, it would nevertheless fail to reflect the particular experiential reality of those who comprise the largest group of moviegoers. Third, and most significantly, fiction films are fundamentally shaped by generic, aesthetic, and philosophical traditions whose continuities may supersede those that exist between fiction and society. Stylistic conventions for showing violence change over time; in THE GREAT TRAIN ROBBERY, for example, "all but one of those shot throw their arms up over their heads before falling down, a gesture unknown today" (Goldberg 49). In order to better understand the meaning of violence in the cinema, I suggest that one reconsiders the doxastic devotion to the idea of the mimetic contract. Art, fiction, and film are all modes of discourse which tend to address the transtextual lineage that has spawned them, and they need not refer to any circumstances beyond the text. "Working with graphic violence," Prince observes, "the filmmaker inherits the history of a stylistic whose conventionalized meanings are readily understood by contemporary viewers" ("Graphic" 32).

The problem of mimesis is certainly no less challenging than the Aristotelian and aesthetic fallacies dealt with in the previous chapters, and I do not aim to present an extended discussion of it here. I shall give short shrift to the numerous works that in various ways have attempted to elucidate the mimetic.[63] First of all, our customary conception of the imitative function of fictional film must be deracinated, or even better, the entire concept of mimesis needs to be recontextualized. But, as Christopher Prendergast has noted, mimesis as a critical term can hardly be disentangled from the numerous theoretical debates it has stirred up throughout its long and complicated history (*Order of Mimesis* 5). An examination of this history is beyond the confines of this discussion, but I shall briefly point to a significant semantic rupture in the early understanding of the term.[64] In a pre-Platonic context, the meaning of *mimeisthai* signified not imitation but performance, and was exclusively related to dance and music. The Platonic sense of mimesis has nonetheless remained unchallenged, particularly in the French and Anglo-American traditions (Spariosu, iii). Aesthetic criticism, therefore, is better served by a pre-Platonic understanding of the mimetic, one which is inclined more toward poesis, play, and performance than toward reflection or representation.

Films do not imitate any reality other than that of cinema's own history. Within the discipline of art history, Collingwood has written perceptively on the subject of imitation: "A work of art is imitative in virtue of its relation to another work of art which affords it a model of artistic excellence" (42). If we want to understand the workings and meanings of fictional texts, we should not disregard the genealogy of aesthetic compositions, norms and conventions out of which these texts emerge. The scope of this contention transcends matters of mere intertextuality, which are often confined to a superficial textual level. Interrelations of fictional works are not only constituted referentially, but also discursively. That is, a text is always implicated in a dialogue with other texts, with one or more traditions, and the discourse of the text does not address the "real" but the already fictional. The continuous production of fictional texts delineates the contours of a closed topography, intangible, but nonetheless real, a territory settled not by the fictional works themselves but by the world they have unfurled. Though it does not have a name, it is in this world that the narration of a film like NATURAL BORN KILLERS comes to address, imitate and finally absorb preceding texts like THE WIZARD OF OZ (Victor Fleming 1939), BONNIE AND CLYDE, A CLOCKWORK ORANGE, BADLANDS (Terrence Malick 1973), SERPICO (Sidney Lumet 1973), RESERVOIR DOGS and many others. When Stone tries to justify the images of violence he has created by asserting that they are a mirror of the society which encompasses both film and filmmaker, his apologia is nothing but redundant, since an impassable conceptual chasm intervenes between our world and that which Stone's film alludes to. The membrane of the text may be malleable, but at the same time impenetrable. Fiction always turns inwards, toward itself, and is thus a supremely self-centered entity.

What exactly does the mimetic fallacy consist of? It denotes a failure to discern that, as Collingwood writes, "art proper is not and cannot be representative" (42). Fiction is not a reflection of the external world, but a reflection of itself. Writing on expressionist films, Jean Mitry points out that the objects shown are not arbitrated according to "a meaning belonging to a represented world beyond its representation" but to what he calls a "decorative interpretation" (189). This seems to designate the sensuousness of film style. The reason why "we take delight in viewing the most accurate possible images of objects which in themselves cause distress when we see them" (Aristotle, *Poetics* 6) is due not to the appeal of imitation but to our knowledge and appreciation of the rules by which aesthetic processes are made to work. As Hantke relates, "[w]hat appears gratuitous in a strictly mimetic model of textuality can acquire purpose and function in a more open and flexible model" (par. 5). It must be pointed out, however, that this modal self-containment should not be seen as suggesting that art and fiction are immanently disinterested. Feature films, for instance, tend to capture and comment on the politics of the moment, but that does not render them imitations of a particularized social world. As Mikhail Iampolski concedes, "a text always appears to us as emerging from some other text" (15).

How and why our experience and comprehension of artworks differ from our perception of real-life phenomena are complex questions that have been at the center of theoretical analyses for centuries. The modes of reception that art and reality elicit are fundamentally divergent, even disparate. Our capacity for finding pleasure in aesthetic artifacts that contain material which we would find repulsive in real life suggests that there is a discrepancy between our understanding of art as opposed to reality. When the psychologist Herbert Langfeld speaks of the "estrangement from the world of reality" as a characteristic of the "aesthetic attitude" (66), he suggests an ontology of art beyond mimesis. For film historian Barry Salt, the diverse manifestations of film form occupy a spectrum the positions of which all signify a certain degree of distortion or transformation of "the real" (108). With this view, form is simultaneously both detached from and committed to the extra-textual world; it is disengaged because distortion inevitably negates the possibility of mimeticism, but it is also committed because every variant of form embodies a particular relation with reality in its very anatomy, an expressive ethics.

Nowhere is the gap between reality and fiction greater than in the sphere of violence. In real life, violence is an extreme experience, one that threatens the integrity of the individual. When we watch violence unfold on a movie screen we are never further away from it. The proximity of violence as aesthetic fiction demystifies our sense of the unimaginable. Film puts violence on display, confers the logic of narrative upon it, and instills in the viewers the perception that the more violence they see, the further removed they are from the possibility of having to face real violence. The violence that narrative inflicts upon film characters is somehow furtively soothing, it reinforces our sense of remaining unviolated. Watching fictional violence takes on the quality of a ritualistic confirmation of our own security. On-screen violence is also infinitely distant from us due to the inaccessibility of the image. The pastness of the pro-filmic embodies its violence – while its ferocious viscerality is kept in check by the immobility of the individual film frame. Violence is as unreal in fiction as it is real in actual life.

Apart from these ontological differences between real and fictional violence, the latter reveals some aspects which are absent from the former. Simulated forms of violence are conventional, narrativized, and structured. The domain of imaginative life to which simulated violence belongs is cut off from actual life by the particular criterion Roger Fry recognizes as the lack of responsive action: "this responsive action implied in actual life moral responsibility. In art we have

no such moral responsibility – it presents a life freed from the binding necessities of our actual existence" (20). He observes that in the life of the imagination,
"we can both feel the emotion and watch it" (27). Movie audiences have no
difficulty appreciating the special reality status that works of fiction entail,[65]
although it is possible that this appreciation requires a basic measure of aesthetic "literacy" [the inability to negotiate between different kinds of reality is
the subject of a joke in a scene in Jane Campion's THE PIANO (1993)]. The distinct
reality status of fiction also needs to be indicated by the texts themselves, since
much of the appeal of fictional works is based on the recognition of artifice.
According to Jeffrey Goldstein, "violent imagery must carry cues to its unreality
or it will lose its appeal" (221).

In *The Society of the Spectacle* (1967), Guy Debord postulates that "everything
that was lived directly has moved away into a representation" (n.p.). Debord's
assertion, hyperbolic as it may be, relates to the notion of the post-mimetic in
complex ways. First, with regard to the field of fiction, it is questionable
whether anything has become part of a representation that did not already belong to a world of simulations. The degree of image saturation may have inten-
sified during the post-war era (and particularly since the early 1990s), but qualitatively, the nature of the simulation – and the relation of that to the real – may
not necessarily have changed accordingly. Thus, my use of the term post-mimetic is somewhat misleading, since I argue that fiction film in general and film
violence in particular have never really been mimetic.[66] More accurately, the
notion of the post-mimetic refers to the critical and theoretical discourse attendant on works of fiction, a discourse which would gain from redefining the fictional as non-mimetic. Spectacle exists, but not necessarily in the way that Debord conceives it, as "a social relation among people, mediated by images" (n.
p.). There is a phenomenological dimension beyond spectacle, beyond simulation. The world is not all text.

However, this is a subject that will not be pursued here. Instead, we will pursue the contention that film fiction, and more specifically film violence, does not
entail a real-life referent. Fictional worlds do not index any non-fictional counterparts. Jan Mukařovský appears to have understood this well: "The influence
of aesthetic value is not that it swallows up and represses all remaining values,
but that it releases every one of them from direct contact with a corresponding
life-value" (89). It is at once the most difficult and the most obvious, but it is the
first thing we need to understand about fiction. If art and fiction are representations, they represent something that does not exist save within the boundaries
of the fictional itself.

The positing of a mimetic relation between the fictional world and the real
world seems particularly obsolete and simplistic in the case of audiovisual
forms of violence. As previously mentioned, the majority of viewers have no

experience with the more extreme manifestations of carnage depicted in films like THE WILD BUNCH or NATURAL BORN KILLERS. Furthermore, even documentary footage of actual violent conflicts that is aired on television is to a large extent filtered through the conventions of cinema. A descriptive case in point is the spectacular and sensationalist rendering of the Gulf War by Cable News Network (CNN) in 1991. On the level of reception, the cognitive schemata through which we perceive and interpret a violent action in the cinema are constituted by our accumulated knowledge of film. Violent action in the cinema is therefore not so much the simulation of actual violence as a re-representation of violent images drawn from the intertextual history of the medium. The taxonomy of schemata that viewers activate while watching violence in the movies is to a significant degree textually generated. This suggests that the reception process involved in this type of film viewing must be largely derived from a specifically aesthetic mode of comprehension.

Our approach to fictional violence is not only conditioned by external contexts, but also by the internal context the text itself establishes. That is, the world of the text is in some measure self-contained in that it relates to what Gérard Genette calls the transtextual – "everything that brings [the text] into relation (manifest or hidden) with other texts" – rather than the extra-textual (*Architext* 81). Transtextuality assumes that the relation each work establishes with other works supersedes the relation it may form with the non-fictional. This non-mimetic relation is most palpably present in acts of quotation, otherwise it functions like an abstract structure that cues our reading of the text. In this sense, all fictional texts contain some degree of metafictionality; the apparent mimeticism of the quintessential Hollywood movie is always deceptive. What I refer to as the internal context prompts the viewer to map the relations *within* the text. Since aesthetic perception is a matter of temporal process first, and of spatial process second, reception proceeds through several phases in which the relational web is continuously modified. The first segments of the artwork introduce a specified set of situations which function as a reference point for the gradual unfolding of the text. The expository moment, narratively conceived, provides a form of thesis statement, and its complication throughout produces new relations which can be regularly referred back to the initial proposition. This appears to be a relatively common pattern that even governs the perception of paintings, which we frequently perceive as a spatial art. Because our engagement with a painting necessarily occupies a certain duration, the reception process is open to multiple transformations in the course of our viewing. Most artifacts contain heavily coded conventions, and thus in part depend on external context. In principle, one could imagine artworks that rely so little on conventionality – consider for instance Pat O'Neill's *Decay of Fiction* (2002) – that the internal context more or less single-handedly orchestrates the spectatorial access to the world of the fiction.

Regardless of the type of realism with which any given violent film segment is presented, the nature of the medium and the impact of narrativity transform the shot into an "imitation," which is one step removed from reality. In this sense, fictional violence represents a closed system; it is always a representation of another representation. Although real-life violence occasionally functions as a source for film fiction, the dialectics of the cinematic transfiguration of the actual material assigns the aesthetic product to this closed system.[67] The spectacle is one of the dominant modes that constitute violence in film, narrative is another, and it is these aesthetic elements that distinguishes the ontology of violence in film from that of reality. Ken Morrison has suggested that violence in "the film world" (and by extension, the world of art and fiction) undergoes a process of valorization that sets it apart from violence in the real world. Fiction films, Morrison maintains, provide violence with a certain value which may be compared to a monetary currency: "inside the film medium violence participates in the same political economy as money in the real world in that both create value outside the real and outside human relationships" (314). The nature of this immaterial value, whose coordinates may be aesthetic, moral, rhetorical, cultural or commercial, constantly fluctuates according to the negotiations of textual meaning.

II

Filming Death

I   The Transfigured Image

Every new aesthetic reality makes man's ethical reality more precise.
Joseph Brodsky

In the introduction to part I, I suggested that the approaches discussed in the previous chapters represent dominant positions on the subject of screen violence. With the exception of empiricism, they are neither research methodologies, nor are they as compartmentalized as the present survey may seem to indicate. In analytical practice, elements overlap and intersect. In spite of possible objections, I have nevertheless chosen such an outline, for these fallacies typify predominant approaches to thinking and writing about film violence. Their logic and concepts provide the terms and conditions –the discursive framework – for how scholars come to understand media violence. But their overall deficiency is that they almost invariably fail to address the relevant questions. For instance, to ask whether exposure to film violence is harmful to viewers is really to ask whether exposure to *fiction* in general is harmful. Decontextualization implies reductionism, but it also leaves the scholar with an incomplete object of study.[1] Furthermore, neglecting the contexts of violence inevitably leads to a situation in which it is treated as a given, as a textual component that does not require interpretation or analysis. Film violence, however, cannot have any meaning or significance apart from the larger textual framework into which it is inscribed. As Tania Modleski puts it, violence is "all in the context – in the way the film allows us to understand what we're seeing, in the questions it poses about the place of violence in our culture and about the viewer's investment in the erotics of violence" (B16). Therefore, any analysis of violence needs to start with the films themselves, as well as the genres and traditions of which they are a part. Since fictional texts are dynamic and ambiguous, their meaning is not immediately given.

If the above approaches are largely untenable, what kind of theory should thye be replaced with? First of all, we need to acknowledge the constructedness of the nomenclature we rely upon. "Film violence" only became the subject of "intense public concern" in the late 1960s (Slotkin, *Gunfighter Nation* 555), but remains an abstraction, a term that is afflicted with a particularly recalcitrant set of presuppositions which stigmatize it as something contagious, something that in itself is sufficient to keep moviegoers away from certain films. Suffering from over-use, the term has nearly been drained of any semantic import. 'Film violence' has become an empty term, signifying nothing except its own self-referential blankness. As such, it cannot constitute the object of any kind of examination. However, though "violence" is merely a discursive term in a specific sense, as Bernard Cook argues (4), there are certainly films that contain violence, or, rather, *textualized* violence. It is these texts that are at the center of this study, not the linguistic signifier that regrettably diverts attention from what is really at stake with respect to violent film fictions. One implication of this awareness is that it is only the films themselves that are susceptible to critical and theoretical analyses. Hence, I have had to abandon a premise that initially informed my project: that film violence is an a priori philosophical concept whose existence could be verified independently of concrete texts. But 'film violence' is nothing if not its individual filmic manifestations,[2] which are too diverse to fit into those larger taxonomies that I at one point hoped to generate. When, for instance, we watch the massacre scene in BONNIE AND CLYDE, we may translate the action as "violence," but this is reductionism, a semantic depletion that functions to erase all particularity, all difference, from the phenomenon it signifies.

What informs the subsequent analysis, then, is the intention to restore an interpretive dimension to the discourse on violent cinema and to examine the moral aesthetics which underpins a number of its key films. I shall labor to sidestep the limited rhetoric that reduces the question of textualized violence to a matter of "'film violence'" and its attendant, limited focus on influence and effects. Violence and narrative are part of the same whole, or as Nesbet writes, "[v]iolence is surrounded with meaning-making structures as it is incorporated into aesthetic structures" (48). One cannot examine the violence without at the same time examining the narrative, nor can one speak about the narrative without also engaging with the issue of violence. Evidently, violence may represent an event devoid of meaning, but whenever it is a question of fictional, textualized violence, it is invested with a host of different and occasionally conflicting meanings. This does not imply that critics are free to interpret violent films in any way they like, but only that such texts are powerfully inscribed by multiple meanings from which salient moral positions may be derived. I do not pretend to claim that the films under consideration necessarily subscribe to any common, unifying theme. The idea is rather to show that what one refers to as 'film violence' warrants and in fact requires interpretation and qualitative criticism. I am, therefore, more concerned with the *process* of critiquing textual violence than with attempting to unearth any monolithic or recurring preoccupations which could be shown to constitute a tradition of violent filmmaking in American cinema.

The relationship between terminology and phenomenon is not the only conundrum that requires attention. There is a similar problem with regard to our ways of looking at violence. Cathy Caruth, for instance, writes that "the most direct seeing of a violent event may occur as an absolute inability to know it" (208). If vision is at odds with the knowability of the 'object' under scrutiny, what might the consequences be for an epistemology of violent cinema? As John Berger makes clear, "although every image embodies a way of seeing, our perception or appreciation of an image depends also upon our own way of seeing" (10). In short, our act of looking alters the conception of the object we look at, the implications of which are insightfully addressed by James Elkins in his *The Object Stares Back* (1996). The pure gaze thus remains an impossibility. At least five different elements determine the nature of the image we have before us: the camera's gaze, our own gaze, the sequential context of the image, the relations of the image to those of other films, and everything that we know has been said about the particular image with which we are preoccupied. This impure image, which is the only one accessible to us, is inevitably circumscribed by this set of qualifications.

This discussion will return us to some of the concerns prefigured in chapter five, in which I argue that theory must abandon the notion of the mimetic as a parameter within which to understand film violence. Seeing fictional violence as a representation of real violence is anathema to an adequate comprehension of both phenomena. As a system of mediation, cinema promotes deception through its seeming transparency. The viewer's acceptance of this transparency is more fundamental than a mere suspension of disbelief. That is, the material signs that constitute a film are perceived to appear unobtrusive; as spectators we are given direct access to a world whose recognizable aspects seem to reference the real world. Is not the film image, as André Bazin maintained ("Ontology" 14), a photographic trace of something that once existed in the world? My overriding ambition is to reveal and possibly overcome the inadequacy of the notions of mimesis, imitation, representation and even referentiality that for so long have remained hegemonic in our relation to works of film fiction.[3] If this stance seems uncomfortably reminiscent of old poststructuralist dogma, I would hasten to add that I do not argue that everything must be reduced to text, or textuality. However, fictional texts address other fictional texts, and our manners of engaging with fiction originate in textuality. I would furthermore claim that it is a mistake to over-emphasize the connection between the world of fiction and the world beyond it. In his theory of intertextuality in film, Iampolski notes that wherever "mimesis is violated, we begin to see vigorous traces of semiosis" (30). For Iampolski, it is the act of quotation that facilitates such a transgression: "the quote violates the link between sign and objective reality (the mimetic link), orienting the sign toward another text rather than a thing" (30).[4] Transtextuality is a malleable concept that may profitably be extended beyond direct allusiveness to also encompass the global conventions of tradition, genre, style and narrative; in short, the familiar components which comprise not only a particular work of fiction but the world of fictionality in general. Understanding film fiction, its internal rules and logic, implies a certain measure of training, one which begins with the realization of a work's non-transparency. When, for instance, an adolescent audience responds with laughter while watching the excesses of a slasher movie, the reaction could be an expression of connoisseurship rather than of amorality. In fact, as Steven Alan Carr points out, the industry is so knowledgeable of the existence of the 'knowing' spectator that the notion of (trans)textual competence has already been commodified (96); that is, the appeal to the audience's cine-literacy is intrinsic to the marketability of industry product. A familiarity with the conventions of the genre enables viewers to resist the illusion of transparency that most mainstream pictures strive to manufacture.

Becoming aware of the solidity of film form as a primary and irreducible constituent of textual meaning is a first antidote to offset the influence of the misconceived arguments considered in previous chapters. Empirical, Aristotelian, mythological, mimetic, and, almost paradoxically, aesthetic approaches all tend to ignore the fact that 'screen violence' is not an unproblematic and unmediated entity that may be approached in any direct manner. We never really *see* any "pure" violence, but *forms* of violence, a wide variety of artistic modes in which violence is being conceived, conceptualized and configured audiovisually. Therefore, one should not confuse the ontology of real violence with that of its cinematic forms.

The structure of the argument in what follows emerges from this initial discernment that filmicity is transtextual rather than mimetic, its forms opaque rather than transparent. Although this is a premise which impinges upon the argument in its entirety, it takes on a particular significance for our comprehension of contemporary film violence, and the repercussions and ramifications of the idea will therefore be explored more fully in my discussion of Tarantino's Reservoir Dogs. Supported by a theory which rejects mimeticism and textual transparency, the argument proposes a form-based approach, and further, a tropology of film violence – grounded in the preceding exploration of non-transparent filmicity – with issues of morality and ethics. These, in turn, involve the intersecting concerns of narrative mortification – or what I shall refer to as narrathanatography – and the attendant preoccupation with conceptions of masculinity in crisis, which bears on all five of the film texts examined in the subsequent chapters.

In their *The Popular Arts* (1964), Stuart Hall and Paddy Whannel acknowledged the extent to which one needs to attend closely to qualitative issues involving form and style in order to examine the topic of violence in film and television appropriately (113). A similar approach may be found in Black's *The*

Aesthetics of Murder, where he impugns attempts to comprehend violence as singularly a sociological, pathological or criminological event: "A philosophical approach to murder that tries to account for murder on purely rational grounds ultimately turns out to be as limited as attempts to systematize crime on moral grounds. Once again the aesthetic dimension of crime and violence is overlooked" (8). Furthermore, as Lawrence Alloway proposes, different forms of film violence disclose "transformations of meaning" (7); or, as William Miller notes, we "prefer our violence mediated in certain styles" (87). The notoriously equivocal notion of style regulates the processes of both signification and perception, yet efforts to come to terms with Hall and Whannel's enjoinder have been conspicuously rare. Before I set out to explore in subsequent chapters the implications of what both Bazin and Serge Daney would have called a morality of style,[5] a general exposition of the neoformalist framework which informs this particular theory is in order.

That films like SCARFACE, THE KILLING, and THE WILD BUNCH foreground violent action is immediately evident; what is perhaps less frequently explored is the degree to which these texts also concretize violence as cinematic forms. My use of the term "form" in this context does not recall the narrowly defined concept of many modernist aestheticians, but derives from a somewhat oppositional and marginalized tradition in film theory that I shall refer to as the dialectical approach. From the writings of Eisenstein, one can trace the tentative outline of this tradition through Noël Burch's *Theory of Film Practice* (1969) and to the work of Bordwell and Kristin Thompson.[6] Both in criticism and in film practice, according to the dominant trend, the form/content division has been a powerful concept. As Burch himself notes, filmmakers have tended to think that only the subject was important or that, conversely, only the presentation of it mattered (140). This confrontation between representationalism and formalism figures prominently in modernist treatises such as Wilhelm Worringer's *Abstraction and Empathy* (1908) and Clive Bell's *Art* (1915). Such theories have the assumption that there is a non-dialectical gap between form and subject in common. In a film like LA RÈGLE DU JEU (Jean Renoir 1939), for example, Burch notes that "the form and even the texture of the film derive *directly* from its subject matter" (141). Traditionally, on the other hand, form and style are regarded as mere technical paraphernalia superimposed on a pre-existing subject matter. Burch celebrates Renoir's achievement in LA RÈGLE DU JEU as a possible solution to what he calls "the problem of the film subject:"

> When film-makers finally become fully conscious of the cinematic means at their disposal, when the possibility of creating organically coherent films in which every element works with every other is within sight, surely the subject matter of a film, the element that is almost always the starting point of the process of making a film, must be conceived in terms of its ultimate form and texture (141).

Burch's notion of a dialectical film aesthetic challenges the categories of form and content, although it does not completely abandon the distinction. While Burch admits that films like LA RÈGLE DU JEU are successful because their subject matter is determined by texture and form, the basis for the pairing itself remains unquestioned. Burch's notorious disdain for mainstream Hollywood filmmaking probably prevents him from accepting such texts as formally fulfilled artifacts. In this sense, Burch is arguably closer to modernist formalists such as Bell than to neoformalists like Bordwell. In *Film Art*, Bordwell and Thompson explicitly reject the classic duality of content and form:

> If form is the total system which the viewer attributes to the film, there is no inside or outside. Every component *functions as part of* the overall pattern that is perceived. Thus we shall treat as formal elements many things that some people consider content. From our standpoint, subject matter and abstract ideas all enter into the total system of the artwork. ... subject matter is shaped by the film's formal context and our perceptions of it (43, emphasis in original).

What, then, are the implications of the argument that there is no such thing as a purity of form or content? Is the assertion also feasible in critical practice, or is it primarily a theoretical construct not easily translated into the analysis of films? There are no intrinsic problems with discussing film aesthetics as a fusion of form and content,[7] but it requires a heightened sensitivity to the specifics of textuality itself. A compressed recounting of a film's "plot," for instance, undermines this kind of sensitivity, and impoverishes the authenticity of the film by distilling from it interpretive meanings which usually pre-exist and pre-condition the text from which they are abstracted. What is at stake is not the type of reductionism that closes off the heterogeneous signifying potential of texts but the suppression of a work's materiality by a diversity of synoptic (and often formula-based) interpretations. Discussions of character psychology and of a film's social or political rhetoric represent prototypical instances of what one could call interpretive violence. While I do not claim that these two areas are unimportant to textual criticism or aesthetic theory, they must be studied in relation to the text. This relation could be comprehended as one between symptomatic and formalist readings.[8] Only the latter can pay adequate attention to the film. A corresponding differentiation between interpretation-driven and form-driven critical approaches is brought to light by Eric Arguillére, who contrasts two diametrically opposed film perspectives: "Films that conceive of the external as impenetrable and visualize it ... [and] films that only use the external to go beyond it and thereby render it invisible" (145, my translation). In the latter, the filmic representation is just a surface to be penetrated by the critic; the signifying material is like a key which unlocks the reality of the fiction. Insofar as the interpretive end is thought to exist beyond the textual surface, the materiality of the film is a simple means by which this end may be reached. In contrast with this attitude is the notion of impenetrability; cinematic form functions as a wall obstructing access to that which it putatively signifies. According to Arguillére, films that manifest this function [his own example is Bruno Dumont's *L'Humanité* (1999)] do not assume the existence of an extra-textual dimension that can be found beyond the film, nor do they self-consciously monitor their own signifying act in the manner of, say, BLAZING SADDLES (Mel Brooks 1974) or ANNIE HALL (Woody Allen 1977). The logic of Arguillére's assertion is that by eliminating referentiality and solidifying the surface structure, the film forces us into a new awareness of its materiality. If formal obliqueness replaces mimetic transparency, the effect is an enhanced perceptual sensitivity to film aesthetics. An epistemology of cinema is dependent upon the cultivation of this kind of criticism.

If only a few select films manage to override referentiality, how generally viable is the pursuit of dialecticism in film analyses? Is the theory exclusive to those films Bordwell refers to as parametric?[9] I would argue that it is not, because even "transparent" forms are essentially *forms*.[10] That is, the nature of the information fictional texts mediate is such that it only becomes accessible as a formal configuration. In his *Art as Experience* (1934), John Dewey notes that "there can be no distinction drawn, save in reflection, between form and substance. The work itself *is* matter formed into esthetic substance" (190, emphasis in original). Moreover, our phenomenological experience of the real world is not delimited like the world of fiction. External reality has neither an outside nor a surface; it is infinite and therefore form-less. The central flaw in the form/content model is the illusion of the opposition between exteriority and interiority, wherein a text's informational substance may be found on the "inside" of the surface texture, which is then the form. This relation is fundamentally of the same order as that which governs a plethora of additional, though familiar, dichotomies such as code-meaning, material-message, signifier-signified, or, within the domain of fiction and aesthetics, poetics-referentiality. Although these relations may be helpful as a means of systematization, they make little sense in actual practice. While looking at a painting or viewing a film, how can we possibly distinguish the content from the form or vice versa? The form/content dichotomy represents an artificial (though highly conventionalized) rather than a real epistemological category. One reason for its continued application in interpretive criticism has to do with the fact that formalist terminology is scarce in comparison with, for instance, the language of psychology or sociology. Thus, when analyzing fictional texts critics tend to reflect on the referential aspects of the work, neglecting to consider the material source which allows referential meaning in the first place.

Throughout the history of aesthetic criticism there have been numerous attempts to refine and redefine the meaning of the term "form." One of the most influential contributions is that of Bell, who introduces the notion of *significant form* as that quality "without which a work of art cannot exist" (7). But when does a text have significant form? One way of answering these kinds of questions is to define Bell's term negatively, which he himself appears to be doing when discussing the antithesis of an aesthetic painting – a "descriptive" one: "They [descriptive pictures] leave untouched our aesthetic emotions because it is not their forms but the ideas or information suggested or conveyed by their forms that affect us" (17). This view is similar to that of Arguillére, who deplores the tendency in mainstream film to foreground the narrative's referential aspect at the expense of formal experimentation (160). Both Bell's and Arguillére's arguments downplay the mimetic attraction of texts by stressing the formal, non-representational qualities.

For Bell, "primitive art" represents a prime example of the prevalence of form over mimesis. Three aspects in particular characterize this type of expression. These, he notes, are "absence of representation, absence of technical swagger, [and] sublimely impressive form" (23). Rather than considering the absence of representational content in for instance Sumerian sculpture, pre-dynastic Egyptian or archaic Greek art as a lapse of technical skill, Bell suggests that these misrepresentations are due to what he calls "'wilful distortion'"(24).[11] On the other hand, he explains that in successful mimetic art, "formal significance loses itself in preoccupation with exact representation and ostentatious cunning" (23). To support his claims Bell remarks that people who do not entertain "aesthetic emotions" tend to remember pictures by their subject matter, whereas those who do usually have no idea what the artwork is "about" (30). His conclusion is that "the formal significance of any material thing is the significance of that thing considered as an end in itself" (69). Regrettably, there is one major flaw in this theory: how can we pin down exactly what significant form is? In other words, if we are strongly affected by a given text, how do we know whether it is the representational or the formal element that affects us? Accordingly, Bell implicitly acknowledges the separation of form from content that has already been discarded.

In spite of the problems mapped out above, there is still one sense in which the notion of significant form may be salvaged. Although Bell ultimately fails in attempting to give an accurate explanation of the term, he has nevertheless provided us with a useful concept that may be better understood if one integrates it into other aesthetic theories. Herbert Marcuse's revaluation of Marxist theories of art represents an appropriate contribution in this respect. In *The Aesthetic Dimension* (1977), he elaborates a theory which – although largely overlooked by critics (Carol Becker 123) – has much in common with Bordwell's and Thompson's neoformalism.[12] Like the two film scholars, Marcuse largely abandons the form/content division:

> We can tentatively define "'aesthetic form'" as the result of the transformation of a given content … into a self-contained whole: a poem, play, novel, etc. … A work of art is authentic or true not by virtue of its content (i.e., the "'correct'" representation of social conditions), nor by its "'pure'" form, but by *the content having become form* (*Aesthetic Dimension* 8, emphasis added).

Marcuse arrives at this conclusion indirectly, through his effort to criticize orthodox Marxist theories which maintain that "appropriate" art is that which truthfully reflects the nature of the social relations within an industrial and post-industrial society. For Marcuse, the political potential of art must be located in the work's formal aspect. What above all else identifies the domain of the aesthetic, he argues, is the inherent capacity of fictional text to *protest* and *transcend* the given social relations. Through its form, the artwork represents an alternative sensibility that is transformative of our habitual perception of reality. Herein lies the subversive potential of art. Marcuse explains the process thus:

> Under the law of the aesthetic form, the given reality is necessarily *sublimated*: the immediate content is stylized, the "'data'" are reshaped and reordered in accordance with the demands of the art form … . Thus, on the basis of aesthetic sublimation, a *desublimation* takes place in the perception of individuals – in their feelings, judgments, thoughts; an invalidation of dominant norms, needs and values. With all its affirmative-ideological features, art remains a dissenting force (*Aesthetic Dimension* 7, emphases in original).

It is evident that Marcuse's claims are indebted to the work of both Shklovsky and Brecht (perhaps incidentally, only the latter is acknowledged), and their emphasis on the cognitive component of the aesthetic experience in general, and estrangement in particular. However, it is not primarily the political inflections of Marcuse's essay that constitute the focus of attention, but rather his insistence of the inseparability of form and content. "Aesthetic form," Marcuse notes, "is not opposed to content, not even dialectically. In the work of art, form becomes content and vice versa" (*Aesthetic Dimension* 41). This formulation seems to be a paraphrase of Nietzsche, whom he also quotes: "The price of being an artist is to experience that which all non-artists call form, as content, as 'the real thing' (*die Sache selbst*)" (41, emphasis in original). Marcuse's comprehension of form is more productive than the less dialectical definitions of Bell and Worringer. What sets Marcuse and neoformalists like Bordwell and Thompson apart from modernist aestheticians like Bell is that the former posit a considerably more radical aesthetic ontology than the latter. Despite their formalist affiliation, Bell and Worringer do not question the validity of the form/content division. They simply prefer to focus on the formal aspect, which in itself presumes their acknowledgment of a "pure" content level. Marcuse abolishes the discreteness of form and content, and instead assumes a synthetic structure in which there is only one aesthetic entity.[13] For Bordwell, this is form.[14]

Although all fictional works belong to the field of the aesthetic, not all artworks are equally arresting, which is my re-interpretation of Bell's concept of significant form. However, significant form is not the ontological core of the artwork. Rather, I take "form" to mean the synthesis of style and substance, and "significant" to imply a qualitative and intersubjective valorization of some forms and artworks over others. That a given work fails to exhibit significant form does not necessarily detract from its status as artwork, but is a way of technically classifying it. This argument apparently runs into some of the same problems that mitigate Marcuse's theory of a "constant standard;" on what grounds do we formulate the criteria that underlie the idea of significant form? Admittedly, the negotiation of such premises is to some extent unavoidably mired in decisions that are ultimately subjective. Notwithstanding, not all arguments are equally convincing, and a theory which is viable and functional should not be discarded only because the objectivity of some of its premises seems volatile. Conventional determinants of significant form may be qualities such as textual indeterminacy (the capacity of a text to generate multiple meanings); stylistic acuity (a text's articulation of information that cannot be given in a non-aesthetic mode); and structural coherence (the consistency with which the chosen logic of patterning is sustained throughout the text). Ultimately, the notion of a significant aesthetic form is perhaps best identified negatively, as Krieger appears to do when he sets aesthetic form against conceptual form (213).

The determinants sketched out above have certain advantages. Unlike Marcuse's "constant standards" or Bell's significant form, these three criteria do not distinguish between "high" art and "trivial" entertainment. The three elements also reflect the indivisibility of the represented and the representation, yet the complementary function of the aesthetic is also taken into account in that art's capacity to express knowledge of an alternative kind is underscored. As we may recall, this is one of Marcuse's most salient assertions in *The Aesthetic Dimension*:

> Not only poetry and drama but also the realistic novel must transform the reality which is their material in order to re-present its essence as envisioned by art. Any historical reality can become 'the stage' for such mimesis. The only requirement is that it must be *stylized*, subjected to aesthetic "'formation.'" And precisely this stylization allows the transvaluation of the norms of the established reality principle – the de-sublimation on the basis of the original sublimation, dissolution of the social taboos, of the social management of Eros and Thanatos (44, emphasis in original).

The principle of recognition through differentiation – the aesthetic metamorphosis of a given reality from idea to form and (perhaps) back again – is a key assumption in this revised theory of significant form.

Marcuse resorts to the phrase *stylization* in the above quotation, a term which requires further commentary. When a text is described in terms of "stylization" in cinema studies, the label commonly refers to an aesthetic that is at odds with the dominant code of filmic realism. When, for instance, THE WILD BUNCH was released in 1969, Peckinpah's western – despite the slow-motion cinematography and the flagrant editing – was perceived as considerably more naturalistic than its generic precursors. A CLOCKWORK ORANGE, on the other hand, has since its 1971 release been taken to be the epitome of stylized cinema violence.[15] Formally different as the two films are, should their aesthetic differences be reduced to the single question of realism versus stylization? A comparative study of two relatively recent violent films – Steven Spielberg's SAVING PRIVATE RYAN (1998) and MAN BITES DOG – may help illuminate this question. The former impressed and disgusted moviegoers because of its unusually verisimilar rendering of the violent impact warfare can have on the human body. I suspect that very few people would complain that this film relies on a heavy register of stylization, the numerous tricks of cinematography and slow-motion devices notwithstanding. While Spielberg's epic has been praised for its overwhelming verisimilitude, MAN BITES DOG pushes its documentary aesthetic so far that critics tend to regard it as one of the most "stylized" accounts of cinema violence in contemporary cinema.

The dichotomy of realism and stylization relies on the assumption that mainstream cinema that derives from the classical Hollywood paradigm employs a "zero degree" narrative and stylistic system in which the process of narration appears to be "invisible." Within this mode of filmmaking, "Realism" is thus codified as a set of formal procedures, whose paramount vectors are the canonic story format, continuity (spatial, temporal, causal) and verisimilitude.[16] The rhetoric of realism, as Jeremy Butler holds, implies that "the best style is the style that is noticed the least" (11). Texts which deviate from these standards are frequently defined as "non-realistic", "subjective/psychological" or simply "stylized." It is clear, however, that classical narrative realism is no less a style than any other filmic mode, and it should follow from this that "stylization" is a term appropriate (or equally invalid) for classical and experimental films alike.[17] From a practical or functional viewpoint, one could argue that the distinction between "stylized" and "non-stylized" films is such a critical commonplace that one is hard pressed to avoid it, and that a rejection of the term "stylization" would cause more confusion than it would clarity. Some of these objections are doubtlessly warranted, but nevertheless the fact remains that the term betrays important principles concerning the nature of film form. Insofar as "style" is the manifestation of a selected set of techniques of the medium, there can be no such thing as a film sans style, and the "invisible style" of Hollywood cinema is therefore a contradiction in terms. When we declare that the aesthetic of A CLOCKWORK ORANGE is radically different from that of THE WILD BUNCH, we rely on more refined stylistic concepts than that of "stylization" to account for these differences.

Stylization is, moreover, to a large extent used interchangeably with that of aestheticization. There appear to be vital similarities in the ways in which these terms are drawn upon to describe certain formal effects in the cinema. If a movie is defined as "stylized," we can usually infer that it is also "aestheticized" in some way. Conversely, an "aestheticized" movie typically contains formal elements we readily interpret as "stylized." For better or worse, these are our conventions of description and categorization in the domain of fictional form. Russel's appraisal of BONNIE AND CLYDE and THE WILD BUNCH as aestheticized narratives of death and temporality exemplifies this process: "It is instructive to analyze the representations of death in these films because they are symptomatic of the tendency of the American mythos of 'regeneration through violence' to disintegrate into an aesthetic discourse of 'excess.' *Stylization* takes up where coherent belief systems dissipate ..." (177, emphasis added). Russell's use of the term stylization indicates an adherence to the standard critical approach which more or less arbitrarily assigns a rather unspecified aesthetic value to a kind of textual material which is felt to differentiate itself from the rest of the film. She claims rightfully that the two films in question explore narrative options different from those of the classical American cinema. A problem arises when Russell attempts to describe the phenomenon which has come to supplant the traditional narrative strategies that habitually articulate "coherent belief systems." These are the so-called closed texts of the classical period. When in the late 1960s cinema's textual structures of death and closure part ways, Russell addresses the nature of this split in terms of "stylization," thus implicitly suggesting that there is a lack of stylization (the zero-degree system) in the earlier cinema. I do not deny that there are significant differences of form between the two types of cinema, but the concepts used to clarify them are highly unfortunate. The absence of an acknowledgment of the relativity of style, or stylization, sanctions the "naturalness" of classical Hollywood cinema while at the same time it exaggerates the "otherness" of alternative aesthetics. BONNIE AND CLYDE and THE WILD BUNCH do not, after all, exhibit a consistently parametric or art cinema norm. In many ways they must be considered traditional Hollywood films with a less familiar rhetoric and a different kind of ending.

It should be evident that a re-conceptualization of the notions of style and stylization is long overdue, and in *On the History of Film Style* Bordwell starts his investigation with the following definition of style:

> In the narrowest sense, I take style to be *a film's systematic and significant use of techniques of the medium*. Those techniques fall into broad domains: mise en scène (staging, lighting, performance, and setting); framing, focus, control of color values, and other aspects of cinematography; editing; and sound. Style is, minimally, the texture of the film's images and sounds, the result of choices made by the filmmaker(s) in particular historical circumstances (4, emphasis added).

This explication greatly assists our endeavor to make a viable distinction between form and style in a theoretical and a practical sense. In principle, all stylistic aspects of a text constitute its form, whereas not all formal parameters are part of the category of style. Moreover, stylistic elements of a film are identifiable as concrete, phenomenal manifestations. Structures that do not necessarily leave explicit traces in the surface of the text, but which can only be generated inferentially as abstract entities, belong to the larger formal level. Narrative phenomena on the level of story are examples of such "invisible" formal principles. A brief analysis of Bordwell's definition may further clarify what the concept of style entails. Five qualifications are particularly prominent in this respect. Firstly, in Bordwell's view, style is effected by medium-specific resources, which he plainly but appropriately calls techniques. There are four main typologies – editing, cinematography, mise en scène and sound – and at least the first is unique to the audiovisual arts. Style thus depends on medium-specific features.[18] Inevitably, film style is inherent in the very fabric of the cinematic materials. Bordwell's conceptual precision is one of the strengths of his argument. By relating the issue of style to intrinsic capacities of a medium, he manages to avoid the broad use of the term frequently encountered in critical discussions of both filmic and literary texts.

Secondly, Bordwell moderates his proposition by introducing the requirement of *systematicity*. That is, if textual elements are to be considered vehicles of style they must be deployed in methodical and recognizable patterns throughout the film. Formal – as opposed to specifically stylistic – phenomena need not fulfill this qualification in an absolute sense. As a textual construction, every film must have a formal dimension. The transmutation of ideas and stories from the level of thought and feeling to the level of artistic expression only takes place through the concreteness of a medium. Hence, all audiovisual constructs from the most intricate and well-crafted fiction film to the crudest home video exhibit a formal system. When it comes to style, the situation is more complex. To state that there can be films with no discernible style is a hazardous and insupportable assertion; however, there is a significant sense in which the perceived presence of film style is somewhat more fragile than that of form. This is partly due to the fact that, as previously mentioned, the concept of form involves factors such as narrative, which are generally not taken to be properties of style. In addition, the perception that style, at least quantitatively, appears less commanding than form is not so far-fetched, since the most pervasive film mode – classical Hollywood cinema – has traditionally been defined in terms of an "invisible," or "zero-degree" style. This is of course a fallacious assumption. Hollywood films are no less stylistically defined than other cinemas. Nonetheless, in a relational perspective, it is methodologically useful to posit one particular type of filmmaking practice as a contrastive background against which other stylistic modes might be scrutinized. In the case of the classical American cinema, this "normative" sample is unquestionably dominant and representative enough.

Thirdly, a key word in Bordwell's explication of film style is *significant*. A film's utilization of any given technique which the medium has at its disposal should not only be systematic but consequential as well. The qualification winnows away many texts that fail to distribute their technical devices in a consistent and meaningful pattern. Thus, a single occurrence of deep space staging which turns out to be of no consequence for the overall architecture of the film, for instance, will be interpreted as a formal rather than a stylistic design. Such apparently arbitrary uses of cinematic effects not only fail to sustain a coherent system, but their semantic function tends to emerge as artificial.

It should be noted that not all inconsistent uses of film techniques are susceptible to the sort of criticism outlined above. Occasionally, the haphazard utilization of a particular filmic technique or device seemingly performs a narrative or differentiational function in the overall text. The use of a wide-angle lens during the rape scene in STRAW DOGS, for example, is a specific technical option that best expresses the horrified point of view of the rape victim: Charles's distorted features facilitated by the wide-angle shot is taken to represent Amy's subjective perception of her attacker. Here the use of cinematic technique is merely formal and not stylistic, since the use of the wide angle lens is motivated by local rather than global concerns. To paraphrase, the use of the wide-angle lens does not fall into an integrated and sustained textual pattern, but is implemented mainly as a practical answer to an immediate functional problem.

There are two more significant qualifications in Bordwell's formulation, the first being that of *directorial choices*. Although a self-evident fact, it receives due emphasis in Bordwell's definition. Particularly because the conventionality of the zero-degree style of classical Hollywood cinema has been naturalized to such an extent, people often tend to forget that it too is the result of carefully calculated formal and stylistic decisions. What one may call *authorial choices* bears equally on both the larger formal level as well as the narrower stylistic one, but there has also been a marked tendency throughout film history to associate particularly assertive and original stylistic contributions with the oeuvres of certain filmmakers. While different varieties of film form have been attached to large-scale categories such as genre, narrative versus non-narrative cinema, silent versus sound cinema and popular versus art cinema, critics and historians have tended to talk about the filmographies of canonized directors when discussing taxonomies of style. Thus, much has been made of the use of close-ups in Dreyer, dialectical montage in Eisenstein, deep focus cinematography in Welles, and the long take in Angelopoulos.

Last but not the least, Bordwell makes room for the contextual embeddedness of caches of film stylistics in the significance he assigns to the role of *particular historical circumstances*. The inclusion of material conditions as part of the history of film style is indispensable, and signals a readiness to go beyond a constricted formalism. The interaction of narrative forms with diachronic parameters (technological evolution, social and economic sanctions and censures of the movies), is of vital importance to cinema violence. By exploring the aesthetics of violence from SCARFACE to FIGHT CLUB, we can arrive at a deeper understanding of the nature of American cinema, but no such survey can be complete without also attempting to account for how certain developments on the textual level have come about.

2   Narrating Violence, or, Allegories of Dying

The problem of death in representation always leads straight to
the question of form.

Garrett Stewart

Audiovisual fiction that shows us death by violence is embroiled in a curious contradiction. By presenting death as violent form, the film violates – or, rather, curtails – its own act of representation. Nagisa Oshima says that "filmmakers want to shoot the dying" (257), but in doing so they also terminate the conditions for the possibility of representation as such. Film violence, therefore, is in a sense a subject that tests the limits of representationality and by implication narrativity. Marking the beginning of infinite stasis, violent death is conceptually at the opposite pole from representation, which involves being. Death and violence, conversely, signify non-being. Though we may have established that violence can be seen as an attempt to seize the process of dying – a visualization of the inexpressible, the embodiment of non-being – the representation itself is in a relation of asymmetricality to the represented. Whatever else it may be about, violence is thus also about performativity; it folds back into a meditation on storytelling.

Several theorists have contemplated the linkage between narrative form and death, Walter Benjamin and Peter Brooks notable among them. For Brooks, in his *Reading For the Plot* (1984), mortality seems to be at the core of temporality (246), and as such it can best be explored by narrative. The faculty of storytelling is thus essentially necrological. Structurally, death represents a form of closure that confers a sense of meaning upon lived life, a lapse of the closural implies an open-ended trajectory where meaning is still continuously susceptible to change (Benjamin, "Storyteller" 93). Moreover, narrative is the only available source of knowledge of death, and it is this aspect of narrative that attracts us to stories. Benjamin, however, holds that our narrative competence has deteriorated, and also that the consciousness of death and dying has increasingly become more fragile ("Storyteller" 93). One hypothesis that may explain the current obsession with fictional violence is that it re-incites audiences that are losing the ability to listen to and receive knowledge from narratives. In his *L'acte photographique*

(1983), Philippe Dubois draws upon the term thanatography to describe the writing, or inscription, of death by photography. This act, as he names it, must however be precipitated by the ocular consciousness of a narrative agency. A particular strata of American cinema, this thesis suggests, originates in a thanatographical gaze, and the relation this cinema sustains with violence is of an essentially cathexic nature. The thanatographical gaze governs the kinds of narrative structures found in this cinema, disclosing an aesthetics one could refer to as narrathanatography; the narration of death. By all accounts, violence seems to be the preferred way of representing death in the cinema. Film thanatography is transgeneric, but has a special purchase on the western and the gangster/ crime genres.

Fictional texts, however idiosyncratic, depend upon conventions and codified structures, and, as E.H. Gombrich has pointed out, the formal and the normative have always overlapped significantly (*Norm and Form* 81). Any specific aesthetic form simultaneously represents a set of norms, while formal genres and classifications evolve historically out of normative evaluations. Formal designations like the gothic or the baroque, Gombrich reminds us, are constructed rather than "natural" categories, and were first used normatively with a derogative connotation that later was harnessed into a formal evaluation (84). It was only in the 19th century that "the idea gained ground that styles are distinguished by certain recognizable morphological characteristics ... and that these terms could safely be applied stripped of their normative connotation" (86).[1] The inevitable conventionality of film modes, genres and individual movies rests on what Bordwell sees as "the relative stability and coherence of ... sets of norms" (*Narration* 150). A certain constellation of extrinsic norms engender the dominant style of any given period, a process Munro details in the following way:

> Each artist takes something from the artistic traditions and cultural environment he inherits, and, if he is creative, he adds to them or alters them in some significant way. His work will have certain generic traits of style in common with that of other artists, and certain more or less distinctive ones. His individual style or styles will help to make up the styles of his cultural group at a certain time (*Form and Style* 240).[2]

The idea that there should be some degree of what Josephine Miles refers to as a "working unity" in any generationally defined period of art may provide a helpful template for grasping the interrelations between the configuration of a formal mode and its contexts of production (63).[3] As Gombrich makes clear, stylistic conventions came to be seen as "manifestations of that spirit of the age which had risen to metaphysical status in Hegel's vision of history" (*Norm and Form* 87). The putative influence of the zeitgeist upon the evolution of a particular artistic mode has also been noted by Heinrich Wölfflin, who once coined the phrase "the national psychology of form" to indicate the inextricability of cultural mentality from aesthetic properties (9).

The individual films that I shall examine in subsequent chapters broadly span three eras of American filmmaking, epitomized by that of Hawks and the studio era, that of Peckinpah and the Hollywood Renaissance, and that of Tarantino and the "New," hyper-modern, Hollywood. Unquestionably, the depictions of violence became progressively more explicit from the 1930s to the 1990s, and this singular fact has tended to overshadow more pressing issues in previous examinations into the nature of violent film style. This is regrettable since such myopia leaves large areas within the poetics of violence unexplored. Moreover, studies that are mainly concerned with the brutalization of American cinema usually stop short of any interpretation of the possible meanings of any particular style of violence. Critics seem content merely to observe and document the escalation of violence according to degree rather than kind. David A. Cook's survey of the evolution of American film violence exemplifies this trend. As a result of the relaxation of the enforcement of the production code during the Second World War, Cook reasons, a shift occurred in the intensity and form of violence in the immediate post-war cinema ("Ballistic" 133). War-time movies such as Edward Dmytryk's HITLER'S CHILDREN (1943), Andre de Toth's NONE SHALL ESCAPE (1944), and Frank Lloyd's BLOOD ON THE SUN (1945) paved the way for a new aesthetics of cruelty in the noirs and gangster films of the late 1940s, and the audience's level of tolerance was affected correspondingly (134).[4] As John Cawelti has noted, the emergence of new forms and genres of film violence usually incites widespread public concern ("Myths of Violence" 522); the Payne Fund Studies (1933) were conducted in the wake of the cycle of gangster films of the early 1930s, and the report from The National Commission on the Causes and Prevention of Violence (1968-69) was to a significant extent a response to the rise of the new movie violence of the 1960s. The commentary by Cook and Cawelti is emblematic of a certain way of approaching the issue of violence and style without really discussing it. This is not intended as a criticism, however, because there is certainly reason to suspect that the existing analytical language of film criticism and theory is insufficient with regard to capturing the complexities of forms that in fact seem inclined to escape or even defeat language.

While it is true that violent American films have become increasingly explicit over the years, what needs to be emphasized is that this development should be described with reference not only to a new permissiveness but also to a transformation of formal conventions. Even the most shocking depiction of violence is ultimately a product of a particular stylistic idiom, a norm; the violence in RESERVOIR DOGS, for instance, is neither more nor less "realistic" than that in

SCARFACE. We become aware of this when we manage to see through (no pun intended) the duplicitous transparency of the film image.

If style, intrinsically constitutive of violent film form, is non-transparent and interpretable, what precisely does it signify? Sobchack's explication of the function of aesthetic violence is representative of what appears to be a dominant view on the subject. Violent style, she writes, "give[s] our senseless death some sort of significance and meaning. ... The moment of death can be prolonged cinematically ... so that we are made to see form and order where none seems to exist in real life" ("Violent Dance" 118).[5] This interpretation equates film violence with what one may provisionally call cinemortality; violence is treated as a method of inspection, as a figure, or metaphor, for processes of death and dying.[6] For Sobchack, it is the fear of the unknowability of death which, sublimated into curiosity, best explains our fascination with violence ("Violent Dance" 115). Assuming the validity of Sobchack's view, one may construe violence in the arts as thanatomimetic, a concept that Robert Kastenbaum and Ruth Aisenberg invoke in their *The Psychology of Death* (1972), to describe the game of feigning death: "The child who playfully intends the thanatomimetic state is learning how to accommodate the meaning of death into his general outlook on life" (149).[7] In this perspective, the cathexic nature of American movie violence may be understood as the articulation of the desire for the impossible epistemology of death. In his analysis of the relation between art and murder, Black writes that murder (and by extension violence) – because it defeats reason – "could only become minimally comprehensible *as* art" (102, emphasis in original). Art, as Lawrence L. Langer so laconically observes, presents us with characters who "'know how to die'" (9). On this account, styles of violence become legible as different methods of inspecting the imponderable event of death.

One should bear in mind that the forms of film violence are not limited to style alone. They also possess narrative components,[8] albeit of a different kind. Because violence is embedded in their narrative structures, films such as those examined here seem essentially concerned with narrating death. They both arise from and produce a kind of thanatographical consciousness, an awareness of finality, of the unrepresentable. The styles of violence give the process of dying a spatial and temporal form; the narration of violence confers a sense of causality upon death in the figuration of moral meaning. Style and narrative combine to generate what I shall call *narrathanatographical* film form.

Why is there so much violent death in the art of the past century? Scholars such as Geoffrey Gorer, Ernest Becker and Vicki Goldberg have all argued that there is a correlation between the disappearance of death as a visible, public event on the one hand, and the escalations of depictions of death in fictional works on the other. "While natural death became more and more smothered in prudery," Gorer writes in 1960, "violent death has played an ever growing part in the fantasies offered to mass audiences" (405). Gorer's observation is more elaborately examined in Becker's *The Denial of Death* (1973), whose premise is that modern society, in its increasingly neurotic relations to the fact of death, has banished its image from our field of vision. Philippe Ariès reaches a similar conclusion in his equally influential *The Hour of Our Death* (1977). The "disappearance of the individual," Ariès observes, "no longer affects [society's] continuity" (560). Death has become invisible. More recently, in an article in *Why We Watch: The Attractions of Violent Entertainment* (1998), Goldberg speculates that "[t]he popularity of images of violent death ... conceivably has something to do with its relative rarity in real life: it is 'safer' to fantasize about something unlikely to occur than about death from cancer or Parkinson's" (43).[9] It appears that the more actual death is removed from sight, the more simulated death comes to the fore. Reduced to a mere "technical phenomenon" (Sobchack, "Inscribing" 285), mortality passes into the realm of storytelling and fiction. We may all ponder, as film critic David Thomson does (13), the meaning of the fact that while we must have seen thousands of dead bodies on film, most of us have seen very few in real life.

It is difficult to ascertain whether the correlation between the invisibility of real death and the omnipresence of fictional death is causal or simply symptomatic, but in any event the crux of the matter is that the simulation of violence in art and fiction appears to be thoroughly inter-connected with issues of mortality. As Elisabeth Bronfen and Sarah Webster Goodwin write, "the alienation of death has led to a fascination with it" (16). Importantly, however, it should be stressed that, as a cultural phenomenon, the narrativization of death in the movies does not serve any cathartic purpose. Watching characters die on the screen does not primarily induce catharsis, but is a means of imagining, or imaging, that which always already escapes definition in real life. Nothing appears as formless, as monstrously amorphous, as the notion of death. The desire for visualizing it – for giving it a shape through aesthetic form – is therefore epistemic rather than cathartic. Cinema violence, Sobchack states, "gives death a perceptible form" ("Inscribing" 289). If, as Jacques Derrida has stated, "every culture entails a treatise or treatment of death" (43), that of death by violence may be the American discourse. But simulated mortality does not necessarily allay the fear of dying. On occasion it may even exacerbate it, but at the very least the performance of fictional death by violence satisfies the need to see the ineffable formalized. If epistemophilia is the engine of narrative, as Brooks suggests in *Reading for The Plot*, it would follow that the narration of death desires knowledge rather than release.

What appears to be an obsession with violence and death in American culture and in film – or what Mark Seltzer dubs "addictive violence" (253) – should not be conflated with the Freudian idea of *Todestrieb* as introduced in *Beyond the*

Pleasure Principle (1920), and developed further in *Civilization and its Discontents* (1929). In the latter work, Freud ruminates over the possibility that "besides the instinct to preserve living substance and to join it into ever larger units, there must exist another, contrary instinct seeking to dissolve those units and to bring them back to their primeval, inorganic state" (65). Though, as C. Fred Alford points out, Freud never used the term *thanatos* in his writings (63), it is clear that his identification of a death instinct and its possible manifestations as aggression and destructiveness bears a certain superficial resemblance to the concept of thanatography understood as cinemortality. Freudian readings of American violence are no doubt a tempting enterprise for some critics. Denis Duclos, for example, alleges that American society is defined by what he calls a "werewolf culture," a state of vacillation between an appetite for destruction and a need for order (120). America's fascination for "uncommon killers," Duclos states, can be seen as "a manifestation of the death instinct" (11). Schlesinger, Jr. renders this Freudianism rather melodramatically with the following statement:

> When we refuse to acknowledge the existence of this other strain [violence], we refuse to see our nation as it is. We must recognize that an impulse to destroy coexists with our impulse to create – that the destructive impulse is in us and that it springs from some dark intolerable tension in our history and institutions (10).

But an artistic accentuation of mortality does not presuppose or gesture toward a death instinct, nor is there any reason to assume that the alleged Todestrieb of culture is played out vicariously in the realm of fictional representations. It could perhaps be added that this latter claim is a discernment that proceeds by way of implication from the aforesaid rejection of any theory of imitation. Violent films do not suggest a drive toward death but a drive toward some kind of apprehension of death. This is a crucial distinction. In a treatise on German literature, Theodore Ziolkowski performs a reading of thanatographic themes, which eludes the predictable implication of a death drive. A literary probing of mortality, Ziolkowski holds, bespeaks an inclination to contextualize the consciousness of death historically; the gravitation toward death in modern literature becomes a means with which to test the conditions for and limits of subjectivity grasped in its temporal dimension (222). Ziolkowski is keenly aware of the historical contingency of the cultural and literary preoccupation with mortality, and points out that an awareness of death "is most acute in periods of social disintegration" (223). This appreciation stands in marked opposition to the mainly ahistorical underpinning of Duclos's and Schlesinger's inferred Freudianisms.

The impulse to capture the elusiveness of mortality seems in fact to be a driving force not only in the cinema but also in significant strata of 20th century American literature. Wolfe has rightfully noted that the genesis of American movie violence was "decidedly pre-cinematic" (1: 518). Sidney Finkelstein, in *Existentialism and Alienation in American Literature* (1965), recognizes the existence of a peculiar "death-hauntedness" in American fiction. Similarly, in *Love and Death* (1963), Gershon Legman makes a parallel discovery: "Brandes, writing in his *Hovedstrømninger* today, would find only one main current in our literature ... deathward" (95).[10] This travel, however, does not take the form of a romanticist yearning for release but of an almost Melvillian confrontation with, and investigative defiance of, the threat of extinction. It is the latter attitude that most plausibly explains the ferocious violence with which American cinema has tended to explore the problem of mortality. According to Kenneth Lynn, critics from D. H. Lawrence in the 1920s to Leslie Fiedler in the 1960s have identified violence as the main theme in American literature (134).[11] Lynn maintains that there is evidence of a literary genealogy of violence from Southwestern humorists like Augustus Baldwin Longstreet to E. P. Roe, Ignatius Donnelly, Wilbur F. Hinman, Jack London, Stephen Crane, Ambrose Bierce and Ernest Hemingway (134-142). W. M. Frohock supports Lynn's thesis with his claim that a majority of the novels written between 1920 and 1950 fall into the categories of either erosion or violence (3). "Time and again," Frohock writes, "the hero finds himself in a predicament from which the only possible exit is the infliction of physical harm upon some other human being" (8). Frohock links the theme of violence in 1930s-and-1940s literature both to contemporary issues (the Depression, the labor disputes, the Second World War) and to the literary tradition: "There is of course a sense ... in which Faulkner, and perhaps others, can be said to exploit an awareness of evil which was already present in Melville and Hawthorne" (13). Furthermore, Richard Chase has maintained that what defines the American novel is its "contradictions and ... extreme range of experience" (1). The "profound poetry of disorder" that characterizes this literary tradition, Chase suggests, emanates from a series of oppositions intrinsic to American experience, such as that between tradition and progress, past and future, Europe and America, and liberalism and reaction (6). Chase writes: "The fact is that many of the best American novels achieve their very being, their energy and their form, from the perception and acceptance not of unities but of radical disunities" (6). Nothing indicates that this tradition has become any less relevant in contemporary fiction. On the contrary, as James Annesley intuits, there is at the turn of the millennium a sense of intensification in the exploration of "new forms and subjects" (1). In its excessively perverted subjectivity, a text such as Bret Easton Ellis's AMERICAN PSYCHO (1991) illustrates this trend perhaps all too convincingly.

The insight of Gorer, Becker, Goldberg and Sobchack alluded to above – that the contemplation of mortality appears to have altogether moved into the realm of storytelling – is thus substantiated by a rich undercurrent of violence and transgression in American fiction and film. This proliferation of thanatographic textuality reiterates a process in which the image of death and the image of violence become one. What these texts seem to be communicating is that if we do not know anything else about death, at least we will know that its occurrence is somehow associated with a moment of violence. The relation may be one of treacherous metonymy, in that acts of violence become the face of mortality. But, the rage with which characters die in fiction films – the violence of their deaths – could also be comprehended as a violence directed against the very notion of death itself. By having the characters die violently, the films attempt to violate death and its inevitability. By inscribing the cinematic forms of death onto the frames of the film, by signifying thanatographically, the text at the same time deconstructs and destroys it. Death implies absence, but since it becomes the object of a visual spectacle it is brought into being and, hence, paradoxically eliminated. In Leo Charney's view, film violence must be linked to the sense of absence, a "lost intimacy with present moments," suggested by the very nature of the image:

> The force of violence externalizes and renders as a kinesthetic effect the rolling hunger to face the present, to feel it and see it and re-present it. But as this effort fails, and fails over and over again, as it can only do, the need to reassert it by force becomes more and more the domain of what could only be called a hysterical impulse. Violence becomes more and more intense in the effort to restore the possibility of having an effect, creating a shock, providing a response…. We can understand the violence … of American cinema only in its link to this modernist sense of the loss of tangible presence in whose context it arose and which its phantasmic form has ratified in perpetuity (49)

Though willfully oblique, Charney's proposition is in step with those of a coterie of theoreticians whose work coalesces in a shared focus on the inter-relations of the photographic image, violence, death, and narrative. The photographic moment envelops the pro-filmic event in stasis, the big freeze, death. In 1972, Roberto Rossellini wrote: "I have faith in everything, except cinema… . I'm convinced that if it's not dead, it's on the point of dying" (165). Paolo Usai, in his *The Death of Cinema* (2001) – a paean to the evanescence of film – defines cinema as "the art of destroying moving images" (4). The conditions Usai refers to involve the fragile nature of the image and the inevitability of new technologies that will supplant cinema. Unlike many other carriers of visuality, photographic film stock is susceptible to processes of deterioration. Each projection of the film image, Usai notes, "will hasten its demise" (67). The life span of the image can even be quantified. In terms of projection, each discreet frame can be expected to last one and one-third seconds before it disintegrates (4). The photographic image is "inherently subject to endless mutation and irreversible destruction"

(Usai 67). Cinema's intimate association with corporeality and with its own decay suggests that it may be death, often transmitted through acts of violence,
which constitutes the essence of cinematicity.[12] Its ephemeral quality, the in-
eluctability of its decay, indexes the medium's own mortality and makes cinema
a violently elegiac art form.

The assumption that violence and death are intrinsic to the ontology of the
cinematic apparatus is not part of a full-fledged, theorized approach, but is
rather the aggregate of miscellaneous claims that understand violence to be essential to the language and the technical processes that define the medium.
Rothman's paraphrase of Griffith is emblematic of this position: violence is internal to the nature of cinema ("Violence and Film" 39). Paul Virilio has developed this argument the furthest,[13] but fragments of a similar reasoning surface
in the writings of Eisenstein, Stanley Cavell, Janet Bergstrom, Tom Gunning,
Russell, Slocum and Prince.[14] Eisenstein, according to Rothman, believed that
"every frame of every film had, as it were, the blood of the world on it, due to
the violence of the camera's original act of tearing pieces of the world from their
'natural' place'" ("Violence and Film" 39). Some mechanical procedures which
the filmmaking process entails are infused with a violent nomenclature (shoot,
shot, cut, fade, dissolve), as are also camera movements (often sudden and unprecedented, as in, for instance, the films of Lars von Trier) and editing (with all
the rapid, incessant perspectival alterations caused by cutting). Moreover, as
Usai has noted, the process of projecting the film represents in itself an act of
violence against the image (49). Pondering this association of the apparatus
with violence, Philip French notes that "the very idea of montage, make[s] films
– irrespective of their subjects – a violent experience for the audience" (329). A
commentator like Horsley suggests that violence constitutes the essence of the
cinematic (1: 41), whereas Wolfe speculates that

> The pervasiveness and durability of screen violence may stem in part from the
> graphic power and plasticity of motion pictures, their ability to register the visceral
> impact of aggressive movement…. The appeal of violence in films, hence, can be
> viewed as a logical extension of the attraction of movie audiences to kinetic spectacle
> (1: 512).

So deep-rooted is this belief in the intrinsic connection between violence and
apparatus that some critics, like Prince, question even the possibility of formu-
lating a critique of violence through the medium of cinema: "Filmmakers who
wish to use graphic violence to offer a counterviolence message … may be
working in the wrong medium. The medium subverts the goal" ("Graphic" 29).
In his *L'acte photographique*, Dubois envisages photography as a form of thanatography, and the photographic act as analogous to murder.[15] In what he refers to
as a process of medusification, a fraction of an instant is cut loose from the flow

of time and given its own temporality, which is separate and symbolic rather than referential (160). Violent as it may be, the photographic gesture for Dubois is an act that merits a positive evaluation, since the immobile temporality of the photographed instant protects it from its own loss. By murdering the instant, photography paradoxically preserves and perpetuates it. Dubois's conception of photographic thanatography is heavily indebted to Bazin, and Dubois openly relies upon one of Bazin's key terms from "The Ontology of the Photographic Image" – *mummification* (Dubois 161). For both Bazin and Dubois, photography represents a method for capturing that fugitive moment where mortality is nullified through its inscription as textual form.

As Bronfen and Goodwin have declared, textual configurations of death can act as "metatropes for the process of representation itself: its necessity, its excess, its failure" (4). This is also Sobchack's point of departure in her meditation on the ethical spaces of filmic mortality: "The representation of the event of death is an indexical sign of that which is always in excess of representation, and beyond the limits of coding and culture: Death confounds all codes" ("Inscribing" 287). What both Bronfen and Goodwin and Sobchack emphasize in their reflection on the phenomenologies of death is the paradox that "[r]epresentation presupposes an original presence" (Bronfen and Goodwin 7). Death, however, is non-presence. There seem to me to be two solutions to this apparent aporia. One can either continue to revel in the paradox of an impossible representationality (the idea that a representation in effect becomes a representation of nothing), or one can jettison the notions of representation and mimesis, which I already did in the first chapter. We may now come to realize the value of choosing the subjects of violence and mortality for the formation of what I call an amimetic theory of film fiction. It is not only that the depictions of violent death in the movies have no other reference than similar depictions in film history, but also that the event of death in real life is inaccessible to representation. There can therefore never be a mimetic textuality of death in the sense that there can at least potentially be a mimetic textuality of, say, the activities of playing a game of soccer or going to the mall. Sobchack fortifies this position when she writes that depictions of death refer "significantly only to themselves" ("Inscribing" 287), and that "[t]he most effective cinematic signifier of death in our present culture is violent action inscribed on the visible lived-body" (288). Though there are evidently images of death not explicitly connected to violence in American film, one would be surprised to find how frequently violence features as intrinsic to the depiction of mortality. Even an uncharacteristically introspective film like IN THE BEDROOM (Todd Field 2001) – an exploration of the grief that accompanies the unexpected loss of a child – seems unable to envision death without violence.

The tradition of thanatographic violence in film and fiction exhibits one central quality that is possibly so obvious that it fails to register: violence in the arts is an almost exclusively male prerogative.[16] One reason is that film genres such as war, detective, gangster, science fiction and the western – forms that are "unimaginable without their idiosyncratic violent signatures" (Greenberg 50) – overwhelmingly sustain the textual turf of male characters. Not only is it impossible to ignore the gendered aspect of movie violence, but, conversely, the violent aspect of the construction of the male gender may provide important cues for examining the gestation of masculinity in key films of the American cinema. The images of violence can thus be rewardingly re-considered as tropes not only for the conception of mortality but for the codification of a specifically masculine ethics. In sum, the amimetic, narrathanatographical filmicity appertaining to a particular praxis in American filmmaking collates issues of mortality, ethics and masculinity in tropes of violence.

If some forms of film violence can be understood as tropes which resignify particular constellations of masculinity, it may be possible to hypostatize a continuity between the films discussed here and general movements within American culture and letters. That is, the tradition of violent film masculinities may profitably be contextualized with reference to a wider aesthetic and psychological orientation. A number of critics have pinpointed and analyzed what Paul Seydor has termed "the masculine principle in American art," whose origin he traces back to Emerson's *Nature* (1836) (*Peckinpah* 316).[17] The various permutations of the discourse on a masculine ethos are evident as an artistic-philosophical trajectory involving Cooper, Hawthorne, Clemens, Melville, Hemingway, Mailer and Peckinpah. Essential to this discourse, Seydor writes, is a near pathological attraction toward the extremes of experience, and the belief that knowledge can be gained in pure and unmediated ways (316). Attendant upon this masculinist tradition is a more or less explicit negation of the entrapments of the female sphere, which is identified with "the force that says no, that tries to make one suppress one's deepest feelings and substitute ersatz or false feelings" (316). David Savran sees the personification of this principle in the figure of the "American existentialist" who inhabits the fiction of someone like Mailer, and who in, for instance, *The White Negro* (1959) rebels against the deadening forces of conformity (4). There are numerous fairly recognizable avatars of this persona, from Thoreau's speaker in *Walden* (1854) to the narrator in Fincher's FIGHT CLUB.[18] Savran's existentialist closely resembles that of Finkelstein, who cites Camusian and Jasperian leitmotifs like the absurdity of existence and the disillusion with modernity and progress as the key concerns of this brand of masculinist thinking (12-13).

Above all, it appears to be modernity itself which provokes the immersion of masculinity in fantasies of violence and dreams of mortality. Writing about

Charles Grayson's *Stories for Men* (1936) Marilyn C. Wesley makes the following pronouncement: "Although the practice of violence is plotted as a necessary response to the conditions of modernity, it generally destroys rather than develops protagonists" (75). This is what she terms the "paradox of virility" (75). The genres which most forcefully and eloquently manifest this plight of the masculine ethos are the hard-boiled detective genre and film noir. For Jopi Nyman, the motor of hard-boiled fiction is the "reaffirmation of a disrupted masculine social order" (3), as well as the attempt to "defend the ideal of the autonomous male" (4). For all the oppressive cruelty inherent in these genres, their ambivalent depictions of masculinity appear to be invested with a certain nostalgia, a cynical romanticism, which is the result of the futility of attempting to reclaim a loss of power brought on by modernity. In the words of Joe L. Dubbert, "[t]he old frame of reference of the frontier and a high degree of individualism, which men used to validate their masculinity in the past, simply does not exist any more" (7). Modernist protagonists, as Alan W. Friedman notes in a study of D. H. Lawrence, are often portrayed as "devitalized and emasculated" (225), and violence affords the male protagonist an opportunity for self-creation, for reasserting a "positive masculine identity" (Wesley 77). While the inter-connectedness of violence and creativity has been acknowledged also by others, notably and unsurprisingly Mailer (in Theodore Gross 196), Wesley underlines the curious paradox that "the very literature which celebrates the definition of masculinity through violent action consistently suggests its failure" (86).

As we shall see below, there is ample evidence to suggest that a similar contradiction infuses the construction of masculinity in the fiction film as well. Projections of the male which extol a violence that is ultimately shown to be defunct suggest a rhetoric of defeatism, or at least of affliction. Tony Camonte in SCARFACE, like Cagney's gangster Cody Jarrett in Raoul Walsh's WHITE HEAT (1949), unveils a murderous rambunctiousness that more than hints at the hysterical; George Peatty in THE KILLING de-sublimates his neurosis into violence and destruction; Pike Bishop in THE WILD BUNCH embodies a weary, masochistic vitalism throughout the whole narrative; the criminals in RESERVOIR DOGS, hyper-conscious of their own self-creation as gangsters, parade their paranoia in bouts of eroticized violence; and Tyler Durden in FIGHT CLUB insistently advocates a return to primitivism as the only response to the general effeminacy that he thinks characterizes his generation of men. In a 1988 special issue on "Male Trouble" in *Camera Obscura*, editors Constance Penley and Sharon Willis focused on the extent to which images of men in contemporary culture "seem particularly organized around hysteria and masochism" (4). However, what the editors fail to address adequately is the fact that, as Savran writes, "there is no transhistorical essence of masculinity" (8). Audiovisual constructions of masculinities are continuously in the process of being reimagined, redefined and –

as viewers and critics compulsively return to older texts –reinterpreted. As film theorists, we should be wary of participating in a kind of facile criticism that confuses the term with the image.

Narratives engulfed by violence may be seen as allegorizations of processes that (de)construct masculinity, that disclose the conditions of a masculinity in modernist and postmodernist ruins. As Mark Ledbetter proposes, the violated body can itself be read as a text, which "serve[s] as microcosm to the larger 'body' of the text" (18), and the ways in which violence affects the body in different film-historical periods may thus be found to reflect historicized ideas concerning masculinity and its modes of being in the world. The cinematic body as an aesthetic construct, as a cultural construct configured by diverse social operations, reveals a set of masculine moralities which – though interpretable – are inseparable from film form.

Cinema violence as a death trope constitutes itself as much through narrative as through style, and the relation between mortality and narration is so compelling that it has lead Stewart to pronounce that "death has more recently become the patron saint of some of the most influential theories of narrative form" ("Thresholds of the Visible" 33). The form of the fiction film embodies what Sobchack understands as *narrative space*, an iconic or symbolic entity the structural reverse of which would be documentary space, which is indexical ("Inscribing" 293). Confined to the screen, narrative space is amimetic and non-referential. The difference between Sobchack's two designations may be clarified with reference to divergent modes of violence in Peckinpah's PAT GARRETT AND BILLY THE KID (1973). A much criticized scene in the film involves the shooting of chickens, an event which according to Sobchack's thesis would denote an indexical kind of violence extending into documentary space. The killing of the movie's characters, on the other hand, represents an iconic/symbolic type of violence whose spatial parameters are singularly narrative. Importantly, the notion of narrative space is valuable not only for a theory of amimetic filmicity, but also as a theoretical specification that elegantly unifies the two senses of aesthetic form (in Bordwell's neoformalist parlance these are, as we recall, style and narrative).

In a gloss on Brooks's theory of plot, John S. Rickard speaks of the narrative's desire to "seek its own cure in the death of the plot, a death that can only come … after the text has remembered and worked through its own original and repressed secrets and traumas" (in Brooks 1994, 6).[19] Though it seems somewhat inadvisable to anthropomorphize narrative in this manner, Rickard's emphasis on mortification is suggestive of the point Stewart makes above. Narrative violence and death constitute closely interlacing figurations in theories of narration, though not necessarily in a Brooksian fashion. Death, Benjamin says in his seminal essay on the work of Nikolai Leskov, is "the sanction of everything that the storyteller can tell" ("Storyteller" 94). On a more technical note, Randi Gun-zenhäuser describes the structural similarity of plotting and death: "A reciprocal relationship exists between discursive plotting and real death: all plots move toward their end, are constructed with a sense of their ending, the absolute, irreversible, and 'natural' solution of life and its plot being death. Death is the point where nature and telling seem to coincide" (81). It may be that the spatio-temporal organization of any plot is determined by how the narrative is going to end.

III

Male Subjectivities at the Margins

3   Mean Streets: Death and Disfiguration in Hawks's SCARFACE

Deathliness is in the mise en scène.
David Thomson

Consider this paradox: in SCARFACE, THE SHAME OF THE NATION, violence is virtually all encompassing, yet it is a film from an era before American movies became really violent. There are no graphic close-ups of bullet wounds or slow-motion dissections of agonized faces and bodies, only a series of abrupt, almost perfunctory liquidations seemingly devoid of the heat and passion of the spastic Lyle Gorch in THE WILD BUNCH or the anguished Mr. Orange, slowly bleeding to death, in RESERVOIR DOGS. Nonetheless, as Bernie Cook correctly points out, SCARFACE is the most violent of all the gangster films of the early 1930s cycle (1: 545).[1] Hawks's camera desists from examining the anatomy of the punctured flesh and the extended convulsions of corporeality in transition. The film's approach, conforming to the period style of pre-BONNIE AND CLYDE depictions of violence, is understated, euphemistic, in its attention to the particulars of what Ledbetter sees as "narrative scarring" (x). It would not be illegitimate to describe the form of violence in SCARFACE as discreet, were it not for the fact that appraisals of the aesthetics of violence are primarily a question of kind, and not of degrees. In Hawks's film, as we shall see, violence orchestrates the deep structure of the narrative logic, yielding an hysterical form of plotting that hovers between the impulse toward self-effacement and the desire to advance an ethics of emasculation.

SCARFACE is a film in which violence completely takes over the narrative, becoming both its vehicle and its determination. As the story's backbone, Camonte's rise to power and his subsequent and inevitable fall rely on violence as the common denominator. In the opening of the film, Camonte assassinates Castillo, the leader of the mafia in charge of the city's South side district. The killing of Castillo propels Camonte's superior Lavo to the position of chief of the South side mob. From the beginning, however, it is clear that Camonte has higher ambitions, and gradually he takes control of the business as Lavo retreats to the background. Camonte also initiates a romance with his boss's wife Poppy, which complicates his relationship to Lavo. Subsequent to Castillo's murder, Camonte sets out on a rampage to assume control over the city's bootlegging business. An escalating chain of violent events ensue as Camonte terrorizes and eliminates rivals, dissenters, and associates who attempt to take more than their share of the profit. Eventually he takes on the North side gangsters (fig. 2), and soon becomes the most powerful criminal boss in the city. From this point on his aggression and hubris gradually defeat him, as he kills Lavo and then his loyal right-hand man Rinaldo who has just married Cesca without Camonte's knowledge. In the end, the film attains narrative symmetry as Camonte's execution of Castillo in the beginning is reversed when Camonte himself is killed while trying to escape from the police.

Fig. 2. Bowling for the north side. Camonte perfunctorily assassinates Gaffney, the leader of the rival gang. Frame enlargement.

The narrative of Camonte's trajectory is immersed in images of violence. Sheer force is what places him in power, and also what ultimately removes him from power. He sustains control of the city through the use of violence, his most important asset as well as his fatal flaw. Likewise, the narrative is organized around the multiple violent events that occur at frequent intervals. Camonte's accelerating violence is presented as a cavalcade of assassinations, in which enemies are executed on the streets, inside bars, in back alleys, in automobiles, in bowling alleys and even in hospitals. In one evocative image, the passage of time is represented by leaves falling off the calendar to the sound of gun shots, a meta-textual device whose non-mimetic quality resembles the disclaimer at the beginning of the film. All these violent segments drive the narrative forward. Although they are not temporally protracted like the violence in, for instance, BONNIE AND CLYDE and THE WILD BUNCH, their recurrence and frequency lend a certain omnipresence to the violence.

SCARFACE has a complicated and sinuous production history.[2] Loosely based on a 1930 novel by Armitage Trail (a pseudonym for Maurice Coons) and a screenplay by Ben Hecht, Hawks's film was shot in 1930 but was not released until 1932. Preceded by Mervyn LeRoy's LITTLE CAESAR (1930) and William A. Wellman's THE PUBLIC ENEMY (1931), SCARFACE was the last of the three major gangster movies of the early 1930s. These films resonate with an historical significance beyond themselves because they provoked the establishment of the Production Code Administration in 1934 (Prince, "Graphic" 4), Although the first-known case of film censorship was reported as early as 1908, when THE JAMES BOYS OF MISSOURI – produced by the Essanay Film Manufacturing Company – was charged with 'criminalizing' history (Hoberman 118), legal censorship of the movies was not sanctioned until 1915. In the case of *Mutual Film Corporation v. Industrial Commission of Ohio*, the Supreme Court denied the film medium First Amendment privileges on the grounds that it was purely a business venture. The cinema was thus neither acknowledged as a part of the mass media nor as an organ of public opinion (Lyons 7). This decision augmented both state and city censorship. It was in response to these threats that the motion picture industry proposed a system of self-regulation. Essentially, these systems were contracts which provided filmmakers with basic, informal rules that would determine the limits of film content. The first embodiment of the self-regulatory system was the "Thirteen Points" and twenty-six other subjects established by the National Association of the Motion Picture Industry (NAMPI) in 1916. In 1922, this system was modified into the "Don'ts and Be Careful," which was instituted by the Motion Picture Producers and Distributors of America (MPPDA), a trade organization led by Will H. Hays (formerly Postmaster General during Warren Harding's presidency). Finally, partly as a response to silent gangster films like Josef von Sternberg's UNDERWORLD (1927) and THE DOCKS OF NEW YORK (1928), the Hays Office formulated a revised MPAA Production Code in 1930 (Hoberman 118).[3] However, the industry was initially quite lenient in enforcing the regulations of the code, and from March 1930 to July 1934, as Thomas Doherty points out, "censorship was lax, and Hollywood made the most of it... More unbridled, salacious, subversive, and just plain bizarre than what came afterwards, [the films] look like Hollywood cinema but the moral terrain is so off-kilter they seem imported from a parallel universe" (2). Due to increasing pressure from the Catholic Legion of Decency, in 1934 the industry eventually established the Production Code Administration Office, which was run by Joseph Breen and whose Seal of Approval governed film production in Hollywood until its disintegration in 1961. All of the film studios supported the Production Code, which made it nearly impossible for filmmakers within the industry to try and release a film without the Seal of Approval.

Before the onslaught of the gangster trilogy, the Hays Office had been concerned mainly with issues of sex and nudity rather than with violence (Hoberman 118), a remaining priority both with the Production Code and the later rating systems. In a 2001 study of 125 censored Hollywood movies, Dawn B. Sova finds that only six were censored due to their violent content alone, whereas forty-nine were banned or cut because of their sexual content (347-348).[4] SCARFACE belongs in the former category, which also includes Roland West's THE ALIBI (1929), James Whale's FRANKENSTEIN (1931), De Palma's DRESSED TO KILL (1980), Stone's NATURAL BORN KILLERS, and Steven Spielberg's AMISTAD (1997). With regard to SCARFACE, the Hays Office attempted to curtail the production of the film both on account of the violence it portrayed, and because it insisted on a connection between public officials and criminal activities. In their evaluation of Hecht's script, the Hays Office came to the following conclusion:

> Under no circumstances is this film going to be made. The American public and all conscientious State Boards of Censorship find mobsters and hoodlums repugnant. Gangsterism must not be mentioned in the cinema. If you should be foolhardy enough to make SCARFACE, this office will make certain it is never released (in Lyons 13).[5]

Howard Hughes, the film's producer, nonetheless opted to make the film.[6] When, upon its release, New York State censors cut a large number of violent scenes, Hughes filed a lawsuit against the censors and defeated them in court. However, despite the verdict, SCARFACE was banned in Chicago and other cities. Hawks's film finally opened in New York on May 20, 1932, after several revisions had been made to accommodate the Hays Office.[7] The most significant of these were the inserted indictment of gangsterism in the very beginning; a scene directed by Hawks's assistant Richard Rosson, in which politicians and officials convene to discuss how to fight crime in the city; and a change in the film's title, which, according to Gerald Mast, was "merely a public-relations tactic" (*Howard Hawks* 73). The Hays Office had also wanted a different ending, one that depicted the apprehension and execution of Camonte, but the suggestion was abandoned before the film's release. Moreover, in Hecht's script, according to Todd McCarthy, "the story was much harsher, more cynical about human motivations and behavior, more jaundiced about political realities, and more forthright than the finished film would be" (136). Although it became a box-office success, SCARFACE did not recoup its production costs quickly, which was mainly due to the fact that the film was still prohibited in some states even after its general opening. In Chicago, SCARFACE could not be seen until over a year after its release, and, as Carlos Clarens notes, the film was not widely distribu-ted abroad (91). Some time after its initial theatrical run, Hughes withdrew all legal prints of the film, making the movie difficult to view even in the United States until it was reissued by Universal Studios in 1979.

The altercation over SCARFACE and its condemnation by the Hays Office was an exception in the history of the censorship of violence and crime in the mo-vies. Few films made between 1934 and 1968 (when the new rating system was first introduced) were denied a seal of approval, and legal censorship of vio-lence in the movies declined similarly. It is notable that throughout the classical period the concern with violence appears to have been correlated more specifi-cally with criminality, whereas from the 1970s onwards, the preoccupation shifted to violence and violent behavior in general (Lyons 14). Maltby, on the other hand, assumes that the censorship efforts of the early 1930s were targeted mostly at spectacle rather than narrative, since by convention the criminal was always punished in the end anyway ("Spectacle of Criminality" 124). What makes the case of SCARFACE stand out is the fact that violence has never been a particularly salient target for censorship struggles, be it from legal censorship boards or from the industry itself.[8] Seldom has a film been singled out as objec-tionable due to its depiction of violence. The subject of violence has never in-cited as much protest from special pressure groups as have issues of the depic-tion of sexuality, ethnicity and religion on the screen. In this perspective, the treatment of Hawks's film by the Hays Office and by local regulatory councils appears unprecedented.

Despite the critical and cultural reputation that SCARFACE enjoys,[9] the film's most distinctive facet is the set of contradictions and ambivalences which ani-mate the narrative. There is a gap between the statement in the preface and the intentions of the film itself; the images are suffused with a violence that, by being shown, conceals; the concern with contemporary social issues and didac-ticism indicated by the preface seems precariously at odds with the insular car-tography of the gangster cosmos; and, most significantly, the ebullient bravado that is the trademark of the main protagonist betrays an hysterical underside which conceives masculinity as infantilism. All these internal contradictions ex-pose a violence immanent to the process in which the film organizes itself as a textual event.

The unabashed disclaimer with which SCARFACE begins relates awkwardly to the subsequent narrative. Condemning both the activities of the gangsters and the passivity of the government, the interpolation anchors the film in an instruc-tional promulgation that at least potentially trades in textual pleasure for didac-ticism. But the insert's ambiguity is evident in that, on the one hand, it functions as a self-conscious meta-frame which directly addresses the situation which is later enacted. On the other hand, because the segment itself is positioned within the parameters of the text, it is also a part of the film's total enunciation. Spectators perceive it intuitively as a documentary passage, or as a non-fictional fragment that precedes the fictional story itself. In principle, however, the disclaimer is inescapably caught within the same textual whole from which it attempts to distance itself, and this contradiction produces a complex interaction between different layers of narrative as well as between text, image and story. The segment reads:

> This picture is an indictment of gang rule in America and of the callous indifference of the government to this constantly increasing menace to our society and our liberty. Every incident in this picture is the reproduction of an actual occurrence, and the purpose of this picture is to demand of the government: 'What are you going to do about it? The Government is your government. What are *you* going to do about it?'

The statement is one of the most direct addresses to the audience on the topic of violence in the history of American cinema, and the explicit link between fictional and historical incidents anticipates the modern re-enactment genre. Beginning with a definition of the film's content, the message ends with a provocative appeal to the viewer. Taken as a narrative framing of the diegetic action of the film, the opening titles serve to restrict the heterogeneity of its discourse.[10] What is striking about this short prolegomenon is the way in which it rhetorically integrates a moral dimension into the aesthetic system of the film. It appears as if the narration with one single brushstroke has clarified its ethical position; principle appropriates textuality rather than the other way around.

However, there is a sense in which the mission statement is duplicitous. By denouncing the violence in advance, the responsibility pertinent to showing it becomes less taxing. The disclaimer, as it were, acts as a form of inadvertent validation. Thomas Schatz, for instance, has argued that "the rhetorical power of Hollywood's narrative codes" in fact works against the didactic purpose of the opening statement (93). Schatz's assertion is not necessarily incorrect, but it requires some measure of modification. The narration of SCARFACE courts ambiguity not only in the juxtaposition of the disclaimer and the violence, but also – in a mereological sense – in the incongruent distribution of rhetorical value among each narrative instance and the text as a whole. It is certainly possible to imply, as Schatz does, that SCARFACE tends to romanticize the figure of the gangster (93), but only in isolated segments of plot. As soon as we reach the story's conclusion, narrative mortification materializes as a relentless exposition and a deglamorizaion of gangsterism. The scene where Camonte is killed – no less than the initial disclaimer – is an illustration of what Nesbet sees as an authorial "framing" of textual violence: "Depictions of violence which are strangely or inadequately 'framed' tend to produce anxiety in an observing audience.... The urgency of critics' search for an authorial 'reaction shot' reflects uncertainty about how they are (or should be) reacting to the violence" (vii). Although Nesbet refers to the work of Isaak Babel, the crux of her thesis – that the nature of the aesthetic point of view which underpins fictional violence is vital for our comprehension of the moral import of the depiction – easily appertains to film fiction as well. In fact, Nesbet already implicates the filmic in her metaphorical reliance upon a film term to describe the process of authorial framing.

The policing of filmic perspectives as regards questions of morality and law has of course always been a paramount concern in Hollywood, which the stipulations recorded in the 1930 Production Code testify. Articles 1 and 3 under "Principles of Plot" declare respectively that "No plot or theme should definitely side *with evil and against good*," and "No plot should be constructed as to leave the question of right or *wrong in doubt or fogged*" (Mintz and Roberts 146, emphases in original). Thus, the MPAA seems to have distrusted the intrinsic morality of the film's story, since the producers were compelled to equip the narrative with a preamble. Confrontational subjects like violence are acceptable in proportion to how convincingly the mechanism of authorial framing articulates a morally based censure of these subjects. However, extra-fictional disapproval is frequently insufficient as a means of audience persuasion. A case in point is Stone's largely unsuccessful attempt to publicly define his NATURAL BORN KILLERS as an anti-violence text in the face of what many took to be the film's own evidence to the contrary.

The notion that particular moralities are embedded in the deep structure of crucial components of aesthetic form, like narrative, represents an intricate challenge to theories of film fiction, but it is one that has been confronted – perhaps obliquely –by certain critics. On a general scale, Jean-Pierre Oudart has diagnosed classical Hollywood cinema's preference for firm narrative resolution as a symptom of a cultural desideratum to reconfirm the hegemony of the dominant ideology (5). By re-establishing order, Hollywood films not only achieve a kind of compositional symmetry in the Aristotelian sense but also an eradication of those subversive elements upon which the narrative movement depends in the first place. If this is a legitimate premise, one may allege that the canonic story format propounded and refined by classical Hollywood films provides a structure which is inherently conservative and, moreover, oppressively homogenous. In a discussion of the economy of violence in the exploitation genre, Rodowick to some extent echoes Oudart's proposition in his identification of three global conventions which circumscribe the logic of violence in mainstream cinema. First, the violence of authority, never excessive but always modulated according to the degree of transgression, is invariably justified. Second, the cause of the transgression is assigned to an external agent, an anarchic other who fails to comprehend or conform to the moral rationality which defines the culture authorized to deploy "legal" violence, which for Rodowick is synonymous with bourgeois society. Third, the projection of "unsolicited" violence onto the other fractures the text so that "criminal violence is consumed by legal violence in a closed circuit established by the undermining and restoration of stable ideological positions" (322). For the audience, this narrative structure ensures an ostensibly legitimate and pleasurable experience of a film's violence, one that reinforces dominant beliefs and safeguards the viewers from becoming implicated in the onscreen action. Rodowick posits a design which necessitates some system of appropriate authorial framing, and it seems to be the occasional lapse of such a system that makes narratives such as Stanley Kubrick's A CLOCKWORK ORANGE (1971), Ellis's AMERICAN PSYCHO, and MAN BITES DOG so disconcerting. When the Production Code presided over the dissemination of moving images, film violence mostly consolidated existing values (Slocum, "Violence" 6).

In terms of characterization, a notable aspect of SCARFACE is the absence of the traditional hero. Although the establishment conventionally defeats the transgressor in the end, the film fails to develop its nominal heroes psychologically or even narratively. The viewers are never encouraged to engage with any of the representatives of the law because their role in the story is insignificant and therefore does not invite any emotional investment. Hence, the viewers are left with Rodowick's anarchic other at the center of the narrative, a characterizational effect not unlike those in THE KILLING, THE WILD BUNCH, and RESERVOIR DOGS. In a larger historical perspective, SCARFACE prevails as an early instance of the later tendency to foreground, and give narrative prominence to the figure of the criminal. However, Hawks's film never indulges in the fetishization of the criminal that we find in these later films. In RESERVOIR DOGS in particular, the viewers no longer merely sympathize with morally deviant protagonists, they become celebrants of their actions and behavior, amused by their dialogue and jokes, and are entertained rather than sickened by the violence.

The romanticization of violent perpetrators is a phenomenon that appears to emerge with the rise of the 1930s gangster films, at whose core, Thomas R. Atkins maintains, "the roots of modern screen violence" may be located (7). It is perhaps inescapable that several critics have interpreted the fascination with crime and violence in the movies of this period as a response to the immoderation of the 1920s and to the crisis of the Depression years. Maltby contributes one such symptomatic reading of the gangster flicks:

> The brief cycle of gangster movies made during the 1930-31 production season was part of a broader representational strategy within Hollywood during the early Depression, by which overtly retrospective accounts of the excesses of the previous decade were staged as melodramatic reenactments of the rise and fall of moral chaos. Through such a strategy, Hollywood participated in a more general cultural attempt

to account for the crisis as an alleged permissiveness of the Jazz Age ("Spectacle of Criminality" 119).

According to William Faure, the 1930s became the decade for cinematic examinations of the nature and causes of social violence, examinations that cemented the impression that mass hysteria was a significant force behind the preoccupation with violence and criminals (23).[11] The movies of the early 1930s construe an ambiguous image of the gangster, an image which vacillates between romantic hero and cultural scapegoat. As Maltby contends, the gangster became "a significant part of the sin that was being expiated after the Crash" ("Spectacle of Criminality" 127). But this expiation insinuates an unauthorized undertow which covertly venerated the criminal. Mast has suggested that the world of SCARFACE, its didacticism notwithstanding, fails to interrogate the sociological structure that may be found to promote gangsterism. SCARFACE differs in this respect from LeRoy's LITTLE CAESAR and Wellman's THE PUBLIC ENEMY, which explore the social influences of unemployment and poverty in order to explain the rise of organized urban crime. In Mast's opinion, the point of Hawks's film is the realization that "gangsters and their brutal world exist because they are in fact thoroughly accepted by the very moral, political, and cultural life of modern America, which deplores them only in theory" (*Howard Hawks* 75). If Mast is correct, the more undisguised celebration of the gangster in BONNIE AND CLYDE may not be so much a direct product of the countercultural rhetoric of the late 1960s as yet another manifestation of a more fundamental and historically far-reaching adoration of a particular criminal archetype.

More than a reflection of the authentic gangster who inhabited the streets of urban America in the 1930s, movie characters like Paul Muni's Camonte may be seen as the celluloid pedigree of the figure of the modern criminal, who, as Black reminds us, is principally an invention of the popular media (*Aesthetics* 31). The main channel of distribution for the particular genre that Michel Foucault has dubbed "the song of murder" was the broadsheet (*I, Pierre* 207-208). Genealogically, the murder song can be traced further through the confessions made by criminals at Newgate (subsequently collected in *The Newgate Calendar* and *The Tynburn Chronicle*),[12] the chronicles of the famous trials like François Gayot de Pitaval's *Causes célèbres et intéressantes*, and texts like John Gay's *The Beggar's Opera* (1728) and Henry Fielding's *Jonathan Wild, The Great* (1743) (Black, *Aesthetics* 32). Throughout the 18th and 19th centuries, the criminal act of murder became an increasingly common and refined topic of domestic conversation. An aesthetic valuation of murder, and the conception of the murderer as a kind of artist, occurs in Diderot's *Le Neveu de Rameau* (written in ca. 1761, but unpublished, though translated by Goethe as *Rameaus Neffe* in 1805), in Schiller's essay "Reflections on the Use of the Vulgar and the Lowly in Works of Art" (1827), and finally, in De Quincey's "On Murder Considered as One of the Fine Arts" (1827) (Black, *Aesthetics* 35).[13] As Black is anxious to point out, the criminals are never seen as artists per se; it is the fictional narrators who aesthetically reconstitute them as artists of murder (*Aesthetics* 38).

SCARFACE features a classically deluded hero who is consumed and destroyed by his own hubris and lack of insight and self-control. Hecht's original draft delineates even more insistently these aspects of Camonte's character, who lives to see some of the concluding gunfire, but the Hays office objected to this suggestion which appeared as a glorification of the criminal (McCarthy 139). Muni's performance is instrumental in exteriorizing and calibrating the excessiveness of the artistic murderer-as-gangster. Robin Wood finds that Camonte is defined by an "essential innocence," in that the primitivism of his behavior and mentality is that of a child (*Howard Hawks* 59). Grouping the film with Hawks's comedies [BRINGING UP BABY (1938), HIS GIRL FRIDAY (1940) and MONKEY BUSINESS (1952)], Wood claims that the combination of farce and horror is indicative of the principal theme which structures SCARFACE: the psychology of total irresponsibility (67). Other critics have also emphasized the co-existence of such traits in Camonte's persona. Leland A. Poague, for instance, writes that the character's "exercise of power is simultaneously playful and brutal" (97), whereas Schatz proposes that "[his] primitive brutality, simple-minded naiveté, and sexual confusion made him a figure with little charisma and with virtually no redeeming qualities" (91). In the context of Hawks's oeuvre this portrayal of giddy irresponsibility becomes especially revealing. While Hawks cultivates a certain laxity in his comedies – the exhilaration accompanying the free play of solipsistic impulses – the heroes of his adventure films share a strong sense of communal accountability. The prototypical Hawksian protagonist represents values such as loyalty, courage and endurance. In SCARFACE, however, it is a strangely careless sensibility that informs the characterization of the main protagonist. Even the nihilism of Bishop and his partners in THE WILD BUNCH falls short of the absolute lack of social commitment of a Camonte. Nonetheless, one of the peculiar effects of Hawks's film, Wood writes, is that the viewers are still able to commiserate with Camonte despite the unspeakable cruelty of his actions. Comparing the film to Godard's LES CARABINIERS (1963), Wood makes the following suggestion: "Though utterly different in style and method, both [films] have leading characters who consistently perform monstrous violent actions which the films never condone, yet who retain the audience's sympathy to the end, and for similar reasons" (58). The reasons alluded to involve the way in which the film presents its protagonist as if he were "an innocent immune from moral judgment" (58). But this narrative strategy does not mitigate the violence of Camonte: "Far from weakening the statement of horror and despair, this intensifies it" (Wood 58).

Irrespective of the many putative references to historical events,[14] the film's violence is essentially amimetic, as the references neither imitate nor represent any extra-fictional reality, but address instead the transtextual tradition from which they emerge. "Despite this claim to social commitment," Eva Bueno, José Oviedo and Michael Varona write, "SCARFACE posits its own 'reality', [sic] one which limits itself to gangsters and those who would censure, control or profit by their activities" (113). In turn, the generic and narrative codes provide a quotational repository for many later films. Ray's PARTY GIRL (1958), Billy Wilder's SOME LIKE IT HOT (1959), Denys de La Patellière's DU RIFIFI À PANAME (1966), De Palma's remake SCARFACE (1983), as well as his THE UNTOUCHABLES (1987), and Coen's MILLER'S CROSSING (1990) are only some among a slew of texts that in various ways reference Hawks's film. Perhaps the most mesmeric intercinematic quotation of SCARFACE takes place in anthropologist Eliane de Latour's BRONX-BARBÈS (2000), in which the criminal trajectory and self-image of a young West African hoodlum are constantly focalized through the characterizational tropes established by Hawks's and DePalma's texts. Although the transtextualism of SCARFACE is a long way from the thoroughgoing pastiche of a Tarantino, Hawks's film is still imbued with a host of generic and individual intertexts. Bueno, Oviedo and Varona apprehend their relationship thus:

> The opening sequence of the film establishes a set of semiotic texts which will continue to generate meaning throughout the movie in various innovative articulations. These semiotic texts, replete with their own internal grammars and contradictions are woven into the deep structure of the film through the use of specific cinematographic techniques (114).

Previous gangster and crime films from Griffith's short silent THE MUSKETEERS OF PIG ALLEY (1912) to Sternberg's UNDERWORLD (written by Hecht) and THE DRAGNET (1928) had already provided a narrative template for the genre. Hawks's film appropriates these generic stock features rather profusely, which is perhaps what stirs a critic like Stephen Louis Karpf to speak of the "derivative" quality of the narrative (87).[15] More particular to SCARFACE is a set of infective motifs culled from a variety of cultural and textual sources. One of the most immediately resonant is the sustained connection to THE GREAT GATSBY (1925), whose thematic ideas underlie the development of both the story and the character of Camonte. There is a scene in SCARFACE in which Camonte tries to impress Poppy with his collection of silk shirts, a moment which, as Doherty has pointed out, directly acknowledges its subtext (148).[16] What appears to be Camonte's credo – "Do it first, do it yourself, and keep on doin' it" (fig. 3) – is an evident though distorted reformulation of the ethos of the self-made man so abundantly associated with Fitzgerald's novel, and the suave licentiousness of the gangster's world is highly reminiscent of the decadence of THE GREAT GATS-

BY. In SCARFACE, Doherty writes, there is a sense in which "the fresh green breast of the New World has rotted on the vine, the cultural metaphor of 1925 having become the economic report of 1932" (148). Hawks's deeply ironic gesture, eloquently rendered in the billboard sign slogan "The World is Yours," seems to be as much a repudiation of the politics of the self-made man as a deromanticization of the gangster figure specifically.

Fig. 3. Fight Club. Camonte pummels a rebellious gang member.
Frame enlargement.

The scene in which the allusion to THE GREAT GATSBY occurs is also revelatory of a major subtext that threads through Hawks's film. Caressing his silk shirts, Camonte performs a gesture which divulges the tension at the core of the film's codification of masculinity. As it turns out, Scarface is not only a childlike gangster, but an effeminate one as well. His vanity only matched by his brutality, Camonte is time and again portrayed as being obsessed with clothing and with his appearance (we first see him inside a barbershop). Furthermore, Camonte is highly unpredictable and he is given to exaggerated, uncontrollable bursts of emotion, traits which are conventionally associated with the feminine. Camonte's melodramatic tinge is somewhat aberrant within the context of a genre which, like the western, values masculine restraint. When juxtaposed with more paradigmatically phlegmatic gangsters like Vito Corleone in THE GODFATHER or Tom Reagan in MILLER'S CROSSING, Scarface's hysterical features emerge even more transparently. Camonte's persona, ambiguously situated between violence and hysteria,[17] appears to illustrate the decentering of masculine subjectivity that David E. Ruth in his book on the invention of the gangster claims to have occurred with modernity. Implying a correlation between violence and particular forms of social change, Ruth writes: "Men celebrated aggression at the same time that the ongoing organization of society rendered aggression increasingly counterproductive" (92). The cycle of gangster movies that appeared in the early 1930s may be seen as a response to the transformations of the notion of masculinity which took place at the time. Muni's complexly engineered gangster could feasibly be read as a symptom of this transformation.

Some of the violence in SCARFACE is signaled not only by the cross symbolism but also by an accompanying aural cue, which is first heard in the film's initial sequence. In an unbroken, uncharacteristically elaborate tracking shot that climaxes with the murder of Castillo, we first hear Camonte's signature whistling, a recurring sound trope that surfaces shortly before he is about to kill someone. Hecht's script indicates that the melody Scarface whistles is a version of the popular 1930s song "Come Back to Sorrento," written by Ernesto de Curtis in 1904 (Hagemann 40), but as Clarens has suggested, the theme used in the film is that of the sextet from Gaetano Donizetti's opera *Lucia di Lammermoor* (93). The musical excerpt was by no means chosen at random. Donizetti's opera, which is based on Sir Walter Scott's *The Bride of Lammermoor* (1819), revolves around the illicit love affair between Lucia and her power-mad brother Enrico's adversary Edgardo. There is much to indicate that Cesca's relationship with her brother is substantially modeled on that of Lucia (Lucy Ashton) and Enrico (Lord Henry Ashton) in Scott's narrative. The text of Camonte's leitmotif, furthermore, translates as "What restrains me in such a moment?" (Clarens 93), a pithy rhetorical question whose self-reflexivity extends beyond the character of Camonte to implicate the film – and its perspective on violence – as a whole. In a conspicuous sense, the text of the melody seems to mock the address to the audience in the beginning of the film, as if to defy the disclaimer's concerned tone with a rejoinder that is equally cynical and sinister. The phrase's temporal designation, "in such a moment," may be taken to denote not only the narrative time of violence but also the historical time of the film's production, thus restating the question in terms of who restrains the filmmaker in showing the audience images of violence. Finally, the aural trope circuitously supports yet another chain of transtextual signification. As Hawks himself discloses in an interview with Peter Bogdanovich, the conception of the relationship between Camonte and Cesca in plainly incestuous terms was a conscious decision on the part of the scriptwriters,[18] as was the use of the Borgia family in late 15th-century Italy as a model for that relationship (52). Hecht even refers to Cesca as a "Borgian wench" in his script (Hagemann 40).[19] Incidentally, prior to *Lammermoor* Donizetti had composed the opera *Lucrezia Borgia* (1833), and in Camonte's effortless whistling the connotations to the Borgia family and to Scott's novel merge.

In a manner not entirely different from Tarantino's cannibalizing of 1970s soul music in RESERVOIR DOGS, SCARFACE achieves a seamless integration of a melange of references to popular music, alongside its narratively prominent quotation of high art. These include Louis Armstrong and Kid Ory's "St. Louis Blues," which is heard on the soundtrack in the "Paradise" sequence, Sophie Tucker's "Some of These Days," (written by Shelton Brooks, 1910) to which Cesca dances in front of Rinaldo in the same sequence, and Cesca's performance of 'Casey Jones" in the scene leading up to Rinaldo's murder. The last two songs in particular portend the later destruction of Cesca and Rinaldo's relationship by Camonte's consuming jealousy. Brooks's lyrics intone the imminent grief which befalls the speaker when s/he is left behind by a lover, and "Casey Jones" chronicles the tale of the eponymous train engineer who is killed in a wreck between Memphis and Canton in 1900.[20] More than mere ornamentation, these musical references both foreshadow plot events and help expand the intertexual range of the film.

All of these allusive patterns in SCARFACE participate in a process of textual self-consciousness, one that the extra-artistic amendments such as the opening disclaimer unwittingly enhance. By underscoring the film's relation to "reality," the insert's irrevocable self-consciousness paradoxically annuls it. As Iampolski has shown, acts of quotation – which in my view become signs of self-consciousness whether they are intended or not – work to promote semiosis at the expense of mimesis (30). Quotationality bolsters a text's amimetic aspects. In Hawks's movie there is an additional sequence in which transtextual citation and narrative self-consciousness converge in the same semiotic space. Some time after the Valentine's Day massacre (fig. 4), Camonte and his companions attend a theatre performance of Somerset Maugham's *Rain*, a morality tale first published in the collection *The Trembling of a Leaf* (1921).[21] Camonte has to leave in the intermission because his men have located the whereabouts of Gaffney, the leader of the gang that were murdered on Valentine's Day. However, Camonte orders one of his men to stay behind and watch the rest of the play to find out which of her two suitors Sadie eventually chooses. The scene in which Gaffney is shot in a bowling alley precedes the scene at the "Paradise" restaurant. Asking for a light, Poppy chooses Camonte's match over Lovo's lighter, a move which, prefigured by the Maugham quotation, indicates that she has now left her former lover for Camonte.

In terms of narrative organization, violent action in SCARFACE is protracted globally but compressed locally. Brutal events take place at short and even intervals, but their duration is brief. Peter Brunette's description of the violent grammar of the Three Stooges films may apply equally to that in SCARFACE: "this narrative of violence ... acts as a kind of punctuation, a system of commas, periods, and paragraph breaks, for the syntax of the ostensibly plotted, 'larger' narrative" (176). For Donald C. Willis, this punctuation system asserts itself so vigorously that it in fact dissolves the film's proper narrative (132). In contrast, violence in a film like THE WILD BUNCH is expansive within the sequence, but occurs less frequently and systematically between different scenes and parts of the film. The anatomy of the violent movement is dissected into detailed fragments, shown from different positions in space and prolonged in time beyond the actual story duration. Similarly, the images of violence establish their own temporality in the concluding shots of BONNIE AND CLYDE, which is not concomitant with that of the represented event. The narration of SCARFACE, conversely, does not linger on its violent images. If Penn and Peckinpah conceive of violence as scenes, Hawks presents it as summary. Furthermore, the graphic imagery in SCARFACE is so cautiously conceptual that it hardly qualifies as carnage at all. Even THE KILLING, which is fairly sanitary in this respect, suggests a certain level of explicitness in the depiction of violence which is absent from Hawks's film. On the other hand, violence in SCARFACE is highly prolific. In the course of the narration there are twenty-eight sequences which feature violent action, and these produce a structuring taxonomy which corresponds to the progression of narratively salient plot phases. Although SCARFACE's violence is rarely developed into the kinds of spectacle found in THE WILD BUNCH, it nonetheless performs a primary aesthetic function in that it shapes and configures the narrative of the film. Violence in Hawks's film is not a consequence of unresolvable conflicts, a product of the action, but rather, the narrative action becomes a result of the violence.

Fig. 4. The scene of violence as shadow-play. Frame enlargement.

The classical and hence extrinsic norms for visualizing violence that inform Hawks's narrative rely to a significant extent on abstraction, on a certain dematerialization of the body – in short, on contour rather than texture. As Browne states, prior to the 1960s, American movie violence was generally codified in "certain dramaturgical conventions ... functioning most notably by suggestion (narrative indirection or simple symbolism), diminishment, or usually the elimination of the details of the actual wounding" ("Aesthetics" 1: 548). In the war films of the 1941-1945 period, James William Gibson describes what he terms "a highly abstract approach to violence": "wounds are relatively painless and bloodless. No one screams in agonizing pain. Even death is discreet, signified by a small red dot on the chest" (22). Because the violence in SCARFACE – and by extension that of the classical cinema as a whole – works by implication, it becomes in a sense even more threatening than the later, graphic depictions. Since an abstract approach omits the impact of violent force upon the body, both the nature and consequences of violence become an enigma, something that entices due to its inarticulate elusiveness. The effort toward ever more explicit portrayals of disfiguration can be conceptualized as an increasing desire to rid classical violence of its unbearable invisibility. When filmmakers like Peckinpah, Scorsese and Tarantino show us images of graphic bodily laceration, their spectacles function as an epistemological delimitation. The violence shown inscribes its own limits in the act itself, as if the images were saying: violence may be this, but at least it is nothing more. Classical cinema's approach to violence – because it involves abstraction and indirection – cannot guarantee such a delimitation, and this renders the impact of violence potentially infinite.

The murder scene with which the narrative begins makes palpable the aesthetics of abstraction that defines the narration of violence in SCARFACE. Shot so that the camera stays behind in the adjacent room through which Camonte first enters, the murder is only shown in silhouette, as a configuration of shadows on a white canvas illuminated by the light. The violence thus achieves the texture of a pantomime, to borrow Infante's phrase (48). Here is how Mast elucidates the scene:

> we see the murder clearly and are capable of recognizing its brutality; but we do not experience that brutality fully, distanced by the murder's shadowy indirectness, so that we do not come to loath or detest the man who performs it. It is a shadow, a two-dimensional shape, not a man, who is the brutal murderer. Nor do we feel deeply for the shadow's victim, since the victim's moral and emotional life is as vague and blurry as the shadowy killer (*Howard Hawks* 81).

We identify Camonte as the killer on account of his trademark whistling, but the sequence does not reveal his face. The killing initiates the narrative, and becomes an emblem of the ways in which violence is presented throughout the film; it takes place in off-screen space, or in spaces where all substance and detail are removed from the image. The lack of bodily definition in the moment of murder formalizes the violence and heightens its conceptual rather than its material suggestiveness (fig. 5). As I have already suggested, this stylistic technique is paradoxical, as it presents a visualization of a violent act that is not shown.

Fig. 5. Camonte executes Costillo in the semi-abstract figuration of cinematographer Lee Garmes's sepia-toned silhouette. Frame enlargement.

Conceptually, the violence in SCARFACE involves acts of intended erasure on multiple levels. There is the prudent erasure of gunshot wounds, there is the incessant wiping out of narrative characters, there are the expository titles in the beginning which, in effect ban the ensuing imagery, and there are the political initiatives to prevent the film from being made in the first place. These acts of deletion find a stylistic correlative in the film's pervasive use of the X motif, a literalization of the multi-layered erasures, the means of which is the mutilation of the textual body. Even the film's title gestures toward an awareness of an aesthetics of disfiguration in its adumbration of a Hawthornian badge of disgrace. The cross-shaped scar on the face of main protagonist Camonte is an inscription of a violence, a *de-facing*, at the same time as it is also the symbolic locus to which all of the narrative's other X's refer back. Each individual manifestation of the emblem in the various spaces of the film, each instance of violation, enters into a metonymic relation with its conceptual source, the master scar on Camonte's face. A remarkable contradiction, the scar as a sign simultaneously performs the acts of imprinting and crossing out.

The form of SCARFACE is not prototypically Hawksian. As McCarthy concedes, such "stylistic flourishes" would not often be seen later in the director's long career (155). Whether he has been celebrated as one of the greatest American film artists (as he was by the *Cahiers du Cinéma* critics in the mid-1950s), or dismissed as a mere "entertainer" [which seems to have been the opinion of Raymond Durgnat in a re-evaluation of the director in 1977 (18)], two aspects of Hawks's practice are continuously repeated: his enormous versatility with respect to genre and subject matter, and the absence of an idiosyncratic film signature. Jean-Pierre Coursodon, however, points out that Hawks worked within "a fairly narrow range of expression," always returning to the same plot and the same characters (160). He explains the director's unevenness as a consequence of the impossibly high standard he set for himself in his few true masterpieces, such as SCARFACE, ONLY ANGELS HAVE WINGS (1939), HIS GIRL FRIDAY, TO HAVE AND HAVE NOT (1944), THE BIG SLEEP (1946), RED RIVER (1948) and RIO BRAVO (1959). The originality of Coursodon's thesis derives from his readiness to maintain that Hawks's forte was his "stylistic richness" rather than his thematic fluctuations. Hawks's style, Coursodon argues, manifests itself as "an extraordinary density, a permanent tension generated by verbal and visual economy and the functional necessity of every shot and every cut" (164). Even Durgnat, who in the aforementioned article does his best to de-canonize Hawks, admits that the director's style possesses a "pantherine grace" (16). In a more recent estimation, Larry Gross reinforces this view when he postulates that Hawks's style "is not a discernible, material phenomenon" but a "distinctive unity of a world that synthesises disparate rhetorical, verbal, visual and dramaturgical capacities" (13).

The film is also Hawks's most expressionistic – Jonathan Munby labels the visual style of the film "documentary expressionism" (56) – evidence of which can be found in the movie's "violent chiaroscuro, tight grouping within the frame, and fluid, staling camera movement" (Clarens 93). It is a testament to the filmmaker's dexterity that the cross-shaped token so richly employed functions both as a symbol and as a stylistic trait within the diegetic world of the film. While on occasion Hawks uses the iconological figure quite self-assertively – as in the St. Valentine' Day massacre scene – at other times its incorporation is subtle and barely noticeable. There is the X on the wall in the police office early in the film, on Cesca's face in the balcony segment, on the curtains in the hospital sequence, and on Cesca's back as she dances in the Paradise restaurant. Poague writes that the cross metaphor – furnishing the story with "a point of moral reference on what might otherwise be seen as a remarkably immoral movie" (96) – also reflects the intertwining plot structure in which two paths of action, Camonte's rise to power and his incestuous relation to Cesca, together form an X.[22] The sign also elicits a sense of the impermissible, of the censured – connotations cross-fertilized with its capacity to signify a lack of substance, identity or information. A semiotic blank, the sign ultimately evokes the unfathomable void of death, but, even more significantly, it is also a disfiguration of the photographic image itself, which is also a kind of violence.

In the introduction to this chapter, I suggested that the plotting in SCARFACE is hysterical, and in the closing section, I intend to return to this idea. The murderous yet almost childlike psychopathology of the main protagonist, the narrative's ambivalence toward its own depiction of violence, and the film's fixation with contradictory acts of erasure and disfiguration – these elements all point to, and are suggestive of, a meaning which can only be particularized on a larger interpretive level. Coursodon has proposed that what fuels Hawks's cinema is a "neurotic denial of death" (168), and it is this obsession that seems to provide the thematic corollary for SCARFACE's formal mode. Death, Coursodon writes, "is the unacceptable, that which must not be shown" (168). Daney, that seminal *Cahiers du cinema* editor and critic, detected this aspect of Hawks's poetics early. In a review of RIO BRAVO, he states that "[L]e rapport à la mort – passage par excellence – est toujours pensé ainsi: *un* mort, ce n'est jamais *la* mort et la mort, ce n'est jamais qu'être absent, plus précisément: être *hors-champ*" (23, emphases in original). Hawks's relegation of death to zones off-screen, to the out-of-frame, is an act of evasion that may account for the hysterical impulse that informs both the film's plot and characterization. Relying on a Lacanian reading of film violence, Guy C. Rittger finds that the totality of classical Hollywood cinema in fact is founded on a similar act of repression: "the libidinal economy of cinematic action film, prior to 1967, can be characterized as 'neurotic,' organized around potentially traumatic glimpses of a Real which remains precariously veiled" (357). The "Real" that Rittger has in mind here is the fact of mortality. If SCARFACE is a "death-dance," as Durgnat has stated ("Hawks" 18), its choreography is tentative, its rhythm timorous. It is as if the filmmaker over-compensates for the repression of death on a conceptual level by reducing it to a spectacle on a literal level. In this regard, violence becomes the only possible method of dying because the event of violence itself is so horrible that it tends to re-direct our attention away from death. By repressing death, violence thus becomes a lugubrious means of coping with it.

4 Kubrick's THE KILLING and the Emplotment of Death

Desire is the product of incomplete knowledge.

Thomas Mann

As far as the issues of violence and mortality are concerned, the work of Kubrick exhibits none of the neurotic prevarication which both Daney and Coursodon claim characterizes the Hawksian approach. Kubrick's films have leaned toward a kind of reluctant misanthropy which reveals the capability for self-destruction as the linchpin of man's existential predicament. Some of the most memorable images and defining moments in Kubrick's cinema foreground this nexus of violence and civilization: the seven-minute long execution sequence in PATHS OF GLORY, the nuclear montage which concludes DR. STRANGELOVE (1964), the confrontation between the prehistoric apes in 2001: A SPACE ODYSSEY (1968), Alex's menacing glance at the viewer in the first shot of A CLOCKWORK ORANGE (1971), and the close-up of the demented Jack Torrance as he pursues his wife and son in THE SHINING (1980). Focusing on a much less exposed film like THE KILLING in light of this exceptional fund of violent imagery may seem like an incongruity. There is little explicit violence in Kubrick's second film noir (the first was 1955's KILLER'S KISS). Yet within the thematic purview of violence, narrathanatography and masculinity, THE KILLING is one of his more apposite movies. Even A CLOCKWORK ORANGE – praised by among others Alexander Walker as "the first landmark study of the 'Violent Society'" (*National Heroes* 44) and by Seth Cagin and Philip Dray as "the definitive investigation into the ontology of violence" (*Hollywood Films* 173) – refuses the stringent inextricability of death and plotting which recommends THE KILLING as a key text on violence in the classical era. Kubrick's trademark preoccupation with what Thomas Allen Nelson has termed "the aesthetics of contingency" (1) and with the fallibility of man (which in a Kubrick film always means the fallibility of the male), meshes with the equally fatalistic universe particular to the genre of film noir.[1] THE KILLING also foreshadows what Marsha Kinder takes to be the central project of A CLOCKWORK ORANGE: violent form and "its consequences for subjectivity" ("Violence American Style" 72). THE KILLING conjures violence as a way of seeing, as an aberration and a disfiguration of the filmic gaze that represents a peculiar challenge to the narrational consciousness of the text. For instance, it is no accident that the massacre toward the end of THE KILLING is the only scene in the entire film that is shot from a subjective point of view.

Adapted from Lionel White's 1955 novel *Clean Break*,[2] a book Kubrick's producer James B. Harris chanced upon while browsing the shelves of a New York bookstore (LoBrutto 111), THE KILLING was released at a time when the Production Code was still in effect, although its pressures were declining. Kubrick's film, like SCARFACE, is a rare example of an independently produced movie in the studio era and was subject to few external limitations save the securing of the Motion Picture Production Code Seal and the film's approval by the Catholic Legion of Decency (Kagan, *Cinema of Stanley Kubrick* 33). Daniel De Vries has stressed the audacious aspects of the movie's depiction of violence:

> The carnage, if not quite so graphic and prolonged as the famous sixties massacres in Arthur Penn's BONNIE AND CLYDE and Sam Peckinpah's THE WILD BUNCH, is perversely effective. Unlike BONNIE AND CLYDE, here one hardly sympathizes with the victims. … Coming when it does, THE KILLING is remarkable for its nastiness (14-15).

The intrepid element of Kubrick's violence is possibly due to a general relaxation of the censorship climate in the latter half of the 1950s.[3] As Charlie Lyons notes, several films released in this decade and in the early 1960s challenged the increasingly anachronistic Hays Code (8). As early as 1953, Otto Preminger's THE MOON IS BLUE was released without the seal of approval, as was Sidney Lumet's THE PAWNBROKER (1965). Discussing these two releases, Lyons claims that the industry "was finally responding to social reality. By 1968, with all of the code's provisions abandoned, the U.S. screen appeared freer from censorship than ever before" (8). However, the contextualization of the massacre in THE KILLING is consonant with the dictates of the code. All the criminals in the film either die unheroically or are unmasked as deplorable losers. Although violent action in THE KILLING is explicit for its time, the effect is balanced by the film's overall conformity with the moral maxims of the Production Code. Both SCARFACE and THE KILLING contextualize violence with reference to an unambiguous moral framework which invariably punishes the culprits in the end.

The restrictions that the production Code imposes concern the filmic quantity, methods, and nature of violent death. There is an acknowledgment of the *narrative* function which murder fulfils in advancing film plot. From the point of view of the Code, violence is conceived as an abstract phenomenon much in the same way as Seymour Chatman defines "events" as plot actions to be configured into a concrete form (*Story and Discourse* 43). Once the context is the actual rendition of murder in an audiovisual medium like film, the concept of violence immediately becomes more problematic. As the Code's paragraph six, article (b) notes, ferocious violence ought not to be depicted "in detail" (in Roberts and Mintz 148). In this respect, the Code functions as an authoritative formula for the aesthetic depiction of crime, violence, sexuality, etc. This formula supervises and limits film practice to such an extent that one may consider it part of a film's intertext. That is, the relative independence of the artwork is compromised by the qualifications of the Code.

For a 1950s audience, the sheer experience of watching a film like THE KILL-ING upset the acquired norms for understanding Hollywood narratives. Perceived as a violation of sorts in itself, the film's nonlinear temporality was unprecedented at the time and perplexed spectators unfamiliar with its complex use of the flashback structure. "The story begins with the end," Maurice Blanchot has written, "and that is what forms its troubling truth" (112). Due to negative responses from colleagues and friends prior to the film's release in June 1956, Kubrick re-edited the film according to a more conventional narrative design, but eventually went back to the original format.[4] Though the filmmaker himself tailored THE KILLING for art-house exhibition, United Artists opted for commercial distribution, and subsequently ended up as a box-office failure (LoBrutto 126). Notably, one of the film's taglines – "Like No Other Picture Since SCARFACE and LITTLE CAESAR!" – makes the explicit reference to Hawks an integral part of the promotion of the film.

Violence in THE KILLING is a narrative and visual trope for masculine moralities. It is the character of George Peatty (Elisha Cook Jr.) rather than that of gang leader Johnny Clay (Sterling Hayden) who emerges as the most significant male protagonist. An embodiment of noir anxiety and repressed anger, Peatty's eventual recourse to violence flaunts and affirms the defeatist deviancy which undergirds the kind of floundering masculinity frequently found in the immediate post-war cinema.[5] Peatty is a weak character in every way, easily bullied and ridiculed by his manipulative wife Sherry, the film's femme fatale. In her first scene she is lying on the bed, patronizing Peatty with sarcastic requests ("go ahead and thrill me, George") which take on a darkly ironic resonance in the face of later events. Peatty's timidity finds a visual equivalent in a later, medium-shot composition within the same sequence, in which Sherry towers over Peatty's small figure in the left corner of the frame. She berates him for his financial shortcomings and lack of ambition, which makes Peatty reveal parts of the heist scheme to Sherry. In narrative terms, this is the fatal error in Clay's otherwise seemingly impeccable stratagem. As in most of Kubrick's films, the capricious human element makes the entire operation capsize. Not only does the plan go awry, but it also obliterates almost everyone involved. The act of plotting leads to violence and death.[6]

The source of violence in Kubrick's film is found as much in the afflictions of a particular form of masculinity as in the malevolence of a contingent universe. While the former etiology anchors its causes in the social and the corporeal, the latter imbues violence with a metaphysical dimension. In its clinical explorations of the conditions and nature of violence, Kubrick's cinema tends to espouse a mechanism which transforms the phenomenon into a transcendental entity; concrete manifestations of brutality become signifiers of an abstract Violence whose fundamental mode of being is metaphysical. Films like DR. STRANGELOVE, 2001, A CLOCKWORK ORANGE and FULL METAL JACKET (Stanley Kubrick 1987) – in their insistence on man's destructive impulses in a hostile cosmos – particularly underscore Kubrick's transcendentalist conception of violence and evil. His first feature FEAR AND DESIRE (1953), long out of circulation at his own behest, features an off-screen narrator who vocalizes what could pass for a philosophical thesis that informs much of Kubrick's later work:

> There is a war in this forest/Not a war that has been fought, nor one that will be/But any war/And the enemies that struggle here do not exist/Unless we call them into being/For all of them, and all that happens now/Is outside history/Only the unchanging shapes of fear and doubt and death/Are from our world/These soldiers that you see keep our language and our time/But have no other country but the mind.

Kubrick's pretension to explain human violence as an innate potentiality is tempered by the generic element; violence in film noir is commonly attributed to specific human and social agencies.[7] What makes Kubrick's film so valuable as an object of analysis is its dual emphasis on violence as both a metaphysical given (as a product of man's fallibility) and a social, historicizable feature (as an effect of a maladjusted masculinity). All the male characters in THE KILLING, and Peatty in particular, embody traits of the quintessential noir anti-hero. Clay's gang consists of discontented, but ineffectual, small-time crooks, fatigued, disillusioned and self-abasing men. In comparison with the film's female counterparts, they appear inadequate and pathetic. When Peatty finally comes unhinged, violence ensues as the expression of his existential impotency. In this regard, the thematic preoccupations of film noir seem to blend seamlessly with Kubrick's notorious pessimism. The films of this genre, Michael Walker contends, "portray a society in which the American dream of success is inverted, alienation and fatalistic helplessness being the dominant moods, and failure the most frequent outcome. In this, the films show the accommodation of a 'European' sensibility which is also reflected in the films' expressionistic mise en scène" (38). Not surprisingly, Kubrick found an appropriate expression for his own emerging interest in the fallibility of man in a violently contingent universe, a theme which is arguably more immanent to film noir than to any other genre.[8]

Released at a time when the genre was moribund, THE KILLING is more than a standard noir. In a much-quoted essay, Paul Schrader delineates the essential properties of film noir's last stage (the 1950s):

> After ten years of steadily shedding romantic conventions, the later *noir* films finally got down to the root causes of the period: the loss of public honor, heroic conventions, personal integrity, and, finally, psychic stability. The third-phase films were painfully self-aware; they seemed to know they stood at the end of a long tradition based on despair and disintegration and did not shy away from the fact ("Notes on Film Noir" 12, emphasis in original).

Schrader considers the complex temporality of many later noir films to be a narrative device which signals and intensifies the feeling of hopelessness already present in the genre. Along with Welles's TOUCH OF EVIL (1958) and Kubrick's own KILLER'S KISS, THE KILLING highlights the ironically unpredictable and often brutal events the male protagonists fall victim to. It is possible to consider the inherent cynicism in such texts as a form of generic exhaustion, prefiguring the narrative mortification that Russell recognizes in the New Wave Cinemas of the late 1950s and onward.

The interconnection between narration and death is no less pertinent to film noir than to the New Waves. In the first serious study of the genre, Borde and Chaumeton discern that "[i]n every sense of the word, a *noir* film is a film of death" (19). In this particular genre, however, deathliness is not only in the mise en scène, to modify Thomson's phrase slightly ("Death and its Details" 15); it forms part of the narrative fabric of the text itself. Non-linearity and the peculiar use of the voice-over are the two principal aspects of THE KILLING which lends the narration a funereal quality. Hardly a coincidence, it is in film noir that one finds some of the most memorable voice-over narrations in American cinema: the dying Walter Neff reciting his story into a Dictaphone in DOUBLE INDEMNITY; Joe Gillis's voice-over from beyond the grave in SUNSET BOULEVARD (Wilder 1950); and, more recently, Ed Crane's lethargic telling of his murder story from death row in Coen's neo-noir THE MAN WHO WASN'T THERE (2001). The narration of a story in flashbacks and voice-over, Robert G. Porfirio suggests, "enhance[s] the aura of doom. It is almost as if the narrator takes a perverse pleasure in relating the events leading up to his current crisis, his romanticization of it heightened by his particular surroundings" (88). Though Porfirio is addressing the technique of first person narration specifically, there is no reason to assume that a third person narration like that of THE KILLING produces any markedly different effects. This is partly due to the kind of heterodiegetic narrator often found in film noir, which is one whose style and inflection borrow substantially from the *Highway Patrol* television series (1955-59), as well as *The March of Time* newsreels of the 1930s-and 40s (Wilson 77) and semi-documentary films like HOUSE ON 92ND STREET (Henry Hathaway 1945), both produced by Louis de Rochemont. The voice of the reporter, who recounts events after the fact (thus contributing to a sense of the inevitable), achieves largely the same effect as that of the homodiegetic narrator who is also a character in the story.[9] Temporality rather than perspective is crucial for the emergence of narrative mortality; who tells the story is subordinated to the temporal relation between the teller and the tale, and to the mood and tonality of the narrative voice. In a literal fashion, this voice belongs to Arthur Gilmore, an announcer for numerous movie trailers from the 1940s to the 1960s. His presence in Kubrick's movie adds yet another semantic layer to the narration, since the voice evokes a particular style of presentation which at the same time is both sensational and highly knowledgeable of narrative endings, to use Bordwell's phrase (*Narration* 57).

Though often taken for granted or even vilified as a clumsy narrative device, the voice-over has become a staple of noir storytelling. In THE KILLING, Wilson argues that the voice-over becomes an agent of the heist itself, being present in twenty-six out of thirty-five segments, and that the scenes where it is absent "signify particular junctures where the plan will break down" (78). The narrator withdraws in those scenes in which characters with an incomplete knowledge of the heist are introduced. Examples are sequences such as Sherry's clandestine meeting with her lover Val in the beginning of the film and Clay giving instructions to more peripheral players like Nikki and Maurice. The narrator's absence also indicates a lapse of control and planning, allowing the accidental free play in disrupting Clay's meticulously regulated schedule. An implication of Wilson's thesis is that the clockwork precision of the voice-over functions as a protection against the chaos of the unplotted; the departure of the narrator punctures the coherence of the conflated structures of planning and plotting. Moreover, the fact that the only male authority in the film is a *dis*embodied subject is on a figurative level indicative of the disempowerment of masculinity which defines film noir in general and Kubrick's film in particular. Gilmore's impersonal voice-over, "all surface and no depth, time-bound and blind to spatial nuances" (Nelson 34), contrasts sharply with the *em*bodied subjectivity of the faltering protagonists.

In its temporal trajectory, THE KILLING proceeds as an allegorization of a crisis of action. Due to the film's overlap structure, what Stephen Mamber terms a "series of elliptical goings-back," there is no real progress to the narrative (par. 2). The exhaustion with which the protagonists are afflicted is made palpable by the film's emplotted paralysis, which in the end leaves those who are not already dead in a virtually apraxic state. All Johnny Clay can muster in the last shot, as two officers walk slowly toward him, is a final resignation underscored by the words "what's the difference." Unlike Camonte in SCARFACE, Kubrick's desolate gangster makes no attempt at a desperate escape. His immobility characterizes the plight of the noir male in terms of devitalization and apathy. This sense of inaction results in no small measure from the knowledge that, within the universe of THE KILLING, all actions are subject to a predetermined conclusion. While a linear emplotment of temporality foregrounds causality – the protagonist's ability to influence the pattern of cause-and-effect – a nonlinear notion of temporality adds contingency and promotes reflection on action rather than action itself. A conventional conception of masculinity in terms of agency is incompatible with nonlinear structures like that of The Killing, since such temporalities deprive the male protagonist of the possibility of intentionality and action.

In an interview with French cinematographer and director Pierre-William Glenn, whose 1993 film 23H58 was heavily influenced by THE KILLING, Chris Drake notes that violence and death in Kubrick's film are "something that's already arrived at, an abstract potential in the shape of money, which then sweeps through a room like a gale, leaving only bodies in its wake" (24). Drake's observation is an acute one, conceiving violence neither as cause nor consequence but as the reification of that contingency which so pervasively pertains to Kubrick's cinema. More than violence itself, it is the textual movement toward it that the narrative accentuates. "The anxiety in film noir," Borde and Chaumeton write, "derives more from its strange plot twists than from its violence" (23). In THE KILLING, the fatality of plotting is further enhanced by the juxtaposition of two contradictory dispositions: on the one hand, the rigorousness of the planning of the heist, and on the other, the chaos that follows in the wake of its execution. The chess metaphor, as Steve Jenkins points out, acts metadiscursively to flaunt the narrative's "perverse desire for a limitless excess of plotting, with repetition substituted for suspense and the robbery's development blocked by the very methods used to chart its progress" (par. 3). The dispassionate order of the design throws the violent disruption into even starker relief, or, as Mamber puts it, "[t]he problem lies in the difference between the elegant conceptual construction and the need to use human beings to execute that construction" (par. 12). THE KILLING exposes the underlying fissures of an apparently fail-safe system and deconstructs in the process the faith in human rationality. In the film's alignment of violence and logic, Kubrick prefigures his extended exploration of this intersection in DR. STRANGELOVE and 2001 particularly.

THE KILLING contains only a small number of violent incidents, yet the mood of the film evokes a heightened sense of fatalism and doom. As previously stated, this is largely due to the way in which the narration structures the temporal relations within the film, and also to the presence of an ominously detached voice-over which infuses the narrative with a relentless irreversibility. In his analysis of the film, Mario Falsetto underlines the formal intricacy of the *syuzhet* construction:

> The fragmenting of narrative information is one of the film's most radical elements, although it does not detract from narrative momentum or intelligibility. THE KILLING illustrates the tension in Kubrick's work between the conventional and the unconventional, between classical storytelling techniques and a more modernist narrative mode (*Stanley Kubrick* 2).[10]

The process of shattering a straightforward plot progression is counterbalanced by an authoritative, extradiegetic narrator who appears to be omniscient though not always fully communicative. In presenting story information gradually – and sometimes elliptically – while at the same time creating the impression that the protagonists' scheme is going to be ill fated, the voice-over succeeds in impregnating the images with a tantalizing sense of a violent crisis that never seems to happen. The most uncomfortable aspect of the violence is precisely its continuous suspension. Critics like Gene Phillips have also noted that the prospect of disaster, in spite of the pedantic, authoritatively administered voice-over, is telescoped onto the very opening of the film. He writes that

> [i]t is clear from the outset ... that the tawdry individuals whom Johnny Clay has brought together ... comprise a series of weak links in a chain of command that could snap at any point. Add to this the possibility of unexpected mishaps that could dog even the best of plans, and the viewer senses that the entire project is doomed from the start (30).

In effect, Phillips traces the cause of the disaster to the intrinsic shortcomings of the particular type of manhood that Clay's team embody. Alexander Walker helpfully compares Kubrick's protagonists with those of John Huston in THE ASPHALT JUNGLE (1950), and concludes that the former embraces an incomparably less commiserating view toward his male characters: "A director like John Huston ... would probably pay respect to the courage of men of action, even when they are criminals. He might allow them some individual decency in death. Not Kubrick ... he stays detached, cynical" (*Stanley Kubrick Directs* 68). With respect to characterization, Walker's assessment of Huston is reminiscent of the narrator's slant vis-à-vis the characters in Peckinpah's movies. While Huston and Peckinpah both manage to mobilize affection for their protagonists even when they are brutal killers, there is little evidence of any empathy in Kubrick.

The scene toward the end of the film which culminates with the killing of most of Clay's gang – Kennan, O'Reilly, Unger – forms the acme of violent action in the film. After the heist at the racetrack, Clay's partners are awaiting further instructions at a secret hiding. George is among them, revealing clear signs of nervousness and anticipation as he is pacing restlessly around the room. The other men remain quiet in their seats, talking and smoking. When they hear the sound of the elevator in the apartment, they get up and approach the door. As O'Reilly opens the door, two men with guns enter. This sequence proceeds from a slightly low-angle shot of O'Reilly to a reverse shot of the two gunmen. The camera then cuts to a long profile shot where the intruders start searching Clay's men, upon which follows a frontal medium shot of Kennan, O'Reilly and Unger holding their hands in the air. Concurrently, George is rummaging around in an adjacent room. Val Cannon, one of the two men who is also Sherry's lover, expects George to be there with the rest of Clay's gang, and, in a low-angle shot, asks them where he is. The subsequent frame reveals in medium shot an empty doorway into which George enters with a shotgun. Positioned a little to the right of the frame, he fires the gun, and the camera cuts to Cannon, who, upon firing back, is hit in the shoulder by the impact of George's gun; his body twists and contorts, he falls back against the door which trampolines him forward. In medium shot we see him falling leftward onto his knees, his head dangling to the right. We next see George firing maniacally into the room. This is a very brief shot that only lasts about a quarter of a second. Val is shown again in the next frame, collapsing and grabbing hold of a lamp, and then swerving in the opposite direction. In a medium-close shot we see him finally lying outstretched on the floor. The following frame in the sequence presents us with George in medium shot firing his gun. Eventually, the shooting desists, and George stares horrified at the havoc he has caused. He leans his head against the wall, eyes transfixed on the scene before him. The next cut establishes an eyeline match, long-to-medium shot, in which the dead bodies of Kennan, O'Reilly and Unger are surveyed from George's optical point of view. In an eccentric tracking movement the camera seems to inspect the dead bodies; O'Reilly stoops over the couch, his head in the pillows and his feet sticking up from the furniture; Kennan lies face-down in the foreground of the frame. The camera tracks to the right, then to the left and closer toward the victims. It tracks in on O'Reilly, then on Kennan, blood running down his face. Tracking further left, the camera reveals one of the intruders, his face smeared with blood, and his left arm, clutching a pistol, rests on his chest. His hat lies beside him as the camera continues tracking further in on his head, lingering a while on his lifeless face, before it tracks in to a near close-up of Cannon. The space of this violence discloses what Nelson describes as "a grotesquely disordered room of carnage" (36).

I have described this sequence in such detail because the narration seems to emphasize it – through the bizarre camera technique, which is restricted to this scene only – to such a degree that the segment takes on a highly self-conscious air. It is as if the camera is straying pensively, yet carelessly, over the dead bodies. After it has examined Cannon, it continues its tracking motion, revealing next the naked floor, the door in close-up as a hand reaches out for it from the left of the frame. The movement of the camera is here even more fluid, almost zig-zagging across the room. As one might expect, the entire sequence represents George's subjective perspective as he watches the five dead men lying scattered about the apartment. He is badly wounded himself as he staggers around the floor. The shot series is also characterized by George's breathing and the jazz score on the soundtrack, bracketing the moment as the focal center of crisis and violence in the film. It is notable that the narration dwells much longer on the consequences of violence than on the act itself. The determination with which the camera surveys the victims is striking in itself; the effects rather than the causes are what the narration highlights. It is also significant that this twenty-three second shot, which was handled by Kubrick himself (LoBrutto 120), is the only subjective point of view shot in the entire film. Falsetto notes that the segment also forms a stylistic counterpoint to the tracking shots, which to a certain extent dominate both this narrative and all later Kubrick films: "It [the subjective point of view shot] penetrates the space in a qualitatively different way than the smooth tracking shots most often used in the film. As the world erupts into the chaos of the massacre, the film appropriately reverts to a hand-held, individualized POV shot" (*Stanley Kubrick* 112).

According to Black – who draws on sources as disparate as De Quincey and Auden – it is precisely the subjective focalization of the act of murder that elevates the textual depiction to aesthetic status (*Aesthetics* 60). As I argue in chapter three, however, it makes little sense to parade the pedestrian aestheticization argument for specific passages of a text that in its entirety is an aesthetic object per definition. There is no reason to assume that a subjectively focalized mediation of violence is any more aestheticized than an objective one. Whatever significance THE KILLING's sole subjective sequence has derives from its oppositional relation to the voice-over. There is order as long as the narrative point of view stays disembodied, but with the subjectively focalized sequence the film's greatest disruption occurs. Sobchack, in her phenomenological theory of cinema, stresses the degree to which the medium engages "*modes of embodied existence* (seeing, hearing, physical and reflective movement) as the vehicle, the 'stuff,' the substance of its language" (*Address of the Eye* 4, emphasis in original). Peatty's point of view in the killing scene represents a subjectivized totality of such an embodiment; the scene not only amounts to a narration *about* the body (the corpses that occupy Peatty's field of vision) but is also a narration *by* the body (Peatty's consciousness as embodied existence). Significantly, the shift to embodied narration substitutes the almost compulsive order associated with the disembodied narrator with violence and disorder.

There is a sense of restraint in the way in which Kubrick orchestrates the violence in THE KILLING. Immersed in a narrative sensibility of ironic detachment, Kubrick's economical handling of the violence defamiliarizes and distances the viewers on one level, while engulfing them on another. This is partly due to the accidental nature of the killings and to George's aberrant behavior. In the scene where he shoots Sherry, the narration further attains a measure of self-reflexivity. Indifferent to the causal chain that propels the action forward, the sequence unfolds almost as if it were a meta-textual commentary on the issue of self-destructive masculinity around which the previous narration has revolved. The violence in the scene is a narrative bifurcation in which one line of action, Sherry's murder, is subordinated to the events in the main plot. George's killing of his wife is an act of violence which takes place in the margins of the story, but for this same reason the act may be construed as a moment of self-consciousness on the part of the narration. Sherry's last remark, "A bad joke without a punchline," might be taken as an ironic statement on events in the narrative; the preceding bloodbath, her own murder, and the intervention of chance when Clay's suitcase bursts open at the airfield.

The conflation of plot and planning in THE KILLING contributes to the manufacturing of a closed, impermeable and self-referential text, temporally delimited by the event of mortality (the narration begins at a point in time when most of the characters are already dead and roughly ends with these same deaths). Hence, the film does not merely narrate *a* story but recaptures the story of its temporal consumption, its own decay. However scrupulously Kubrick choreographs this self-containment, it is the film's continuity with the themes and moods of film noir that provides the impetus for this absence of mimesis. Schrader, who also presents a list of the genre's most characteristic stylistic facets,[11] is particularly perceptive regarding its artificiality:

> [film noir] tried to make America accept a moral vision of life based on style. That very contradiction – promoting style in a culture which valued themes – forced *film noir* into artistically invigorating twists and turns. *Film noir* attacked and interpreted its sociological conditions, and, by the close of the *noir* period, created a new artistic world which went beyond a simple sociological reflection, a nightmarish world of American mannerism which was by far more a creation than a reflection (13, emphases in original).

The transtextualism of THE KILLING, furthermore, is specific as well as generic. In terms of character and casting, both Cook and Hayden reprise parts they played in THE BIG SLEEP and THE ASPHALT JUNGLE, respectively, and Kubrick's Peatty – according to Nelson – was deliberately modeled on the Harry Jones character in Hawks's film (30-31). Kubrick also quotes THE TREASURE OF THE SIERRA MADRE (1948), another Huston film, toward the end of THE KILLING, where the cash from the robbery literally vanishes into thin air like the gold dust in Sierra Madre. Arthur Gilmore's film-trailer represents yet another allusive layer which serves to distance the text further from the notion of mimesis while consolidating its semiotic process. Finally, the referentiality of The Killing also encompasses later texts such as Reservoir Dogs, 23h58, Chasing Amy (Kevin Smith, 1997), Jackie Brown (Tarantino 1997), Silent Rain in the Ninth (Jacob Rosenberg, 1998), Lock, Stock and Two Smoking Barrels (Guy Ritchie, 1998), Star Wars: Episode 1 – The Phantom Menace (George Lucas, 1999), Le Fabuleux destin d'Amélie Poulain (Jean-Pierre Jeunet, 2001), Minority Report (Spielberg, 2002), Panic Room (Fincher, 2002) and Kaante (Sanjay Gupta, 2002), films that all in their own ways quote The Killing. Most contemporary viewers will have seen Reservoir Dogs prior to Kubrick's film, thus inverting the original order of influence. For a theorist like Iampolski, however, a lack of chronology is no challenge to the process of quotation:

> the intertextual field of certain texts can be composed of 'sources' that were actually written after them.... in some way a later text can serve as the source of an earlier text. This reverse chronology is of course only possible from the perspective of reading, which is precisely the basis of an intertextual approach to culture (246).

Part of the attraction of Iampolski's thesis stems from its emphasis on reception rather than production, which permits a kind of multi-directional intertextuality that is more flexible and dynamic than a production-centered intertextuality of the kind that mechanistically traces the references in a given text to a previous one. Iampolski's conception of the intertextual also seems to be closer to the actual logistics of textual consumption; readers and viewers often begin with whatever texts are current at the moment and then work their way back to older texts. From the point of view of reading, therefore, intertextuality may frequently imply (as it does in the Reservoir Dogs-The Killing case) a reversal of the relation between source and allusion.

Like the gangster movie and the western, film noir is a genre which presents an entirely self-contained textual universe that is hardly tangential to an extra-fictional world. Even without their densely allusive texture, the films that belong to these genres would be positively amimetic. The narration of violence that by itself serves to determine the structure of the genres in question suggests a particular form of allegoricity, a reading strategy, whose object is the examination of cultural fantasies concerning death, masculine identity and the body. It is critical that the canvas onto which this discourse inscribes itself is something else than a reflection, or representation in the conventional sense of the word. The gap which arises between text and life – the epistemological distortion which occurs when films violate mimesis – is required in order to generate that enunciatory space where the domain of the real is assayed. The difference is the

condition of articulation and discourse; representation in the mimetic, reflective
sense merely duplicates, creating nothing but sameness and identity. This is
why textuality must advance beyond mimesis in order to enunciate. The world
of film noir, like that of the gangster movie and the western, does not signify
any corresponding universe beyond itself, but should be comprehended instead
as a storehouse of images and narratives which project and explore the contents
of different subjectivities. A sign rather than a transparent reflection, the depiction of violent masculinity that these genres invest in becomes tangible only as
allegory.

One of the crucial observations that Borde and Chaumeton make in their pio-
neer study of film noir is that "[t]he primary reference point of earlier days, the
moral center, is completely skewed" (25). In this respect, noir narratives an-
nounce the emergence of a type of cinematic characterization that adds subtler
shadings to the depiction of male protagonists than had been common in the
earlier American cinema. As Porfirio submits, "[t]he word 'hero' never seems to
fit the *noir* protagonist, for his world is devoid of the moral framework necessary to produce the traditional hero" (83, emphasis in original). Clay's demand
in THE KILLING that he wants "a guy that is a 100% dependable" becomes in this
genre of black fictions yet another of Kubrick's cynical ironies. There are few
dependable characters in a film where femininity represents a fatal threat and
masculinity in turn is enshrouded in permanent crisis. The source of the protagonists' demise, galvanized by Kubrickian contingency, is always related to the
psychological errors which inhere in the individual male characters (Nelson 31).
In THE KILLING the nature of these flaws is psychosexual: it is Peatty's jealousy
and fear of the feminine that release his violence, and it is Unger's frustrated
desire for Clay that has him end up drunk on the day of the robbery, thus jeo-
pardizing his boss's seemingly foolproof plan. Kubrick's working title for the
film was BED OF FEAR (Nelson 34), a metaphor more descriptive than THE KILL-
ING of the narrative's probing of the pathology of desire and anxiety.

Released in the middle of a decade of conformism – the year after Ray's REBEL
WITHOUT A CAUSE – Kubrick's film also anticipates the subject of entrapped
masculinity so significant to THE WILD BUNCH (and, in effect, to most of Peckinpah's films) and FIGHT CLUB. This is an issue that has been largely glossed
over in previous criticism of THE KILLING. All of the male characters in the film
are figuratively imprisoned, spatially as well as temporally, and from the very
beginning the narration seems to associate disillusion with domesticity. Both
Peatty and O'Reilly derive their criminal motivation from domestic predica-
ments, Peatty from the need to satisfy Sherry's material appetite, O'Reilly from
the need better to provide for his ailing wife. Images of confinement are legion
in the narrative, and Nelson even finds that the cinematography itself enacts an
externalization of the state of entrapment: "The film combines a series of hori-

zontal tracking shots with repeated vertical compositions to create a spatial grid that suggests both a chessboard and a cage" (34). Notably, most of the film's violence breaks out within the perimeters of the domestic sphere, and the mise en scène of both the massacre sequence and Peatty's killing of his wife is configured in terms of an oppressive enclosure. The characters are also metaphorically trapped in a temporal sense of the term, since their defeat is already a foregone conclusion thanks to the peculiar narrational delineation of the plot. In the film's last shot, the motif of entrapment culminates in the image of the two detectives approaching Clay, who does not even consider the possibility of escape. The narration of masculinity in THE KILLING, as in most noirs, employs the rhetoric of resignation.

Film noir's fetishization of dejection and defeat, along with its conspicuous lack of happy endings, makes the genre an appropriate vehicle for allegorizations of mortality. The noir heroes, Porfirio suggests, "fear death but are not themselves afraid to die; indeed a good deal of what dignity they possess is derived from the way in which they react to the threat of death" (89). Though the aesthetics of violence in film noir generally and in THE KILLING in particular is couched in the same euphemistic register that characterizes all depictions of violence in the classical period, the genre's concern with deviant masculinity and with the forms of death looks forward to the New Wave's increased awareness of these issues. Durgnat in fact sees the "obsession with violent death in all forms and genres" in the 1960s as the legacy of film noir, eventually seeping through the narrative texture of more commercially popular genres ("Paint it Black" 51).

5   Blood of a Poet: Peckinpah's THE WILD BUNCH

Whatever you set your mind to, your personal total obsession, this is what kills you.
Poetry kills you if you're a poet, and so on. People choose their death whether they
know it or not.
Don DeLillo, *Libra*

Only a sadist or one who is mentally deranged would enjoy this film.
Text written on one of the response cards distributed to the audience at THE
WILD BUNCH's sneak preview in the spring of 1969

Even more than BONNIE AND CLYDE, THE WILD BUNCH represented a definite departure from classical cinema's euphemistic portrayals of the violated and wounded body. By showing the vulnerability of the flesh, as well as the "physical fact of death by violence" (Pechter 92), Hollywood cinema was finally able to produce an image of *real* bodies. It is difficult to overstate the historical and cultural importance of THE WILD BUNCH. Signifying is in Peckinpah's film illimitable, its structure nearly collapsing from the weight of its own narrative vision. Hyperbolically praised as the MOBY DICK of westerns (Slotkin, *Gunfighter Nation* 594),[1] and saddled with presumptuous epithets like "THE WILD BUNCH is America" (Kitses 168), the film has come to occupy an unassailable position as a key text not only in American film but in American art at large. Epic yet personal, anarchic yet moral, despairing yet humanistic, THE WILD BUNCH internalizes a set of contradictions that are endemic to the cinema of violence, a kind of schizophrenia that Devin McKinney claims is "unique to the male American artist" ("THE WILD BUNCH" 178). Though criticism of the film emerged rather slowly, Peckinpah's autumnal magnum opus has become one of the most discussed American movies of the post-classical period.[2] THE WILD BUNCH is a work of mourning. A self-reflexive elegy not to the past as such but to the pastness of the past, the film is Peckinpah's CAMERA LUCIDA. THE WILD BUNCH is in a fundamental way about death: the death of the characters, of an epoch, of an ethics, of the west, of a certain form of masculinity, of a genre, and of narrativity. The ensuing examination will revisit a host of crucial issues that pertain to Peckinpah's movie, but the awareness of the text's thanatographical passion will invariably be at the core of my discussion.

Excepting Welles, there has hardly been a Hollywood filmmaker with a more mythologized reputation than Peckinpah's, and even the neo-formalist would have to doubt if it is in any way possible to examine his work without taking into account the temperament behind it.[3] Referring to the man as a "pop socio-aesthetic entity," Richard Jameson suggests that Peckinpah's name has super-seded the films themselves (34). Though the concept of the auteur now seems as dated and anachronistic as the world eulogized by THE WILD BUNCH, Peck-inpah is in many ways more deserving of the designation than most, not be-cause his oeuvre necessarily achieves a greater stylistic or thematic unity than that of say Ford or Huston, but because his entire artistic enterprise was crea-tively fueled by his antagonistic relationship with the industry of which he was a part.[4] Peckinpah's work, which can easily be read as one extended critique and indictment of corporatism, has polarized critical opinion to an almost un-precedented degree. On the one hand, Peckinpah's work was panned by a ma-jority of reviewers and academics for its putative misogyny and unbridled de-piction of violence. On the other, a coterie of critics came to reappraise his films, insisting that they be included in an American "Great Tradition." Both evalua-tions, as Tony Williams remarks, are equally crude (55).

The violence with which most of the director's films are associated has tended to obfuscate their numerous moral, philosophical and poetic qualities. With the sole emphasis on the bloody elements of his films, Peckinpah was a director few critics wanted to study, and it was not until the 1990s that re-invigorated read-ings of his work began to emerge. In the case of THE WILD BUNCH, it would take a whole decade before the controversy subsided and critics could come to ap-preciate the substance of form, style and ideas that had been obliterated by the singular discussion of violence (Parrill 40). In spite of the numerous publica-tions on Peckinpah's oeuvre that have appeared during the last decade, there are thus still avenues of inquiry left to be explored. As a matter of fact, one of Tony Williams's main objections to Bliss's monograph is its absence of "modern critical approaches" (63). In his review of Prince's anthology *Screening Violence*, Mark Gallagher arrives at a similar conclusion, calling for a "new critical ap-proach" to the study of contemporary film violence (par. 5). Though I shall ne-glect Williams's implicit enjoinder to read Peckinpah with reference to Foucault or Kristeva (63), I intend to re-evaluate both THE WILD BUNCH and its well-established frames of critical interpretation in light of narrative mortality, mas-culine moralities and an amimetic theory of screen violence.

Few films have invited so many tendentious readings as THE WILD BUNCH. All of the fallacies discussed in part I have been invoked in analyses of the film; Russell, for instance, brings up the notion of stylization in her otherwise percep-tive interpretation of the film (177); and Slotkin deploys his colossal mythologi-cal structure to explain Peckinpah's argument (*Gunfighter Nation* 594). Others have stressed the film's mimetic realism (Jacobs 38). My skepticism with regard to these readings should not be understood as a wholesale rejection but rather as an unwillingness to let debatable explications obscure issues that I hope to show are imperative for an informed appreciation of THE WILD BUNCH.

Due to the film's unusual magnitude, unwieldiness and aesthetic affluence, my reading of Peckinpah's requiem requires a centering point of departure, a kind of trope for the processes of death and mourning which it recounts. THE WILD BUNCH is a lacerated film, its own "body" mutilated by the many incisions made to Peckinpah's 190-minute rough cut.[5] On the narrative level, the film reveals a fundamental ambivalence toward its own act of signification, posing what could be construed as a threat of violence to the moving image itself: "If they move, kill 'em." The line is of course William Holden's well-known injunction to his men in the beginning of the film, spoken as the frame freezes and Peckinpah's directorial credit flashes across the screen.

Read in the context of the *form* of the film's initial segments, however, Holden's statement comes off as an address to the relentless flow of images, or what Lee Mitchell calls "the problem of memory and historical accuracy" (*Westerns* 241). As each member of the central cast is introduced, the image turns to black and white and freezes for a moment, as if the narrative is barely able to proceed. Stewart's term for this process is *photo-gravure*: "film's static impress of its own death as narrative" ("Photo-Gravure" 23). For Stewart, the freeze-frame is film's own Barthesian suspension, not photography's but cinema's punctum (*Between* 141). The basic conflict is one between two different temporalities or historical imaginings, that of the photograph and that of the moving image. While the former is commemorative and implies preservation, the latter is ephemeral and epitomizes irreversible change. As Stewart points out, recent theories of the image have tended to associate the image-in-movement with life, and the stilled image with death and termination.[6] Stewart writes that "[e]ven the radical stasis of a freeze frame is more likely to inscribe the death *of* rather than the death *in* film.... . the freeze frame ... [is] a trope for death's violent arrest of time" ("Photo-Gravure" 13, emphasis in original). Peckinpah's characters are ensnared by the impossibility of remaining at the intersection of these temporalities, which is what ultimately decimates them. From this point of view, Holden's threat can thus be taken as an instance of meta-textual self-consciousness; the violence in the narrative extends to the images, which, because they move and hence connote change, must be destroyed.

The stasis of the freeze-frame implies death, but also a kind of immobility desired by the text. While the stilled image suggests mortality, it also preserves the static moment for posterity by chemically embalming it. Thus, in terminating movement (and by extension life), the photographic image paradoxically retains it. The moving image, on the other hand, causes the death of the moment simply by moving. Strangely, therefore, it is the static photograph rather than moving image that best is able to resist death. "The nostalgia of old photographs," Cavell says in *The World Viewed* (1971), "is the perception that mortality is at some point to be stopped in its tracks" (75). Barthes has also stressed this double and seemingly contradictory meaning of the photographic act as that which "produces Death while trying to preserve life" (*Camera Lucida* 92).[7] Photography, perhaps more so than film, is a medium hospitable to processes of memory and mourning, largely because it provides the condition of spatio-temporal closure that these processes entail. This aporia – preservation by destruction – represents the philosophy at the center of Peckinpah's film, the dialectic that somehow holds all the disparate textual elements together. Tropologically speaking, THE WILD BUNCH is therefore a wounded and bleeding text, its blood gushing forth in the form of semiotic rifts and ruptures that inscribe the contradictions that both allow and embody the narration of mourning.[8]

The modal shift between moving and still images in the film's credit sequence, punctuated by a corresponding shift in color values (from color to black and white), may also be interpreted as signaling transformations of moralities. Susan Marshall proposes that the use of the freeze-frame represents the effort on the part of the narration to "imagine the past" (17), and when the image escapes the freeze-frame and starts to move, it implies a future-directedness which, in overcoming the past, negates it. For Marshall, violence provides "a central narrative power or value through which Peckinpah accomplishes transformation" (63).

A study of the violence in THE WILD BUNCH must begin with the meta-textual gesture signified by the sole emergence of the film on June 18, 1969. More than just a thorough deconstruction of the western, the film was Peckinpah's act of genrecide, the end of an illusion whose premier vehicle was the fiction of Hollywood.[9] The notion of the mythic West was exposed as "an invention of the modern, urban (California) mind," as Kenneth Cameron puts it (150). Hence, what THE WILD BUNCH mourns is not so much the past as the loss which follows from the realization that the past "was probably always a deceit" (Sharrett, "Peckinpah" 104). Much of the film's sound and fury derives from this recognition, which is constitutive of Peckinpah's overarching vision; in one way THE WILD BUNCH allegorizes the confused and angry consciousness of a child at the threshold of gaining the insight that the world is all a charade.

The structuring irony in Peckinpah's relation to the western is that he can strip the genre of its illusionism only by misreading it. According to Harold Bloom's influential (no pun intended) *The Anxiety of Influence* (1973), the most passionate poets purposefully misinterpret the work of their predecessors in order to "clear imaginative space for themselves" (5). The scope of Peckinpah's vision – of his deconstructionist agenda – required more imaginative space than the format of the conventional western could offer him. With particular reference to the legacy of Ford, it may be argued that Peckinpah in THE WILD BUNCH teraciously attempts to overstep Ford's methods, perspectives and perception of the West. Reviving a genre that already in the 1960s was becoming increasingly anachronistic must have represented a formidable challenge, one that he could only meet by directing what is possibly the most magnificent failure in American film. Although he was hailed as Ford's successor, it is not inconceivable that Peckinpah at one point may have been intimidated by the hegemonic vision of the West engraved onto the Fordian image in numerous westerns, from his first silent THE TORNADO (1917) to CHEYENNE AUTUMN (1964). This willful misreading, the ferocious deconstruction of the received myth, seems to have been the result of the filmmaker's ambivalence vis-à-vis the tradition from which he emerged. Both in theme and method, THE WILD BUNCH overturns every convention of the western. Soldiers turn out to be outlaws, the lawful are worse than the criminals, children are sadistic and violent, women and children are dispatched just as carelessly as the men, and nearly everyone is killed in the end. In its dismantling of the genre, THE WILD BUNCH is one long cinematic epiphany.

The deconstructive surge of THE WILD BUNCH produces a referential field that is hyper-charged and breathtaking in its scorching re-interpretation of the western. In the 1960s, the genre found itself in a transitional period, and the films released exhibited a certain ambiguity in the relation to their antecedents as well as to the larger frontier framework that had previously encapsulated westerns. Some critics have dismissed their revisionist impulse as merely "stylistic" (Cameron 227).[10] If the first sixty years had been homogeneously characterized by romanticized interpretations of the past, the films of the sixties waxed critical of the basic assumptions that were implicit in the master story. A shift in tone from jubilant excitement over the frontier project to estranged disillusionment over its social and cultural impact accompanied this transition. Partly a result of a generic fatigue and the need to interrogate the received versions of national experience, the westerns of the sixties articulated a bleak and pessimistic view of history. To some extent the types of protagonists that inhabit these narratives epitomize the emerging nihilism that later culminated with THE WILD BUNCH. Essentially, there are two kinds of heroes in the sixties westerns. The image of condemned, anachronistic men who have lived beyond their time is a recurrent motif in THE MISFITS (Huston 1961), LONELY ARE THE BRAVE (David Miller 1962), THE MAN WHO SHOT LIBERTY VALANCE (Ford 1962), RIDE THE HIGH COUNTRY (Peckinpah 1962) and HUD (Martin Ritt 1963). The rhetoric of these films reads as an indictment of modern urban civilization as dehumanizing and destructive. At the same time, they paint a sympathetic picture of aging men "threatened by the encroachment of a new social order" (Lenihan 159). The confrontation between the prototypical western individualist and the forces of modernization thus becomes the central narrative conflict. Antagonism toward the inevitability of progress appears to be proportional to the pace with which the world of the frontier recedes into history. Contrary to subsequent westerns, however, the dominant mood of the transitional texts is more one of sadness and melancholia over the disappearance of old ways than of the piercing cynicism which characterizes the so-called "anti-western" of the late sixties.

Toward the end of the decade the revisionist tendency of films like THE MIS-FITS solidified into a form that could be termed the "anti-western." Substantial parts of the setting of BUTCH CASSIDY AND THE SUNDANCE KID and THE WILD BUNCH (Peckinpah 1969) – two of the most significant texts of this period – were not the mythic American west but early 20th-century Bolivia and Mexico, respectively. The dislocation of the spatial and temporal frames suggests an alienation from the generic tradition. While RIDE THE HIGH COUNTRY and LONELY ARE THE BRAVE expose the plight of men who have become anachronisms in their own time, the two 1969 films narrate the story of characters who have survived it and are therefore utterly displaced in the increasingly technology-driven modernity in which they are trapped. THE WILD BUNCH is the last western, marking the acme of transgression in the series of films that interrogate the underlying ideological assumptions of the genre. Apart from a few central texts that followed in the wake of Peckinpah's film – LITTLE BIG MAN, SOLDIER BLUE (Ralph Nelson 1970), MCCABE AND MRS. MILLER, THE GREAT NORTHFIELD MINNESOTA RAID (Philip Kaufman 1972) and Peckinpah's own PAT GARRETT AND BILLY THE KID – the seventies westerns increasingly adopted a more sanitized and compromising perspective on the past where sentimentality and nostalgia occasionally came to substitute the savage frenzy that we find in THE WILD BUNCH. They inevitably became self-parodies. The exploration of violence in post-Peckinpah American cinema has mainly occurred in other genres, notably the road movie and the gangster film. In the 1970s, the number of westerns produced decreased significantly, a development which in 1974 lead Pauline Kael to declare the genre dead (Lenihan 148). Jim Hitt thought the reason for the decay of the genre to be the usurpation of western conventions and mythography by other genres like science fiction and the urban crime film (294).[11] The mid-1980s saw a slight resurgence with the so-called "post-revisionist" films like PALE RIDER (Eastwood 1985) and SILVERADO (Lawrence Kasdan 1985), emulated in the early 1990s with the big-budget epics DANCES WITH WOLVES (Kevin Costner 1990), UNFORGIVEN[12] and GERONIMO (Walter Hill 1993).[13] The calcification of the myth of the old west in films such as the above is indicative of the comatose state in which the genre survives after THE WILD BUNCH.[14]

One of the defining traits of the quintessential Peckinpah protagonist, Rita Parks writes, is the "paradox of individual isolation in the midst of a group" (116). In THE WILD BUNCH, as in most of the director's films, this subject ties in with the overall critique of modernity that gives his work its dominant tenor. Non-conformity, alienation and loneliness are facets of several of Peckinpah's key characters, that of Joel McCrea in RIDE THE HIGH COUNTRY, Holden in THE WILD BUNCH, and Steve McQueen in JUNIOR BONNER, to name a few. Symptomatic of the times, these features are also part of the filmmaker's personal obsession. "The Bunch's cynical disillusionment," Weddle suggests, "reflected that of America in 1967" (*If They Move* 317). Michael Harrington described how modern progress had eluded large segments of the population in *The Other America* (1962), and philosophers like Marcuse mourned in his *One-Dimensional Man* (1964) the shortcomings of an increasingly technocratic society. With the cultural upheaval and political commotion that were to dominate the 1960s, the relative stability of the preceding decade exploded into its antithesis. In the face of assassinations, race riots, the Vietnam war, campus violence and mass murder, "concepts of special national destiny," Coyne remarks, "had become redundant" (142). In part, the ideological contests that ensued were defined in terms of generational warfare. One of the primary oppositions that feed into THE WILD BUNCH is the relationship between personal and institutionalized violence, as well as the antagonistic discourse between the establishment and the counterculture at the time of the movie's release. The disillusionment with the mainstream institutions and values of American society was fuelled by the accelerating barbarity and futility of officially sanctioned violence as witnessed in numerous contexts in the sixties and seventies. The bombing of Cambodia, the shooting of students at Kent State University and Jackson State College in 1970, the prison revolt of Attica that claimed forty-three dead in 1971 and the intense bombing of Hanoi in 1972 were all documents to the central function of institutionalized forms of violence as viable responses to political confrontations. As Coyne argues, the meaning of violence as officially determined implies a different set of ethical and political problems than does individual violence (161). If we grant some measure of probability to Slotkin's thesis that "[v]iolence that can be purchased by the wealthy is oppressive; violence that proceeds freely (and in a sense disinterestedly) as a response to injustice is redemptive" (*Gunfighter Nation* 603), the economy of violence in THE WILD BUNCH appears to be Sorelian and Paretian in nature.

Violence has always been intrinsic to the western, but in the New Wave period it wholly overpowers the narrative, becoming, as Deleuze has suggested, its "principal impetus" (*Cinema 1* 167). Since violence is an end in itself, in a film like THE WILD BUNCH it emerges as a distinct event uncontaminated by the narrative teleology that the classical western conventionalized. Hence, the image of violence becomes a kind of meta-image. Freed from the constraints of Hollywood's moral dramaturgy, Peckinpah's violence tends toward the self-referential.[15] It is even more antithetical to the notion of mimeticism that is the classical film aesthetics. THE WILD BUNCH is highly self-conscious about its amimetic quality, which is perhaps what defines the film as post-classical. Peckinpah's achievement is to have deconstructed all the tropes and conventions of the genre only to reassemble them as rhetorical patterns whose transparency has been lost. Richard Schickel has admitted that he doubts whether the film "can be widely tolerated … without some understanding of the new set of feelings about the frontier that it, unlike the films that established this tradition, *consciously,* and therefore artfully, summarizes" (*Second Sight* 244, emphasis in original). There is an unmistakable allegorical instinct to Peckinpah's method (Galperin 171), and like Benjamin's concept of allegory, the governing propulsion in THE WILD BUNCH is the accumulation of (textual) fragments without any clearly articulated teleology (*Origin* 84).[16] The film interrogates the legitimization of violence that the traditional western has promulgated (Calder 133), but the syntax of this inquiry is never fixed, so that it is not obvious what THE WILD BUNCH is an allegory *of*.[17] Allegoricity, as Jorge Luis Borges has stated, produces fables of abstraction (229), and, in the words of Russell, operates "to smash false appearances, to 'transfigure' and bring into visibility new possibilities of the material world" (18). The tendency toward abstraction, moreover, is for Douglas Pye characteristic of the western:

> The simultaneous presence of the solid surface and a high degree of abstraction elsewhere causes an oscillation or response from one level to another, an awareness that the narrative flow is not the sole source of meaning, but that it is accompanied by another dimension, intimately tied to it, but supplying another kind of meaning (203).

One productive way of reading this other presence in the text is to conceptualize it as a figural embodiment of an ethical discourse or worldview, though it is crucial that this interpretation does not hinge on a simplistic dichotomy which pits aesthetics against politics, form against content or, at the level of reception, transformation against propaganda. Ideational and aesthetic patterns coexist in the violence of films like THE WILD BUNCH and STRAW DOGS; violence is, in fact, their vehicle. As Russell has suggested, this violence is a form of historical allegory interpretable within the context of narrative mortality (27). In THE WILD BUNCH, the philosophical resides in the aesthetic, the aesthetic in the philosophical.

The western is a genre where violence has become a pure figure, or sign, and as such it belongs exclusively to the regime of the aesthetic and transtextual. But the question still remains what this figure of violence signifies, and rather than interpret it as a metaphor for the political and social issues of its time,[18] I propose that the film's violence should more appropriately be read in the broader context of an allegorization of a less time-specific ethics that involves masculinity and mortality. Peter French has contended that the spirit of THE WILD BUNCH contains "an extreme consciousness of death" (84). As a western, the film's ethics emerges from a particular conception of mortality; it is the narration of death which comes to codify what kind of ethics is sanctioned (French 49). Illustrative of the characters' "anarchic integrity" (Sragow, "Homeric Power" 122), the violent deaths that are a staple of Peckinpah's art denote within the psychological parameters of the genre "a moral victory" (Engel, "Sam Peckinpah's Heroes" 27). The locus of this morality that materializes as violent action is a subjectivity that is both corporeally and metaphysically fashioned; corporeally because the protagonist's body itself is a palimpsest, a mise en scène of scarification and decay; and metaphysically because the western hero bases his moral worldview on a personal law that he finds by "[l]ooking sincerely within himself" (Hine 324). A key tenet in Peckinpah's screen code, which recalls that of the ancient epics as well as Joän Guimarães Rosa's THE DEVIL TO PAY IN THE BACKLANDS (1963) (Parrill 38), is morality's absolute independence vis-à-vis institutional law and social tradition. For the filmmaker, to act morally means not to "bend from [his] beliefs in order to survive" (Andrews 69). Thus, individual responsibility provides the rationale for Peckinpah's distinctive brand of existentialism, a philosophy that can be transcribed as a variety of moral idealism. Part of the violent excess that characterizes much of the director's work derives from this impulse to create dramatic situations in which his definition of morality may be confronted. Kael, one of Peckinpah's supporters, has even hinted that narrative action is only the director's pretext for promulgating a particular ethical vision ("Notes" 70).[19] Always a morality play, a Peckinpah film is "concerned with exposing the fallibility of collective morality and with testing the reality and strength of an individual's moral decisions by placing him in a crisis situation.... Moral decisions taken in extremis are authentic and revealing precisely because they are spontaneous" (Andrews 70). The indivisibility of individual choice and morality engenders a subjectively conditioned ethics whose essential mode of operation is the rejection of compromise. For the bunch, meaning arises in the violent spaces where the solidity and scope of this rejection can be tested. However, as Mitchell points out, the moral idealism which influences Peckinpah's ethics will always be engulfed by the dominant disparity between the ideal and the actual, an incongruity that in THE WILD BUNCH imbues the narrative with a sense of "ubiquitous amorality," "modern aimlessness," and "the absence of anything larger than the self and its fleeting desires" (Westerns 245). Mitchell's interpretation buttresses familiar readings of the film in terms of anarchic solipsism, and may be counterposed to Marshall's conception of the moral vista of THE WILD BUNCH, which is decidedly (and unexpectedly) a positive one. In Marshall' view, the ethics of the bunch materializes in the form of group unity, responsibility of leadership, ability to reflect, and coherence and continuity as a body (27). Marshall even suggests that Peckinpah's kinesiological camera eye reflects this ongoing conflict between the main moral positions of unity/solidarity on the one hand, and disunity/selfishness on the other. The dramatic progression of the movie, Marshall holds, is facilitated by an interplay of sequences dominated by what she calls "camera convergence" and sequences of fragmentation. As an example, she calls to mind the Starbuck scene, in which the camera emphasizes initial convergence in the spatial and narrative unification of different actions – the bunch's arrival, the bounty hunters awaiting them on the rooftop, and the march of the Temperance Union. When the shooting begins, however, this visual-narrative integration collapses into a kaleidoscopic form of spatiality that epitomizes disunity (13). Marshall's analysis is commendable for its sensitivity to the morality of aesthetic form, but her occasionally too facile, literal parallelisms between ethical stance and film technique need to be modified in accordance with a theory of film form that abolishes the separateness of the idea and the material.

The insistence on individual morality as the only viable ground for thinking the ethical as well as the desire to disrupt conventionally accepted beliefs aligns Peckinpah's work with an artistic tradition Fiedler has termed *tragic humanism* (432). In his *Love and Death in the American Novel* (1960), Fiedler maintains that writers like Hawthorne and Melville were not so much Transcendentalists as tragic humanists, whose "vision of blackness" was motivated by, and found expression as, the intention to "*disturb* by telling a truth which is always unwelcome" (450, 432, emphasis in original). Fiedler's concept is apposite to Peckinpah's imagination, and Seydor in fact evokes a similar designation when he refers to the filmmaker as a "tragic idealist" ("Sam Peckinpah" 18).[20] Seydor himself traces the genealogy of Peckinpah's art to the American Renaissance writers, asserting that the director's work "is fully understood only against the backdrop of this tradition" (*Peckinpah* 363).[21]

More specifically applicable to the western, however, is another cultural context whose historical permutations may be found to complement the non-conformist ethos of the tragic humanists. Peter French alleges that the genre's values were formed in opposition to what he identifies as "feminized Christianity" (15).[22] The hero in the anti-westerns of the 1960s establishes a relation to mor(t)ality that is predicated upon an inversion of Judeo-Christian principles: he is indifferent to the notion of God's existence; he does not believe in the afterlife; and he values the loyalty of friendship over the comfort of familial relations. Renouncing religion, the ethics of the western is anchored in an "annihilation conception of death" that might be "more vigorous, more life-affirming" than an ethics based on Christian doctrines (70). French's thesis has a precedent in

Jane Tompkins's *West of Everything* (1992), where the author holds that a fear of emasculation became the genesis of the western: "the Western owes its popularity and essential character to the dominance of a woman's culture in the nineteenth century and to women's invasion of the public sphere between 1880 and 1920" (Tompkins 44). Within this frame of comprehension, the genre's central project seems to rest on the de-domestication of American masculinity. During the late 19th and early 20th centuries, women became involved in a range of social activities, campaigning for suffrage, higher education, the prohibition of alcohol and a host of other issues. The feminization of the public domain implied the corrosion of traditional masculine values and created a need to reclaim one's manhood by embracing violence and confronting death, and the western became a fictional outlet for this fantasy. As Tompkins suggests, the genre's "real antagonist" was the Christian domesticity advocated by best-selling authors like Harriet Beecher Stowe, Susan Warner and Maria Cummins, whose novels embraced all the values that western fiction called into question: Christian virtue, emotionalism, and altruism – in short, the cultural signifiers of an emergent civilization. In spite of THE WILD BUNCH's general deconstruction of the genre, the film retains an element of the politics of de-domestication, as for instance in the staging of the San Rafael massacre in the beginning, where the Temperance Union literally becomes the target of the men's violence, but incorporates it into a more wide-ranging critique of corporate society. It is not so much feminized Christianity as a technocratic, consumerist modernity that is Peckinpah's main adversary. In FIGHT CLUB, as a subsequent chapter will make clear, Peckinpah's concern with the process of masculinization reappears alongside a revitalized negation of domesticity.

It has often been noted that THE WILD BUNCH affords the viewer a particular set of problems with respect to what may be recognized as the indistinguishability of ethics and aesthetics.[23] If, as I maintain above, the westerner's outlook on death shapes the ethical foundation of the genre, what seems to be needed is an interpretive template that gauges the reciprocity of the ethics/aesthetics interface. A significant aspect of Stewart's argument in *Death Sentences* (1984) offers such a theoretical contribution. Working from the assumption that depictions of mortality in fiction represent that textual region where aesthetic form comes most distinctively into view, Stewart concludes that "[d]eath in fiction aspires beyond mimesis to an absolute poesis" (5). While Stewart focuses on the literary medium, his thesis may fruitfully encompass death by violence in the medium of film (violence is here comprehended as indexing death metonymically). The mutuality of the relation between violence and form in the cinema has been discerned by several critics of the American new wave. Jacques Rivette, for example, detects a correspondence between screen violence and the rejuvenation of aesthetic style (95), and Robert Sklar suggests that, beneath the surface, the key violent works of the late 1960s really enact a "commentary on the making of visual images" (51).[24] In its dissection of the nature of violence, THE WILD BUNCH is therefore also a meditation on form; Doug McKinney argues that the film in fact invites "a complete confrontation between form and audience" (97).

The concept of the west is in itself tinged with intimations of death, and THE WILD BUNCH's destruction of the western can be conceived as an attempt to come to terms with the genre's ingrained "necrological impulse" (Mitchell *Westerns* 172), or death worship (Horrocks 81). Death's imminence is woven into the fabric of the plot, and, as Tompkins points out, to die in the western is somehow different from death in other violent genres (24). Containing terms such as "transfigurati[ve]," "spiritual," "ritualized," and "sacramental" (24-25), the lexicon that Tompkins resorts to in order to describe death in a genre based on the renunciation of Christianity is, ironically, religious. What this nomenclature attests to is the inclination to refer the exhausting experience of watching Peckinpah's violence to the domain of the transcendent. The violence in a film where "death has almost become the only thing" (Tompkins 26) represents an act of going beyond both mortality and the idea of redemption in the afterlife. As Peter French puts it, "[t]he death of the West is the death of death" (143), and in killing the western, Peckinpah sublimates this contradiction. Rejecting both death and religion, the only alternative that is left for THE WILD BUNCH is that of memory as absolute form. Fictional death, Stewart writes, "is the fullest instance of form indexing content, is indeed the moment when content, comprising the imponderables of negation and vacancy, can be found dissolving to pure form. Death in narrative yields, by yielding to, sheer style" (*Death Sentences* 3). The process of violence in Peckinpah is the submission of thanatography to the kind of *moral ecstasy* only aesthetic form can provide.[25]

One of the most influential readings imposed on THE WILD BUNCH has been that of regeneration through violence,[26] and despite the questionable mythological base which underpins this interpretation, it is too important to be entirely discarded. The most immediate difficulty with myth-based theories of violence in fiction – to reiterate my objections from a previous chapter – is the way they subsume all textual particularities under one grand interpretive formula. Moreover, the organicist metaphor upon which Slotkin's thesis relies also invites a more specific kind of criticism. The "rich regenerative violence" that William Carlos Williams writes of in 1925's *In the American Grain* (130), and that informs theories of regeneration is, if not metaphysical, at least immaterial, or discarnate. When critics mobilize an organic tropology and consider violence a means of societal renewal and rebirth, they unwittingly mask (and erase) a set of contingencies with respect to agency. History, society, culture are not living organisms, or "agents," in the sense that regeneration thesis suggests. Violence cannot be appropriated by any such institution. The grand theory of regenerative violence misleadingly implies that the use of violence is a collective process while it is, in fact, one profoundly circumscribed by particular historical subjectivities. Slotkin's account, for all its meticulous attention to historical detail, is surprisingly ahistorical in that it replaces cultural and temporal specificity with a generalized mythology that is insensitive to the ways in which violence is embedded in contexts which are by nature resistant to meta-narrativity. That is, violence is not the expression of society's intrinsic need to regenerate itself, but rather the manifest discourse of particular masculinities at particular historical junctures. Narrative violence is not a reflection of a self-perpetuating cultural impulse, but a sign – in the form of allegory – of something else, and this "something" is always historically variable, impermeable to the constancy of grand mythologies.

I¹ violence is a primary concern in western narratives, it entails a dimension that appears to escape the mythological in Slotkin's sense of the term. As Seydor notes while discussing violence in Mailer and Peckinpah, redemption by violence is only possible on an individual basis (*Peckinpah* 318). While for Slotkin violence is envisioned as a means by which to regenerate society itself (thus interconnecting violence and progress) (*Regeneration* 15), it would seem that, in the western, violence is only relevant *in relation to* the individual. If the metaphor of rebirth has any bearing at all on our understanding of western fiction, it must be on the level of individuality rather than on that of collectivity. Other violent genres like the gangster film and film noir exhibit similar patterns; violence is the prerogative of the individual, who, even when acting on behalf of the community, is wont to employ it gratuitously as a means of self-creation. An interpretation of aesthetic violence grounded in mythology is therefore largely infelicitous. Not only is the theoretical recourse to myth impervious to the capriciousness and fluctuations of historical context, but it is equally ineffective in elucidating those phenomena that the trope of violence is perhaps most essentially about – subjectivity and corporeality. The intractableness of the violated body does not conform easily to the rigid structure of myth.

If fictional violence as a form of writing on the body is circumscribed by irreducible particularity, how is it possible to theorize film violence, to establish a generalizable interpretive framework? In other words, how do we establish a theory that is at the same time sufficiently sensitive to capture the particularity of any instance of textualized violence and broad enough to give a sense of coherence to the historical and formal variability of aesthetic violence? Speaking of the western, Mitchell notes that the genre's fundamental concern is with the "making of masculinity" (*Westerns* 4), a statement which by no means is critically unprecedented. Mitchell's thesis, however, may in a somewhat modified way represent a tentative response to the questions posed above. The trope of violence – not only in the western but in other genres as well – seems to be related to the process of *un*making masculinity, to the extent that violence is both a destructive and a deconstructive act whose moment of literal impact becomes constitutive of the notion that masculinity is an interminable construction. The crucial question Mitchell asks is: "Is a man's face and body little more than a gendered mask, in need of being destroyed and reshaped to confirm that manhood exists beneath?" (*Westerns* 182).[27] According to Mitchell, the western, in its obsession with violence, aims to reaffirm the notion that manhood is in fact a biological process rather than a culturally acquired mode of behavior. Regardless of the underlying agenda that may be found to inform the issue of masculinity in the western, the fact that it is being explored, deconstructed and reassembled is in itself sufficient evidence to flaunt the inherent constructedness of manhood. In its indication of this process, film violence performs an unmaking of masculinity, a radical undermining of the conditions upon which the fabrication of manhood is founded.

If film masculinity is merely an enactment, a tropologically mediated interrelation of particular narratives and images, the question of identity becomes increasingly perplexing. A sense of extreme dislocation percolates through THE WILD BUNCH, and it is the character of Don Jose who aphoristically gauges the nature of this crisis when he says that "[w]e all dream of being children again, even the worst of us. Perhaps the worst most of all." Some critics have maintained that Don Jose's remark crystallizes the main idea of the film (Horsley, 1: 49), which should not be misconstrued as a plea for a return to an infantile state. In the context of Peckinpah's overpowering melancholia, the longing for childhood is a figurative yearning for a place that never was. As Brooks reminds us, implicit in the notion of nostalgia is the certainty that "paradise is always lost" (*Psychoanalysis* 120). The frangible and faltering masculine identity that THE WILD BUNCH tentatively adumbrates is a projection of the confluence of the ideas of dislocation, nostalgia, mourning and violence. For Peckinpah, masculinity seems to become manifest as a relation between a consciousness of permanent displacement and the subjectivity of the male protagonist. Immersed in melancholia, masculine identity in THE WILD BUNCH exists – as in most of Peckinpah's films – only as an awareness of belatedness and terminality.[28] The sense of grief that this recognition entails threatens to collapse the boundaries between the elegy and the violence, thus mediating a sensibility of weary vitalism unique to Peckinpah's cinema. In his virtual conflation of the processes of mourning and violence, Peckinpah appears to embrace Nietzsche's postulation in *On the Genealogy of Morals* (1887) that "[m]an could never do without blood, torture, and sacrifice when he felt the need to create a memory for himself" (61).

So irrepressible is the filmmaker's concern with a defeatist masculinity that it leads Neale to proclaim that a Peckinpah western may be read as a reification of "doomed male narcissism" ("Masculinity" 15). Despite the vulgar psychoanalytical inflections of Neale's analysis, his attribution of the notion of male narcissism to a film like THE WILD BUNCH appears to be incisive enough. As Devin McKinney has argued, Peckinpah overstates the mode of nostalgia – a kind of neurosis that has serious repercussions for the constitution of an identity that is more than this awareness of that oppressive space between belatedness and finality ("THE WILD BUNCH" 189). Amin Maalouf has suggested that problems of identity tend to instigate acts of violence (30). Like Arendt and Pareto before him, Maalouf examines the ways in which disempowerment may result in violent conflict, and it is not difficult to see how the exhausted masculinity of THE WILD BUNCH solicits a relation between violence and lack of power or identity. In this regard, the apocalyptic Agua Verde gunfight is a paradoxical way for the bunch to maintain a sense of continuity of self in the chaos of historical change. Violence becomes in effect constitutive of what may be referred to as post-identity a gestation which forms in the wake of what Coursodon terms "disturbances of such magnitude that nothing after them can ever be the same again" (262).

In the celluloid necropolis that is THE WILD BUNCH, the amimetic ontology of film violence becomes more overt than in earlier films, in part because Peckinpah was one of a generation of filmmakers who were vigorously self-conscious with respect to their cinematic heritage (Armes 103).[29] Peckinpah's reconfiguration of generic tropes and transtextual imagery results in a self-reflexivity at the same time so excessive and subtle that it tends to confound any audience not accustomed to the hyper-quotationism of a Tarantino or a Fincher. Few critics have been able to discern this meta-textual quality of his method, mistaking it instead for a certain idiosyncratic heavy-handedness. Mark Crispin Miller has argued that Peckinpah deliberately distorts convention in such a way that his irony either passes unnoticed or is misapprehended as sheer exaggeration (5). Though there is no question that his attitude toward his characters is one of reverence, there is also a competing element of travesty in his homage: "Peckinpah mocks his characters, their machismo, his own admiration, and finally even himself" (Horsley, 1: 48). When the process of self-referentiality becomes so pointed as in THE WILD BUNCH, narration itself takes on an air of performativity; it is no accident that Kinder evokes the term "performative numbers" when she discusses the choreography of violence in BONNIE AND CLYDE, THE WILD BUNCH and A CLOCKWORK ORANGE ("Violence American Style" 68). Kinder, however, reads the violence in these films as an equivalent to the song-and-dance sequences in musicals, whereas I would suggest that the notion of performativity also applies to the films in their entirety. THE WILD BUNCH not only produces but actively performs its own transtextuality, its own work of semiosis. What animates Peckinpah's narrative method are the figural movements of "implication, allusion, suggestion, and metaphor" (Slotkin, *Gunfighter Nation*

594). In thinking through the conditions of this approach, one does well to keep in mind Jean Mitry's qualifications with regard to the idea of filmic metaphoricity:

> Film does not establish its significations with metaphors. It *builds* them by contrasting facts and actions in juxtapositions, created most often in editing and whose connotations always have to be deciphered. The metaphor is not *presented*; it only exists as such (its meaning) in the mind of the audience (197, emphases in original).

There is an unruly surplus of significational value in THE WILD BUNCH – the film engenders more information than is required to sustain the narrative trajectory – and this excess implements a rhizomatic destabilization of perspectival singularity.[30] Seeping out of the narrative dimension is a fragile yet primary contiguity of allusive segments that form a thematic circuitry that escapes translation in linguistic terms. The concept perhaps most descriptive of the poetic and semiotic process in THE WILD BUNCH is that of irreconcilability: the aporia of the film emerges in its vitalistic thanatography, its vacillation between the glorification and the condemnation of violence, its simultaneous deconstruction and celebration of a particular kind of masculinity, its melancholic cynicism, and its disillusioned nostalgia. Defying paraphrase and finite interpretive apprehension, THE WILD BUNCH is a work of figurality, a visual poetics in the sense described in the introductory chapter.

The extent to which the film's discrete blocks of textural form are not amenable to acts of re-articulation is perhaps best illustrated by way of exemplarity. One of the most distinctive aesthetic features of Peckinpah's cinema is his allegorical use of tableau composition,[31] and one such configuration – the much analyzed ants-and-scorpion sequence in the beginning of the film – offers a case in point. Trading glances with the approaching bunch, the children – whose vantage point in the Starbuck massacre externalizes that of the viewer[32] – are staging a spectacle of their own in which a scorpion is being devoured by an anthill.

The tableau, evidently, is a narrative omen, though one whose conception appears to have been largely spontaneous. It was actor Emilio Fernandez, who plays General Mapache in the film, who first conjured up the image of the ants and the scorpion because the Starbuck ambush reminded him of a similar game he used to play as a child (in Weddle, *If They Move* 330). Fernandez's suggestion provided Peckinpah with an immediate, instinctive trope; whether or not the filmmaker was consciously aware of the symbolic import of this imagery at the time does not deflect from the fact that this 'allusive segment' operates on narrative, metaphorical and intuitional levels. While the tableau does little to advance the narrative, the irregular juxtaposition of two separate emblems of death in a single constellation renders palpable the self-assertive impenetrability of the image as a purely self-referential entity.[33]

The tableaux imagery notwithstanding, Peckinpah is both aesthetically and conceptually first and foremost a montage director, and his means of expression is what Linda Nochlin has called "the signifying power of the fragment" (55). Her reading of the notion of *the body in pieces* as a metaphor for modernity and the loss of wholeness seems a supremely appropriate analogy to Peckinpah's embittered rejection of the modern world which incites his furious montage. Furthermore, the strictly cinematic process of constructing a totality from splicing individual pieces of film complements the abstract notion of producing a new whole from the symbolic particles and textual ruins of other sources. THE WILD BUNCH is voracious in this respect, feeding on an expansive gamut of references both deliberate and inadvertent, obvious and opaque. In addition to generic precursors like Huston's THE TREASURE OF THE SIERRA MADRE and Peckinpah's own RIDE THE HIGH COUNTRY and MAJOR DUNDEE (1965), THE WILD BUNCH is substantially indebted to two seminal Kurosawa films – RASHOMON and SEVEN SAMURAI (1954) – as well as Elia Kazan's adaptation of A STREETCAR NAMED DESIRE (1951), and finally Lean's THE BRIDGE ON THE RIVER KWAI (1957). Hedling notes that Curtiz's THE CHARGE OF THE LIGHT BRIGADE (1936) and Aldrich's VERA CRUZ also exhibit striking thematic similarities with Peckinpah's film.[34] However, there are more oblique allusions in THE WILD BUNCH as well. On the literary side there is Camilo José Cela's *La Familia de Pascual Duarte* (1946), a novel that exerted a major influence on Peckinpah (Schrader 28), and which he also at one point wanted to adapt (Kinder, *Blood Cinema* 184). From "the violent gaze" of Saura's LA CAZA (1966), the director learned "how to use violence to structure not merely an individual sequence but the stylistic and narrative design of the entire film" (Kinder, *Blood Cinema* 160; "Violence American Style" 65).

Apart from the artistic heritage that THE WILD BUNCH draws on, there exists a wealth of historical material that informs the film both on a thematic and on a structural level. Peckinpah does not so much recreate a prototypical image of the old west as a compelling iconography of a crucial period of transition in Mexican and American history. In this respect, the film exploits motifs from stories, legends, folklore and chronicled reports patterned into a coherent filmic design. The film's wild bunch is partly modeled on Butch Cassidy's Hole-in-the-Wall gang, i.e., a historical syndicate of bank and train robbers active approximately during the same period in which Peckinpah's film takes place. The movie also incorporates the conflict between Pancho Villa and the Mexican army, an historical reference which contextualizes the diegetic world of the film. Ultimately, the backdrop for the whole narrative, and the incentive that informs the decisions the bunch makes, is the transitory process of the West as a geographical, cultural and mythic space. At the time of the film (1913), the horrors of World War One were imminent, the civil war in Mexico was raging, and in the lapse of time since the frontier officially closed, the Unites States had just been through the Spanish-American War. The turbulence and confusion of local and international warfare coexist with the historical shift from a primitive, agricultural to an industrially sophisticated society; together these elements contribute to creating an atmosphere of impending apocalypse and disaster. In the midst of this commotion, innovations in technology become perhaps one of the most significant metaphors for the violence of the period. The machine gun is presented as an uncontrollable, almost animate force which, as Jason Jacobs puts it, "has overwhelmed its user" (39). The omnipresence of the bullet-spraying gunfire is reminiscent of the accumulation of images produced by the excessively rapid cutting used in the film's final scenes. The destructive technology of the machine gun is also a product of the same industrial culture that generated the art of cinema. Griffith's THE BATTLE AT ELDERBUSH GULCH (1913), depicting an Indian attack on a white settlement, was an early example of the command of the code of continuity editing. Released the same year in which the action of THE WILD BUNCH takes place, Griffith's film places the impact of the role of the technological innovations in the Peckinpah film into a wider cultural perspective. The mentality of the bunch becomes anachronistic in the encounter with a burgeoning modernity that leaves men like Pike and Dutch with very few options.

The diegetic world of THE WILD BUNCH thus contains a violent vortex of different stratifications of culture that compete for control of space, be it territorial or ideological. Seydor argues that the vision of the film is one in which organic and mechanical, or human and technological forms of energy act and react within the same topos: "the theme is not of diminishing space, but of fixed and limited spaces becoming increasingly crowded, which then only multiplies the possibilities for conflict and violence." (136).[35] As a consequence of the consummation of the frontier project – which according to Turner was completed in 1890 – the force of the westward movement was redirected beyond the borders of the nation. In the case of the wild bunch, the values which they embody might be conceived of as a vestige of an era which has become antiquated practically overnight. For the gang, Mexico represents the space in which they are reterritorialized. However, before long Mexican space is also packed with people whose values are antithetical to those of the bunch. Chased by the bounty hunters, the gang falls into conflict with the American army, Pancho Villa's insurrectionists and Mapache's soldiers. The constant violence is always a correlate to the negotiation of spaces. All the different groups that converge and fight each other in this limited Mexican space create an irrational disorder which on the level of the image explodes in the fracturing of filmic space.

The average shot length of THE WILD BUNCH is unusually short, and the film consists of a remarkable number of individual shots,[36] making it one of the fastest-edited films of its time. If the long take, as Bazin maintains, is indicative of a regard for the unity of space, then Peckinpah's frantic cutting exposes a profound ambivalence about the possibility for recovering a homogeneous and constant space. The sanguineous confrontation at the end of THE WILD BUNCH is an orgy of spatial displacement. Evidently, the logistical configuration of the sequence suggests that violence is ubiquitous, but the kinesthetic structure of the scene also conveys the impression that the indivisibility of the film-narrative space is mortified in the process. In terms of the multi-perspectivism at the conclusion of THE WILD BUNCH, the plethora of points of view amounts to a complete deterritorialization of narrative authority. The rapid flow of images resists pausing, so that a stable perspective is rendered impossible.

Insofar as narration in the cinema is manifested as a production of spatial segments (Branigan, *Point of View* 57), certain sections of THE WILD BUNCH may threaten to undermine the narrative function of the film. The scene in which Pike, Dutch, Lyle and Tector decide to reclaim their tortured companion Angel is one that eventually allows spectacle to supersede the story. The politics of excess materializes in the rhythmic explosions and convulsions of a cine-space that shatters and disintegrates completely. A significant function of this process of fragmentation is the sense in which violence and dying are felt to be everywhere. Russell writes that "violent death involves a melodramatic displacement of the desire that cannot be sustained or fulfilled in the narrative" (183). She thus seems to suggest that there exists a close link between narration and desire, perhaps to such a degree that the two must be considered components of the same whole. If the desire that is intrinsic to processes of narration is curtailed for some reason, the narrative drive might be arrested. This implies a shift in formal definition; the storytelling quality of the text deteriorates and metamorphoses into absolute spectacle. In THE WILD BUNCH, this excess has infamously been labeled a "celebration of violence" (183). It is the failure of subjectivity and desire, Russell claims, that causes the overwhelming sense of stasis in conventional narrative representation, and she traces the origin of this failure back to the closing of the frontier: "narrative mortification allegorizes an inability to 'return home' to homogeneous cultural nationalism" (183). The transitional period in which the action of THE WILD BUNCH is set thus registers the passing of the old society of relative consensus, and importantly, of the shared ideological bedrock that is manifest destiny. Allison Graham conjectures that Peckinpah's heroes "are probably among the few in recent American film who confront emotionally the brutal fact of the finality and exhaustion of the American vision" (69).[37] In this perspective, it is perhaps not so much desire itself as the presumed teleology of desire that is waning.

One of Russell's essential claims in her discussion of death and closure in the new wave cinemas is that spectacle – particularly of a violent coloration – overturns narrative closure and "destabilize[s]" representation (2). When the film fails to terminate the narrative process according to convention, the text comes to embody the aesthetic of narrative mortality. A cinema of this configuration, Russell writes, aspires toward "a radical politics of filmic narrativity" (2). The schema of narrative mortality is radical in more than one sense since the abandonment of closure through violent spectacle mediates "an 'undoing' of the ideological tendency of death as closure" (2). Claiming that classical films tend to 'tame' death in their strategies of closure, Russell sees death and narrative closure in film as an aesthetic vocalization of a covert system which naturalizes the act of closure as a temporally inherent narrative and historical event (2). Narrative, Russell holds, "is the means by which Thanatos is 'appropriated' by social forces" (9). What the nature of this appropriation might be is unclear, and I suggest that Russell's reasoning may be delineated in the following manner. Narrative is, more than anything else, a social activity [consider Benjamin's conception of the act of storytelling in terms of having "counsel" ("Storyteller" 86)], with a set of governing conventions and structures that are relatively constant. The event of death, though affecting the social, is principally an individual phenomenon (the passage from animate, volitional subject to inanimate object is also a passage out of and away from the social sphere) that is fundamentally baffling to the living. By confining death to a highly manipulable system like narrative, Thanatos is tamed, or rendered less threatening, due to the meaning-making aspect of storytelling. While narrative thus contains and regulates the socially disturbing event of death, death, in turn, lends the structurally significant component that is closure to the act of narration. The process by which films are narratively terminated, however, is not a natural given but a culturally produced practice that functions as a means of wrapping things up, as a rationalization of the events of the narrative, and as an attempt to impose a structure on the infinite play of filmic signifiers. Many New Wave films can be read as reactions to this tradition. By centering on narrative ambiguity and open endings, these films flaunt the arbitrariness of textual processes of closure. Thus, texts like Godard's WEEKEND (1967), Oshima's BOY (1969), BONNIE AND CLYDE, Peckinpah's STRAW DOGS, and Altman's NASHVILLE interrupt the isomorphism of death and closure. The violence in these films may be perceived as a protest against or even a denial of the historical dependence on the sense of an ending.

Wherever the concept of ending is contested, the meaning of death loses its contextual grounding in dominant forms of rationality, the consequences of which are severe for a "human imagination [which] seems unable to exist without hope for a purposeful death" (Langer 15). The separation of closure and death implies that the two terms must be understood on the basis of different temporalities; the closure of abstract time does not follow from the closure of lived time. However, in the kind of classical cinema against which the new waves react, the end of narrative time – which, within the world of the diegesis, constitutes a fictional slice of abstract time – is reconciled with the end of lived time. Hence, the conclusion of the story lends a sense of inevitability and purpose to both violent and non-violent forms of dying; death is safely contained. Evidently, the fictional agents require a narrative space in order to exist. Once that space has reached its teleological destination, or structural vanishing point, the death of the protagonists is resolved as a natural function of that movement. One might say that life and narrative, history and identity, have collapsed. With the New Wave cinemas, the teleological dimension of narration is in rapid decline.[38] Films exhibit dysfunctional narrative structures that fail to provide a form of closure that is acceptable in the conventional sense. The texts end technically, but not structurally. Whereas the lives of the characters might be brought to an end through various manifestations of dying, the narrative itself fails to reach a resolution. This disparity, Russell notes, is interpretable as a "freeing of historical time from the mythic time of human mortality" (4). In her dissertation on morality and narrative in Peckinpah, Susan Marshall makes a related but nonetheless different argument. For her, death in THE WILD BUNCH signifies the death of old moralities. Thus, Marshall claims,

> Nothing simply *ends* in Peckinpah's imagination. A dying always entails a transformation into something new and into a new way of seeing. Or, in other words, "the end" never makes an end in these movies, it "completes" in the etymological sense of coming to fullness. Peckinpah's moral method generates an art of beginnings, not an art of annihilation (9, emphasis in original).[39]

Where Russell tends to conceive of the ending of THE WILD BUNCH as a denial of closure, Marshall sees it as immediately giving way to a beginning. Presumably, this divergence arises out of the fact that Marshall seems to define closure as closure-of-something. Russell, conversely, espouses a much more abstract notion of the phenomenon, one in which the separateness of temporality, narrativity, death and desire appear to collapse. Some New Wave films, she maintains, respond to the lack of ending by resorting to spectacle. One could hypothesize that the hostilities and aggression in films like BONNIE AND CLYDE and THE WILD BUNCH are the eruption of a violence directed at the defective narrative structures. Spectacle becomes emblematic of the cinema of narrative mortification, whose designation appears somewhat paradoxical. On the one hand, the concept refers to the deterioration of conventional story structure, hence the term mortality, or mortification. On the other hand, the reaction to this process of disintegration is one of escalating, and occasionally apocalyptic violence. In this respect, the spectacle of violence produces a correspondent process of mortification. There is a strong sense of reciprocity between filmic violence and narrative mortality, and the two might best be conceived of as dialectical phenomena that are mutually reinforcing.

When death can no longer be rationalized by reference to narrative closure, the spectatorial relationship to the film changes significantly. Russell makes the argument that the desire (for meaning) that informs narration is also a desire for meaningful death (3). However, the death of a protagonist is generally regarded as less meaningful if it occurs outside of the erotetic, teleological framework of classical narrative. Films that split death from closure therefore have a potential for subverting the kind of desire spectators usually entertain during film viewing. As briefly noted above, it is probable that a cinema of narrative mortality generates different experiences of desire than those which arise from the narrative seductions of classical film.

Although Peckinpah's film represents a core illustration of the mortification of narrativity at work in the new wave cinema, the aesthetic is traceable back to the post-Second World War period and texts like Lang's *Beyond a Reasonable Doubt* (1956). Russell maintains that the separation of death and closure is "a key means by which filmmakers have represented the social transformations of the second half of the twentieth century" (3). She argues that significant sociopolitical and philosophical issues in the post-war era – the Cold War divisiveness of the 1940s and 1950s, the antiauthoritarianism and Vietnam protests of the 1960s, the "death of myth" in the 1970s and finally the "death of the subject" in the 1980s – have been reworked in the New Wave cinemas in images of narrative mortification.

It is possible to view the sense of spectacle accompanying filmic violence as a logical product of the obsession with visibility that is associated with postmodern culture. As a technology of sound and vision, cinema itself is perhaps one of the most historical-material manifestations of this obsession. On a general level, the medium is spectacle in its very essence. However, it is clear that some films revel more lavishly in, and experiment more gratuitously with subversive imagery; thus one could speak of a specific type of spectacle. What is at any one time regarded as transgressive cinema evidently varies according to historical and contextual determinations. The socio-cultural processes which generate these variables therefore constitute a part of the analysis of the aesthetics of such a cinema.

One way of theorizing the spectacle of violence in THE WILD BUNCH is to consider it not as a provocation or a cause in itself but rather as a way of responding to a different phenomenon that for some reason escapes direct representation in the text. Russell suggests that ultraviolence in film could be taken as an "excessive overcompensation for the unrepresentable, unknowable, invisible event of death" (18).[40] Viewed in this context, the final shootout in Peckinpah's movie becomes a fetishistic way of confronting mortality. The impossibility of knowing, representing or overcoming death turns into a kind of fixation upon the process of dying. On a first viewing, the compulsive histrionics of Peckinpah's ending risks being perceived as nothing short of exploitation or titillation. The largely infamous sequence, however, makes sense when it is put into the context of Russell's argument. The scene, which takes up approximately five minutes of screen time, is shot through a variety of lenses, speeds, distances and angles. The juxtaposition of slow-motion cinematography, exceptionally rapid editing and a total fragmentation of point of view combine to protract the process of dying. The interplay of a kinetic mise en scène and an extravagant editing technique creates a filmic iconography of death which is, in Russell's words, "baroque in its excess" (187).

In The Wild Bunch, the protagonists' goal of redemption becomes virtually indistinguishable from its attendant corollary, death. The demise of the bunch is an ending that might make sense on a psychological level (the idea of the death wish as character motivation), but this logic is less appropriate within a narrative context. This has got to do with the global relations of causality in the text. In introducing death as the allegorical destination and fulfillment of the story – and hence the death wish as the narrative catalyst – the film eliminates the structure that produced this particular teleological end in the first place. By desiring its own end, and by subsuming narrative termination to character death, the text cancels the movement which is the source of this desire. In other words, the negative teleology of death becomes an impasse within the framework of the story. The desire for a textual ending through death is simultaneously the death of the desire that requires it. The Wild Bunch, however, recoils from this trajectory by setting up two surrogate endings which transport the text beyond the stalemate of the fatal massacre. Diegetically, the text provides a condition for the metaphorical endurance of the bunch's values by having Sykes and Deke Thornton, the oldest and only remaining members, team up with the Villistas in the aftermath of the slaughter. Sykes, who preserves the outlaw ethic of loyalty, thus brings the morality of the bunch with him into the company of Pancho Villas's revolutionaries. His conversion, a bizarre rite of passage, is ritualistic in that it institutes the spirit of the bunch into a new social framework.

Stylistically, the ending of The Wild Bunch circumvents the narrative impasse of the massacre by closing the film with the images of the bunch superimposed over the shot of Syke and Deke as they ride away with the Mexicans. After their diegetic deaths, Pike, Dutch and the Gorch brothers are thus restored to the viewer, as they are captured in one of the happier moments departing Angel's village. The sentimental mode of the sequence notwithstanding, the stylistic resolution seems to indicate that the film refuses to surrender wholly to the effects of narrative mortality. Both the diegetic and the stylistic endings attempt to resurrect an enduring image of the bunch and their way of life despite the terminality of their departure. As the focus wavers between the graphic exultation of a violent end and the naïve promise of regeneration, the film deconstructs its own narrative conclusion.

The camera records the various phases of disintegration to create a monstrous cinematic mosaic, a montage of abomination. What the film accomplishes more profoundly and more dramatically than any other western preceding or succeeding it is the capture of the distinctiveness of the body in a state of transition. As the bunch and the Mapachistas are demolished, they are momentarily suspended in a limbo where they are neither fully alive nor entirely dead. The architecture of corporeal decay is exposed as a process of repulsive proportions. In temporally extending the process of dying, the film tends to emphasize the effects of violence upon the body in ways unfamiliar to the majority of motion pictures trafficking in it.[41] The prototypical Hollywood violence may be brutally gory, but, at the same time, the films are likely to sidestep that intermediary movement which comes between the animate and the inanimate states, the stage of in-betweenness that Kristeva has identified as the potential site of both the abject and the sublime (4). Death in the conventional American cinema is abrupt and sudden, and the distinction between the two ontological conditions is bifurcated in an absolute sense.

Contrary to what is often assumed, the function of the slow-motion device in Peckinpah is not to linger on the visceral gore of the violence in any exploitative manner, as the inserts are much too brief to serve that purpose. The salient focus of these shots, therefore, is not the explosion of blood but the body's loss of control over its actions and movements. At the same time, both lyrical and grotesque, the convulsing, spinning body captures a paradoxical state of being in that it is technically dead yet it continues to move. As Sobchack has stated, "the moment of death can only be represented in a visible and vigorous contrast between two states of the physical body: the body as lived-body, intentional and animated, and the body as a corpse" ("Inscribing" 287). In THE WILD BUNCH, the body is kept moving by the violent impact that so savagely terminated its volitional movements in the first place. The sudden lack of intentionality in the body effects a release of anarchic transgression in which being and movement become uncontrollable, chaotic elements. There are many instances of such imagery in THE WILD BUNCH, but also in later Peckinpah films like PAT GARRETT AND BILLY THE KID and CROSS OF IRON (1977), as well as in Penn's BONNIE AND CLYDE. Penn's film shows Bonnie's rotating, dying movements as she is shot repeatedly while sitting in the car, while in THE WILD BUNCH the effect is manifested in the images of dying men falling off the rooftops of San Rafael, of the U.S. soldiers shot off the train, and of the maniacal Gorch brothers shot to pieces but nonetheless kept standing by the force of the bullets fired by Mapache's soldiers. These images vividly dramatize and specify the phenomenality of death, not simply as non-being, but as a non-being where its implications are laid bare; particularly the loss of volition and intention. In Peckinpah's cinema, death is certainly not reduced to an analogy of sleep, but rather externalizes the ontological consequences of its onslaught.

The most valuable achievement in this context is arguably the construction of a new viewing position for the audience of film violence. It is in this area that Peckinpah's project may be salvaged. His persistently mobile camera works against the notion of spectacle. In the dynamism of Peckinpah's editing scheme, the viewer is shaken out of the safe confinement of any stable point of view regarding the action. In the San Rafael and Agua Verde scenes the perspective is exploded; it fragments into a constantly fluid everywhere.[42] The three types of montage employed in THE WILD BUNCH and STRAW DOGS destabilize perspective and thus block out any sustained or singular focus on the violent action. If the fascination with mimesis can be broken, the configurations of violent acts in the images appear to lose their narrative prominence, which nullifies the viewers' aesthetic attraction to the representation of violence. The overall aesthetic purpose of Peckinpah's stylistic assemblages is to facilitate a screen discourse that is less a mediator than a critique of violence.

6   As I Lay Dying: Violence and Subjectivity in Tarantino's RESERVOIR DOGS

> *Film directors want to shoot the dying.*
> Nagisa Oshima

Violent films, like the public and critical turbulence they generate, seldom emerge in cycles. The peak of screen mayhem that was part of the New American Cinema – and whose token conclusion arrived with Scorsese's TAXI DRIVER – left in its wake a hiatus in the evolution of violent form. Perhaps the most conspicuous legacy of the Renaissance films in the field of violence was the injection of increasingly graphic depictions into what David Robinson calls "prestige productions" that were distributed by major companies (76). Prior to Peckinpah's challenging of the norms for rendering violence in the classical cinema, such explicit portrayals had been limited to the domain of the exploitation film. After a decade of hackneyed, comic strip carnage that offered little in the way of aesthetic experimentation or ideational novelty, the 1990s ushered in a new cycle of movie violence that has earned various monikers such as "the new brutalism" (Shelley, "Boys are Back" 7), "neo-violence" (Rich, "Art House" 6), and simply "new violence" (Slocum, "Violence" 1). These nondescript labels are richly suggestive in that they underline both the extent to which critics perceived the films in question to be genuinely innovative and the attendant lack of precision in signaling what the changes consisted of. Somehow American screen violence appeared to have re-invented itself, and RESERVOIR DOGS, according to Bouzereau, was the film that initiated this new era in movies (71). Critics have been divided on the question of the New Wave's relation to its tradition; where Prince emphasizes the continuity of the 1990s violence with that of the New American Cinema (1998, *Savage Cinema* 2),[1] Sharrett postulates a fundamental discontinuity between the two ("Afterword" 414).

The criticism of the Tarantino aesthetic has been almost uniformly negative, the principal charges being shallowness and nihilism both on a formal and a moral level.[2] Lester Friedman, for example, deplores the alleged "amorality" of Tarantino's fictions (7), whereas Giroux castigates the director's films for "[emptying] violence of any critical social consequences" (*"Pulp Fiction"* 308).[3] For Bogue and Cornis-Pope, what is new about screen violence in the 1990s is "the cynical self-awareness that accompanies it," a quality they see as the product of "a disintegration of cultural values in an age of expanding communication" (2). Unsurprisingly, some of the pundits who voice the most incendiary opposition tend to use Peckinpah's treatment of violence as an analytical benchmark for an appraisal of the cinema of Tarantino and his contemporaries like Coen, Stone, Roger Avery, and Tony Scott. "One great difference between [Peckinpah] and his imitators," Seydor holds, "lies in how deeply and passionately felt his violence is, and how securely it is tied to character, to milieu, to story – in a word to meaning" ("Sam Peckinpah" 20). For Sharrett, what most of all distinguishes Peckinpah's cinema from that of Tarantino's is the former's bleak but unswerving humanism: "Peckinpah's great compassion for the human condition and for the characters he created is something totally alien to the glacial movie-brat worldview of a Tarantino" ("Peckinpah" 79). The conditions for this disillusionment with the screen violence of the 1990s are ultimately rooted in a theoretical misconception that may be exemplified by Bernard Cook's diagnostic statement regarding the cause of the deteriorating standards of screen violence post-Taxi Driver. What increasingly happened throughout the 1980s and 1990s, Cook writes, was that "[t]he sign of film violence became severed from the referent of real violence" (296). But such a shift in the macro-economy of signification has not really occurred, since real violence has never been the referent of the "sign" of fictional violence. In principle, Scarface depends no less on artifice, quotation and the conventionalization or codification of a particular choreography of the body than does Reservoir Dogs. Tarantino's film may simply contain more citations or exhibit a more pronounced self-referentiality than Scarface, but these are differences not of ontology but of degree. It would be a mistake to preclude the possibility that the pessimistic but dominant analyses of films like Reservoir Dogs and Pulp Fiction in terms of concepts such as depthlessness and pastiche may be an offshoot of deeply entrenched (and largely) poststructuralist practices of reading. What I mean to suggest is that one needs to be aware of the extent to which an aesthetic text might become hostage to the prevailing terms of discourse that dominate any given historical context. Anxious to amplify the perceived newness of the kind of film form found in texts like Reservoir Dogs or Natural Born Killers, critics tend to brush aside considerations of similarity and continuity. It is disputable whether the Tarantinian approach to violence is predicated upon a notion of filmicity that is fundamentally different from that which underlies the classical and new wave narratives. Strenuous as it may be to go beyond the patina of critical hype which enmeshes a film like Reservoir Dogs, a revision of the premises that have governed the reception of the film seems long overdue. My argument, however, involves not so much a refutation of the established readings of Tarantino in terms of an aesthetics of intertextuality and self-referentiality as the assertion that such an aesthetics does not represent a radical departure from the tradition of American movie violence.

RESERVOIR DOGS, like all of the films previously considered, is concerned with the reluctant construction of what could be termed an amimetic body, reluctant because the immutable presence of the body is the only aspect of film fiction which partially resists the overall semiotic movement toward the hermetically transtextual. Regardless of the demands of amimesis, fiction, performativity and acting, an inescapable fact about the filmic body is that it remains within itself, a part or dimension of it oblivious to the narrative context that enwraps it. A mode of being, or ontology, which subjects everything to the regime of the transtextual must necessarily and at least to a certain degree suppress the ambiguous existence of the body.[4] Shaviro's term for this ontology is "simulacral incorporeality" (28), which produces an image "at once intense and impalpable" (26). Sobchack has suggested that the violence of the 1980s and 1990s may be a reflection of the increased influence and dominance of technology vis-à-vis the human body:

> The excessive violence we see on the screen, the carelessness and devaluation of mere human flesh, is both a recognition of the high-tech, powerful and uncontrollable subjects we (men, mostly) have become through technology – and an expression of the increasing frustration and rage at what seems a lack of agency and effectiveness as we have become increasingly controlled by and subject to technology ("Violent Dance" 122).

Sobchack's symptomatic reading may be of some relevance for a comprehension of the screen violence of the last two decades, though I would argue that the problem of agency in relation to the cinematized body's intentionality and volition arises not from the tyranny of technology in particular but from the technology of signification in general. The violated body that fictions like RESERVOIR DOGS and FIGHT CLUB present is evidence of a resistance to the process of textuality, a resistance that is impossible yet irrepressible. Violence, to cite screenwriter Larry Gross, has become "a secondary symptom of a primary disease, the sheer pollution of representational imagery" ("Exploding" 8). As I have contended throughout this text, fictional images cannot sustain a relation to the notion of representationality as traditionally conceived, although Gross's statement launches the hypothesis that particular forms of film violence may be grasped as a response to the nullification of the body by amimetic processes. According to Paul Smith, the body surmounts the repressive empire of textualization and narrativization only in the interstices of what he calls a "residual" male hysteria:

> The hysterical moment I am stressing marks the return of the male body out from under the narrative process that has produced what appears to be its transcendence,

but that in fact is its elision and its forgetting. In other words, although there is in these [action] movies a conservatively pleasurable narrative path which finishes by suppressing the masculine body and its imaginary, the body nonetheless returns from beneath the weight of the symbolic. What I mean to point to as this hysterical residue, then, is an unresolved or uncontained representation of the male as it exceeds the narrative process (92).

Smith's thesis seems to say that there is an element of the male body that is "unsymbolizable" and that evades the trappings of signification, narrative, and iconography. Thus problematized, the fascination with fictional violence can be attributed to the need of the modern subject to re-connect with the realm of physicality, a hypothesis already proposed in Fraser's *Violence in the Arts* (63).

RESERVOIR DOGS pivots to a remarkable extent on the vagaries of language, its contingencies and gaps. Not only is the film rigidly dialogue-driven – most of the narrative consists of men talking to each other in warehouses, lavatories, offices, restaurants, and cars – the title itself exposes the incompatibility of sign and reference, of perception and its objects. The combination of words in the film's title appears nonsensical, bearing no obvious relation to the text or, apparently, to any idioms or expressions in the language. Tarantino evidently nods to films such as Peckinpah's STRAW DOGS and Lumet's DOG DAY AFTERNOON (1975) (the latter film is also about a failed heist), but the reference of the first part remains enigmatic. The linguistic conundrum stems from a particular species of what Iampolski calls misquotation: "Any kind of quotation that brings further anomalies into the text" (51), and that "smuggles a puzzle into the text that is nigh impossible to solve" (52). In the case of Tarantino's film, the puzzle derives from the director's mispronunciation of the title of Louis Malle's AU RE-VOIR LES ENFANTS (1987) (Bernard 171), which in an extended metathetical enunciation, Tarantino reconstitutes as the first word of his film's title. Allegedly one of Tarantino's favorite films, AU REVOIR LES ENFANTS is set in a Catholic boarding school in Nazi-occupied France and examines the politics of male friendship and betrayal, themes which reappear prominently in RESERVOIR DOGS. Malle's film also shares with the later text a preoccupation with fake names and mistaken identities, so there is more than just the linguistic misquotation that connects the two movies. Once the irregular title is introduced, it generates additional layers of connotations that harmonize resourcefully with the film's narrative action. The term *reservoir* implies a strict delimitation of space, a space that may potentially burst, and by way of associative contiguity the warehouse in RESERVOIR DOGS seems to evoke a similar confinement of spatial energy. Further, reservoir also designates a place in the body where fluids accumulate, and the film's name is thus also suggestive of the pool of blood oozing from Mr. Orange's belly throughout the narrative.

The fixation on the instability of the interrelations of language, storytelling and identity permeates Reservoir Dogs on other levels as well, and although the body is always present in the frame, the perpetual process of abstraction which the linguistic indulgence promotes tends to deny it its sovereignty. Arbitrariness features significantly in this process, for instance, in Joe Cabot's naming of the members of his gang according to a pre-determined color scheme of "pure signifiers" (Botting and Wilson 52),[5] and in the fictitious "Commode story" that Mr. Orange recounts to Joe and Eddie Cabot and Mr. White to bolster his own credibility as a career criminal. More generally, allusions to a *poploristic* textuality dominate almost every conversation in the film, a method which contributes to making what is absent (the referent) present, or primary, and what is present (the embodied, speaking subject) absent, or secondary. Subjectivity in its fully embodied form only seems to come alive in the most excruciating moments, such as the scene in the beginning in which Mr. Orange has just been shot and the scene where Mr. Blonde torments the policeman.

It is in their staging of the violated body that films like Reservoir Dogs truly become "pulp fictions," narratives of the flesh (from the Latin *pulpa*) in an ecstatic agony which, to use Elaine Scarry's phrase, "does not simply resist language but actively destroys it" (4). Critics who discredit Tarantino's film based on its fetishistic quotationism tend to overlook the acutely corporeal dimension which escapes the logic of the sign even as it is suppressed by it.

If violence in Hawks, Kubrick, Penn and Peckinpah overwhelmingly dictates film narration, in Tarantino violence and narration can no longer be kept apart as two separate entities. As Amy Taubin pointed out, Reservoir Dogs is a film whose temporal and dramatic unity is principally determined by "the length of time it takes for a man … to bleed to death in front of our eyes" ("Men's Room" 3). While violent death is pervasive in the films of someone like Peckinpah, it is nonetheless swift and instantaneous, enfolded in the choreography of what Kinder terms "performative numbers" ("Violence American Style" 68). Like in Scarface, The Killing and Bonnie and Clyde, the patterns of narrative violence in The Wild Bunch are structured rhythmically in a dialectic of explosions and pauses. In Reservoir Dogs, on the other hand, the entire narrative (except for the preface) unravels as Mr. Orange lies dying on the warehouse floor. The film's temporality is thus conceived as one extended moment of death. Tarantino's characters, most of whom do not survive the act of narration, seem to occupy what Blanchot's has called *death's space*, a notion that the film in a sense literalizes since the warehouse which provides the primary location is in fact a morgue (there are coffins everywhere, and Mr. Blonde is sitting on an old hearse, not a crate). In a discussion of Kafka's protagonists, Blanchot propounds the idea that "not just when they die but apparently while they are alive Kafka's heroes carry out their actions in death's space, and ... it is to the indefinite time of 'dying' that they belong" (92). Blanchot's concept is apposite to a reading of RESERVOIR DOGS which proposes that death by violence is not only limited to discrete narrative moments but has come to immerse the spatio-temporal continuum. In the beginning of the film (after the introductory scene in the diner and the slow-motion presentation of the "dogs"), the first utterance following the cut from black screen to the medium shot of the wounded Mr. Orange is "I'm gonna die," which is repeated several times. Beneath the tone of desperation there is a hint of an acknowledgement of the imminent, and one may see the remaining part of the narrative as the process toward what Blanchot might have called the achievement of one's own death (96). Addressed to Mr. White, Mr. Orange's subsequent lines – "I'm sorry," and "I can't believe she fucking killed me, man" – further underscore his awareness of the temporality of death into which he has entered. Like Noé's IRRÉVERSIBLE, RESERVOIR DOGS utilizes the principle of *irreversibility* as a conceptual template for narrating mortality.

That Tarantino's movie in effect collapses its own *syuzhet* with the process of death resonates well with the overall signifying practice of a thoroughly transtextualized filmicity. In the era of hypermodernity, films such as RESERVOIR DOGS, PULP FICTION, and NATURAL BORN KILLERS represent what could be termed *archival cinema*, a kind of cinema defined above all by the incessant recycling of particles of older texts[6] - some critics have even hinted that violence is "the principal instrument that holds all the fragmented postmodernist fictions together as coherent narratives" (Morrison 314). The case of Tarantino amply illustrates the logic of consumption which regulates the proliferation of the archival. Unlike that of directors like Peckinpah (who had an industry background before becoming a filmmaker), or Scorsese (who is a film school graduate), the foundation for Tarantino's film education was the years he worked as a clerk in the Video Archives in Manhattan Beach (Dawson 43).[7] The omnivorous accumulation of references to the texts of popular culture history – what Pat Dowell has referred to as the director's "pop-culture erudition" (4) – reconstitutes his films as archives in their own right, as a reservoir of quotations which have come to signify a textual morgue.[8] Intrinsic to Tarantino's cinematic sensibility, therefore, is the gravitation toward the forms and modes of mortality both in a literal and a figurative sense. The uninhibited reprocessing of old images suggests textual stagnation, decay, and finally death.

Attractive as it may be, an interpretation of RESERVOIR DOGS by way of analogy with the notion of the textual archive, or morgue, is also indicative of a particular indignation with the kind of sublimated transtextuality that dominates contemporary cinema. Dowell's comparing of Tarantino's aesthetics of quotation to that of Godard epitomizes this resentment:

Godard borrowed with a difference – to comment, to satirize, to discredit, to examine, to open up other possibilities. Tarantino borrows to create cultural cul-de-sacs, places of intellectual safety and anesthesia.... he is first and foremost an ingenious curator displaying his collection of cultural trivia (4).

Fred Botting and Scott Wilson, furthermore, buttress this perception when they write that, in Tarantino, "[c]ultural reference, omnipresent and obvious, offers no depth, no deeper insight or significance" (10). On the basis of similar observations, some critics extrapolate what they discern to be an absence of morality in the works of Tarantino (Lipman 51),[9] which I believe is an error caused by the conflation of value judgment and the particulars of film form. When a perceptive critic like Giroux dismisses the director's films for "reordering the audience's sense of trauma through a formalism that denies any vestige of politics" ("*Pulp Fiction*" 308), he elides the question of the ethics of both masculinity and spectatorship that is inseparable from the formal fabric of the texts. One may legitimately conjecture that the real though hitherto not fully articulated object of the critics' concern is this: films like RESERVOIR DOGS make explicit the amimeticism that has always been integral to the ontology of the fiction film. In a sense, the art of Tarantino reifies the gospel of someone like Jean Baudrillard, who in *The Evil Demon of Images* (1987) has this to say regarding the referentiality of the image:

> "Above all, it is the reference principle of images which must be doubted, this strategy by means of which they always appear to refer to a real world, to real objects, and to reproduce something which is logically and chronologically anterior to themselves. None of this is true" (13).[10]

The logic by which the image functions, he continues, is that of "the extermination of its own referent" (*Evil* 23). Baudrillard's postulation is of course tiresomely familiar, exhausted, and would not merit reiteration were it not for the fact that it serves as a welcome reminder of the mimetic fallacy.

My uneasiness regarding the criticism that commentators such as Dowell, Amanda Lipman, and Giroux level against Tarantino's films is twofold. There is not sufficient support for the suggestion that hyper-quotational cinema inaugurates an entirely new kind of film narrative; and there is nothing about the form of the films in question which eliminates any engagement with morality or ethics. As Baudrillard maintains, cinema constantly reproduces and "plagiarises" its own history (*Evil* 33), and the politics of multi-referentiality is thus not something that has only emerged since the postmodern era. Grant's statement, however, condones precisely this view:

> American cinema has arrived at the postmodern point where it is at once fully aware of its history regarding such contentious issues as representations of violence and at

the same time able to mock the treatment of violence in these films, and other media, while employing their very same techniques ("Landmark" 1: 524).

The overstating of the increased self-consciousness of Tarantinian cinema is subsidized by a teleological understanding of the evolution of film aesthetics, whereby one conceives formal developments as stages in a process toward some kind of ultimate realization of the medium's essence.[11] For the postmodern millenarianist, the notion of the end of cinema as the attainment of a state of suffusive self-awareness complements the idea of the end of history. As Robert Stam reminds us, "we dwell in the realm of the already said, the already read, the already seen" (305). As much as Stam is correct in pointing this out, we may very well have been occupying this realm for some time already. This inertia of historical vision, if that is what it is, is neither the cause nor the effect of transtextuality in the cinema, but it does seem to participate in an interrogation of the epistemological conditions that facilitate the mediation of history in terms of images.

More to the point, the phenomenon that filmmakers like Tarantino exposes is both the unavoidability and necessity of re-appropriating and re-interpreting cultural texts according to the exigencies of the moment. RESERVOIR DOGS, for instance, is invariably involved in acts of hypothesis-making and theorizing, from the opening exegesis of "Like a Virgin" to the ongoing rationalizations regarding the failed heist. The psychology of pulp hermeneutics does not so much repress history as reassemble its components within textual relations of simultaneity and contingency. If the erosion and extension of the past into the present risk curtailing the sense of historical movement, which, among others, Sharrett seems to claim ("Introduction: Crisis" 8), they also contribute to a deconstruction of the myths of historical teleology. In Sharrett's account, the key failure of apocalyptic film violence lies in its inability to provide narrative closure, instead it promotes the hegemony of spectacle and historical travesty.

Sharrett proposes that the new American apocalypticism in the cinema from the 1970s onward is based on a crisis of epistemology, and implies that the postmodernist texts essentially read as a retrograde millennialism. In attempting to come to terms with this hypothesis, Sharrett identifies some of the conditions that cast postmodernity as a crisis scene. Among these, the most salient is the disregard for traditional narrative and all forms of representation, a "death of totalization" which defines the crisis as one of legitimation ("Introduction: Crisis' 3). For Sharrett, the lapse of meaning is not an effect of what he refers to as "our poststructuralist-trained imaginations" but rather the outcome of processes of depoliticization and irresponsibility ("Introduction: Crisis" 4). Sharrett appears to believe that the emergence of crisis cinema is an extension of the general cultural and political decline that Jameson discusses in his *Postmodern-*

ism, or, The Cultural Logic of Late Capitalism (1991). The equivocation of apocalyptic cinema – the fact that it recycles old notions of millennial violence *and* neutralizes its historical import – clearly suggests that it flounders in its attempt to validate itself as an ideologically consistent discourse. In decomposing history and discrediting the efficacy of grand narratives, the post-eschatology of what Sharrett terms apocalyptic cinema forgoes historical vision to "retreat into aesthetic liberation" ("Introduction: Crisis" 3). Sharrett impugns contemporary crisis cinema for severing any relation to the world outside its own fictional diegesis, an invective abundantly mandated by the majority of Tarantino's critics. This is a cinema, the argument goes, unwilling to participate in the social and political discourses of its time; it is a cinema that has become self-absorbed and self-sustained (hence its penchant for irony, metafictionality, and the mirthful unveiling of its own artifice). What is perceived to be the premiere target of this new cinema is, ironically, something that has only existed as a deception, an irresistible misunderstanding, perhaps: the idea of mimesis.

While the trademarks of a hypermodernist cinema[12] – self-consciousness (Rich, "Art House" 6), playfulness, perspectival multiplicity, identity politics, irreverence, eclecticism and self-reflexivity (Todd 41) – emblematize nothing less than a significational dystopia for many critics, there are others who project a more affirmative valorization of this particular aesthetic. Kinder, for instance, praises the reflexiveness of films like Natural Born Killers and Pulp Fiction ("Violence American Style" 77), and W.J.T. Mitchell applauds the meta-textual aspect of Stone's movie for "offer[ing] a place in which critical reflection on this issue [violence] may be carried out" ("Representation" 3: 46).[13] A film's self-awareness of its own fascination with violence betrays what could be conceived as a meta-aesthetic project, or what Valerie Fulton names with reference to Tarantino "meta-violence" (178). The violent imagery in Reservoir Dogs and Pulp Fiction, Fulton holds, is "a decorative surface – familiar to viewers because similar images have appeared to them in previous films" (178). In Mitchell's and Fulton's view, Tarantino's films are approachable as depictions of depictions of violence, and as such they demand a mode of viewing that is authentically participatory and self-evaluative. The production of a spectator who "is not only seeing differently, but is aware of seeing himself/herself see," to quote Cristina Degli-Esposti (5), is one of the key contributions of a film like Reservoir Dogs.

At a certain stage the discussion of the kind of cinema that Tarantino represents will have to gravitate toward the primary conflict that hypermodern film violence animates, namely that between ethics and aesthetics, history and textuality. In contemporary culture, as Black sees it, "the aesthetic realm of the hyperreal" has supplanted "the ethical world of the real" (*Aesthetics* 138).[14] Like Baudrillard, who proclaims that the logic of the image is "immoral," "beyond good and evil, beyond truth and falsity" (*Evil* 23), Black posits an insuperable discord between the two domains of text and ethics. Notably, the "immorality" that Baudrillard speaks of has more to do with the conditions for the construction of the image than with any thematic qualities which inhere in it. In short, the most fundamental provocation that the hypertextual image offers crystallizes in Patrick Fuery's insight that "[t]he cinematic sign is more real than anything we find in the world" (128). Fuery's declaration is arguably indebted to Baudrillard's own pronouncement that simulation, or the hyperreal, not only negates reality but – perhaps more importantly – negates illusion itself (*Evil* 52). If neither the real nor the illusory is possible, the image becomes its own authority

There may be similarities between Baudrillard's theory of the hyperreal and the concept of the amimetic that I have tried to establish, but, it should be pointed out, they are largely superficial. Unlike the notion of simulation, which by nature complicates the relation between the consciousness of reality and the consciousness of textuality, amimeticism does not imply a negation of extra-textual modes of sensation or being. Much less ambitiously, the amimetic position challenges the existence of the real (as a model or extratextual signified) within the fictional text, not the existence of the real altogether. However, the fragmentary repackaging of film and television history that the quotational promiscuity of Reservoir Dogs undeniably luxuriates in does seem to abolish historical linearity and to encourage a commodification of cinema's transgressive expressivity. Dowell, for instance, has suggested that the originality of Tarantino's method lies in the way in which his films require a mode of viewing which mimics the experience of being a "consumer" (4). In the celluloid archives of hypermodern film, the viewer can shop around for transtextual capital like a customer in a mall or a surfer on the web.[15] Describing the parameters of such a viewing experience, Botting and Wilson make this concession: "Cultural reference, omnipresent and obvious, offers no depth, no deeper insight or significance... If the movies invite an enthusiastic filmspotting, their dizzying range of allusion suggests that ultimately the task could be infinite, so constantly overlaid, multiple and unreflecting are the references" (10).[16] If Dowell is correct when he writes that a film like Pulp Fiction "exists only in terms of other movies" (4), hypermodern cinema does not merely undertake an "ironic rethinking of history," to recall Linda Hutcheon's phrase (5), but dismantles the belief in the past's authenticity. How, one might ask, would someone like Benjamin have responded to the densely allusive syntax of a film like Reservoir Dogs?

It is to some extent in their relation to history that the narrations of violence in Reservoir Dogs and Pulp Fiction depart from the approach of earlier filmmakers like Penn and Peckinpah. Tarantino's films, William DeGenaro has pointed out, destabilize the past by "subvert[ing] the notion that nostalgia establishes 'reassurance and direction'" (57). Particularly THE WILD BUNCH, one remembers, renders nostalgia an overwhelming presence in which both melancholy and violence are embroiled, but also the early 1970s cycle of deeply nostalgic movies like THE LAST PICTURE SHOW and AMERICAN GRAFFITI convey a sense of the past as something temporally continuous, morally coherent and phenomenologically reliable. In hypermodernity, however, nostalgia survives only in the form of parody or irony; the desire for unbounded quotation seems incompatible with the desire for history. The "catastrophe" of the postmodern, Sharrett says, is "the simultaneous affirmation and denial of historical views of reality, the nostalgia for the past simultaneous with its derision" ("Afterword" 421). For some analysts, the order of spectatorship that hypermodern film invites is one hamstrung by what Jameson has called the "waning of affect" (*Postmodernism* 16),[17] or "compassion fatigue," to evoke Sissela Bok's comparable term (68). On a related note, Richard Falcon has asserted that cinema's potential for offending the sensibilities of its audience is in fact diminishing. Pondering the extreme, misanthropic violence and morbid eroticism in some films from the late 1990s – notably ONE AGAINST ALL (Noé 1998), SITCOM (François Ozon 1998) and THE IDIOTS (von Trier 1998) – Falcon seems to infer that transgression is no longer attainable in the cinema:

> [these films] share an aggressive desire to confront their audiences, to render the spectator's experience problematic. But the difficulties involved in this desire to attract exposure through transgression ... are not without irony. This winter [1998-99] has seen the hugely successful re-release of THE EXORCIST to a new generation of cinemagoers. Does their curiosity about Friedkin's film relate to the current orthodoxy that THE EXORCIST represents a decade of authentically transgressive film-making since lost to a Hollywood dominated by feelgood and genre movies? ... FilmFour has transmitted MAN BITES DOG uncut and other more recent films in a 'Savage Cinema' strand. We can conclude perhaps that transgressive cinema – canonified, exhibited in the museum and the object of nostalgia – ain't what it used to be (11).

In an article on the use of popular music in RESERVOIR DOGS, Marcus Breen cites a passage from Pier Paolo Pasolini's THE ASHES OF GRAMSCI (1954) – "will I ever again be able to act with pure passion when I know our history is over?" (Pasolini 23) – which may be construed as a rhetorical encapsulation of the hypermodern impasse that the waning of affect has brought about. What Falcon essentially addresses is the nature of the cultural and textual processes that have transformed film violence from a transgressive act to a commodity. From such a perspective, Tarantino's effortless regurgitation of film history is beyond homage, beyond the mourning of a time in which film art was still capable of subversion; the act of commodification is ultimately a form of textual necrophilia.

If hypermodernized film violence has surrendered its transgressive impact, can it still be a purveyor of ethical knowledge? Critics like Grant and Prince seem distrustful of the prospect and are adamant that contemporary screen violence lacks the moral framework that in various forms always has been a staple of American storytelling (Grant, "American Psycho" 37; Prince, "Graphic" 33). They find support in Carol Becker's charge that the aesthetics of pastiche, irony and cynicism forfeits the social responsibility of art (125),[18] and in Tom Whalen's claim that the Tarantinian sensibility is all style and no substance (2). Sobchack is likewise suspicious of the critical potential of neo-violence: "[the] heightened sense of reflexivity and irony that emerges from quantities of violence, from 'more,' is not necessarily progressive nor does it lead to a 'moral' agenda or a critique of violence" ("Violent Dance" 121). All of these reservations, however, seem like a dead end. Fortunately, film violence does not lead to any "agenda" (the idea would presuppose a message-oriented and hence reductive view of film fiction), and there is furthermore no need for a critique of violence since there would be few objectors to the claim that violence is an inherently intolerable phenomenon in and of itself. What is needed is a critique of the formal conventions that configure images of violence and of the modes of consciousness for which violent action serves as a trope. The strategies of hypermodern cinema are not antithetical to processes of ethical semiosis; on the contrary, aesthetic form cannot help signifying ethically. It is not as surprising as it may seem, therefore, that Botting and Wilson choose to call their book on Tarantino's cinema *The Tarantinian Ethics* (2001), thus displaying an awareness of the centrality of an ethics of form for the comprehension of film violence.

Like THE WILD BUNCH, RESERVOIR DOGS invests its violence with a tropological inference which, more specifically, involves masculinity and its relation to questions of identity, trust, and death. Images of violence, as it were, project fictitious constellations of manhood by placing the protagonists in circumstances that are extreme. The narrative of RESERVOIR DOGS comes close to suggesting that violence is constitutive not only of the expression of ethical experience but also of the enactment of masculinity. A key paradox in Tarantino's film is the unmasking, or de(con)struction, of the masculine through acts of playful performativity. Acting or pretending comes to replace being as an existential foundation, thus obliterating the conditions for the achievement of a coherent, homogeneous identity. When Clint Burnham interprets Harvey Keitel's "wondrous, polyvalent, unmated moan" at the film's conclusion as the symbolization of a "lack" in the masculine self (116), his observation could gainfully be seen in connection with the complexities of manufacturing subjectivity solely from the ephemerality of performance.[19] The incarnation of the film's proclivity for the rhetoric of pretending is British actor Tim Roth, who plays an American detective who plays one of the crooks. His policeman persona's "commode" story, a

carefully rehearsed anecdote that he has been instructed by his boss to tell Cabot's men to cement his own credibility as a criminal, is the prime example of
the significance of performance in the movie.[20] Seamlessly merging storytelling
and acting, the syntactically meticulous flashback structure of the sequence
shows Roth preparing his story in various surroundings; on a rooftop, in his
apartment, in front of a graffiti wall, in a bar with Cabot, Eddie and Mr. White,
and even in the men's room (in a flashback within a flashback). "You gotta be as
naturalistic as hell," Roth's mentor explains as he eggs him on to perfect his act.
In a later segment which footnotes Robert de Niro's crazed mirror scene from
TAXI DRIVER, Roth speaks to his reflection and compares himself to Baretta.[21]
The architecture of performativity is foregrounded in other scenes as well, as
for instance, when Mr. Blonde and Eddie pretend to fight in Cabot's office, and
when Mr. Blonde tortures the policeman, perhaps the single most cited moment
of violence in all of the 1990s American cinema.

The sense of a fractured subjectivity and of the absence of a holistic male
identity appears to be essential to the ways in which Tarantino's narration
brings together violence and ethics. According to John Fried, violence in RESER-
VOIR DOGS signifies "the fear associated with the revelation that masculinity is
all artifice, sans substance" (6), an assertion that could easily have provided the
epithet for all the films that this study examines. In the moment of confession
and death, all that the Roth character is able to reveal about himself is the scope
of his charade, the hemorrhage as the only substance of his maleness. The transtextual and exceedingly amimetic form of RESERVOIR DOGS is particularly ger-
mane to the notion of masculinity as a composite, amorphous, untotalizable, or
even blank construct:

> Character, in Tarantino, is not produced as an effect of a representation being judged
> 'true to life,' as if the life of characters existed outside representation. Rather, character
> is the effect of a representation being 'true to itself' in relation to other representa-
> tions. Which is to say that it is true to itself as a representation through the citation,
> adoption and deployment of other representations in a distinctive or singular way.…
> For Tarantino … character has little to do with cinematic representation of 'novelistic'
> characters, even if it has everything to do with 'writing' in an expanded sense (Bot-
> ting and Wilson 13).[22]

Contrary to what its detractors maintain, the hypermodern film aesthetic of un-
constrained quotationality does in fact capture a significance beyond itself; the
eclecticism of a film poetics based on referentiality is reflective of the idea that
masculine identity is nothing but a construction culled from the multiple fictions that the cultural imagination has narrated. The relative coherence of the
identity of the male hero in classical cinema has in the hypermodern era given

way to a drastic decentering where character has become a matter of "disjointed signs," to borrow Burnham's description of the Keitel persona (122).

Masculinity in RESERVOIR DOGS is also interlaced with an ethics of trust reminiscent of that which regulates the relationship between the men in THE WILD BUNCH. Irwin has identified the "criminal code of honor and professionalism" as the most prominent subtext in the film (76). Similarly, Botting and Wilson stress the ways in which "the ethics of professionalism" provide the bedrock for the film's meditation on masculine morality. Throughout the narrative the characters of Mr. White and Mr. Pink repeatedly lament what they perceive as an inexplicable betrayal of this ethics: "What you're supposed to do is act like a fuckin' professional," Mr. White intones while looking at himself in a mirror, an imploration Mr. Pink reproduces immediately before the final shootout. Keitel's character, however, in fact confuses the principles of professionalism with those of ethics, as Botting and Wilson also appear to do in their argument. Drawing on the work of Emmanuel Levinas, they maintain that "[e]thics precedes ontology and the moral law which is associated with symbolic regulation and desire" (48). While ethics is defined by individual responsibility and "care for other persons" (Botting and Wilson 50), morality implies principles and acts of institutional intentionality. Hence, according to this philosophy, morality is secondary to ethics. When Mr. Pink accuses Mr. White of compromising his professionalism by revealing his real name to the dying Mr. Orange, the conflict between individual commitment and moral code becomes palpable as the conflict between ethics and professionalism.

In Botting and Wilson's view, Mr. White "invests personally," as opposed to professionally, in Mr. Orange's agony, and the reason that enables him to do this is his recognition of Mr. Orange as the other in Levinas's sense; "the neighbour and double, that one loves as oneself" (64). For Botting and Wilson, Mr. White's decision that the wounded Mr. Orange is his personal responsibility occasions an ethical moment in the film (64), and the inevitable outcome of this act is violence: when at the end of the film Mr. White is forced to relinquish his trust in either Mr. Orange or his old friends, he chooses to pursue his ethical commitment to the other even if it entails self-destruction. Not unlike the Agua Verde scene in THE WILD BUNCH, the violence which erupts at the conclusion of RESERVOIR DOGS derives directly from the embrace of an irreversibly ethical stance. The scene thus epitomizes the notion of *an ethics of violence*. Aesthetic violence, as Botting and Wilson express it, "becomes ethical if it opens a gap within representation which questions the complicity of desire and law" (70).

On a certain level, then, the main dynamic that energizes the ethical world of the characters in RESERVOIR DOGS is that between suspicion and trust, professionalism and responsibility.

When Botting and Wilson submit that it is the omnipotence of pop culture allusionism which permits intersubjectivity in the film (46), they neglect to take into account the constant re-negotiations of this dialectic. Much of the dialogue in the warehouse scenes centers on issues of betrayal, culpability and distrust as the characters increasingly become involved in forming hypotheses regarding the identity of the informer among them. Tarantino cinematizes the transactions of trust, doubt and fear which take place among the various members of the group according to the logistics of ethical space. I adopt this concept from Roger Poole's *Towards Deep Subjectivity* (1972). Sobchack's interpretation of the term – "the visible representation or sign of the viewer's subjective, lived, and moral relationship with the viewed" ("Inscribing" 292) – may with a slight alteration prove feasible for a renewed appreciation of the inter-dependence of aesthetic form and ethics in a film like Tarantino's. There is, in addition to the viewer's perspective, a spatio-narrative perspective which establishes a relation with that which is put on view. As Branigan has pointed out, it is the look that is "the activating instance or cause" of the image displayed on the screen (*Point of View* 57).[23] For Sobchack, moreover, the act of looking has ethical ramifications in itself in that "[t]he visible representation of vision inscribes sight as a moral insight" ("Inscribing" 291). In Reservoir Dogs, this process finds perhaps its most explicit expression in the exchanges between Mr. Blonde and the policeman and in Mr. Orange's witnessing of Mr. Blonde's cruelties against his victim.

When Mr. Orange interrupts the abuse by shooting the perpetrator, one may comprehend his action as the logical extension of his gaining of moral insight; his act of looking at the mistreatment of the cop – his spatial sightline – becomes an ethical way of seeing. In recognizing the suffering of the other, Mr. Orange, unlike Mr. Blonde, also recognizes the subjectivity of the other.

Reservoir Dogs is a film in which the notion of ethical space is more than a mere catchphrase; it materializes in the spatial coordinates of the image itself. First, as Thomas Beltzer has argued, the warehouse setting indicates "an unreal, timeless environment" of "mutual alienation and isolation" (par. 3), where characters seemingly behave in accordance with Garcin's misanthropic assumption at the end of Sartre's *No Exit* (47). The space of action is neither literal nor figurative but an embodiment of ethical situationality. In a series of images that have since become iconographic – Mr. White and Mr. Pink pointing their guns at each other; the triangular configuration at the end in which Mr. White, Eddie and Joe aim their weapons at each other in a closed circuit; and the dying Mr. White heaving himself onto Mr. Orange – violent encounters encode a set of ethical values as spatial inscriptions. The way in which the mise en scène organizes the space between the characters reveals relational patterns of power, (dis)trust, and intimacy; in the film's last scene the inter-personal space collapses as Mr. White crawls on top of Mr. Orange, their wounded bodies blending into one corporeal unity. When Mr. Orange discloses his true identity, the ethics of allegiance which the recognition of the subjectivity of the other prompts gives way to senseless revenge, the seamless transition of which Sharrett has described as a merging of "eros with thanatos" ("Peckinpah" 87). It may be a temptation to read these images as a flaunting of homoerotic desire, which Jacobs does by rhetorically asking, "Would Mr. White ... tenderly comb Mr. Orange's hair ... in RESERVOIR DOGS if Orange wasn't bleeding to death?" (39).

Jacobs's implication, evidently, is that violence enables the kind of male intimacy that this imagery exhibits. Being within death's proximity legitimates acts of erotically charged contact that would have been unthinkable in virtually any other context. It is a mistake, however, to imply the existence of a sexual subtext in this sequence. Like Robert Alan Brookey and Robert Westerfelhaus in their predominantly gay reading of FIGHT CLUB (29), Jacobs seems all too prepared to superimpose an aesthetics of homoeroticism whenever images of physical interaction between men is highlighted. Keitel and Roth's embrace is affectionate but not erotic, their bodily exchange a cinematic figuration of a common consciousness of the process of dying. But even in this most private moment in the film, Tarantino cannot refrain from quotation: though the most transparent allusion is to the films of John Woo, the director also invokes the scene in Peckinpah's *Ride the High Country* in which Gil Westrum caresses his dying friend Steve Judd's bleeding abdomen, as well as the image in THE WILD BUNCH where Bishop and Engstrom cling to each other before they die.

The second crucial instance in RESERVOIR DOGS that demarcates filmic spatiality as an ethical relation is the one in which Mr. Blonde severs the policeman's ear and tries to incinerate him. It may appear inconceivable that this scene has anything to do with ethics, but in spite of its spectacular inhumanity, the situation contains an unfulfilled ethical potentiality. Immobile and helpless, the cop is in a state of absolute vulnerability and dependence, and his only hope is that Mr. Blonde eventually discerns the nature of the ethical relation between them and identifies him as the other of himself. What defines this sequence as an extreme moment in the narrative is the immensity of the demands placed upon both of the protagonists. Marvin, the policeman, has little choice but to trust his tormentor's capacity for discontinuing the torture; Mr. Blonde is in a position which requires him to make the right ethical decision. But the gangster Marvin is reduced to being just a part of his self-conscious performance, like a found object around which Mr. Blonde's horror show is orchestrated. The arrangement of film space in the scene concretizes the perpetrator's failure to recognize the intersubjective space which connects him ethically to his victim. Chopping off the cop's ear and gagging him, Mr. Blonde symbolically conveys his dehumanization of his victim and his own lack of desire to interact. The rejection of Marvin's only request – "just talk to me" – pinpoints the essence of Mr. Blonde's dementia, his inability to respond ethically to the existence of other subjectivities. Referencing Alex's "Singing in the Rain" in A CLOCKWORK ORANGE, Mr. Blonde's iniquitous dance movements as he prepares to pour gasoline on the cop enact a choreography of cruelty and complete ethical indifference.

The ethical space in RESERVOIR DOGS is a fluid entity that easily reconstructs itself according to the fluctuating intentions of the narration. When Mr. Blonde amputates Marvin's ear, for instance, the camera pans leftward to linger on an empty section of the warehouse while the victim's wailing continues on the soundtrack. The act of looking away denies the spectator the kind of illicit punctuation which makes the razor blade scene in UN CHIEN ANDALOU and the slicing of the nostril in CHINATOWN (Roman Polanski 1974), so disconcerting to watch. Throughout the film, Tarantino's narration tends to emphasize the postures of the body in the aftermath of violence rather than the exact moment of violent infliction, as in Peckinpah. Tarantino's interest is in the interplay between wounded and dying men; the glances, silences, and short verbal exchanges – as in Mr. Orange's and Marvin's tentative communication – which define the being-within-violence as an intersubjective experience.

In terms of the notion of narrative mortification, RESERVOIR DOGS pushes the limits of the cinematic visualization of dying beyond any previous efforts. The process of death has already begun when the narrative proper is introduced and, centering on the character of Mr. Orange, the remainder of the film charts the trajectory along which the animate body slowly turns into a corpse. Death, according to Levinas, "marks the end of the subject's virility and heroism" ("Time and the Other" 41), and it is the repercussions of this admission that the film struggles to enunciate. By cutting from the slow-motion montage which establishes the cool and seemingly indestructible masculinity of the villains to the image of the injured Mr. Orange imploring Mr. White to hold him, Tarantino draws attention to the masculine self's loss of nobility in dying by violence. How the consciousness of violent film death has been altered from the classical to the hypermodern period may be revealed by the fact that dying in SCARFACE and THE KILLING takes only a fraction of a second, whereas in RESERVOIR DOGS it takes almost the entire narrative.

7 One-Dimensional Men: Fincher's FIGHT CLUB and the End of Masculinity

*As if the only choice they have left is how they're going to die
and they want to die in a fight.*
Chuck Palahniuk

One of the most memorable performances of masculine bravado in classical Hollywood cinema takes place in Ford's "Irish" epic THE QUIET MAN (1952), in which the character of Sean Thornton (John Wayne) instigates a mock fistfight with his brother-in-law Will Danaher (Victor McLaglen). As the two men pummel each other around haystacks, streams, and hillsides, even stopping for a pint at a nearby pub, they seem to respect what I believe is the seventh rule of FIGHT CLUB: "fights will go on as long as they have to." Conceptually as well as rhetorically, this particular sequence from Ford's movie comes across in retrospect as a narrative blueprint for the masochistic spectacle of excessive corporeality which constitutes the centerpiece of Fincher's visceral tour de force. Though Gavin Smith has proclaimed it "the first film of the next century" ("Inside Out" 58), FIGHT CLUB may also be appreciated as the logical culmination and synopsis of a century-long discourse in American arts and letters on the meaning and substance of violence and masculinity. The notion of split subjectivities which undergirds Fincher's narration exteriorizes the schizophrenia afflicting the male protagonist of countless Hollywood fictions. FIGHT CLUB lays bare the identificational rift that has remained implicit or unpresentable in preceding exhibitions of violent masculinity. From Camonte to Mr. White, the characters' perspective has tended to be that of FIGHT CLUB's Durden; and Fincher's film renders explicit the constructedness of this fantasy. One of the reasons that makes FIGHT CLUB such a landmark event in the cinema of violence is that it represents the acme of a tradition in which the awareness of the artificiality and performativity of this violent Other has emerged only slowly and tentatively.

In the introduction to this book, I propose that a film narrative may rewardingly be construed as a form of theory in its own right, as a form of reflection akin to what Bogue, with reference to Deleuze, has called a "non-representational semiotics of cinema" (77). If the film itself is a way of thinking, textual analysis in the conventionally hermeneutic sense of the term is no longer necessarily the only way of approaching the text. Throughout my readings of the selected films I have attempted to elicit their constitutive theoretical assumptions and to continue their act of theorizing within discursive parameters that, perhaps unfeasibly, are both constrained by and excede the films themselves. In view of such a methodological operation, the idea of *film theory* demands that viewers place themselves into a critical position which generates intra-filmic reflection: by films theorizing other films. By devoting the last chapter to a re-appraisal of FIGHT CLUB, I will examine this film in light of the recurring preoccupations that inform the crux of my study: the narration of masculinities, violence, and death.

As both a practice and a sign, violence in FIGHT CLUB is poised between being and nothingness. "You just had a near-life experience," Tyler Durden tells Jack after he has poured an acid solution on the latter's wrist, thus implying a conflation of the particular mode of pain and the general mode of existence. Unwittingly, the Durden persona subsidizes an ethical philosophy that in some respects is indebted to Levinas's postulation that suffering implies "the impossibility of nothingness" because to feel pain means to be "directly exposed to being" ("Time and the Other" 40). For the characters in Fincher's film, the experience of agency and autonomy begins with the deliberate submission to acts of physical injury. What distinguishes FIGHT CLUB from other violent movies, and what makes it so supremely equipped to function meta-discursively vis-à-vis its tradition, is the film's abandonment of any narrative pretexts save that of violence itself. In Hawks, Kubrick, Penn, Peckinpah, and even Tarantino the use of violence seems unavoidable yet accidental; that is, the characters of these earlier narratives become enmeshed in the vortex of violence while pursuing other ends and activities. The principal attachment of Fincher's heroes, on the other hand, is to the teleology of the fight.

Even more brazenly so than THE WILD BUNCH, FIGHT CLUB is a thesis-driven narrative whose mindset is focalized through the narrator's and Durden's polemical commentary, much of which is fashioned as aphoristic statements concerning the putative marginalization of Masculinity in hypermodern society. Dubbed "ersatz-Nietzschean" by Gavin Smith ("Inside Out" 58), Durden's puerile rhetoric is ambiguously lodged between sincerity and parody:

> I see in fight club the strongest and smartest men who've ever lived. I see all this potential, and I see squandering. God damn it, an entire generation pumping gas, waiting tables; slaves with white collars. Advertising has us chasing cars and clothes, working jobs we hate so we can buy shit we don't need. We're the middle children of history, man. No purpose or place. We have no great war. No Great Depression. Our Great War's a spiritual war ... our great Depression is our lives.

You're not your job. You're not how much money you have in the bank. You're not the car you drive. You're not the contents of your wallet. You're not your fucking khakis. You're the all-singing, all-dancing crap of the world.

We're designed to be hunters and we're in a society of shopping. There's nothing to kill anymore, there's nothing to fight, nothing to overcome, nothing to explore. In that social emasculation this everyman is created.

Self-improvement is masturbation. Now self-destruction, that may be the answer.

Giroux's stigmatization of the film as "reactionary" is not altogether unprecedented in light of Durden's unabashed indictment of what he perceives to be the feminization of culture ("Private Satisfactions" 7),[1] but Giroux overlooks the extent to which Fincher satirizes what Smith sees as "the absurd excesses of the men's movement" ("Inside Out" 58). FIGHT CLUB is no less a travesty than for instance A CLOCKWORK ORANGE, and it would be a mistake to take the narrator's axioms at face value. Though the film is certainly *about* those maxims, one should be careful not to confuse the values of the protagonists with the politics of the film itself. In my own reading of FIGHT CLUB, I shall contextualize its ideological purchase with reference to the artistic tradition from which it emerges and furthermore argue that Fincher, in attempting to denaturalize the notion of an essential, masculine subjectivity originating in the masochistic body, inadvertently projects a critique of the cinematic proclivity for assigning a liberating potential to acts of violence.

The crucial conflict which FIGHT CLUB dramatizes is the repossession of masculinity as a rejection of the world, a negation the site of which is the body and its capacity for violence. What I would first like to draw attention to is the unanticipated conjunction in Fincher's film of two distinct but complexly interrelated historical tendencies in American fiction and film: the enduring tradition of dissent and the late-20th-century development that Annesley in his book of the same name has termed *blank fiction*. Characterized by what Munby refers to as the "continuity of discontinuity" (223), the first phenomenon signifies an artistic impetus of ideological dissonance that in some ways intersects both with Fiedler's notion of tragic humanism and with the project of re-masculinization that we have seen Tompkins and Peter French claim dominates the western. Suzanne Clark has proposed that if a film like FIGHT CLUB "reasserts a masculine identity threatened by the feminization of American culture, then it reiterates a theme more than a hundred years old" (413). Violence has provided the foremost means of expression and the most salient metaphor for the tradition of discontinuity. Paradoxically, the male body prior to Peckinpah was at least quite intact within this aesthetic. This is arguably in no small measure due to the influence of literature and art on film. As Fraser has noted, the body "has been suspect much of the time in American literature" (69), a circumspection that has contaminated Hollywood's staging of the body not only with regard to sexuality but to the wider domain of the textual regulation of the corporeal. For Shaviro, this fear of the material continues unabated in postmodern western culture which is anxious to "keep thought separate from the exigencies of the flesh" (127). However, the advent of blank fiction heralded what appeared to be a genuine breach with the tradition of portraying the body euphemistically. In the novels, imagery, and music of some contemporary American artists, Annesley holds, there is a peculiar obsession with sex, death, and brutality ("Commodification" 143). The literature of writers such as Jay McInerney, Dennis Cooper, Donna Tarrt, Tama Janowitz, and Brian D'Amato glides toward "the extreme, the marginal and the violent" where "[the] limits of the human body seem indistinct, blurred by cosmetics, narcotics, disease and brutality" (*Blank Fictions* 1).[2] FIGHT CLUB could easily be seen as the pinnacle of what one might define as the Ellis-Tarantino syndrome in American culture, as Fincher's work affords perhaps the first sustained and commercially successful attempt at situating this fiction of aberration within an explicit philosophical framework. In some ways, FIGHT CLUB represents a microcosm of the major concerns that have invigorated the tradition of dissent as well as that of the 1990s blank fiction.

A discussion of FIGHT CLUB can scarcely avoid the subject of modernity. Like THE WILD BUNCH before it, Fincher's narrative is a vehement indictment of what Gavin Smith describes as "the inauthenticity and mediocrity of modern life" ("Inside Out" 60). The sheer pretension and scope of such a critique are however propitiously modulated by the film's self-parodying slant, by its mockery of conventional anti-materialist alternatives (anarchy and situationism for instance), and by its obdurate insistence on violence and the body as the only available venues for authentic experience. In FIGHT CLUB, masculinity itself is a crisis scene, society "an urban nightmare labyrinth disrupted by the seething, denatured and corralled male ego it was built to control" (Whitehouse 46). The beginning of the film effectively captures the depth of this crisis in the image of the narrator with a gun in his mouth, and the timeline of the story proper extends from this sequence to the moment when the gun goes off. In the meantime Jack's unnervingly unaffected narration revisits in a "dissociative" mode the past events that have culminated in the present emergency (Smith "Inside Out" 60). Emblematized by Jack's insomnia, the narration of FIGHT CLUB – not unlike that of RESERVOIR DOGS – opens with a perception of liminality, of being exposed to the existential interval between agency and mortality.

In simultaneously reveling in and parodying the nexus of masculinity and violence, FIGHT CLUB seems to propose a radical decentering of the identity politics of the male hero, perhaps to the extent of admitting that masculinity is not only a construct but in fact an empty signifier. When even the last possibility for regaining a sense of durable manhood – bodily violence – ultimately falls short, it is tempting to read Jack's execution of his alter ego at the end of the film as the completion of a long process of symbolic divestiture. Evacuated of the violence which brings coherence to Jack's tenuous gender identity, the narrative ends on an ambiguously apocalyptic note where the foreclosure of masculinity-as-violence is accompanied by images of collapsing skyscrapers. This conclusion is richly polyvalent, overlaid as it is by a string of disparate connotations; the demolition of the buildings suggests both an immobilization of the phallic and a return to Durden's vision of a prehistoric civilization of men "stalking elk through the damp canyon forests around the ruins of Rockefeller Center."[3] Fincher evokes and blends two distinct conceptions of the masculine in this sequence: the dysfunctional and corporate modern male, and the primeval figure of the warrior that Gibson in his *Warrior Dreams* (1994) claims is increasingly populating the unofficial regions of American culture. The Durden character and the fight club phenomenon seem to emulate part of the ideology of resignation which spawned the growth of the warrior culture throughout the 1980s and 1990s. Gibson argues that the death of the regeneration myth in Vietnam resulted in a "crisis of self-image" (10), the rehabilitation of which was made possible by embracing the warrior myth from ancient times and from the nation's frontier past. The dream of the warrior, Gibson writes, represents "a flight from the present," inaugurating a new masculinist and paramilitary culture in which "[t]he whole modern world was damned as unacceptable" (12). While Peckinpah's arraignment of modernity and corporatism has its sources elsewhere, Gibson's notion of a warrior culture has already found expression in the cinema with Scorsese's Taxi Driver, whose main protagonist, Travis Bickle, may be seen as a harbinger of the frustrated male collective that frequents Durden's fight clubs. "The imaginary New War that men created," Gibson holds, "is a coherent mythical universe, formed by the repetition of key features in thousands of novels, magazines, films, and advertisements" (13). Particular to this new warrior culture is the sense in which violence and death no longer relate to a general cause but acquire meaning in and of themselves. According to Giroux, this is also the thesis that informs Fight Club: "violence is the ultimate language, referent, and state of affairs through which to understand all human events, and there is no way of stopping it" ("Private Satisfactions" 18).

A study of the ethics of Fight Club risks immersion in an analytical loop in which a problematization of the film's violence leads to a consideration of the structuring of masculinity and vice versa. Most of the existing criticism on the movie has predictably though pertinently addressed the question of Fincher's gestation of the masculine.[4] I have adumbrated Fight Club's textual lineage above, though it must be added that the film's rhetorical economy also resonates compellingly with that of a number of roughly contemporaneous texts that all in various ways converge on the subject of masculine malaise. What I have in mind, more specifically, are both critical works such as Robert Bly's *Iron John* (1990), Sam Keen's *Fire in the Belly: On Being a Man* (1991), and Susan Faludi's *Stiffed* (1999), novels like Ellis's *American Psycho*, and films like Neil LaBute's *In the Company of Men* (1997), Todd Solondz's *Happiness*, and Sam Mendes's *American Beauty*. A unifying diagnosis in relation to these texts is that of "social emasculation," a concept Durden himself explicitly invokes at one point in Fight Club.[5] The unremitting vulnerability of the male self-image that these writers and filmmakers thematize, however, possesses a critical urgency because it necessarily has to dispense with the notions of coherence, constancy and closure in the mediation of gender identities. Robert Paulson and Jack's awkwardly affirmative dialogue as they first meet at the support group for men with testicular cancer – "We're still men. Yes, we're men. Men is what we are" – is ironically suggestive of the insubstantiality of the masculine. Contemporary manhood, Sally Robinson has argued, is hysterical, and the male body is "the canvas on which repressed trauma is written" (136).[6]

If masculinity, as among others, David Gilmore (11), Judith Butler ("Melancholy Gender" 32), and Giroux ("Private Satisfactions" 19) seem to imply,[7] is ultimately a performance rather than an immanent psychic structure, it follows that any analysis of this performance as it manifests itself in popular texts must historicize rather than universalize the narration of men in crisis. Michael Kimmel and Savran have both duly emphasized the degree to which particular subjectivities and positionalities are entrenched in historical circumstances that may explain but certainly cannot justify the emergence of destructive masculinities. It is "historical and social changes," Kimmel writes, that "create the conditions for gender crisis" (123). A historically aware contextualization of Fight Club, for instance, would reveal that the Durden character's confused grievance in the bathtub scene ("We're a generation of men raised by women. I doubt if another woman is what we really need") is merely a reiteration of the antifeminist sentiment that was one of the central responses to the late-19th-century crisis in masculinity. The remasculinization of the American male around the beginning of the 20th century, epitomized by deeply symbolic cultural phenomena such as Roosevelt's "rough rider" persona and the founding of the Boy Scouts of America in 1910, was according to Kimmel a reaction against a late-19th-century development in which the socialization and education of children increasingly became the responsibility of women (141). Savran, likewise, underscores the historical underpinnings of the late-20th-century masculine discontent by correlating it with the Mailerian concept of the "white negro." The contemporary "male moral masochist," Savran holds, is an outgrowth of the "marginalized and dissident masculinity of the 1950s" that in the post-Vietnam era has become the prevailing male figure in American culture (5). The Norton character in FIGHT CLUB is evidently a forceful embodiment of this despondent everyman.

The crisis of masculinity which Faludi analyzes on a general level and Giroux with reference to FIGHT CLUB appears as an exhaustion of feeling, or what Hanson terms a "spiritual sadness" (15), producing dysfunctional men for whom the strategies of apathy apparently have become the only seduction. "Which is worse," the narrator of Chuck Palahniuk's novel asks, "hell or nothing?" (141). In both its literary and filmic renditions, FIGHT CLUB identifies the logic of consumerism and its persistent colonization of subjectivity as the root causes of this gendered malaise: Jack's disaffected life, as Giroux sees it, is reduced to being "an extension of a reified and commodified culture" ("Private Satisfactions" 8).[8] The argument of Fincher's movie collapses, however, when it interprets Jack's crisis – his existential desolation and disenfranchisement – as the effect of the disappearance of the conventionally masculine in the post-industrial era. Hence, the target of the film's cultural critique, Giroux is led to believe, is not only an expanding commodification but also that of domestication and feminization ("Private Satisfactions" 15). In his caustic but poignant evaluation, Giroux indicts Fincher's narrative for conflating the processes of consumerism and emasculation: "If Jack represents the crisis of capitalism repackaged as the crisis of a domesticated masculinity, Durden represents the redemption of masculinity repackaged as the promise of violence in the interests of social and political anarchy" ("Private Satisfactions" 13). It is worth noting that Giroux's analysis, incidentally, aligns FIGHT CLUB's rhetoric with that of Christopher Lasch in his *The Culture of Narcissism* (1979). Ostensibly like Fincher, Lasch holds the feminization of masculinity and the culture of commodification accountable for what he sees as a degeneration of manhood in the wake of the counterculture. Against this image of the narcissistic, emasculated male he pits that of the "rugged individualist" (38), a cultural opposition that finds a parallel in FIGHT CLUB. What Giroux's criticism fatally neglects to take into account, however, as I have previously suggested, is the extent to which Fincher parodies not only the socially emasculated everyman enslaved by his "nesting instinct" but also the bruised and bloodied – in other words remasculinized – members of Jack's Fight Clubs. This is the privilege but also the limitation of the thoroughly transtextualized, hypermodern film: that its unbounded meta-consciousness – its playful awareness of cultural and cinematic history – cannot help but focalize its discursive import through a detached and ironic lens.[9] Drawing upon an almost unparalleled arsenal of visual effects (i.e., underexposure, resilvering, grainy footage, fluorescent coloration, flash frames), FIGHT CLUB creates what Gavin Smith sees as "a mocking sense of flux and liminality in its attitudes and values both formally and conceptually" ("Inside Out" 60). In its very form, then, the movie parodies and ridicules with equal force a range of targets, from the fetishistic quotationism of a Tarantino to the revamped machismo of the fight clubs, the culture of sensitivity, self-improvement and quasi-spirituality, and perhaps even the academic fondness for the concepts that Smith mentions above. FIGHT CLUB, like RESERVOIR DOGS, is thus a frivolous yet profound text, one that entails a (possibly new) mode of viewing that is susceptible to the semiotic complexities of film form rather than to the facile conclusions of first impressions which arise as a consequence of an inability to see film as a non-transparent entity.

More specifically, in order to be able to discern the impenetrability of aesthetic form the viewer must be attuned to the tropological aspects of a film's significational flow, and in this regard I would like to call attention to a key segment in FIGHT CLUB, which much of the criticism of the film inexplicably seems to have glossed over. During one of the support group meetings that Jack compulsively attends at the start of the narrative, the participants are asked by their group leader to venture into their "caves" to find their "power animal."

Next, in a subjective shot, Jack encounters his own power animal, which turns out to be a cheerful penguin whose cryptic message to Jack is to let it "slide". Moreover, when Jack re-enters his cave later in the film, it is the chain-smoking Marla Singer, repeating the penguin's advice, who incarnates his power animal. These two scenes, while flagrantly mocking the new age, pop enlightenment gibberish of the group leader, present incisive tropes for the kind of masculinity that observers like Lasch and Savran claim has become hegemonic in late-20th-century American culture.

In his meditative moment, Jack deploys what Peter Middleton, in his book of the same name, has termed "the inward gaze,"[10] an only moderately successful act of self-examination on the part of the puzzled male subject. Reflexivity, Middleton asserts, "works imperfectly for men because they don't see what they are seeing when they see themselves" (11). Jack sees a penguin, a benevolent but ludicrous being that becomes an urgently appropriate image for the masculine predicament in FIGHT CLUB. The animal's connotational values starkly negate the dream of empowerment and agency that Jack desires, and, at the same time, the figure of the penguin also serves as a mirror of Jack's entrapment. The penguin, a bird incapable of flight, provides an especially resonant symbol of the processes of environmental dislocation and costly adaptability.

By connecting the penguin narratively and conceptually with the seductive, feline Marla, Fincher comes close to suggesting that it is the feminine sphere that is responsible for re-fashioning millennial masculinity in the guise of a penguin. This reading ostensibly corroborates Giroux's incendiary assertion that the film erroneously blames the politics of domestication for the current gender crisis which the narrative plays out ("Private Satisfactions" 19). But the fantasy sequence featuring the penguin is fraught with internal ambivalences, for it presents Jack's power animal as a creature at once enchained by civilized servility (the "tuxedo") and drawn toward anarchic imprudence (the slide). Its brief message could doubtlessly be construed as a rebellious entreaty to escape the white-collar inertia of Jack's Ikea reality, though it could also be taken as an untimely reaffirmation of his lack of agency or self-determination. As a distinctively cinematic trope, finally, the function of the image of the penguin lies beyond the conjecture of conventional interpretation. The film trope, as Stern has pointed out, does not "represent" something else, but is sufficient onto itself as "a form of process, of cinematic energy" (266).

In what remains of my reading of FIGHT CLUB, I shall turn to explore in more detail issues such as the correlation between violent embodiment/masochism and subjectivity, Fincher's use of violence as a master trope, and what Annesley refers to as "the complex relationships that have developed between commodification, violence and the body" ("Commodification" 150). As Paul Smith rightfully points out, film theory has historically paid short shrift to the plurality of male subjectivity in the cinema, choosing instead to sponsor a "monolithic view" of masculinity (88). This uniform emphasis, as far as the study of heterosexual male protagonists is concerned,[11] has typically yielded criticism of depictions of various kinds of machismo.[12] Giroux's conceptualization of FIGHT CLUB as a "celebration of hyper-masculinity and violence" is a case in point ("Private Satisfactions" 15). Calling for a more complexly heterogeneous understanding of masculine film subjectivities, Smith cites the work of Bersani, Silverman, and Studlar as a fountainhead of gender research capable of unraveling the monolithic views of well established film-theoretical discourse on the image of the male.

Tropes of masculinity and violence accrete meanings by way of their "narrative disposition" (Smith 80), which is to say that analyses of aesthetic violence must not only tolerate but, in fact, take advantage of the interpretive spaces of what could be conceived as a liquid contextuality. There is a different rhetorical economy at work in the scene in THE QUIET MAN where Sean Thornton and Will Danaher beat each other senseless than in the fight sequences in Fincher. External similarities notwithstanding, the specificity of the formal and semiotic process of troping the violence in FIGHT CLUB imbues it with a morality which diverges significantly from that of Ford's movie. While the fight scene in THE QUIET MAN is to some extent good-humored, even whimsical at times, those in FIGHT CLUB have a persistent intensity to them, which announces a disconcerting inseparability of pain and pleasure unknown to Ford. The statement that Giroux assigns to FIGHT CLUB, "[m]ale violence offers men a performative basis on which to construct masculine identity" ("Private Satisfactions" 19), paraphrases the tropological value of Thornton and Danaher's fist fight. Violence in

THE QUIET MAN is affirmative of the stability of a certain masculine identity, whereas the violence in FIGHT CLUB attempts to do away with it. Masculinity in the latter film, therefore, is more closely related to Huston's presentation of the destitute male in a film like FAT CITY (and in turn to film noir) than to the histrionics of Ford's macho posturing.[13]

How and to what end, one may ask next, does Fincher employ the trope of violence in his narrative? To begin with, FIGHT CLUB dismantles what Paul Smith identifies as "the orthodox structuring code" inherent in Hollywood's dissemination of images of hegemonic masculinity (83). In an article on the semiotics of the Eastwood persona, Smith shows that this code hinges on the application of a "masochistic trope" (88), by which the male body is routinely subjected to a process of eroticization, destruction, and regeneration. Needless to say, this corresponds with the overall narrative structure of scores of western and action movies.[14] Just as manhood is something that the subject can only attain by becoming a warrior (Donald 127), lasting masculinity may likewise only be guaranteed through acts of intermittent testing by violence. The narrative dynamic of the action genres derives largely from this "demonstration of masculine destructibility and recuperability" (Smith 81). However, the masochistic trope appropriates the violated body in a way that is devoid of any critical significance, since the temporary alterations of the body through acts of brutalization are not complemented by analogous transformations in the realm of consciousness or sensibility. The body of the hero of the quintessential action movie is damaged only to confirm and preserve the dominant, one-sided masculinity inhabiting the psychology of the film's narrative origin. Such violence is fundamentally conservative; no real modification of subjectivity occurs. Anne Jerslev has fruitfully juxtaposed the organization of the body in the action and horror genres, concluding that while the body in the action film remains "solid," the horror genre displays a body "constantly in the act of becoming, without borders or outlines, constantly transforming into another" (42). This corporeal transmutability provides an important condition for the critical, and as we shall later see even philosophical, potential of film violence. Though it has been all too rarely seen in non-generic films, the troping of the body according to the rationality of transformation suffuses the narration of FIGHT CLUB.

When Giroux, in his scathing assessment of FIGHT CLUB, broaches the subject of the corporeal, it seems that he makes an observation that is partly valid while nevertheless drawing the wrong conclusion: "Given Fincher's suggestion that men have no enduring qualities outside of their physicality, resistance and affirmation are primarily taken up as part of a politics of embodiment that has little concern for critical consciousness, social critique, or democratic social relations" ("Private Satisfactions" 15). The point that Giroux misses is that acts of (re)embodiment and critical consciousness form an entity that is indissoluble. FIGHT

CLUB, as Gavin Smith has stated, is a movie about thought ("Inside Out" 62), which the film's opening shot – disclosing the interior of Jack's brain – does little to discount.[15] In one fervid, unbroken take, Fincher's elastic cinematography undoes the spatio-temporal interval that isolates the brain from the body and the gun, thus interconnecting thought, corporeality and violence in a closed circuit.

As an art form (rather than as a technology), cinema is constantly preoccupied with the phenomenology of the body, with investing it with a significance as permeable as its own celluloid tissue.[16] However evanescent and abstract the cinematic image, corporeality remains the essence of the mise en scène. Unlike literature, for instance, the constitutive fiction of filmicity is the fiction of the body. Its gestures and tantalizing expressivity are both the subject and the material of film form, and grasping the semiotic system of cinema has much to do with being able to discern the multifarious and often subtle implications of corporeal movement. In *Body Work* (1993), Brooks sees the body as a "vehicle of mortality," inescapably inscribing and being inscribed by narrative (1). Storytelling and the meaning of narratives, Brooks holds, are sustained by the presence of the body (xii). The specifically cinematic body, however, is not just narrative, not only symbolic, but evokes simultaneously a palpably ethereal iconicity and indexicality that other, non-photographic types of narratives do not share. Contrary to exclusively verbal narratives, film presents the body not only as the object but also as the material of signification. The flesh, Shaviro writes, "is intrinsic to the cinematic apparatus," and constitutes "at once its subject, its substance, and its limit" (256).[17] To a greater extent than the theatrical body, the cinematic body suggests mortality and non-being; it is a body that, due to what Arnheim sees as film's "ghostly incorporeality" (5), is impossibly both there and not there at the same time. Furthermore, the body that so vibrantly enacts the narrative on the screen represents in a certain sense a ghost. Watching THE WILD BUNCH more than thirty years after its initial release, most of the bodies that we see are already dead, forever outlasted by their own moment of execution. Inherent in the cinematically narrativized body is an ambiguous fragility which connotes mortality, but also permanence. Self-consciously or inadvertently, narratives of violence are fictions that dramatize the body, perhaps more so than other narratives, and certainly more explicitly. Violence codifies the knowability of the body according to how it is constituted in its transition from animate subject to inanimate object. Like calligraphy, violence is in a sense a textual inscription on the body, a semantic possibility that requires both the body and the violence in order to become a sign. The disfiguration of the everyday body is analogous to the process of moulding the text; like the materiality of the artwork, the body becomes an object of manipulation with violence as its prime manipulator. Violation curtails the integrity and continuity of the body as a "natural" object.

Fincher's opening shot provides an exceptional visual metaphor for the dual process of embodying thought and turning the body into a mode of thinking. In what I take to be a vital passage in his *Cinema 2*, Deleuze envisions a new philosophy of filmic reflection sensitive to processes of embodiment:

> The body is no longer the obstacle that separates thought from itself, that which it has to overcome to reach thinking. It is on the contrary that which it plunges into or must plunge into, in order to reach the unthought, that is life. Not that the body thinks, but, obstinate and stubborn, it forces us to think, and forces us to think what is concealed from thought itself, life (189).[18]

For Deleuze, it appears that the body is instrumental in facilitating and recharging processes of reflection (the term "the unthought" may also be understood in the sense of the-not-yet-articulated), and this, I would add, is achieved by endowing the body with tropological substance. What Shaviro calls "the aesthetics of the flesh" (127) is the corollary of Eugenio Barba's concept of the "decided" body (94), an irretrievably textualized body recognizable yet fundamentally different from our own bodies.[19] The co-optation of the body by the camera, the scenography, the direction – in short, by the structures of film – reconstructs the body and confers upon it traits and characteristics which are endlessly re-exploitable within the symbolic economy of the narrative. In cinematizing the body, "film is continuing a line, originally found in painting and sculpture, of exposing the body, transforming it as distinct from re-presenting it" (Fuery 72). What Fuery implies by his notion of "cinematization" is equivalent to what I have claimed to be the filmic body's ineluctable amimeticism. The "decided" body is a changed body, and it is on the basis of the transformative potential of the aesthetic troping of this body that a reflection on film violence may ensue. Shaviro, in fact, approaches the position of Deleuze when he suggests that film theory as a whole should be "a theory of the affects and transformations of bodies" (257).

Granted its multiple instances of bodily transformation, perhaps FIGHT CLUB itself could be conceptualized as such a theory. The imagery of the fights aside, there are numerous other indications of acts of irregular alterations of the body in the film: violent intimations of ugly deaths in airplanes and cars recur throughout the film; men grow breasts; several of the support groups that Jack and Marla visit are attended by victims of cancer; one of Durden's anarchic pastimes involves the splicing of frames of subliminal pornography into family features (an alteration both of the body of the film and the bodies in it); Jack and Durden make off with human fat from liposuction clinics to render soap (a trope that at once suggests civilization, barbarity, and melodrama); Jack's hand is horrendously charred by acid; the skull of the Robert Paulson character gets cracked open so that its contents gush forth; and, finally, Jack shoots himself through the head. As if this litany of violent modifications of the body was not enough, there is Jack's gradual physical deterioration as he accumulates scars and bruises. His corporeal decline, made all the more noticeable by its juxtaposition to the overwhelming sterility of the workplace, metaphorically disowns what Martha P. Nochimson sees as "the otherness of body ... to American corporate culture" (2).

The best way of making sense of the variegated transmutations and disfigurations inflicted upon the body in FIGHT CLUB may be to consider them as cinematic tropes that gauge the nature of the fluctuating relation between subjectivity and masculinity.

What is central to this relation, as Savran and Butler, among others, have argued (174; "Melancholy Gender" 32), is the awareness of some unspecified "lack," one which Silverman believes constitutes "the irreducible condition of subjectivity" (84). This intimation of an unarticulated absence triggers a "perpetually deferred masculinity" which "produces a sense of profound anxiety and is connected both discursively and behaviorally to violence" (Savran 178). However, it is not just any kind of violence. Rather than venting his anger and frustration by turning against his Other, this new post-masculine male turns against himself. Even those only vaguely familiar with Fincher's film need hardly be reminded of its decisive narrative ploy – the revelation that Jack and Durden are the same person – and the concomitant spectacularity of the scenes in which Norton's character beats himself up. The sequence where Jack pounds himself to pulp in his boss's office – perhaps the most significant and epochal images of violence in all of American cinema – facilitates a subversion of the "masochistic trope" that Paul Smith has identified as the engine of classical portrayals of masculinity-cum-violence. Jack does not expose himself to physical pain to substantiate his masculinity but, inversely, to overcome it. Giroux's description of the first fight between Jack and Durden (which retrospectively turns out to be an act of violence against oneself) in terms of "exhilaration" and "blissful[ness]" thus amounts to a fundamental misreading of the nature of the brutality that the film transmits ("Private Satisfactions" 10). The violence in FIGHT CLUB still falls within the purview of what Studlar has termed the "*masochistic aesthetic*" (9, emphasis in original), but it also challenges the narrative paradigm of "destructibility-and-recuperability" that has traditionally allayed Hollywood's portrayals of masculinity and violence.

The masochistic aesthetic that comes to fruition with FIGHT CLUB is both in a philosophical and rhetorical sense a progeny of films like BONNIE AND CLYDE and THE WILD BUNCH. By "dismembering the pure, integrated flawless body of classical aesthetics, and exposing the unsettling 'truth' of the body *qua* vulner-able, eviscerable, material Thing" (Rittger 357, emphasis in original), Penn's and Peckinpah's films reconstituted the body as a symbolic terrain where the as-sumed coherence of concepts such as masculinity could be probed and interro-gated. One of the (accidental) functions of screen violence, as Brian Caldwell has noted, is to make the spectator cognizant of masculinity as something con-structed, or affected (139). FIGHT CLUB represents an advancement on this reali-zation, as it must ultimately be seen in light of the "ruination of masculinity" that Silverman discusses in relation to Fassbinder's BERLIN ALEXANDERPLATZ (1979) and IN A YEAR OF THIRTEEN MOONS (1978) (214).[20] In de-idealizing and mutilating the male body, the former film performs a violence which "seems expressive of a textual desire for a movement outside the vicious circle of end-less repetition, and specifically for the transformation as the site of male subjec-tivity" (270). Jack's chillingly acquiescent (and Baudrillardian) statement at the beginning of FIGHT CLUB – "Everything's a copy of a copy of a copy" – precisely summarizes the existential, masculine plight that Silverman claims may be transcended by the "masochistic ecstasy" of a violence that transforms subjec-tivity by transforming the body (275).[21] The implication of the two Fassbinder films, according to Silverman, is that masculinity "can only be abolished by era-dicating its corporeal referent" (216), a conclusion which seems equally valid for an analysis of the purpose of violence in FIGHT CLUB. Jack's self-inflicted gun-shot at the end of the film is a metaphorical deracination of the masculine theol-ogy that Tompkins has referred to as the "Wild West of the psyche" (6), and it is the symbolic killing of the one-dimensional men of American cinema from Paul Muni's Scarface to Harvey Keitel's Mr. White.

Postscript

The principal relevance of the concept of violence, I have come to believe, is its instrumental and heuristic value. Like most other concepts, violence is philosophically functional; it represents a theoretical intermediary which, in turn, prompts us to pursue and problematize a range of other concepts. For this reason, the subject of my inquiry concerns perhaps as much the possibilities of a particular interpretive methodology as it does the theme of violence. For Slocum, film violence is "the lazy signifier" ("Violence" 2), indicating semiotic opacity, or a certain elasticity of meaning. Whatever multiplicity of significations the concept invites, we may productively reconceptualize it as a tropological structure, as a special system of representation that escapes the narrowly mimetic. In that they are ultimately about something else, depictions of violence fulfill a function similar to that of the metaphor. Screen violence, for instance, may be read as a symptom, indexing a collapse of viable moralities. The current crisis in ethics paves the way for violence as the metaphorical embodiment, or imaging, of a new morality. In this context, violence is both the symptom of an ethical crisis and a mediation of a renewed ethical commitment.

A *poethics* of screen violence would not reference the real as much as the textual. Violent movies affirm, challenge, and transform the mythological and artistic tradition of which they are a part, thus manufacturing a form of discourse that is fundamentally extra-mimetic. The relationship between film violence and real violence is therefore hardly ever tangential. Film violence inhabits a realm of textual self-containment. It is a ritualistic, semi-mimetic parastructure whose conditions of operation are independent of the exigencies of violence in real life. While the transtextual, pastiche-like, and self-conscious aspect of screen violence is particularly resonant in contemporary films, it has to varying degrees always been part of the rhetoric of movie narrations.

Apart from the insufficiencies of conventional approaches, there is another, overarching impetus for a radical reframing of the question of methodology in relation to the study of violence in the arts. Mary Boelcskevy pinpoints the magnitude of this inducement in her recognition that "[a]ll our reading practices break down in the face of violence" (60). If at the outset the subject of violence presents itself in the guise of a metaphor for the impossibility of reading – or the impossibility of particular ways of reading in any case – we should feel encouraged to revise not only the principles but also the preconditions of film interpretation. As Kaja Silverman intuits in *The Threshold of the Visible World* (1996), visual texts are capable of "reeducat[ing] the look" (5), but only after the viewer has apprehended the nature of that perceptual mode in which such a re-education becomes both desired and achievable. The look cannot afford to be paralyzed by the overwhelming silence of the image.

This ultimately brings me to a series of interlocking issues that unquestionably merit a study of their own. It appears that the distressing fact of violence in turn gives rise to questions that are in themselves distressing, namely those of pleasure, ethics, and the phenomenology of looking. Violence in the arts, as Lee Mitchell grants, has been treated "with so much imaginative vitality that fascination rather than fear seems to have been the inspiration" ("Violence" 177). Others, as well, have suggested how the audience's desire is both aroused by and in turn gravitates toward aesthetic renderings of bodily violence.[1] One is loath to confess that one enjoys looking at images of violence, whether they are paintings or movies, but must the source of this kind of pleasure be illicit? First, I suppose that the reasons for our attraction to depictions of violence may be the same as those which lure us to the screen in the first place, the gratifications of narrative and of form. Second, violent images hone our ethical proficiency in that they implement a liturgy of looking which tests our moral experience by transgressing or enlarging it. Aesthetic violence teaches us the libidinous economy of cinema which seals the spectator's relation to the screen no matter what the screen shows. The image of violence educates the viewers in the art of filmic appreciation by having them infer and revel in the screen's opacity. Film violence, according to Goldstein, "induce[s] reflexiveness in viewers – we become aware of the camera, of the music, or of special effects, and in every case are aware of our status as viewers" (3). Forthcoming studies of violence and film must abandon the exhausted and ill-advised question of whether fictional violence promotes or deters real violence. What should be asked, instead, are eminently "improper" questions (in Ray's sense of the word), such as 'what may account for the pleasures inherent in watching violent films and how is that pleasure related to other aesthetic pleasures?' We are in need of a new poethics of screen violence. The argument in this text only contributes the most embryonic sketch of such a project. My intention here has been to undertake a critique of some approaches that may advantageously be retired, to advance a theory of film violence that foregrounds its non-transparent modality and that suggests we consider films metapictorially as theories in their own right, and, finally, to provide one possible method for re-reading a group of violent films with an accent on how they can be seen to theorize the problem of death and masculinity.

In the spirit of montage that methodologically invigorates my examination, I shall bring this study to a close by drawing attention to two seemingly disparate claims impinging on the realm of the ethical. Ledbetter, in reflecting on violence and narrative scarring, says that "it is the body violated and broken, and not the body healthy, that provides transforming moments of ethical importance" (9). Emphasizing "the specular foundation of subjectivity" (*Threshold* 195), Silverman insists that "none of us is released from the imperative of looking ethically by the fundamental impossibility of that task" (5). Her call is for an intersubjective ethics of spectating that carries the act of viewing beyond the limits of "the visible world." But what exactly does an ethical way of looking imply, and in what sense may we assertively speak of that which is out of sight, which is not-yet-visible as opposed to invisible? The phrase that lends Silverman's book its name is also fraught with ambiguity. From where does the viewer at the threshold of the visible world look? Is she already enfolded by the visual world, gazing into the void of the not-yet-visible, or does she look from within the obscurity of a pre-visual ambit at some materialization of sight that can only take place in the act of looking? And is ethical insight a way of looking which summons, or incites, the kind of moral awareness that Silverman clearly has in mind in the above quotation? What does it mean to have an ethical experience of violent screen imagery? These are questions to be probed elsewhere, though I shall briefly call attention to possible points of departure. The viewer's awareness of her own status as witness may be one feature of an ethics of looking. In the negotiation with the text, there exists an inherent potential for the spectator's perceptual transformation in the Bazinian sense. Susan Marshall, as we remember, identifies such a potential in some of Peckinpah's images. Those films that accomplish this kind of transformation foster a cinematic morality which facilitates the acquisition of ethical insightfulness. The narrative ethic, Adam Newton has argued, is not a didactic one; it is rather the relation that proceeds reciprocally from the viewer's faith in the sincerity of the narration and the film's faith in the viewer (12). From the point of view of the spectator, this implies that she finds in the film a built-in critique of its own violence. Where this filmic self-critique is covert, the act of viewing will have to dismantle the film. From the point of view of the film, the spectator is trusted to work out the implications of the screened violence for herself. Two textual qualities are therefore inimical to a narrative ethic: the film cannot be exploitative or rhetorically programmatic.

An ethical phenomenology of film viewing may also be established by taking its cue from the literature. Two of the most vocal promulgators of an ethics of reading, Wayne Booth and Hillis Miller, both seem to harbor the conviction that reading literature in itself is an intrinsically ethical enterprise.[2] Booth goads us to make the further assumption that all critical work that is the extension of reading must be ethical in nature ("Are Narrative Choices" 62). Miller, furthermore, writes that "[i]t is an intrinsic feature of written pieces of language that they demand to be read" ("Is There an Ethics" 87) and that "[t]he ethics of reading begins with my response to this demand" (88). When confronted with this command, the reader has no choice but to concede. What is at stake in Booth's and Miller's arguments? First of all, their approach indicates that ethical accountability can only be invoked in the perceptual process of reading. Hence, it is only the text completed by the reader that can be made subject to moral consideration. The novel, play or film in *itself* is beyond ethics (the view presupposes that one makes a philosophical distinction between the phenomenologically realized and unrealized text). This position, in its ultimate consequences, makes censorship irrelevant, in that it is the reader's ethical judgment that impromptu performs the act of censure if need be. A moderate version of this interpretation would suggest that, when faced with offensive material, the reader has the choice of whether or not to read on. In a more uncompromising version, one that Miller appears to endorse, reading becomes genuinely ethical at the moment when one chooses to read on in spite of the fact that the text makes it uncomfortable. The hermeneutic negotiation with texts that challenge our sense of morality – say AMERICAN PSYCHO, MAN BITES DOG or ONE AGAINST ALL – is thus a test rather than a unqualified corruption of our ethical sensibilities.

Booth's and Miller's reflection on the ethics of reading intersects with what I take to be one of the underlying inferences of this dissertation: the theory that aesthetic form is ethical in itself. By renewing cinematic forms through violence, films like BONNIE AND CLYDE and RESERVOIR DOGS are essentially concerned with manifesting what one might term moral tropologies, which also achieve a renewal of ethical vision.[3] "Renunciation of the aesthetic form," Marcuse wrote, "is abdication of responsibility" (*Aesthetic Dimension* 52). One of the ethical lessons of his statement, which also extends to cinema, is how absolutely necessary it is to sustain the love of cinema despite its violence.

Notes

Notes to Prolegomenon

1. For a consideration of the intersecting patterns of violence and tango, see Julie Taylor's *Paper Tangos* (1998). Note that all of the parenthetical references after the title of a work (articles, essays, and reviews excepted) indicate the date of its original publication even if the work was first published in a language other than English. Repeated references to both films and critical works omit the year of release or publication.
2. See, for instance, Gunter, Harrison, and Wykes 89.

Notes to Introduction

1. Insofar as contemporary movies are concerned, it has become increasingly decisive, as Eileen R. Meehan has argued, "to understand them as always and simultaneously text and commodity, intertext and product line" (62). Her suggestion appertains no less to the specific domain of fictional violence.
2. I am only too aware that for some critics the difference between the concepts of representation, imitation, and referentiality is anything but negligible. While it has never been my intention to slash these terms to a straitlaced notion of mimesis, I take their individual distinctiveness to be secondary to the more prominent disparity between the textual and the non-textual, the aesthetic and the extra-aesthetic. A fiction film neither represents nor imitates or mimics or refers to anything external to the sphere of textuality; it is only because it does not copy or reflect the world that it can have a bearing upon it. The rejection of a text's mimetic determination is of course not a controversial notion, and most certainly not with regard to linguistic enunciation. See, for instance, Barthes's *S/Z* 139; Derrida's "The Double Session;" Lyotard's "On the Strength of the Weak;" and, again, de Man's *Resistance to Theory* 10. It should not take the teachings of poststructuralism to acknowledge, however, that visual fiction is no more mimetic than literature. Even Metz grants that the cinema's sense of semblance to the real is merely an illusion the result of which is "a unique impression of familiarity which flatters the emotions" ("On the Impression" 5). For Metz, however, there can be no doubt that the viewer is able to perceive this deceptiveness of the image (11). See also Riffaterre, who takes the longing for referentiality to be an expression of a regressive nostalgia (*Semiotics* 18).

3. In the following passage, Rodowick betrays a keen awareness of the essence of this quandary:
   The historical development of cinema as a signifying practice has been dominated by an ideology of mimesis that, by determining the organization of images according to a schema of spatial continuity, linear exposition, and temporal irreversibility, has privileged film's realist vocation: the direct adequation of images to things. By posing visual representation as that which provides direct access to the real by short-circuiting symbolic expression or the mediation of 'writing,' the exploitation of film's mimetic faculty tends to sublimate signification in favor of iconic presence (90).
   What should be added to Rodowick's otherwise precise explanation is that it is the process of "writing" that in fact produces the "mimetic faculty" in the first place, which means that mimesis is one of the effects, or codes, of the figural rather than its opposite. In a sense, Rodowick tacitly assumes this when he sees modernism as "the last stage of referentiality in the arts" (239).

4. My use of the term figural is a reinflection of the one analyzed in D.N. Rodowick's *Reading the Figural* (2001), which revisits the Lyotard of *Discours, figure* (1971) to make a case for and explain the "new logic of sense" from which modern visual media materialize (x). For Rodowick, the figural represents a new significational topography that liquefies the dichotomy of the linguistic and the visual (2).

5. There have been several attempts in the recent history of film scholarship to explore the tropological aspect of cinema. See, for instance, Trevor Whittock's *Metaphor and Film* (1990), in which the author, focusing on the power of metaphor to articulate "the unnamed" (16), constructs a taxonomy of various types of film metaphors; Thierry Kuntzel, who in his lengthy "Film Work" essay in *Camera Obscura* conducts a psychoanalytic reading of the primacy of metaphor and condensation over metonymy and displacement in film; Lesley Stern, who in an unlikely analytical pairing of THE RED SHOES (Michael Powell and Emeric Pressburger 1948) and RAGING BULL (Scorsese 1980) makes a claim for the medium-specific quality of cinematic tropes (266); and, finally, Steffen Hantke's reading of HENRY: PORTRAIT OF A SERIAL KILLER, in which he writes that film violence can be a "metaphor that needs unpacking" (par. 17), as well as a "dramatic means to concretize an abstraction" (par. 24).

6. Originally published in 1983 and 1985, these texts were translated into English as *Cinema 1: The Movement-Image* (1986) and *Cinema 2: The Time-Image* (1989). It was only a decade later that they started to accumulate commentary by film scholars outside France, and Rodowick's own *Gilles Deleuze's Time Machine* (1997) was instrumental in sparking increased interest in the philosopher's idiosyncratic approach to film theory. I shall return to Deleuze's writings on cinema in chapter 13.

7. Consult again *The Time-Image*, in which Deleuze proclaims that "the essence of cinema … has thought as its highest purpose, nothing but thought and its functioning" (168). For an analysis of Deleuze's "*cinema-thinking,*" see Eric Alliez's article "Midday, Midnight" (293, emphasis in original). Mary M. Litch's *Philosophy Through Film* (2002), a systematic attempt to explore the principal questions of philosophy in readings of popular films such as THE MATRIX (Andy and Larry Wachowski 1999) and BEING JOHN MALKOVICH (Spike Jonze 1999), appeared in 2002. See also Kevin L. Stoehr's anthology *Film and Knowledge* (2002) for a useful introduction to the epistemological applicability of moving images.

8. In his essay "Zentralpark," Benjamin seems to suggest that the fundamental mode of the allegorical is visual: *"Das ursprüngliche Interesse an der Allegorie ist nicht sprachlich sondern optisch"* (686).

9. Birringer relies on Kazimir Malevich's understanding of transfiguration. The Biblical roots of the word, from Old French *transfigurer,* may be traced back to Matthew 17, which refers to the alteration of Christ before three of his disciples. Invoking the term in the context of violence and film is not as unprecedented as it may seem. In his short text on the aesthetics of violence written for the encyclopedia *Violence in America,* Nick Browne applies the concept in a discussion of the concluding carnage in Taxi Driver (1: 549), and Paul Seydor, in an article on the screenplay for The Wild Bunch, writes that at the end of the film, "death really does lead to transfiguration" ("The Wild Bunch" 68). This interpretation of the transfigurative in terms of apotheosis reoccurs in Michael Bliss's analysis of the search of Peckinpah's characters for redemption in violence (*Justified Lives* 16). In his essay "Commitment," Theodor Adorno connects violence and transfiguration in a way which seems to anticipate that of the three film scholars (313). See also Arthur Danto's *The Transfiguration of the Commonplace* (1981), in which he intends the term to signify a process whereby objects from the prosaic world – his example is Andy Warhol's Brillo boxes – are taken out of their familiar context and put on display as works of art.

10. See also Botting and Wilson, who, like Black, apprehend the epistemological effect of a culture in which experience is entirely subsumed by the visual: "The doubling of reality with reproduction presents a founding duplicity, establishing the priority of performance over the real, making reproduction itself original" (44). Their contention is also the basic premise of Neal Gabler's "republic-of-entertainment" thesis in his *Life the Movie* (1998). On an even more pessimistic note, Vilém Flusser laments the condition in which images have "put themselves in place of the world, to the extent that man lives as a function of the images he has produced" (7).

Notes to Part I

1. The need for an interdisciplinary approach in the research on actual violence was acknowledged by Robert Brent Toplin as early as 1975 (*Unchallenged xvii*).

2. It is possible that this lack of faith in the critical judgment of the spectators is an unacknowledged inheritance from the early days of cinema, when the majority of the movie audience was working class, and educators and politicians expressed concern over what they imagined was the boundless susceptibility and naiveté of uneducated viewers. The censuring[censoring??] of film violence may thus metonymically indicate a tendency to condemn film viewing in general. William Rothman writes that "[i]n America, the idea that movies have harmful effects has remained inextricably intertwined with the puritanical notion that movies are intrinsically immoral" ("Violence and Film" 38).

3. The publication of the National Commission on the Causes and Prevention of Violence yielded no evidence of a causal relationship between violence in the media and violent behavior (Eves 42). In the wake of this extensive survey, findings and

opinions have been swinging back and forth between those who believe that media violence does induce aggression and those who do not. Stephen Brody, for instance, concludes that "social research has not been able to[??] unambiguously offer any firm assurance that the mass media in general, and films and television in particular, either exercise a socially harmful effect, or that they do not" (125). More recently, Prince has asserted that cumulative evidence now confirms the existence of a causal link between screen violence and aggression ("Hemorrhaging" 141), and Brad J. Bushman and Craig A. Anderson blame the media for deliberately misinforming the public about the nature of the correlation (486). Others, like Martin Barker, have reached the opposite conclusion (11), and it appears that for every affirmative view on the subject of causation, there is a contradictory one. Few of the critics seem capable of the level of clarity inherent in Thomas Munro's statement that, in order to forge a high correlation between real life violence and art and media, "it would be logically necessary to show a) that a significant proportion of the individuals perpetrating ... crimes had been recently exposed to this kind of [violent] art, and b) that few or no violent crimes of the sort had been committed without prior exposure to it" ("Art and Violence" 318).

4. See, for example, de Tarde's *The Laws of Imitation* (1903), and Fenton's *The Influence of Newspaper Presentations upon the Growth of Crime and other Anti-Social Activity* (1911).

5. Between 1933 and 1935, MacMillan published eight volumes of professional reports on the influence of mass communication on children and adolescents. The title of the series was "Motion Pictures and Youth," though it became widely known as the Payne Fund Studies. Among its notable members were the sociologist Herbert Blumer, the educationalist Edgar Dale and the philosopher Mortimer Adler. Titles such as P.W. Holaday and George D. Stoddard's *Getting Ideas From the Movies* (1933), Blumer's *Movies and Conduct* (1933), and Edgar Dale's *The Content of Motion Pictures* are indicative of the kind of research the PFS represents (in Jowett xxiv). In 1933, Henry J. Forman published a popularized and inopportunely moralizing summary of the PFS findings under the title *Our Movie Made Children*.

6. As Jowett, Jarvie and Fuller note, the research methods of the PFS – which involved the use of questionnaires, interviews, autobiographies, content analysis, and statistical tests – are still "in refined forms" applied today (5).

7. The principle of organization that structures Dale's book is classificatory and content-based, to which headings such as "Murder techniques shown in the 115 pictures" and "Vulgarity in the 40 pictures" testify. That the methods Dale adopts in his 1935 study have not been superannuated is made only too palpable by Gunter, Harrison, and Wykes's *Violence on Television* (2003) – the most comprehensive British study of television violence to date – the captions of which such as "Average Number of Violent Acts per Hour on Terrestrial and Satellite Entertainment Channels" and "Top 10 Weapon Types on BBC Channels" suggest the type of data highlighted by the Payne Fund Studies.

8. Under George Gerbner's management, this commission has monitored prime-time network television programming in the United States since 1967.

9. This organization has compiled a database of relevant literature pertaining to the topic of screen violence and children, which can be accessed at: http://www.nordicom.gu.se/unesco.html.

10.   In *Republic*, Plato voices a concern for the conceivably harmful influence of poetry, which prefigures the rhetoric of the effects lobby:

Our message will be that the commitment appropriate for an important matter with access to the truth shouldn't be given to this kind of poetry. People should, instead, be worried about the possible effects, on one's inner political system, of listening to it and should tread cautiously; and they should let our arguments guide their attitude towards poetry (362).

In *What Is Art?* (1898), Leo Tolstoy articulates an even more virulent criticism of the purpose and influence of art. His Platonic skepticism, in no small part based on the questionable assumption that the governing modality of art is imitative, leads him to the conclusion that if the only art available is depraved or simulated, society is better off without any art at all.

11.   Robert Hughes's *Culture of Complaint: The Fraying of America* (1993) offers a valuable overview of the relationship between political and aesthetic polarizations within the cultural landscape of the United States.

12.   See also Anne Jerslev 39.

13.   It should be noted that the promotion of contextual factors in the study of screen violence has gained currency among some media scholars working within an empirical paradigm. James Potter's *On Media Violence* (1999), for example, advocates the necessity of "recogniz[ing] a broad template for the construct of violence" (2), and argues for a synthesis of biological, ecological, cognitive and interactionist theories in future research on the subject (23).

14.   Brody was an early proponent of the necessity of complementing social science research with qualitative studies, who has pressed for an elucidation of "the meaning and significance of aggression and violence in a broader social and cultural sense" (127). This, he writes, may be accomplished if social scientists begin to take advantage of the studies done by literary and film scholars.

15.   See, for example, Bordwell's aforementioned *Making Meaning*; Branigan's *Narrative Comprehension and Film* (1992); Murray Smith's *Engaging Characters: Fiction, Emotion and the Cinema* (1995); Richard Allen's *Projecting Illusion: Film Spectatorship and the Impression of Reality* (1995); Warren Buckland's anthology *The Film Spectator: From Sign to Mind* (1995); Greg Currie's *Image and Mind: Film, Philosophy, and Cognitive Science* (1995); Joseph Anderson's *The Reality of Illusion: An Ecological Approach to Cognitive Film Theory* (1996); Ed Tan's *Emotion and the Structure of Narrative Film: Film as an Emotion Machine* (1996); Torben Grodal's *Moving Pictures: A New Theory of Film Genres, Feelings, and Cognition* (1997); Carl Plantinga and Greg M. Smith's anthology *Passionate Views: Film, Cognition and Emotion* (1999); and Buckland's *The Cognitive Semiotics of Film* (2000).

16.   Etymologically, the Greek term *katharsis* is derived from *kathairein* (cleanse), which in turn derives from *katharos* (pure). Centuries before Aristotle, the word *katharsis* referred not only to the ritualistic purification required of the murderer but also to that which was required of those who came into contact with him. The origins of the current term signal yet another level of ambiguity in that the pre-Aristotelian concept of *katharma* was interchangeable with *pharmakon*, which means both poison and cure (Twitchell 46).

17. For a scrupulous discussion of the term's exegetical history, see A.D. Nuttall's *Why Does Tragedy Give Pleasure?* (1996). See also Andrew Ford's article "*Katharsis*: The Ancient Problem," and Terry Eagleton's 2003 study *Sweet Violence* 153-177.

18. Sam Peckinpah, for instance, was well acquainted with the *Poetics* long before he made his first feature film (Seydor, *Peckinpah* 345). Marie Selland, the director's first wife, says that "Aristotle's *Poetics* was something that seemed to grab him and he was constantly referring to it" (Dukore 11), indicating that the director seems to have developed a self-reflexive approach to the function of catharsis in his own art. Another filmmaker who somewhat obliquely and eccentrically appears to subscribe to the theory of catharsis is Larry Clark, who in an interview with *Sight and Sound* imparts to James Mottram that "I want the audience to pay for all those fucking stupid movies they watch, where hundreds of people get killed. People have seen the film [*Bully,* 2001] and said, 'It's so violent.' But there's only one killing. You go to other movies and there are a hundred killings, but they mean nothing" (25).

19. Sobchack's insight seems indebted to Dewitt H. Parker's notion of "sympathetic curiosity" which he presents in *The Principles of Aesthetics* (1920). Parker devotes one chapter to an examination of the pleasures to be had from representations of evil in art. What renders evil pleasurable to us, he writes, is its appeal to five different cognitive-emotional proclivities, of which sympathetic curiosity is just one (the others are the tragic, the pathetic, the comic and sensual delight) (84). The concept is not without its merits, as it establishes a relation between the aesthetic pleasure of evil – and by extension, violence – on the one hand, with the notion of epistemophilia, on the other. This correlation could also be pursued further by hypothesizing that the curiosity concerning violence veils an interest in that which usually constitutes the object of violence, namely the body. I shall return to this idea in subsequent chapters.

20. It has been noted, by among others William Faure, that early cinema was in fact incapable of shocking audiences because films were too closely aligned stylistically with the theatre. In Mack Sennett's BARNEY OLDFIELD'S RACE FOR A LIFE (1913), for example, vaudevillian and melodramatic poses and mimicry eliminate the element of shock in the scene of a lady chained to a railway track with three villains looming over her (13). Only D.W. Griffith's BIRTH OF A NATION (1915) gave cinema the form of violent spectacle that it has cultivated ever since.

21. In *The Psychology of Art* (1971), Lev Vygotsky offers an interpretation of catharsis in which the concept comes to epitomize a general theory of aesthetic response, crystallized in a "mutual transformation" of form and feeling: "The law of aesthetic response is the same for a fable as for a tragedy: *it comprises an affect that develops in two opposite directions but reaches annihilation at its point of termination*. This is the process we should like to call catharsis" (214, emphasis in original).

22. Other film theorists have emphasized the role of spectacle in expanding the narrative possibilities of violence. Charles Wolfe, for example, claims that the aesthetic significance of shock for film violence has compelled filmmakers "not simply to enhance or refine stylistic techniques but to toy with the narrative implications of violent acts and test the limits of prevailing taboos" (1: 515).

23. In the *Nicomachean Ethics*, however, Aristotle sustains a specifically ethical interpretation of catharsis, in which it is granted the function of restraining the passions in order to achieve balance in the sense of justice.

24. However, Robert Hughes has remarked that within an American context the therapeutic potential of art has historically been limited to works considered morally and
spiritually edifying (171). Thus it is rather improbable that confrontational art of the
cathartic kind would be recognized as therapeutic by the conservative patrons of art
from the Puritans to the latter-day reactionaries.

25. I have elsewhere drawn attention to the growing body of work on audiovisual reception. See note 14 in the previous chapter.

26. Eisenstein was not alone in assigning a prominent function to the notion of shock in
art. Tretyakov and Benjamin both believed that shock would alter the quality of
perception in the viewer. Andreas Huyssen considers some of Benjamin's work in
the 1930s to be an attempt to establish a connection between the potential for shock
inherent in avant-garde art and the "utopian hope for an emancipatory mass culture" that has never been pursued (14). With postmodernism, the function of shock
has degenerated into a state in which it merely reinforces rather than alters perception (Huyssen 15).

27. The capacity for violence to generate shock, and the notion of shock as a key device
with which to maintain audience attention, are the subjects of William Faure's 1973
book *Images of Violence*.

28. By cruelty, Artaud did not have barbarism in mind, but rather strictness, diligence,
unrelenting decisiveness, irreversible and absolute determination. ... Above all,
cruelty is very lucid, a kind of strict control and submission to necessity. There is no
cruelty without consciousness, without the application of consciousness, for the latter gives practicing any act in life a blood red tinge, its cruel overtones, since it is
understood that being alive always means the death of someone else (80).

29. It testifies to the longevity and consequence of Artaud's concept that it has been
regularly re-invoked in discussions of film violence. See, for example, Jonathan
Romney's review of RESERVOIR DOGS (16).

30. One may note that the idea of cruelty in film was not unknown to André Bazin, who
discerned precisely such a cruel aesthetics in the cinema of Erich von Stroheim, Carl
Theodor Dreyer, Preston Sturges, Luis Buñuel, Alfred Hitchcock, and Akira Kurosawa. See André Bazin's *The Cinema of Cruelty* (1982).

31. Dolf Zillmann has argued that viewers who are compelled to justify their fascination for violent films tend to invoke "claims of aesthetic merit" to support their position (182).

32. The applications of the terms aestheticization and stylization are legion among film
critics and theorists, suffice it here to name those of Thomas Elsaesser (176), Alexander Walker (*National Heroes* 45) and Marsha Kinder ("Violence American Style" 73).
Wead and Lellis's definition of the spectacle film as the embodiment of a "purely
esthetic cinema" is another instantiation of the *entelechial* use of the notion of aestheticization (435).

33. Roger Fry has attempted to refine the notion of beauty by specifying two different
senses in which a work of art may be beautiful: the sensual and the supersensual. It
is within the latter category that representations considered ugly and reprehensible
may be subsumed. Regrettably, Fry is reticent about the nature of this supersensual
kind of beauty, resorting to a vague phrase like "purposeful order and variety" (31).
The formal elements which enable the work to transcend the purely sensual Fry
labels as "the emotional elements of design," but these merely designate the tradi-

tional components of pictorial art (rhythm, mass, space, light and shade, and color) (33).

34. See, for example, how Henry A. Giroux, in the article "Racism and the Aesthetics of Hyper-real Violence," virulently rebukes the films of Tarantino 221.

35. In fact, attempts have been made to account for the obverse of beauty. In her article "Beauty and its Opposites," Ruth Lorand presents a litany of "negative aesthetic concepts:" ugliness, the meaningless, kitsch, boredom, the insignificant, and the irrelevant (399-404). However, as Anne Sheppard points out, "[a]esthetic appreciation would have a very narrow range of objects if it were confined to those objects to which 'beautiful' happens to be applicable" (57).

36. Occasionally, some feature films also set out to self-consciously explore the nature of the relation between art and beauty, like Luchino Visconti's DEATH IN VENICE (1971) and Sally Potter's THE TANGO LESSON (1997).

37. Tan's line of reasoning may be supplemented by George E. Yoos's statement that "sound artistic judgment take[s] place after the appreciation of a particular work of art. Criticism evaluates the recall of the experience of appreciation. Such criticism relates the experience of secondary and discrete values to a primary aspect" (81). In light of this comment, it seems that the mistake critics occasionally make is to attribute the quality of beauty directly to the text rather than to their own perception of it.

38. Kant's theory thus escapes the postmodern relativization of the standards of aesthetic judgment, which has prompted Heidi Kaye and I.Q. Hunter to declare the hegemony of "cultural populism" in the introduction to the oxymoronically titled *Trash Aesthetics* (1997, 1). However, the appeal of a concept like Kant's subjective universality still finds support among some aestheticians, like Nishida Kitar̄o, whose *Art and Morality* (1973) argues for the existence of a "universal validity" and a "transindividual consciousness" in aesthetic judgments (9).

39. On a more confrontational note, Taylor evokes the concept of *entelechy* to divulge the historically and culturally situated origin of the seemingly universal perception of art. Taylor points out that what is generally accepted as a universal standard for the valuation of art is a highly culture-specific invention. "Western structures of feeling," he writes, "are positioned as normative, as the events that give other cultural expressions its global reference point and name" (56). Though Taylor is mainly concerned with non-Western art, it would seem that the logic of his argument is akin to that employed by someone like Noël Carroll (in *A Philosophy of Mass Art*, 1998) who attempts to subsume popular entertainment under the auspices of art. Taylor explains that via entelechy a particular category or phenomenon is promoted to paradigmatic status, which in turn serves to classify "lower" manifestations within the same category. He exemplifies the entelechial process thus: "Certain brand names have gained an entelechial preeminence over a genre of products, like *Xerox*, *Kleenex*, *Webster's*, or *Walkman*.... Western art becomes art, socially approved writing becomes literature" (59). Taylor further claims that entelechy operates by acts of violence and forgetfulness. The first is symbolic and denotes the "seizure of advantages of definition that deprives other people of the capacity to speak of themselves with equal resonance and conviction" (59). An act of forgetting is then necessary to mask the act of violence, and this process is essentially facilitated by the formations of canons and "great traditions." What is intriguing about Taylor's thesis is that it

decenters the idea of art as a transcendent entity beyond the limitations of human judgment, and that it opens it up to a re-interpretation of the aesthetic that has much in common with the efforts of certain theorists of popular culture to undermine the distinction between high and low art.

40. Elsewhere, Bourdieu has also called attention to the historicity of what he calls a "pure aesthetic" ("Historical Genesis" 206). In a diachronic perspective, the implications of the aesthetic are flexible. It is not the subjectivity of beauty that one is concerned with, but the historically subjectivized definitions of the characteristics and functions of art. The affinity of aesthetics with beauty is therefore not a universal given but rather the product of how a specific epoch views artistic texts. Different eras produce different philosophies of, and norms for, the aesthetic. The art of cinema did not even exist at the time when the association of the aesthetic and the beautiful was first made. As Stephen Regan submits in a lucid synopsis of the trajectory of aesthetic thinking, the contingencies of social and historical perception confer shifting values upon the notion of the aesthetic (8). This implies that aesthetic systems are fundamentally dialectical, in that they are, as Berel Lang points out, "open to change from without, as the overall philosophical context varies; and they are also open to change from without as they respond to the demands of aesthetic experience" (45).

41. Recognizing the extent to which "artistic value is far broader than beauty," Francis J. Coleman introduces the concept of "aesthetic pain" to describe the frame of emotion experienced in the transaction with such texts (332).

42. For a discussion of the sublime with regard to violence, see Frappier-Mazur 189, and Huhn 259.

43. The word aesthetics in its current sense was first used by Alexander Gottlieb Baumgarten in his *Aesthetica* (1750), which defines it as "the science of perception". In 1875, it became an entry in the ninth edition of *Encyclopaedia Britannica*, where it replaced Lord Francis Jeffrey's entry for "Beauty" (Regan 5). In a highly polemical critique of modern aesthetic philosophy, Robert Dixon indicts what he refers to as the "Baumgarten corruption" for infelicitously transforming the meaning of the Greek word from "perception" to "taste" (80).

44. Artists' suicides like those of Japanese author Yukio Mishima (1970) and British filmmaker Donald Cammell (1996) are reflective of the degree to which expressions of art and violence may interrelate. Both deaths were elaborately staged as aesthetic "events," and in the latter case the choreography of the spectacle is highly reminiscent of the murder of the Turner character in Cammell's own PERFORMANCE (co-directed by Nicolas Roeg in 1970). Moreover, as Steven Jay Schneider points out, Cammell's 1987 film THE WHITE OF THE EYE appears to be an exploration of the 'murder as art' thesis. In this film, Schneider writes, "particular shots … ask to be 'extracted' from their narrative context and viewed as paintings of a highly disturbing and challenging nature; a cinematic metaphor is effected whereby the killer gets equated with a kind of artist, and the carnage he leaves behind with works of art" (par. 8).

45. Sharrett's collection *Mythologies of Violence in Postmodern Media* illustrates this tendency. See also Bliss's *Between the Bullets*, published in 2002, 33, in which the author reads a sacrificial dimension into John Woo's *Hard-Boiled* (1989).

46. In a review of Slotkin's GUNFIGHTER NATION (1992), Sharrett asserts that the regeneration thesis "has become extremely influential in cultural studies" (Rev. 50).

47. John G. Cawelti has segmented the myth of violence into five large-scale narrative patterns, of which Slotkin's regeneration scenario is only one. The others are the myth of 'crime does not pay,' the vigilante myth, the myth of the hard-boiled hero, and the myth of equality through violence ("Myths of Violence" 530-537). It is noteworthy that Cawelti does not consider the regeneration myth as a structure that informs all myths of violence, but rather as one of many myth narratives centering on violence.

48. Slotkin's conception of the wilderness is decidedly Turnerian. In "The Significance of the Frontier in American History," Frederick Jackson Turner defines the frontier both as a topographical place and as a concept. The frontier demarcates a space in which civilization comes into contact with the wilderness, but it also represents a conceptual locus where the possibilities of the future clash with the actualities of the present (Bliss, *Justified Lives* 2). Richard Hofstadter calls the frontier process a "perpetual rebirth," but points out that the connotations of violence were brought to bear on the idea of the frontier not by Turner but by cultural critics like Lewis Mumford and Van Wyck Brooks (5).

49. The regeneration thesis finds implicit support in the work of some conflict theorists, who argue that "conflict prevents the ossification of society by posing a constant pressure for innovation and creativity. Because conflict has diverse, integrative, and disruptive functions, it can lead to fundamental social change" (Rose 45). See also Georges Sorel's *Reflections on Violence* (1915). The idea of societal renewal through violence is not unique to American thought and letters, although the particular mythology Slotkin describes appears to be. William Butler Yeats, for example, seems to subscribe to a regeneration-through-violence view when he quotes these words from his own character Michael Robartes (from *Stories of Michael Robartes and His Friends* 1931): "'Love war because of its horror, that belief may be changed, civilization renewed'" (*On the Boiler* 20). The rejuvenating aspect of violence has perhaps above all become associated with the name of Frantz Fanon, who in *The Wretched of the Earth* (1963) adjoins violence and creativity. In *On Violence* (1969), Hannah Arendt argues that the glorification of violence in contemporary society is a response to the paralysis of action and the diminishment of individual agency (19).

50. Slotkin himself expresses a certain ambivalence with respect to the place of mythology in American experience. While, on the one hand, he draws attention to the poetic efforts of creating a specifically American mythology from scratch (embodied in texts such as Joel Barlow's *Columbiad* (1807), Timothy Dwight's *Greenfield Hill* (1794), the works of Whitman and Melville), on the other, he also acknowledges the "strong, antimythological stream" that permeates American culture (*Regeneration* 3).

51. There are those who take issue with Slotkin's monolithic framework. Citing Richard Hofstadter, Hugh Davis Graham argues that American violence has never had a particular ideological center: "So various, diffuse, and spontaneous were our patterns of violence that they lacked the cohesion necessary to forge a tradition" (484).

52. This literature is subject to extensive treatment in the first volume of Slotkin's trilogy, *Regeneration Through Violence: The Mythology of the American Frontier, 1600-1860*, first published in 1973 (94-145). See also Gordon M. Sayre's compilation *American*

Captivity Narratives (2000). As regards the politics of purification rites in particular, the regeneration ethos seems related to processes of remasculinization, what Tony Williams calls the "act of ritual cleansing whereby man can purify his masculinity and disavow his feminine side" (129). A more extended analysis of the converging sites of remasculinization, the function of violence in Puritan teleology, and the rhetoric of manifest destiny would require a separate thesis. See also Susan Jeffords's *The Remasculinization of America* (1989), Paula Wiloquet-Maricondi's "Full-Metal-Jacketing, or Masculinity in the Making," and Jane Caputi's "Small Ceremonies: Ritual in FORREST GUMP, NATURAL BORN KILLERS, SEVEN, and FOLLOW ME HOME." Caputi's essay is particularly thought-provoking in its suggestion of an ideological nexus of patriarchal culture and theologies of violence.

53. After I had begun revising this thesis, two new films appeared – one a feature, the other a documentary – that both probed the nature and impact of this rhetorical legacy. Michael Moore's BOWLING FOR COLUMBINE (2002) posits the American culture of fear (of the other) as the primary though oblique cause of violence in real life, while Scorsese's GANGS OF NEW YORK more ambitiously undertakes an ontologization of violence as the manifestation of a response that arises at the intersection of xenophobia and the territorial imperative. Heavy-handed and obsolescent, Scorsese's intention in GANGS to align the birth of the nation with an act of originary violence – in other words, his regurgitation of the regeneration mythos – is surprisingly out of synch with the new narratives of what is rapidly becoming a post-mythological culture. Even Slotkin himself, in his conclusion to the frontier trilogy, acknowledges the bankruptcy of myth: "We are in a 'liminal' moment of our cultural history. We are in the process of giving up a myth/ideology that no longer helps us see our way through the modern world, but lack a comparably authoritative system of beliefs to replace what we have lost" (*Gunfighter Nation* 654). Scorsese's retrograde vision is best seen as the belated yet entirely redundant coda to a historical teleology that American cinema has contested at least since THE WILD BUNCH.

54. Sharrett succinctly describes the function of the scapegoat thus: "During periods of local or national strife, the population could become galvanized against a designated Other; blood sacrifice in the interest of destroying the Other would have a purgative, redemptive effect, and would further ennoble the collective purpose" (Rev. 50).

55. Other scholars have also detected a similarity between the theories of Slotkin and Girard. Sharrett, for instance, notes that Girard's theory of language formation and the social function of violence "complements very well the cultural studies of Slotkin" ("Afterword" 425).

56. For Girard, the difference between *sacrificial* and *reciprocal* forms of violence is crucial. While the former initiates processes of differentiation, the latter abolishes them. Anne Nesbet explains mimetic crisis thus: "The crisis comes when the two kinds of violence are confused; in that confusion, sacrificial violence loses its ability to create differences and indeed all differences disappear, replaced by non-differentiating reciprocal violence" (45).

57. Ardrey is the author of several influential though notorious works on the nature of aggression in human societies. See, for example, *African Genesis* (1961), *The Territorial Imperative* (1966), and *The Social Contract* (1970).

58 As Andrew Thomas Mozina notes, there are two different conceptions of sacrificial killing:
    The same loss of life suggests two opposing interpretations: a just death that stabilizes a community threatened by revolution (the traditional purpose of pagan scapegoating); an unjust death which reveals the community's basis in violence and thus becomes an argument against the existing regime (the traditional purpose of Christian martyrdom) (2).

59 Other theorists have made claims reminiscent of Girard's thesis. Twitchell, for instance, finds that "[t]he willingness to be violent has made the species dominant, but unrestrained violence could undo eons of evolution.... Violence became ritualized, aggression rechanneled, civilization began having its discontents" (32).

60. As Todd Herzog points out, the term scapegoat is first mentioned in Leviticus 16 (3: 96). For an examination of the various traditions of scapegoating, consult James Frazer's *The Golden Bough* (1890). Rikke Schubart discusses Girard's theory of the scapegoat in relation to the action film in her article "Passion and Acceleration: Generic Change in the Action Film."

61. There is a tendency in recent media criticism to distrust the viability of mythological structures. See, for example, Mark Pizzato's "Jeffrey Dahmer and Media Cannibalism: The Lure and Failure of Sacrifice."

62. I am aware that Black has recently used the term "mimetic fallacy" to denote the misconceived belief that viewers learn violent behavior from exposure to mock violence, cf. his thesis that "artificial violence could be mistaken for the real thing only by viewers who are either mentally incompetent or culturally illiterate" (*Reality Effect* 112). The belligerent flavor of his phrasing notwithstanding, I am in entire agreement with Black's assessment, though my own understanding of the mimetic fallacy involves relations of textual signification rather than the relationship between text and audience. Herbert Lindenberger also uses the expression "the mimetic fallacy" in his review essay on the "mimetic bias" in Anglo-American literary criticism (1: 22).

63. This is due to a lack of space, not a lack of concern. I have explored the nature of mimesis and the relation between film and reality elsewhere. See my "The Lying Game? Historical Films and the Re-Invention of the 'Past'."

64. In the first chapter of *The Order of Mimesis*, Prendergast provides an informative account of the ways in which the idea of mimesis has historically been couched in a set of rhetorical figures that have served either its denigration or its celebration. See also Prendergast's *The Triangle of Representation* (2000). For a discussion of the mimetic predisposition in much 20th century literary scholarship, see Herbert Lindenberger's article "The Mimetic Bias in Modern Anglo-American Criticism." See also Erich Auerbach's seminal *Mimesis: The Representation of Reality in Western Literature* (1953), and M.H. Abrams's *The Mirror and the Lamp: Romantic Theory and the Critical Tradition* (1953).

65. Hill's study *Shocking Entertainment*, which I mention in chapter 1, convincingly affirms this hypothesis.

66. In this context, Danto's assessment in *After the End of Art* (1997) that mimetic representations have become less significant than "some kind of reflection on the means and methods of representation" (8) appears somewhat belatedly. Self-reflexivity and non-mimeticism are not exclusive to postmodernity.

67. The relation of aesthetic texts to the external world is not one of reflection, neither visually nor ideationally. As Samuel Alexander explains in his *Philosophical and Literary Pieces* (1939), "the artist will always be having ideas of the subject matter flitting before his mind, and the greater his absorption in the subject the more freely will his imagination play about it. These images, however, are not anticipations of the expression contained in the work of art" (217). Alexander also refutes the claim that the text is a translation of ideas into aesthetic form (211).

Notes to Part II – Chapter I

1. The indispensability of context for the evaluation of violent movie scenes has also been pointed out by scholars like John G. Cawelti ("Myths of Violence" 523).
2. I realize that this contention may make my argument vulnerable to charges of nominalism, but it is intended as a response to a problem that is principally methodological, and by no means indicates an absolute and generalizable recommendation of any nominalistic doctrine.
3. The objection could be raised that, though feature films are fictional, the scenarios they embody might easily be conceived as realities in a hypothetical sense. But a hypothetical reality is no more a reflection or representation of the world than fiction is.
4. In his *Semiotics of Poetry* (1978), Michael Riffaterre anticipates the relation between intertextuality and semiosis (what he calls "ungrammatical constants") that becomes so important to Iampolski's theory (115). Though he seems to imply that the process of semiosis may occur at the expense of a text's referential function, Riffaterre does not, like Iampolski, oppose semiosis to mimesis.
5. See Dudley Andrew 89.
6. Most of Bordwell's and Thompson's work springs out of neoformalist concerns, from their collaboration *Film Art* (1979) and, with Janet Staiger, *The Classical Hollywood Cinema. Film Style and Mode of Production to 1960* (1985), to Bordwell's *The Films of Carl-Theodor Dreyer* (1981), *Narration in the Fiction Film* (1985), *Ozu and the Poetics of Cinema* (1988), *The Cinema of Eisenstein* (1993), and *On the History of Film Style* (1997), and to Thompson's *Eisenstein's* Ivan the Terrible: *A Neoformalist Analysis* (1981) and *Breaking the Glass Armour: Neoformalist Film Analysis* (1988).
7. Judith Genova advocates a more radical position when she argues that "style and meaning are inextricably interwoven; they reflect, express and constitute each other" (323).
8. For an explanation of the notion of symptomatic reading, see Bordwell and Thompson's *Film Art* 51-52.
9. The concept is first introduced in *Narration in the Fiction Film*, and owes its etymology to Burch's use of the word parameter in his *Theory of Film Practice*. Bordwell writes that in parametric narration, "the film's stylistic system creates patterns distinct from the demands of the *syuzhet* system. Film style may be organized and emphasized to a degree that makes it at least equal in importance to *syuzhet* patterns" (275).

10. It is not only texts which deliberately flaunt their opacity, or non-transparency, that should be taken as evidence for the primacy of form over representationality. Critics with a formalist orientation tend to gravitate toward the work of experimentalists such as Stan Brakhage and Michael Snow, or stylists like Yasujiro Ozu and Robert Bresson, artists who self-consciously play with the obtrusiveness of film form. Their filmmaking practice foregrounds the material aspect of the text so that its representational import is rendered inaccessible to the viewer. However, the critic who invokes the taxonomies of such work as manifestations of a type of art that paradigmatically exposes the material qualities of the text, endorses the same form/content division as those critics who only emphasize the subject matter of any work. The problem, therefore, is not that there are too few formalist critics, but that there are too many who are oblivious to the inadequacy of the dichotomy of content and form.

11. This observation is in agreement with that of another modernist aesthetician, Wilhelm Worringer, who in his *Abstraction and Empathy* argues that "[t]he stylistic peculiarities of past epochs are … not to be explained by lack of ability, but by a differently directed volition" (9). The name Worringer gives to this volition is "will to abstraction."

12. Marcuse's treatise, though critical of historical materialist theories like those of Lukács, offers a politically charged account of the aesthetic. This perspective differs from that of Bordwell, whose work has come under attack because of its insistence on a de-politicized agenda.

13. For a systematic consideration of the underlying political inflections of the major aesthetic perspectives from realism to formalism, see Max Rieser's lucid article "Problems of Artistic Form: The Concept of Art."

14. Bordwell's reason for subsuming form and content under the concept of form can be taken as a symbolic move that underscores the author's commitment to the artwork rather than to its symptomatic interpretations.

15. In his review of the film for *Sight and Sound*, Don Daniels assigns an effect of heightened emotional impact to the sequences he describes as stylized. Discussing the "Singing in the Rain-" sequence, he writes that

> Kubrick combines the gang's brutal improvisations with Alex's calculated song and dance: realistic detail and stylised action that reinforce one another and indicate the state of mind that is the subject of the film. Some have found only a technique of estrangement in the stylised violence. I find myself distanced and touched. Somehow the artificiality makes the violence more painful, Alex's coolly committed acts more evil (44).

16. As Bordwell has demonstrated, the particular brand of narrative realism favored by Hollywood can be retraceable to historical forms such as the well-made play, the popular romance, and the late-nineteenth-century short story (*Narration* 157).

17. Jenni Calder exposes the contingency of the realism vs. stylization-dichotomy with the remark that "[t]he whole of recent realism is bedeviled by the assumption that one form of stylisation is *per se* more realistic than another" (139, emphasis in original).

18. There is, curiously, a faint echo of Christian Metz's structuralist taxonomy in Bordwell's thinking, though one should note that key terms such as form mean different things for the two scholars. Those facets of the film whose conjunction establishes

medium-specificity (the image, other graphic material, spoken sound, music and noise) Metz refers to as substance, whereas form he takes to be "the structure of themes" ("Methodological" 87). Metz also makes a distinction between "an extra-cinematic signified recruited by the film" (presumably the pre-filmic) on the one hand and a purely cinematic signification on the other (89, emphasis in original). His argument rests upon the assumption that the signifier/signified split applies to both the level of form and the level of substance individually (94). Like Bordwell (though more explicitly), Metz subsumes the thematic under form but, unlike Bordwell, he seems unable or unwilling to dispense with the Saussurean scheme. The most troublesome aspect of Metz's semiology in this regard is his apparent failure to recognize the profundity and irreversibility of the transformations his "extra-cinematic signified" is subjected to by the filmic process. As both Benjamin and Barthes knew, recording something – even the most aleatory or insignificant – transforms the recorded object. One should hence be careful not to posit the isomorphism of the pre-filmic "referent" and the post-filmic texture that is its transformation. The ontology of the extra-cinematic is not reproducible.

Notes to Part II – Chapter 2

1. An observation by Munro in his seminal *Form and Style in the Arts* (1970) lends support to Gombrich's point (238).
2. There is no reason not to assume that the principles delineated by art historians like Gombrich and Munro are also applicable to all art, including cinema. Munro's postulation is particularly well suited to describe the dialectics of the formation of style in Hollywood films, in which individual style is always vulnerable to the monumental sway of the impersonal and formulaic. To complicate the matter, styles of violence in American cinema have at times also been heavily influenced by European and Asian film aesthetics, notably German Expressionism (film noir and the crime films from the 1920s to the 1950s), the French New Wave (the Renaissance films from 1965-1975), and Hong Kong Action Cinema (contemporary action films) (Wolfe 1: 515).
3. Marcia Cavell reminds us of the seemingly obvious fact that any given text arises out of the conventions of a certain tradition (32).
4. Cook agrees with Alloway's account in *Violent America* (1971) that the depiction of violence in the post-war cinema is prominent in the work of filmmakers like Aldrich, Don Siegel, Anthony Mann, Fuller, Ray and the aforementioned Dmytryk (26). The said directors exhibit what Alloway calls a "cruel aesthetic," betraying a level of nihilism and pessimism previously uncharted by Hollywood (25).
5. For a related argument, see also Jane Tompkins 25.
6. The meanings of this metaphor are historically variable. In the field of literature, R. W.B. Lewis writes, generations of writers can be distinguished by "their manner of responding to the fact of death" (19). Moreover, Bronfen and Goodwin find that a community's conception of itself is inextricably linked to the ways in which it configures death (15).

7. Kastenbaum and Aisenberg's theory may be compounded by Nuttall's validation of the appeal of tragedy as being that of preparing the spectator for the vicissitudes of death (77).

8. This delineation of the concept of form is indebted to Bordwell and Thompson's argument in *Film Art* (42-43).

9. Both Becker and Goldberg date the onset for the elimination of death from public view to the late 19th and early 20th century, and the phenomenon thus coincides not only with the birth of cinema but with the establishment of the two new fields of gerontology and thanatology by Elie Metchnikoff. Studies in the latter emerged only in the 1960s, but at the time of the publication of Becker's influential book, a journal devoted to research on death, dying and grief – *Omega* – had appeared, as had other book-length studies such as Jessica Mitford's *The American Way of Death* (1963), and Elisabeth Kübler-Ross's *On Death and Dying* (1969).

10. Georg Brandes's highly influential book was translated into English as *Main Currents in Nineteenth Century Literature* in 1905.

11. It is perhaps not an unwarranted claim that American art in general has proven peculiarly permeable to the subject of violence. Within the graphic arts, paintings such as John Trumbull's *Death of General Montgomery in the Attack on Quebec* (1788), John Vanderlyn's *The Death of Jane McCrea* (1804), Thomas Cole's *Cora Kneeling at the Feet of Tamenund* (1827), George Catlin's *Buffalo Hunt* (1844), and Frederic Remington's *The Last Stand* (1890) and *The Charge of the Rough Riders at San Juan Hill* (1898) demonstrate that a preoccupation with violent motifs and aesthetics can be evidenced in the pictorial arts long before Porter shot his *The Great Train Robbery*, as do photographic works like Mathew B. Brady's *On the Antietam Battlefield* (1862), Timothy O' Sullivan's *A Harvest of Death* (1863), and Alexander Gardner's *Gardner's Photographic Sketch-Book of the War* (1865-66).

12. That the cinema again seems to be a moribund art form is the subject of Wheeler Winston Dixon's painstakingly argued essay "Twenty-Five Reasons Why It's All Over."

13. See for instance his *War and Cinema* (1989).

14. For Bergstrom, film violence is also "the violence of the cut, that is, violence engineered on the level of film technique" (21).

15. Dubois's insights are also applicable to film, and he himself analyzes an image from Michael Curtiz's *The Mystery of the Wax Museum* (1933) with reference to thanatography (162).

16. I say "almost" because there are obviously exceptions, some of which are analyzed in Martha McCaughey and Neal King's anthology *Reel Knockouts: Violent Women in the Movies* (2001). There is also a current tendency in the European cinema to explore sexualized violence perpetrated by female protagonists, as illustrated by films like Virginie Despentes and Coralie Trinh Thi's *Baise-Moi* (2000), Haneke's *The Piano Teacher* (2001), and Claire Denis's *Trouble Every Day* (2001).

17. References to Seydor's book are for the revised edition published in 1997.

18. For a more detailed account of the non-conformist streak in *The Wild Bunch* and *Fight Club*, see my "Peckinpah's Walden: The Violent Indictment of 'Civilization' in *The Wild Bunch*."

19. As this quoted passage reveals, both Brooks and Rickard approach narrative from within a psychoanalytic framework. I do not see any pertinent reason to refrain

from recontextualizing elements of this model, as they may have a validity in other systems of interpretation.

Notes to Part III – Chapter 3

1. See also Thomas Leitch's *Crime Films* 25.
2. According to Richard A. Blake, producer Howard Hughes was so reluctant to make any compromises based on the suggestions of the Hays Office that the film's release was postponed for two whole years. Blake speculates that "[h]ad he held out another two years, when Hollywood got serious about its production code, *Scarface* might never have been released at all" (131).
3. Although the Code was adopted in 1930, it did not come into effect until 1934. This is how Mintz and Roberts explain the development:
    the producers had regarded it [the Code of 1930] as a public relations device, not as a code of censorship. But in 1933, the newly appointed apostolic delegate to the U.S. Catholic Church, the Most Reverend Amleto Giovanni Cicognani, called on Catholics to launch "a united and vigorous campaign for the purification of the cinema, which has become a deadly menace to morals." Many Catholics responded by forming the Legion of Decency, which soon had nine million members pledged to boycott films that the Legion's rating board condemned. Threatened by fear of boycotts, the producers decided to enforce the production code (17).
4. There are four different forms of film censorship: withholding a finished film from distribution and exhibition (the case of Peckinpah's *Straw Dogs* in the UK affords an example in this respect); overt censure, which implies the termination of a film project for political reasons; covert censure, abandoning a project due to a lack of funding; and post-censorship, the re-editing of a film prior to its theatrical release (Petrie 1).
5. The convention which divides the firing of a gun and its resulting impact into two separate shot segments illustrates the extent to which depictions of violence in Hollywood films prior to the 1960s were subject to extra-aesthetic concerns. In the event that censorship boards might delete the sequence, the convention protected narrative continuity by splitting up the action into several shots. Thus, even though censors would remove part of a scene due to violence, there would still be sufficient material left to ensure that the film did not skip important plot information (Maltby, "Spectacle of Criminality" 121).
6. Howard Hughes was regarded as a threat to the established Hollywood studios. A self-made businessman and millionaire with movie-making ambitions, Hughes financed his own production company, Caddo, which thus became one of the very few – if not the only – independent American film company at the time.
7. E.R. Hagemann gives 26 March 1932 as the date of release (31).
8. After the controversy surrounding the gangster movies of the early 1930s, the issue of screen violence was largely laid to rest until the late 1940s, when, as Hoberman observes, Maxwell Shane's *City Across the River* (1949) was cut according to Production Code advice (120). This film was part of a small cycle of juvenile delinquency

films that flourished briefly around 1950, and which included titles such as Nicholas Ray's *They Live By Night* and *Knock on Any Door* (both 1949), Kurt Neumann's *Bad Boy* (1949) and Joseph H. Lewis's *Gun Crazy* (1950). Despite a few occasional hisses – spurned by the release *of The Blackboard Jungle* (Richard Brooks 1955), *Kiss Me Deadly* (Robert Aldrich 1955), *Rebel Without a Cause* (Nicholas Ray 1955), *Baby Face Nelson* (Don Siegel 1957), *Machine Gun Kelly* (Roger Corman 1958) and *The Bonnie Parker Story* (William Witney 1958) – film violence as a public and media topic would not reappear until the late 1960s with *Bonnie and Clyde*.

9. Andrew Sarris characterizes the film as "the bloodiest and most brutal of the gangster films" ("World of Howard Hawks" 37). Doherty's verdict is that Hawks's film was "the most controversial and violent" of the 1930s cycle (148), and Cuban novelist and film critic Guillermo Cabrera Infante maintains that Hawks's opening sequence set the tone for the entire genre of gangster and crime films that came out of Hollywood in the 1930s (48).

10. For an extended discussion of the preface's rhetorical relation to the narrative, see my "Straitjacketing the Image: Illocutionary Writing and the Obstruction of Cine-Semiosis in Hawks' *Scarface*."

11. According to Maltby, in the classical era the issue of violence was subsumed under the more general category of crime, a fact the Payne Fund Studies also confirm. It was only in the 1960s that depictions of violence came to be viewed as a distinct case ("Spectacle of Criminality" 120). However, as most of the criminal activity seen in the gangster films involves violence, there is no reason to subjugate the prominence of violence to a matter of crime alone; nor is it inconceivable that the priority given to crime over violence is actually interrelated with the seeming "invisibility" of violence from an aesthetic point of view. The hypothesis, then, would be that it is not until violence becomes stylistically "excessive," as in Penn and Peckinpah, that it is considered a category of its own.

12. See Keith Hollingsworth, *The Newgate Novel, 1830-1847: Bulwer, Ainsworth, Dickens, and Thackeray* (1963).

13. The previously mentioned author Yukio Mishima and filmmaker Donald Cammell are examples of artists who carried the romanticization of murder to its extreme conclusion in both art and in life. That there remains an interest in the tradition of the murder song in contemporary popular culture is evident in the work of recording artists like Nick Cave (*Murder Ballads* 1996), The Auteurs (*After Murder Park* 1996), and Kristin Hersh (*Murder, Misery and Then Goodnight* 1998).

14. As much a lurid promise as a warning, the disclaimer's statement that "[e]very incident in this picture is the reproduction of an actual occurrence" refers among other things to incidents like the St. Valentine's Day Massacre in 1929, when Al Capone and his cohorts murdered seven men from Bugs Moran's gang in Chicago, and the Siege of West 90th Street in New York in 1931, in which young criminal Francis "Two-Gun" Crowley was apprehended by the NYPD after a two-hour shootout (Hagemann 40-41).

15. In his 2002 study of the history of the gangster cinema, Fran Mason reads *Scarface* as a meta-generic narrative of excess which puts to use "virtually all the gangster tropes established in the earlier classic gangster films" (24).

16. E.R. Hagemann makes the same observation in an article which predates Doherty's text (33).

17. In the present context, I have in mind the general and pedestrian rather than the academic or clinical sense of the term. I am aware that the notion of hysteria has a controversial history, particularly with respect to the term's association with femininity. Though the linkage is evidently fallacious, there is still a sense in which the clichéd perception, by the recalcitrance of convention, persists as a cultural codification. Needless to say, I do not in any way endorse this connotation. Moreover, when I earlier claim that *Scarface*'s narrative emplotment plotting is hysterical, I mean that the film can hardly be found to obey long established principles of narrative composition, principles which regulate a film's rhythm so that peaks of action may be foregrounded by long, intermittent stretches of relative calm. *Scarface* violates these Aristotelian principles by more or less skipping the tranquil parts, thus skewing what one ordinarily considers to be vital functions of narrative rhythms. In comparison, a text like *The Killing* permits the final act of violence to gather a particular momentum, since the preceding narrative consistently favors the suggestion of a crisis rather than the crisis itself. Conversely, in Hawks's film the omission of pauses that allow narrative progression to accumulate tension results in a plot that is too hurried, or "highly strung" as it were. There is a certain semblance to the movements of hysteria in this, though of course merely on the level of analogy.

18. Other scholars have also commented on the incest motif. See, for example, Clark Branson 71.

19. Lucrezia Borgia (1480-1519) is reputed to have had an incestuous relationship with her elder brother Cesare and her father, Pope Alexander VI. The story of her life was the inspiration for Victor Hugo's prose play *Lucrece Borgia*, written in 1833, the same year as Donizetti completed his *Lammermoor* opera (Hagemann 40).

20. There are several versions of this song, apparently conceived by Wallace Saunders and first published in 1902, and the one used in *Scarface* may be found in H.M. Belden and A.P. Hudson's *The Frank C. Brown Collection of North Carolina Folklore* (1952) (Hagemann 41).

21. Coincidentally, Maugham's text was adapted for the screen and released only a few months after *Scarface*'s premiere under the direction of Lewis Milestone. Another version of the story had been made into the film *Sadie Thompson* (1928), by Raoul Walsh – a key director of gangster films, whose *White Heat* is much indebted to *Scarface*.

22. The range of associations that the sign of the X carries could doubtlessly be extended. I have chosen to pass over the obvious religious resonance of the symbol, which is something that Wood discusses in his book on Hawks. Hagemann, moreover, has suggested that the appearance of the symbol in the first shot resembles a Tau cross, which in art is the insignia of St. Anthony the Great (31).

Notes to Part III – Chapter 4

1. Mario Falsetto is only one of many critics who have remarked upon this consistent thematic strain in Kubrick's oeuvre: "A central theme of THE KILLING, and of Kubrick's work as a whole, is the fallibility of the individual" (*Stanley Kubrick* 12). Writ-

ing twenty years earlier, Gene D. Phillips expresses a similar view: "the novel [*Clean Break*] touches on a theme that is a frequent preoccupation of Kubrick's films: the presumably perfect plan of action that goes wrong through human fallibility and/or chance" (30).

2. White is the author of a series of potboilers in the 1950s-and 60s, including *Flight into Terror* (1955), *Invitation to Violence* (1958) and *Death at Sea* (1961). THE KILLING's affinity with pulp fiction is further augmented by Jim Thompson's dialogue work for Kubrick. Thompson's oeuvre contains now classic novels like THE KILLER INSIDE ME (1952), AFTER DARK, MY SWEET (1955) and THE GETAWAY (1959), the latter adapted for the screen by Peckinpah in 1972.

3. The movies were granted First Amendment rights in 1952, when the Supreme Court in what has become known as the "Miracle Decision" ruled that "'sacrilege' was not a 'viable standard' by which to suppress a movie ... movies from this point on would be considered protected speech" (Lyons 8). The film that led to this decision was Rossellini's THE MIRACLE (1951). Although the Hays Office remained active for 10-15 more years, the Miracle Decision fundamentally changed the official view on the cinema. The gradual liberalization in the depictions of violence seems to be related to this conceptual shift from defining film as pure business to defining it as art.

4. See also Stephen Mamber par. 7.

5. Violence as an externalization of psychic instability seems to have been a common trope in classical Hollywood filmmaking. As Slocum has reported, images of violence often imply nonconformity and deviation ("Violence and American Cinema" 4).

6. See also Hantke, who finds violence to be "the driving force" of Kubrick's plotting (par. 18).

7. Space does not allow for a general account of the history, themes and aesthetics of film noir. The body of literature on the genre is bulky, and over the last fifteen years there has been a deluge of publications on the subject. French cinéphile Nino Frank allegedly coined the term in 1946 (and thus linking the films with the crime novels known as Série Noire), when a number of key films produced and released in the United States during the war finally reached Parisian screens: THE MALTESE FALCON (Huston 1941), LAURA (Preminger 1944), MURDER, MY SWEET (Dmytryk 1944), DOUBLE INDEMNITY (Wilder 1944) and WOMAN IN THE WINDOW (Fritz Lang 1944). The first book-length study of the genre was Raymond Borde and Étienne Chaumeton's *Panorama du Film Noir Américain* (1955). The reader may consult the following titles for further reading: Amir Massoud Karimi, *Toward a Definition of the American Film Noir, 1941-1949* (1976); Ann E. Kaplan, ed., *Women in Film Noir* (1978); Alain Silver and Elizabeth Ward, eds., *Film Noir* (1979); Foster Hirsch, *The Dark Side of the Screen: Film Noir* (1981); Jon Tuska, *Dark Cinema: American Film Noir in Cultural Perspective* (1984); J.P. Telotte, *Voices in the Dark: The Narrative Patterns of Film Noir* (1989); Frank Krutnik, *In a Lonely Street: Film Noir, Genre, Masculinity* (1991); Ian Cameron, Ed, *The Movie Book of Film Noir* (1992); R. Barton Palmer, *Hollywood's Dark Cinema: The American Film Noir* (1994); James F. Maxfield, *The Fatal Woman: Sources of Male Anxiety in American Film Noir, 1941-1991* (1996); R. Barton Palmer, ed., *Perspectives on Film Noir* (1996); James Naremore, *More Than Night: Film Noir in its Contexts* (1998); Eddie Muller, *Dark City Dames: The Wicked Women of Film Noir* (2001); Paula Rabinowitz, *Black and White and Noir: America's Pulp Modernism* (2002); Kelly Oliver and Benigno

Trigo, *Noir Anxiety* (2002); Andrew Dickos, *Street With No Name: A History of the Classic American Film Noir* (2002); and Megan E. Abbott, *The Street was Mine: White Masculinity and Urban Space in Hardboiled Fiction and Film Noir* (2002).

8. See, for example, Mark Irwin, who suggests that noir is essentially about "the mysteries of alienation, capricious fortune, and the possibility of cosmic malevolence" (74).

9. For a meticulous account of different types of narrators, see Gérard Genette's *Narrative Discourse* (1980, 243-259).

10. Kubrick's film appeared at a time when a high modernist film practice was evolving into full maturity. The period from the late 1940s and throughout the early 1960s is generally regarded as the peak of the art cinema mode, featuring landmark texts by accomplished auteurs like Fellini, Kurosawa, Bergman, Buñuel, Bresson, Godard, Truffaut and Resnais. In its complex flashback structure, Kubrick's film displays at least a vague resemblance to Kurosawa's RASHOMON (1950).

11. THE KILLING features most of the trademarks identified by Schrader: a complex temporal order, the narrational pleasure of "reliving a doomed past," scenes lit for night, an expressionistic mise en scène (typically manifested in a preference for vertical and oblique lines over horizontal ones), the emphasis on compositional tension to complement physical action, an obsession with rain, and the equal distribution of lighting on actor and setting (11).

Notes to Part III – Chapter 5

1. The frequent recourse to referencing Melville reveals the extent to which criticism of the film has become almost indistinguishable from the mythologization of it. David Weddle, for instance, drapes his description of the film's production context in a dramatic language that does little to subdue the sense of epic adventure with which the filming of THE WILD BUNCH has been associated: "when Sam Peckinpah set off for Mexico in the spring of 1968 to begin filming, it was with the fanatical passion of an Ahab determined to plant his harpoon in the back of the white whale" ("Making" 45). What future criticism needs is a perspective that will demythologize both the film and its director.

2. THE WILD BUNCH has been recognized as the central text in Peckinpah's cinema by among others William Parrill (29).

3. Several critics have drawn attention to the biographical aspect of the director's work, notable among them Doug McKinney (20).

4. Comparing the director's fate to that of Welles, Horsley claims that Peckinpah was "a victim of the Hollywood system" (1: 52). Unlike Welles, Horsley says, "Peckinpah had an almost perverse desire to squander his own talents" (1: 51).

5. There exist at least four different versions of the film: the 151-minute cut that was shown at the notorious sneak preview in Kansas City in May 1969, the 145-minute European cut, the 143-minute initial domestic version, and Phil Feldman's drastically abridged, 135-minute cut dictated by Warner. Two narratively prominent

flashbacks were excised by the studio, yet reinserted at Paul Seydor's behest in 1980 (Simmons 83).

6. Consult for example Cavell, "What Photography Calls Thinking" 11.

7. See also Silverman's luminous analysis of photography's "screen" in the last chapter of her *The Threshold of the Visible World*. "The still camera," she imputes, "simultaneously 'kills' and affirms; it lifts the object out of life and into representation, and psychically and socially actualizes it. It would thus seem that what we generally think of as 'reality' is on the side of 'death' rather than 'life,' representation rather than being" (199).

8. See, for example, Lesley Stern, who suggests that "film itself can materialise as a body of sorts, a body that bleeds, metaphorically, but with sensible effects, producing for instance sensations of illness, fear, ecstasy" (254).

9. Devin McKinney has also argued that Peckinpah kills off the Hollywood western with THE WILD BUNCH ("*The Wild Bunch*" 195). McKinney, however, does not significantly elaborate on this statement, nor does he place it in the wider context of death and mortality that defines the film.

10. See also Parks, who holds that Peckinpah's revisionism in fact contributes to a re-mythologization of the western hero (115), and Dukore and Slotkin, who make a case for the authenticity of THE WILD BUNCH's act of generic subversion (3) and the film's "demystification of Western mythic structures", respectively (*Gunfighter Nation* 612).

11. For a similar conclusion, see Slotkin, *Gunfighter Nation* 633.

12. Though Eastwood himself has dedicated the film to his mentors Leone and Don Siegel, screenwriter Lem Dobbs considers it an homage to Peckinpah (Richard Combs 16).

13. For a comprehensive survey of the evolution of the western in the 1980s and 1990s, see Neale's article "Westerns and Gangster Films Since the 1970s."

14. For a discussion of how the western myth is still active in the 1990s westerns, see also Douglas J. McReynolds 47.

15. The production of THE WILD BUNCH has its own history – possibly apocryphal – of violence on the set (Bouzereau 16).

16. The way in which the concepts of allegory and melancholy interrelate in Benjamin's thought may also provide a pattern with which better to comprehend the nature of Peckinpah's investment in that selfsame structure. Benjamin writes that if the object becomes allegorical under the gaze of melancholy, if melancholy causes life to flow out of it and it remains dead, but eternally secure, then it is exposed to the allegorist, it is unconditionally in his power. That is to say it is now quite incapable of emanating any meaning or significance of its own; such significance as it has, it acquires from the allegorist. He places it within it, and stands behind it; not in a psychological but in an ontological sense" (*Origin* 183).

17. This openness is a result of the inherent inparaphrasability of aesthetic discourse, or, as de Man puts it, "the impossibility of closure and totalization (that is the impossibility of coming into being) [in] all textual systems made up of tropological substitutions" ("Autobiography" 71). Mitchell's notion of picture theory that I refer to in the introduction may offer a context in which better to make sense of the allegorical "thinking" of a film like THE WILD BUNCH.

18. See Slotkin's *Gunfighter Nation* 591; and Prince's "Hemorrhaging" 140. For an opposing view, see David E. James' book on American cinema in the 1960s, in which he proposes that films like BONNIE AND CLYDE and THE WILD BUNCH should be seen as "de-contextualized" and apolitical (173).

19. See Bliss, "Introduction" xviii.

20. See also David A. Cook for an assessment of the "dark" humanism inherent in Peckinpah's vision ("*The Wild Bunch*" 123).

21. Symbolically significant as it may be, the integration of Peckinpah's work into a specifically American tradition should not deflect attention away from the fact that the filmmaker must have drawn inspiration from a comprehensive agglomeration of sources. Marie Selland, the director's first wife, recalls that Peckinpah was familiar with Shakespeare, Dickens and Cela, and in college and after in fact directed plays by writers like Sophocles, Molière, Congreve, Ibsen, Strindberg, Chekhov, Brecht and Pirandello (Seydor, *Peckinpah* 1980, 256). See also Dukore 3, 11.

22. See also Slotkin, *Gunfighter Nation* 157.

23. See, for example, Bliss, "Introduction" xx; Pechter 91; and Strug 89.

24. Consult also Dukore 75, and Coursodon 257.

25. The expression belongs to Tompkins, who uses it descriptively when discussing the Agua Verde montage (229).

26. The principal proponent of the regeneration mythos is of course Slotkin. See his chapter "Cross-Over Point" in *Gunfighter Nation* for an extended analysis of the myth's relation to THE WILD BUNCH (578-623). For a related argument, consult Seydor, *Peckinpah* 1997, 319; and Robert Shulman 2: 262. Consider also Cawelti's hypothesis that the concept of regeneration was integral to the establishing of the formula for the western in the 19th century (*Adventure* 193).

27. For an analysis of how a "new" masculinity is acquired in a non-western Peckinpah narrative like STRAW DOGS, see Isa Ostertag 666.

28. It is Lee Mitchell who draws upon the concept of belatedness to describe both the setting and the characters of Peckinpah's film (*Westerns* 241). The choice of terminology is well suited to indicate the chasm that has arisen – and that the western relays – between historical inevitability and cultural mentality: "The impetus to roam free … move westward has no object anymore, but the American psyche still wishes to see it enacted" (Shadoian 299).

29. See also Thompson 8.

30. For an explication of the concept of the rhizome, consult Deleuze and Guattari's *A Thousand Plateaus* (1980).

31. For a full examination of the function of tableaux imagery in Peckinpah, read Prince's *Savage Cinema* 170-184.

32. Dukore has termed this self-reflexive strategy a "play-within-a-play" that "mirror[s] and guide[s] audience response" (82).

33. In surrealist literature in particular, ants conventionally symbolize blood and death. See for instance André Breton's *Le revolver à cheveux blancs* 57; Benjamin Péret's *Mort aux vaches et au champ d'honneur* 47; Artaud's *Héliogabale ou l'anarchiste couronné* 139; and of course Buñuel and Dali's UN CHIEN ANDALOU. Among a host of other significations, the scorpion has traditionally been associated with death and self-destruction.

34. Hedling's comment was made as a response to the author's "Violence as Form and Rhetoric: On Reading THE WILD BUNCH as a Narrative of Regeneration," and is a particularly perspicacious observation in light of the fact that Peckinpah allegedly staged his own version of Curtiz's film at age eleven (Seydor, *Peckinpah* 337).

35. For an expansion of the theme of entrapment, read Bliss's article "'Back Off to What?' Enclosure, Violence, and Capitalism in Sam Peckinpah's THE WILD BUNCH."

36. Editor Lombardo claims that the finished film, which was cut from three hours and forty-five minutes to two hours and twenty-four minutes, consisted of an astonishing 3,642 shots, which is six times as many as there are in the average feature film (Simmons 101).

37. On the filmic deconstruction of the myth of manifest destiny, see also Michael Eric Stein 41.

38. The origin of this process can probably be traced back at least to the Italian Neorealism of the 1940s. Films like the paradigmatic THE BICYCLE THIEF (Vittorio De Sica 1948) reveled in a narratively loose and open structure, where many of the plot events were left unresolved. The linearity of the story is defunct, narrative spaces are non-coordinated, and the characters lack a clear sense of purpose or motive for their actions.

39. Marshall's innovative re-reading of Peckinpah suggests a propinquity with Marcuse's argument in *The Aesthetic Dimension* that the determination of artistic form is to engender new moralities.

40. Note how Russell's thesis recalls that of Sobchack ("Violent Dance" 118).

41. The genre of horror films occasionally produces depictions of violence to the body in ways that appear similar to the strategies in THE WILD BUNCH. Peckinpah's manipulative editing, notwithstanding, the western film overall is shot in a "classicist" mode, whereas the horror film explicitly defies notions of conventionalized realism.

42. Incidentally, but nonetheless significantly, in structure Peckinpah's approach resembles the aesthetics of violence found in the neo-Assyrian palace reliefs (900-627 B. C.).

Notes to Part III – Chapter 6

1. For an estimation of the influence of Peckinpah's cinema on popular culture at large, see Richard Luck 15.

2. See, for example, Horsley 2: 229-231.

3. See also Kim Newman, Rev. 51; Lane 95; and Whalen 2.

4. For a discussion of the relation between the materiality of the body, signification, and poststructuralism, see Judith Butler's *Bodies That Matter* (1993), especially 27-31.

5. This concept is itself a reference to Joseph Sargent's crime film THE TAKING OF PELHAM ONE TWO THREE (1974).

6. The wealth of allusions in RESERVOIR DOGS form a veritable catalogue of intertextual shards from films such as THE WIZARD OF OZ, DILLINGER (Max Nosseck 1945), THE BIG COMBO (Joseph H. Lewis 1955), DU RIFIFI CHEZ LES HOMMES (Jules Dassin 1955), THE KILLING, OCEAN'S ELEVEN (Lewis Milestone 1960), THE GREAT ESCAPE (John

Sturges 1963), LE PETIT SOLDAT (Godard 1963), THE PROFESSIONALS (Richard Brooks 1966), POINT BLANK (John Boorman 1967), LE SAMOURAÏ (Jean-Pierre Melville 1967), THE WILD BUNCH, A CLOCKWORK ORANGE, STRAW DOGS, STRAIGHT TIME (Ulu Grosbard 1978), Q (Larry Cohen 1982), VIGILANTE (William Lustig 1982), BREATHLESS (Jim McBride 1983), BLUE VELVET (Lynch 1986), RAW DEAL (John Irvin 1986), THE LOST BOYS (Joel Schumacher 1987), YINGHUNG BUNSIK II (John Woo 1987), and CITY ON FIRE (Ringo Lam 1987), television series like "Honey West" (1965-66), "The Fantastic Four" (1967), "The Partridge Family" (1970-74), and "Get Christie Love" (1974-75), and pop songs such as "True Blue" (Madonna 1986) and "Stuck in the Middle With You" (Stealers Wheel 1973).

7. See also Botting and Wilson 7. As a director who recycles fragments from recent media history, Tarantino is not so much an anomaly as a representative of the generation of American filmmakers born in the 1960s that Hanson terms the "culture vultures" (18). This emerging generation, which includes such notable artists as Steven Soderbergh, Fincher, Paul Thomas Anderson, Todd Haynes, Doug Liman, Bryan Singer, and the Wachowski brothers, consists to an unprecedented degree of "moviemakers whose only frame of reference is movies" (Hanson 40).

8. Giuliana Bruno has in like manner defined the poetics of pastiche as "an imitation of dead styles deprived of any satirical impulse" (238).

9. See also Todd 42.

10. One may note that Baudrillard's skepticism vis-à-vis the image appears to implicate all forms of visuality, whereas my own emphasis in this context is restricted to the domain of the fiction film.

11. The logic of this argument finds its precedent in what Bordwell has identified as "the standard version of stylistic history," now largely discredited. See *On the History of Film Style* 12-45.

12. As John Orr has persuasively argued in *The Art and Politics of Film* (2000), the ineffectual concept of postmodernism in relation to the cinema may advantageously be cast aside in favor of the more informative term "Hyper-Modernism." Orr claims that the neo-modern form of the 1960s and 1970s has evolved into what he calls "Meta-Modernism" in the East (often centering on the clash between tradition and modernity, as in the films of Abbas Kiarostami and Edward Yang) and "Hyper-Modernism" in the West (where a concern with technology and with the proliferation of spectacle recurrently comes to define a broad array of film fictions (1). The notion of hypermodernity suggests a continuity not only with the modernist cinemas but also with widely disseminated propositions such as Debord's "society of the spectacle" and Baudrillard's theory of the hyper-real. Evidently, the formal characteristics which identify hypermodern texts would correspond to those critics like Cristina Degli-Esposti take to be manifestations of the prototypically postmodern:
By morphing into other entities and recreating other narrational centers that constitute layers of *metalepses*, i.e., the worlds and their levels of reality, postmodern films become multivoiced texts ruled by shifting perspectives where puzzle-making and elaborate word/image play become the signifying space in which meaning occur (9). Moreover, the conceptual signposts of postmodernism – the "'dereferentialization of the real'," the "'desubstantialization of the subject'," the "'dematerialization of the economy'," and the "atrophied" sense of history (Stam 301) – likewise overlap with the features of the hypermodern. The term postmodernism, which was already

employed as an aesthetic category in Federico de Onís' *Antologia de la poesia española e hispanoamericana* (1934) and as an historical category in Arnold Toynbee's *A Study of History* (1934), is due to its inherently and "exceptionally protean" quality largely unhelpful as an explanatory concept with regard to the politics of amimeticism (Stam 300). Though the denomination has been current at least since Fiedler and Ihab Hassan used it in the 1960s, and though its genealogy in film criticism can be traced back to BLADE RUNNER (Ridley Scott 1982), Orr's term is more apposite in the present context. See also W.J.T. Mitchell's interview with Christine Wiesenthal and Brad Bucknell, in which he pronounces postmodernism dead and proposes in its place the term "the pictorial turn" (6-9), which I discuss in the introductory chapter.

13. By the director's own admission, NATURAL BORN KILLERS is a "surface movie," a film "about images" (Bouzereau 68).

14. As a process of simulation the concept of the hyperreal, according to Baudrillard, may be envisioned as "the generations by models of a real without origin or reality" (*Simulations* 2).

15. Stam thus explains the logic by which hypermodern cinema negotiates the relation between film and audience:
    The point is to combine references to the most diverse sources possible in a ludic game with the spectator, whose narcissism is flattered not through old-fashioned secondary identification with characters but rather through the display of cultural capital made possible by the recognition of the references (305).
    In RESERVOIR DOGS, the protagonists themselves participate in this game, as in the sequence where Eddie narrates his Elois story.

16. Contemporary cinema's appropriation of references from the vaults of film and media history, Slocum contends, engenders "historically 'depthless' movies whose simulation of and nostalgia for the past are based in existing representations rather than any attempt to re-create a 'real' past" ("Violence" 21). For similar conclusions, consult also Horsley 2: 231, and Devin McKinney, "Violence" 106.

17. See also Grant, "Landmark" 523.

18. According to Hutcheon, who holds that it is the very determination of "postmodern art" to call into question "principles such as value, order, meaning, control, and identity" (13).

19. Burnham's further thesis – that this lack, or "split subjectivity," arises from the colonization of white, heterosexual masculinity by corporate America (120) – is less pertinent to RESERVOIR DOGS than to FIGHT CLUB, and I shall briefly return to this topic in the next chapter.

20. See also Jonathan Romney 16.

21. Baretta was the unconventional cop with a fondness for disguises in the 1975-76 television series of the same name.

22. See also Bal on the different ontologizations of character in "mimetic and constructivist narratology" (483).

23. In his *Point of View in the Cinema* (1984), Branigan delineates the six aspects of the shot in terms of *origin* (the spatial source of an image), *vision* (the material condition which connects the viewer with the viewed), *time* (the relations of chronology or simultaneity between one shot and the next), *frame* (the spatial delimitation of the shot), *object* (what is shown), and *mind* (the kind of subjectivity manifested by the spatial source) (57).

Notes to Part III – Chapter 7

1. Giroux is not the only cultural critic who disprizes the ethos of a cinema of exhaustion, to borrow Sharrett's term. In an analysis even more defiantly symptomatic than that of Giroux, Sharrett himself imputes that the self-reflexive allusionism of a score of canonical 1990s American films (PULP FICTION, SE7EN (Fincher 1995), HEAT (Michael Mann 1995), CRASH (David Cronenberg 1996), HAPPINESS (Todd Solondz 1998), THE MATRIX, AMERICAN BEAUTY (Sam Mendes 1999), and FIGHT CLUB) is in fact in cahoots with a neo-conservative culture industry divulging by this very self-reflexivity "that it has nothing more to say," thus traducing any progressive vision ("End of Story" 330). I do not share Sharrett's sense of pessimism, nor does his equation of historical exhaustion with allusionism seem overly commanding. The fascination with self-consciousness and artifice, as Carroll has persuasively argued (*Philosophical Problems* 4), inheres in the very roots of Hollywood Cinema and is hence not a phenomenon to which late 20th century films can make any definite claim. Secondly, even if the films at stake in Sharrett's essay could legitimately be read as tracts for a neo-conservative masculinity, for the Faustian bargain of textuality itself with the commodification industries, for the decay and exhaustion of Western culture – in short, for all the other millennial diseases that one can possibly imagine – it is not a causal fact that the practice of transtextual quotation should have anything to do with this development. If we look beyond Hollywood, it would transpire that an almost viral allusionism is equally predominant in many other national cinemas apparently shorn of the apocalypticism peculiar to American film.
2. Peripheral yet somewhat connected to this trend is the work of Andres Serrano, whose provocative photographs of dead bodies and appropriation of bodily liquids such as blood and urine as aesthetic material disclose a similar preoccupation with elastic forms of corporeality.
3. In retrospect, Project Mayhem's acts of terrorism against the credit card companies– the icons of capitalist modernity – seem like an uncanny premonition and situate the film's rhetoric within a broader political context of anti-consumerism and globalization.
4. Brookey and Westerfelhaus have even suggested that the negotiations over the meaning of masculinity extend to and are modified by the elaborate DVD package of FIGHT CLUB. The DVD material features interviews with the director and actors Edward Norton and Brad Pitt in which they, according to Brookey and Westerfelhaus, endeavor to redefine the alleged homoeroticism of the film in terms of homosociality (30). Elsewhere, the same critics interpret the violence in FIGHT CLUB as "a means of simultaneously relieving the homoerotic tension in a way deemed acceptable to mainstream sensibilities" (33). As one may recall, Jacobs mounts a similar argument in his reading of the scenes of male intimacy in RESERVOIR DOGS (39). See also Alexandra Juhasz's "The Phallus Unfetished" for another interpretation of FIGHT CLUB's blend of homoeroticism and homophobia.
5. See also Gavin Smith's use of the term, "Inside Out" 61.
6. A conception of the body as a discursive surface has of course become a critical commonplace, and certainly since Foucault's *Discipline and Punish* (1975), in which the author acknowledges the political involvement of the body in power relations

which "invest it, mark it, train it, torture it, force it to carry out tasks, to perform ceremonies, to emit signs" (25). See also Jean Starobinski 353. Insofar as aesthetic depictions of the body are concerned, James Elkins's *Pictures of the Body* (1999) offers one of the most rewarding studies on the subject. The semiotic pliability of the cinematic body, however, has only recently come to be seen as a subject of film theory beyond the horror genre. Barbara Creed's essay "Horror and the Carnivalesque: The Body-Monstrous" may nonetheless be a suitable place from which to begin one's study of how a particular film genre takes the malleability of the body as its primary thematic matter.

7. See also Lola Young, who highlights the degree to which ideas concerning masculinity are always in fluctuation (60), and Homi K. Bhabha, who defines masculinity as "the 'taking up' of an enunciative position, the making up of a psychic complex, the assumption of a social gender, the supplementation of a historic sexuality, the apparatus of a cultural difference" (58).

8. The ubiquity of corporate America in FIGHT CLUB is visually, though subliminally, accentuated by the inclusion of the Starbucks logo in nearly every shot of the film.

9. FIGHT CLUB inscribes a breathless range of sources that seem to surpass even that of Tarantino's archival cinema, quoting films such as THE INVISIBLE MAN (James Whale 1933), CINDERELLA (Clyde Geronimi et al. 1950), THE QUIET MAN, DR. STRANGELOVE, PERSONA (Ingmar Bergman 1966), VALLEY OF THE DOLLS (Mark Robson 1967), THE GRADUATE, PLANET OF THE APES (Franklin J. Schaffner 1968), PERFORMANCE, A CLOCKWORK ORANGE, FAT CITY, TAXI DRIVER, APOCALYPSE NOW, RAGING BULL, BRAZIL (Terry Gilliam 1985), RAISING ARIZONA (Coen 1987), BAD INFLUENCE (Curtis Hanson 1990), TOTAL RECALL (Paul Verhoeven 1990), IN THE LINE OF FIRE (Wolfgang Petersen 1993), FORREST GUMP (Robert Zemeckis 1994), SE7EN, TWELVE MONKEYS (Gilliam 1995), and TRAINSPOTTING (Danny Boyle 1996).

10. The source of Middleton's title is Ezra Pound's "Hugh Selwyn Mauberley: Life and Contacts."

11. Smith's apprehension of the underexplored aspects of film and masculinity is reminiscent of Neale's argument that heterosexual masculinity has been examined to the extent that it has been seen as a structuring norm vis-à-vis women and gay men, but rarely in other contexts ("Masculinity" 9). Film scholarship, however, can boast an important and expansive tradition of queer studies. See for example Parker Tyler's *Screening the Sexes: Homosexuality in the Movies* (1972), frequently regarded as the first such study of its kind, Richard Dyer's anthology *Gays and Film* (1977), Vito Russo's *The Celluloid Closet: Homosexuality in the Movies* (1981), Richard Dyer's *Now You See It: Studies on Lesbian and Gay Film* (1990), James R. Keller's *Queer (Un)Friendly Film and Television* (2002), and Robert Lang's *Masculine Interests: Homoerotics in Hollywood Film* (2002). It is symptomatic of the influence of this research tradition that the notions of homosociality and homosexuality tend to be applied to films (like RESERVOIR DOGS and FIGHT CLUB) that are crucially preoccupied with questions of masculinity, though not necessarily with homoeroticism in particular. In this regard, Alexander Doty's deliberately gay readings of canonic films like THE CABINET OF DR. CALIGARI (Robert Wiene 1920), CITIZEN KANE and PSYCHO in his *Flaming Classics: Queering the Film Canon* (2000) provides an illustrative instance. As we have previously seen, Jacobs's analysis of a scene from RESERVOIR DOGS and Brookey and Westerfelhaus' article on FIGHT CLUB represent examples of this seemingly compel-

ling need to reduce cinematic depictions of relationships between men to a matter of latent homosexuality. I do not claim that such readings are always infelicitous, though it would be refreshing occasionally to come across interpretations of male intimacy in the cinema that are at least marginally less predictable.

12. See, for example, James L. Neibaur's *Tough Guy: The American Movie Macho* (1989), Steve Craig's compilation *Men, Masculinity and the Media* (1992), and the Constance Penley and Sharon Willis-edited anthology *Male Trouble* (1993).

13. For more on the interrelation between the depictions of men in FAT CITY and FIGHT CLUB, see my "Topographies of Defeat: Masculinity and Desolation in FAT CITY and JUNIOR BONNER" 43-44.

14. The scope of this thesis does not permit a consideration of the strategies and aesthetics of the first stage of this process, that is, how films eroticize the body of the male protagonist, but this is a topic that unquestionably merits further attention, with regard to FIGHT CLUB in particular. One may note that, according to Jerslev, "stagings of the male body are the most important signifier in the construction of the appeal of [the action and horror genres]" (41), an assertion whose relevance seems to call for sustained research. See also Lee Mitchell's claim that the notion of the brutalized (and subsequently restored) body is formative of the construction of masculinity in the western (*Westerns* 185).

15. For a meticulous description of the trajectory of the film's first shot, which starts at the brain's center of emotion (the amygdala) and culminates in the image of the gun barrel in Jack's mouth, see Lisa Stanley's "Digital Domain uses Houdini to get Inside Jack's Head." See also Taubin, "So Good It Hurts" 18.

16. See Brigitte Peucker's *Incorporating Images* (1995) for an intriguing account of the centrality of the body for an articulation of cinematic tropes.

17. Shaviro even seems to suggest that an ethics of film should be founded on the aesthetics of the cinematized body, and maintains that the viewing of film bodies has practical consequences in that the omnipresence of mass media bodies has made the viewers perceive their own bodies differently (264). The performing body and the spectator's body, Shaviro speculates, are "inextricably linked in the formation and operation of the cinematic libidinal economy" (82).

18. Deleuze's insistence on the affiliation of philosophy and the body, it must be stressed, has a counterpart in the historically intimate relation between poetics and the body. Aesthetics, as Eagleton has remarked, originated as "a discourse of the body" (*Ideology of the Aesthetic* 13), a proclamation echoed in a slightly altered form by Fuery when he says that "[c]inema's discourse is the discourse of the body" (90). It may be objected that such a privileging of the corporeal disingenuously marginalizes what is incontestably a vital component of film, namely the level of sound. This objection is partly warranted. Sadly, the use of music in film remains an underexplored area of film studies, despite significant recent efforts. See for example Rick Altman's *Sound Theory, Sound Practice* (1992) and Michel Chion's *Audio-Vision: Sound on Screen* (1994). However, it must be pointed out that much non-musical sound in film consists of diegetic speech, whose origin is after all the body. Rather than protesting the hegemony of the body that theorists like Fuery and Shaviro seem to legislate, one could with no small justification argue that film criticism and theory have paid too scant attention to the extra-linguistic (and possibly extra-narrative) discourse of the body, gravitating instead toward the more easily paraphrasable semio-

tics of dialogue, language and narrative. Moreover, it is unlikely that filmicity can survive without the visual and the body the way it could do without sound prior to THE JAZZ SINGER (1927).

19. It is the aspect of performativity which, according to Stern, makes the aesthetic body different from the everyday body: "the particular way of deploying energy ... the presence of an audience, that marking out of a quasi-ceremonial or ritualistic space" (259).

20. One may note that Silverman's concept of "ruination" is intriguingly reminiscent of Russell's definition of the photographic image (with reference to her theory on narrative mortification, as the reader may recall) as a "ruin" of bodily performance (5). There seems to be an intricate overlapping of concepts here which all in various ways gravitate toward the complex interrelation of violence, the body, film aesthetics, and the ontology of the image. Surely this is a correlation that warrants further scrutiny in a different context.

21. See also Taubin's short essay on FIGHT CLUB, "So Good It Hurts," in which she argues that Jack embraces violence as a means "to get out of his own skin" (18). For those interested in the broader ramifications of Silverman's yoking together of subjectivity and violence, I recommend Cynthia Marshall's recent book on Shakespeare and John Ford (among others), *The Shattering of the Self* (2002), in which the author argues that textual processes of the dissolution of the self through violence act as a defense against the demands of the emerging forms of modern subjectivity. It is from the Renaissance, she maintains, that we acquire "not only a violent literary culture but also a notion of subjective identity partly modeled through interaction with textual forms that cast pleasure in terms of dominance and submission" (4).

Notes to Postscript

1. See Shaviro 55, and Cynthia Marshall 47.
2. See also Miller's *The Ethics of Reading* 9; Berys Gaut 182; and Herbert Langfeld 104.
3. See de Laurot 581.

Bibliography

2001: A Space Odyssey. Dir. Stanley Kubrick. Metro-Goldwyn-Mayer, 1968.

Abbink, Jon. "Preface: Violation and Violence as Cultural Phenomena." Aijmer and Abbink xi-xvii.

Abbott, Megan E. *The Street Was Mine: White Masculinity and Urban Space in Hardboiled Fiction and Film Noir.* New York: Palgrave, 2002.

Abel, Sherry, ed. *The Immediate Experience: Movies, Comics, Theatre, and Other Aspects of Popular Culture.* 1962. Garden City, N.Y.: Anchor Books, 1964.

Abrams, M. H. *The Mirror and the Lamp: Romantic Theory and the Critical Tradition.* New York: Oxford UP, 1953.

A Clockwork Orange. Dir. Stanley Kubrick. Warner Brothers, 1971.

Adler, Mortimer J. *Art and Prudence.* 1937. New York: Arno P, 1978.

— *Art, The Arts, and the Great Ideas.* New York: Touchstone, 1994.

Adorno, Theodor W. "Commitment." Trans. Francis McDonagh. *The Essential Frankfurt School Reader.* Eds. Andrew Arato and Eike Gebhardt. Oxford: Basil Blackwell, 1978. 300-318.

Aghed, Jan. "*Pat Garrett and Billy the Kid.*" *Sight and Sound.* 42.2 (1973): 64-68.

Aijmer, Göran. "Introduction: The Idiom of Violence in Imagery and Discourse." Aijmer and Abbink 1-21.

Aijmer, Göran, and Jon Abbink, eds. *Meanings of Violence: A Cross Cultural Perspective.* Oxford: Berg, 2000.

Alexander, Samuel. "Art and the Material." *Philosophical and Literary Pieces.* Ed. J.L. London: Macmillan, 1939. 211-232.

Alford, C. Fred. "Freud and Violence." *Freud 2000.* Ed. Anthony Elliott. Cambridge: Polity P, 1998. 61-87.

Allen, Richard. *Projecting Illusion: Film Spectatorship and the Impression of Reality.* Cambridge: Cambridge UP, 1995.

Alliez, Éric. "Midday, Midnight: The Emergence of Cine-Thinking." Trans. Patricia Dailey. *The Brain is the Screen: Deleuze and the Philosophy of Cinema.* Ed. Gregory Flaxman. Minneapolis: U of Minnesota P, 2000. 293-302.

Allison, David B, Mark S. Roberts, and Allen S. Weiss, eds. *Sade and the Narrative of Transgression.* Cambridge: Cambridge UP, 1995.

Alloway, Lawrence. *Violent America: The Movies 1946-1964.* New York: Museum of Modern Art, 1971.

Alpert, Hollis. "Crime Wave." Wake and Hayden 216.

Altman, Rick. *The American Film Musical.* 1987. Bloomington: Indiana UP, 1989.

— *Film/Genre.* London: BFI Publishing, 1999.

— *Sound Theory, Sound Practice.* New York: Routledge, 1992.

Amis, Martin. "Blown Away." Karl French 12-19.

Ammann, Jean-Christophe. "Violence and Beauty." *Reasons for Knocking at an Empty House*. Bill Viola. Ed. Robert Violette. London: Thames and Hudson, 1995. 13-21.

Anderson, Joseph. *The Reality of Illusion: An Ecological Approach to Cognitive Film Theory*. Carbondale, Ill: Southern Illinois UP, 1996.

Andrew, Dudley. "André Bazin's 'Evolution." *Defining Cinema*. Ed. Peter Lehman. London: Athlone P, 1997. 73-94.

Andrew, Geoff. *The Films of Nicholas Ray: The Poet of Nightfall*. London: Charles Letts, 1991.

Andrews, Nigel. "Sam Peckinpah. The Survivor and the Individual." *Sight and Sound*. 42.2 (1973): 69-74.

Annesley, James. *Blank Fictions: Consumerism, Culture and the Contemporary American Novel*. London: Pluto P, 1998.

— "Commodification, Violence and the Body: A Reading of Some Recent American Fictions." Tim Armstrong 142-151.

Arsen, David. "The Return of a Bloody Great Classic." *Newsweek*. 13 March 1995: 70-71.

Apocalypse Now. Dir. Francis Ford Coppola. United Artists, 1979.

Ardrey, Robert. *African Genesis*. New York: Atheneum, 1961.

— *The Social Contract*. New York: Atheneum, 1970.

— *The Territorial Imperative*. New York: Atheneum, 1966.

Arendt, Hannah. *On Violence*. San Diego: Harvest/HBJ Book, 1969.

Arguillére, Eric. "Bedrar Skinnet?" *Z Filmtidsskrift*. 70 (1999): 145-161.

Arès, Philippe. *The Hour of Our Death*. 1977. Trans. Helen Weaver. New York: Alfred A. Knopf. 1981.

Aristotle. *The Ethics of Aristotle: The Nicomachean Ethics*. 1953. Trans. J.A.K. Thomson. Harmondsworth: Penguin, 1976.

— *Poetics*. Trans. Malcolm Heath. London: Penguin Books, 1996.

Armes, Roy. "Peckinpah and the Changing West." *London Magazine*. 9 (1970): 101-106.

Armstrong, Michael. "On Violence." *Films and Filming*. 15.6 (1969): 20-31.

Armstrong, Nancy, and Leonard Tennenhouse. "Representing Violence, or 'how the west was won'." Armstrong and Tennehouse 1-26.

— eds. The Violence of Representation. Literature and the History of Violence. London: Routledge, 1989.

Armstrong, Tim, ed. *American Bodies: Cultural Histories of the Physique*. Sheffield: Sheffield Academic P, 1996.

Arnheim, Rudolf. *Film Essays and Criticism*. Trans. Brenda Benthien. Madison: U of Wisconsin P, 1997.

Artaud, Antonin. *Héliogabale ou l'anarchiste couronné*. Paris: Gallimard, 1979.

— *The Theatre and its Double*. 1964. Trans. Victor Corti. London: John Calder, 1977.

Arthur, Paul. "Violent Genres." Gottesman and Brown 540-543.

— *The Asphalt Jungle*. Dir. John Huston. Metro-Goldwyn-Mayer, 1950.

Atkins, Thomas R., ed. *Graphic Violence on the Screen*. New York: Monarch P, 1976.

— "Images of Violence. An Introduction." Atkins 1-18.

Auerbach, Erich. *Mimesis: The Representation of Reality in Western Literature*. Trans. Willard R. Trask. Princeton, N.J.: Princeton UP, 1953.

Auteurs. *After Murder Park*. Hut, 1996.

Badlands. Dir. Terence Malick. Warner Brothers, 1973.

Bailey, John. "Bang Bang Bang Bang, Ad Nauseum." Prince, *Screening Violence* 79-85.

Baker, Robert K. *Mass Media and Violence; a report to the National Commission on the Causes and Prevention of violence, by David L. Lange, Robert K. Baker and Sandra J. Ball.* Washington, 1969.

Bal, Mieke. *Looking In: The Art of Viewing.* Introduction. Norman Bryson. Amsterdam: G +B Arts, 2001.

— *Quoting Caravaggio: Contemporary Art, Preposterous History.* Chicago: U of Chicago P, 1999.

— "Snow White in the Wrong Story: Cultural Analysis, Aesthetics, and Catastrophic Culture." *Aesthetic Theory, Art and Popular Culture.* Ed. Jostein Gripsrud. Bergen: Høyskoleforlaget, 1999. 33-71.

— "Toward a Harshavian Poetics." *Poetics Today.* 21.3 (2000): 479-502. *The Ballad of Cable Hogue.* Dir. Sam Peckinpah. Warner Brothers, 1970.

Barba, Eugenio. *Beyond the Floating Islands.* New York: PAJ Publications, 1986.

— *The Dilated Body.* Trans. Richard Fowler. Rome: Zeami Libri, 1985.

Barker, Francis. *The Culture of Violence: Essays on Tragedy and History.* Manchester: Manchester UP, 1993.

Barker, Martin. "Violence." *Sight and Sound.* 5.6 (1995): 10-13.

Barnouw, Eric. *Tube of Plenty: The Evolution of American Television.* 1975. New York: Oxford UP, 1990.

Barr, Charles. "*Straw Dogs, A Clockwork Orange* and the Critics." *Screen. The Journal of the Society for Education in Film and Television.* 13.2 (1972): 17-31.

Barthes, Roland. *Camera Lucida: Reflections on Photography.* 1980. Trans. Richard Howard. New York: Hill and Wang, 1981.

— "Rhetoric of the Image." *Image, Music, Text.* Trans. Stephen Heath. New York: Hill and Wang, 1977. 32-51.

— *S/Z.* 1970. Trans. Richard Miller. New York: Hill and Wang, 1974.

Bataille, Georges. *Literature and Evil.* 1957. Trans. Alastair Hamilton. London: Marion Boyars, 1985.

— *Visions of Excess: Selected Writings 1927-1939.* Trans. Allan Stoekl with Carl R. Lovitt and Donald M. Leslie Jr. Ed. Alan Stoekl. Minneapolis: U of Minnesota P, 1985.

— *The Battle at Elderbush Gulch.* Dir. D.W. Griffith. Biograph, 1914.

— *Battleship Potemkin.* Dir. Sergei Eisenstein and Grigori Aleksandrov. Amkino Corporation, 1925.

Baudrillard, Jean. *The Evil Demon of Images.* Sydney: Power Institute of Fine Arts, 1987.

— *Simulations.* Trans. Paul Foss, Paul Patton, and Philip Beitchman. New York: Semiotext(e), 1983.

— *Symbolic Exchange and Death.* 1976. Trans. Iain Hamilton Grant. Introduction. Mike Gane. London: Sage Publications, 1993.

Bauman, Zygmunt. *Postmodernity and its Discontents.* Cambridge: Polity P, 1997.

Baumgarten, Alexander Gottlieb. *Aesthetica.* 1750. Hildesheim: Olms, 1970.

Baxter, John. *Hollywood in the Sixties.* London: The Tantivy P, 1972.

Bazin, André. *The Cinema of Cruelty: From Buñuel to Hitchcock.* 1975. Ed. François Truffaut. Trans. Sabine d'Estrée. New York: Seaver Books, 1982.

— "The Crisis of French Cinema, or *Scarface* and the Gangster Film." *Bazin at Work: Major Essays and Reviews from the Forties and Fifties.* Ed. Bert Cardullo. Trans.Alain Piette and Bert Cardullo. New York: Routledge, 1997. 109-112.

— "The Ontology of the Photographic Image." *What is Cinema? Vol. 1.* Trans. Hugh Gray. Foreword by Jean Renoir. Berkeley: U of California P, 1967. 9-16.

— "The Western: Or The American Film Par Excellence." *What is Cinema? Vol. 2.* Trans. Hugh Gray. Foreword by François Truffaut. Berkeley: U of California P, 1971. 140-148.

Beardsley, Monroe C. *Aesthetics: From Classical Greece to the Present.* 1966. Tuscaloosa, Ala: U of Alabama P, 1975.

Beardsmore, R.W. *Art and Morality.* London: Macmillan, 1971.

Becker, Carol. "Herbert Marcuse and the Subversive Potential of Art." Becker 113-129.

— "Introduction. Presenting the Problem." Becker xi-xx. (ed.) *The Subversive Imagination: Artists, Society, and Social Responsibility.* New York: Routledge, 1994.

Becker, Ernest. *The Denial of Death.* New York: The Free Press, 1973.

Bénar, Henri. *Reservoir Dogs* Press Conference, Toronto International Film Festival 1992. Peary 35-40.

Belden, H.M., and A.P. Hudson, eds. *The Frank C. Brown Collection of North Carolina Folklore.* Durham: Duke UP, 1952.

Bell, Clive. *Art.* London: Chatto & Windus, 1915.

Bell, David F. "Introduction. Reading Violence." *Substance: A Review of Theory and Literary Criticism.* 27.2 (1998): 3-4.

— "Reading Corpses: Interpretive Violence." *Substance: A Review of Theory and Literary Criticism.* 27.2 (1998): 92-103.

Bellour, Raymond. "The Unattainable Text." *Screen.* 16.3 (1975): 19-27.

Belton, John. *American Cinema/American Culture.* New York: McGraw-Hill,1994.

Beltzer, Thomas. "Dogs in Hell: *No Exit* Revisited." *Senses of Cinema.* 6 (2000). 29 Oct. 2002. .

Benjamin, Walter. "Critique of Violence." Trans. Edmund Jephcott *Reflections: Essays, Aphorisms, Autobiographical Writings.* Ed. Peter Demetz.. New York: Schocken Books, 1986. 277-300.

— *The Origin of German Drama.* Trans. John Osborne. London: New Left Books, 1977.

— "The Storyteller. Reflections on the Works of Nikolai Leskov." Trans. Harry Zohn. *Illuminations.* 1955. Ed. Hannah Arendt.. New York: Schocken Books, 1968. 83-109.

— "Zentralpark."*Gesammelte Schriften.* Eds. Rolf Tiedemann et al. Vol. 1, 2. Frankfurt am Main: Suhrkamp, 1974. 655-690.

Berger, Gilda. *Violence and the Media.* New York: Franklin Watts, 1989.

Berger, John. *Ways of Seeing.* London: British Broadcasting Corporation & Penguin Books, 1972.

Berger, Maurice, Brian Wallis, and Simon Watson, eds. *Constructing Masculinity.* New York: Routledge, 1995.

Bergstrom, Janet. "Violence and Enunciation." *Camera Obscura: A Journal of Feminism and Film Theory.* 8-9-10 (1984): 20-31.

Bernard, Jami. *Quentin Tarantino: The Man and his Movies.* London: HarperCollins Publishers, 1995.

Bernstein, Matthew. "Model Criminals. Visual Style in *Bonnie and Clyde.*" Friedman 101-126.

— 'Perfecting the New Gangster. Writing *Bonnie and Clyde.*" *Film Quarterly.* 53.4 (2000): 16-31.

Bersani, Leo. *The Freudian Body: Psychoanalysis and Art.* New York: Columbia UP, 1986.

Bersani, Leo, and Ulysse Dutoit. *The Forms of Violence: Narrative in Assyrian Art and Modern Culture*. New York: Schocken Books, 1985.

Bhabha, Homi K. "Are You a Man or a Mouse?" Berger, Wallis, and Watson 57-65.

Bingham, Jonathan B., and Alfred M. Bingham. *Violence and Democracy*. New York: The World Publishing Company, 1970.

Biró, Yvette. *Profane Mythology: The Savage Mind of the Cinema*. Trans. Imre Goldstein. Bloomington: Indiana UP, 1982.

Birringer, Johannes H. "Constructions of the Spirit: The Struggle for Transfiguration in Modern Art." *Journal of Aesthetics and Art Criticism*. 42.2 (1983): 137-150.

— *Birth of a Nation*. Dir. D.W. Griffith. David W. Griffith Corp., 1915.

Black, Joel. *The Aesthetics of Murder: A Study in Romantic Literature and Contemporary Culture*. Baltimore: Johns Hopkins UP, 1991.

— *The Reality Effect: Film Culture and the Graphic Imperative*. New York: Routledge, 2002.

Blake, Richard A. *Screening America: Reflections on Five Classic Films*. New York: Paulist P, 1991.

Blanchot, Maurice. *The Space of Literature*. 1955. Trans. Ann Smock. Lincoln: U of Nebraska P, 1989.

Bliss, Michael. "'Back Off to What?' Enclosure, Violence and Capitalism in Sam Peckinpah's *The Wild Bunch*." Prince, *Sam Peckinpah's* The Wild Bunch 105-129.

— *Between the Bullets: The Spiritual Cinema of John Woo*. Lanham, Maryland: The Scarecrow P, 2002.

— "The Conclusion of *The Wild Bunch*." Bliss 158-168.

— (ed.) *Doing it Right: The Best Criticism on Sam Peckinpah's* The Wild Bunch. Carbondale: Southern Illinois UP, 1994.

— Introduction. Bliss xv-xxiii.

— *Justified Lives: Morality and Narrative in the Films of Sam Peckinpah*. Carbondale: Southern Illinois UP, 1993.

Bloom, Harold. *The Anxiety of Influence: A Theory of Poetry*. London: Oxford UP, 1973.

Blum, William. "Toward a Cinema of Cruelty." *Cinema Journal*. 10.2 (1971): 19-33.

Blumer, Hebert. *Movies and Conduct*. New York: Macmillan, 1933.

Bly, Robert. *Iron John: A Book About Men*. 1990. Shaftesbury, Dorset: Element, 1991.

Boelcskevy, Mary Anne Stewart. "Towards a Poetics of Violence." Wright and Kaplan 60-63.

Bogdanovich, Peter. Interview with Howard Hawks. Hillier and Wollen 52- 53.

Bogue, Ronald. "Word, Image and Sound: The Non-Representational Semiotics of Gilles Deleuze." *Mimesis in Contemporary Theory: An Interdisciplinary Approach*. Ed. Ronald Bogue. 2 vols. Philadelphia: John Benjamins, 1991. 77-97.

Bogue, Ronald, and Marcel Cornis-Pope. "Introduction: Paradigms of Conflict and Mediation in Literary and Cultural Imagination." Bogue and Cornis-Pope 1-17. eds. *Violence and Mediation in Contemporary Culture*. Albany: State U of New York P, 1996.

Bok, Sissela. *Mayhem: Violence as Public Entertainment*. Reading, Mass.: Perseus Books, 1998.

Boltanski, Luc. *Distant Suffering: Morality, Media and Politics*. 1993. Trans. Graham Burchell. Cambridge: Cambridge UP, 1999.

Bomar, F. Albert, and Alan J. Warren. "Midsection: Sam Peckinpah." *Film Comment*. 17.1 (1981): 33-48.

Bonnie and Clyde. Dir. Arthur Penn. Warner Brothers, 1967.

Booth, Wayne C. "Are Narrative Choices Subject to Ethical Criticism?" Phelan 57-78.
— The Company We Keep: An Ethics of Fiction. Berkeley: U of California P, 1988.
Borde, Raymond and Étienne Chaumeton. Panorama du Film Noir Américain. Paris: Editions de minuit, 1955.
— "Toward a Definition of Film Noir." Trans. Alain Silver. Silver and Ursini 17-25.
Bordwell, David. The Cinema of Eisenstein. Cambridge, Mass.: Harvard UP, 1993.
— The Films of Carl-Theodor Dreyer. Berkeley: U of California P, 1981.
— Making Meaning: Inference and Rhetoric in the Interpretation of Cinema. Cambridge, Mass.: Harvard UP, 1989.
— Narration in the Fiction Film. Madison: U of Wisconsin P, 1985.
— On the History of Film Style. Cambridge: Mass.: Harvard UP, 1997.
— Ozu and the Poetics of Cinema. Princeton: Princeton UP, 1988.
Bordwell, David, and Kristin Thompson. Film Art: An Introduction. 1979. New York: McGraw-Hill, 1993.
Bordwell, David, Janet Staiger, and Kristin Thompson. The Classical Hollywood Cinema: Film Style and Mode of Production to 1960. New York: Columbia UP, 1985.
Borges, Jorge Luis. "From Allegories to Novels." Borges: A Reader. Eds. Emir Rodriguez Monegal and Alastair Reid. New York: E.P. Dutton, 1981. 230-232.
Botting, Fred, and Scott Wilson. The Tarantinian Ethics. London: Sage Publications, 2001.
Bourdieu, Pierre. Distinction: A Social Critique of the Judgement of Taste. 1979. Trans. Richard Nice. London: Routledge & Kegan Paul, 1984.
— "The Historical Genesis of a Pure Aesthetic." Journal of Aesthetics and Art Criticism. 46. Special Issue (1987): 201-210.
Bouzereau, Laurent. Ultraviolent Movies: From Sam Peckinpah to Quentin Tarantino. Secaucus, N.J.: Citadel P, 1996.
Branigan, Edward. Narrative Comprehension and Film. London: Routledge, 1992.
— Point of View in the Cinema. Berlin: Mouton Publishers, 1984.
Branson, Clark. Howard Hawks: A Jungian Study. Santa Barbara: Capra P, 1987.
Braudy, Leo. The World in a Frame: What We See in Films. Garden City, N.Y.: Anchor Books, 1977.
Breen, Marcus. "Woof, Woof: The Real Bite in Reservoir Dogs." UTS Review: Cultural Studies and New Writing. 2.2 (1996): 1-9.
Breton, André. Le revolver à cheveux blancs. Paris: Editions des Cahiers libres, 1932.
— The Bridge on the River Kwai. Dir. David Lean. Columbia Pictures, 1957.
— Bring me the Head of Alfredo Garcia. Dir. Sam Peckinpah. United Artists, 1974.
Brite, Poppy Z. "The Poetry of Violence." Karl French 62-70.
Brode, Douglas. The Films of the Sixties. Secaucus, N.J.: Citadel Press, 1980.
— Money, Women and Guns: Crime Movies from Bonnie and Clyde to the Present. New York: Carol Publishing Group, 1995.
Brody, Stephen. Screen Violence and Film Censorship: A Review of Research. London: H.M.S. O., 1977.
Bronfen, Elisabeth, and Sarah Webster Goodwin. Introduction. Death and Representation. Eds. Sarah Webster Goodwin and Elisabeth Bronfen. Baltimore: The Johns Hopkins UP, 1993. 3-25.
Brookey, Robert Alan, and Robert Westerfelhaus. "Hiding Homoeroticism in Plain View: The Fight Club DVD as Digital Closet." Critical Studies in Media Communication. 19.1 (2002): 21-43.

Brooks, Peter. *Body Work: Objects of Desire in Modern Narrative*. Cambridge, Mass.: Harvard UP, 1993.

— *Psychoanalysis and Storytelling*. Oxford: Blackwell, 1994.

— *Reading For the Plot: Design and Intention in Narrative*. Oxford: Clarendon P, 1984.

Brown, Kenneth R. Rev. of *The Wild Bunch*, dir. Sam Peckinpah. *Cineaste*. 3.3 (1969/70): 18-20.

Browne, Nick. "Aesthetics of Violence." Gottesman and Brown 548-552.

— (ed.) *Francis Ford Coppola's* Godfather *Trilogy*. Cambridge: Cambridge UP, 1999.

— *The Rhetoric of Filmic Narration*. 1976. Ann Arbor: UMI Research P, 1982.

Browne, Ray B., ed. *Popular Culture and the Expanding Consciousness*. New York: John Wiley & Sons, 1973.

Bruner, Jerome. "The Narrative Construction of Reality." *Critical Inquiry*. 18.1 (1991): 1-21.

Brunette, Peter. Interview with Quentin Tarantino, 1992. Peary 30-34.

— "The Three Stooges and the (Anti-)Narrative of Violence. De(con)structive Comedy." *Comedy/Cinema/Theory*. Ed. Andrew Horton. Berkeley: U of California P, 1991. 174-187.

Bruno, Giuliana. "Ramble City: Postmodernism and *Blade Runner*." Sharrett, *Crisis Cinema* 237-250.

Buckland, Warren. *The Cognitive Semiotics of Film*. Cambridge: Cambridge UP, 2000.

— (ed.) *The Film Spectator: From Sign to Mind*. Amsterdam: Amsterdam UP, 1995.

Bueno, Eva, José Oviedo, and Michael Varona. "Sarface [sic]: The Erasure of Society and the Narrative of Prophecy." *Sociocriticism*. 5.1 (1989): 113-117.

Bullough, Edward. *Æsthetics: Lectures and Essays*. Ed. Elizabeth M. Wilkinson. London: Bowes & Bowes, 1957.

Burch, Noël. *Theory of Film Practice*. 1973. Trans. Helen R. Lane. London: Secker & Warburg, 1983.

Burgess, Jackson. Rev. of *A Clockwork Orange*, dir. Stanley Kubrick. *Film Quarterly*. 25.3 (1972): 33-36.

Burke, Edmund. *A Philosophical Enquiry into the Origin of Our Ideas of the Sublime and Beautiful*. 1757. Ed. David Womersley. London: Penguin, 1998.

Burkert, Walter. *Homo Necans: The Anthropology of Ancient Greek Sacrificial Ritual and Myth*. 1972. Trans. Peter Bing. Berkeley: U of California P, 1983.

Burnham, Clint. "Scattered Speculations on the Value of Harvey Keitel." *Boys: Masculinities in Contemporary Culture*. Ed. Paul Smith. Boulder: Westview P, 1996. 113-129.

Burwick, Frederick. "De Quincey and the Aesthetics of Violence." *The Wordsworth Circle*. 27. 2 (1996): 78-86.

Buscombe, Edward. Rev. of the Re-release of *The Wild Bunch*, dir. Sam Peckinpah. *Sight and Sound*. 5.10 (1995): 62.

Bushman, Brad J., and Craig A. Anderson. "Media Violence and the American Public. Scientific Facts Versus Media Misinformation." *American Psychologist*. 56.6-7 (2001): 477-489.

Butch Cassidy and the Sundance Kid. Dir. George Roy Hill. 20th Century Fox Film Corporation, 1969.

Butler, Judith. *Bodies That Matter: On the Discursive Limits of 'Sex.'* New York: Routledge, 1993.

— "Melancholy Gender/Refused Identification." Berger, Wallis and Watson 21-36.

Butler, Jeremy Gaylord. "Toward a Theory of Cinematic Style: The Remake." Diss. Northwestern U, 1982.

Butler, Terence. *Crucified Heroes: The Films of Sam Peckinpah*. London: Gordon Fraser, 1979.

Cagin, Seth, and Philip Dray. *Born To Be Wild: Hollywood and the Sixties Generation*. Boca Raton, Florida: Coyote: 1994.

— *Hollywood Films of the Seventies: Sex, Drugs, Violence, Rock 'n' Roll & Politics*. New York: Harper & Row, 1984.

Calder, Jenni. *There Must be a Lone Ranger*. London: Hamish Hamilton, 1974.

Caldwell, Brian. "Muscling in on the Movies: Excess and the Representation of the Male Body in Films of the 1980s and 1990s." Tim Armstrong 133-140.

Cameron, Ian, ed. *The Movie Book of Film Noir*. London: Studio Vista, 1992.

Cameron, Kenneth M. *America on Film: Hollywood and American History*. New York: Continuum, 1997.

Camus, Albert. *The Rebel: An Essay on Man in Revolt*. 1951. Trans. Anthony Bower. New York: Vintage International, 1991.

Camy, Gérard. *Sam Peckinpah: un réalisateur dans le système Hollywoodien des années soixante et soixante-dix*. Paris: Harmattan, 1997.

Caprara, Valerio. *Sam Peckinpah*. Florence: La Nuova Italia, 1975.

Caputi, Jane. "Small Ceremonies. Ritual in *Forrest Gump, Natural Born Killers, Seven*, and *Follow Me Home*." Sharrett, *Mythologies* 147-174.

Carr, Steven Alan. "From 'Fucking Cops!' To 'Fucking Media!' *Bonnie and Clyde* For a Sixties America." Friedman 70-100.

Carroll, Noël. *A Philosophy of Mass Art*. Oxford: Clarendon P, 1998.

— "Art, Narrative, and Moral Understanding." Levinson 126-160.

— "Defending Mass Art: A Response to Kathleen Higgins's 'Mass Appeal'." *Philosophy and Literature*. 23.2 (1999): 378-386.

— Introduction. *Theories of Art Today*. Ed. Noël Carroll. Madison: The U of Wisconsin P, 2000. 3-24.

— *Philosophical Problems in Classical Film Theory*. Princeton: Princeton UP, 1988.

Carson, Diane. "'It's Never the Way I Knew Them:' Searching For Bonnie and Clyde." Friedman 42-69.

Cartmell, Deborah, I.Q. Hunter, Heidi Kaye, and Imelda Whelehan, eds. *Trash Aesthetics: Popular Culture and its Audience*. London: Pluto Press, 1997.

Caruth, Cathy. "Traumatic Awakenings." de Vries and Weber 208- 222.

Casarino, Cesare. "David Wojnarowicz, AIDS, and the Cinematic Imperative." *Raritan*. 20.4 (2001): 148-157.

Cave, Nick. *Murder Ballads*. Mute/Reprise, 1996.

Cavell, Marcia. "Taste and the Moral Sense." *Journal of Aesthetics and Art Criticism*. 34.1 (1975): 29-33.

Cavell, Stanley. "What Photography Calls Thinking." *Raritan: A Quarterly Review*. 4 (1985): 1-21.

— *The World Viewed: Reflections on the Ontology of Film*. 1971. Cambridge, Mass.: Harvard UP, 1979.

Cawelti, John G. *Adventure, Mystery and Romance: Formula Stories as Art and Popular Culture*. Chicago: U of Chicago P, 1976.

— "Myths of Violence in American Popular Culture." *Critical Inquiry*. 1.3 (1975): 521-541.

— "Reflections on the New Western Films." Nachbar 113-117. Champlin, Charles. *Hollywood's Revolutionary Decade: Charles Champlin Reviews the Movies of the 1970s*. Santa Barbara: John Daniel and Company, 1998.

— Rev. of *The Wild Bunch*, dir. Sam Peckinpah. *Filmfacts: A Publication of the American Film Institute*. 12.10 (1969): 220.

— *The Charge of the Light Brigade*. Dir. Michael Curtiz. Warner Brothers, 1936.

Charney, Leo. *Empty Moments: Cinema, Modernity, and Drift*. Durham: Duke UP, 1998.

— "The Violence of a Perfect Moment." Slocum 47-62.

Chase, Richard. *The American Novel and its Tradition*. Garden City, N.Y.: Doubleday Anchor Books, 1957.

Chatman, Seymour. *Coming to Terms: The Rhetoric of Narrative in Fiction and Film*. Ithaca: Cornell UP, 1990.

— *Story and Discourse: Narrative Structure in Fiction and Film*. Ithaca: Cornell UP, 1978.

Cheyenne Autumn. Dir. John Ford. Warner Brothers, 1964.

Un Chien andalou. Dir. Luis Buñuel. Video Yesteryear, 1929.

Chinatown. Dir. Roman Polanski. Paramount Pictures, 1974.

Chion, Michel. *Audio-Vision: Sound on Screen*. Ed. and trans. Claudia Gorbman. New York: Columbia UP, 1994.

Christensen, Claus. "Ondskabens Strategi: Amerikanske Thrillers I 90'erne." *Kosmorama: Tidskrift for Filmkust og Filmkultur*. 219 (1997) : 100-109.

Ciment, Michel. *Kubrick*. Trans. Gilbert Adair. London: Collins, 1983.

Clarens, Carlos. *Crime Movies*. 1980. New York: Da Capo P, 1997.

Clark, Arthur B. Rev. of *The Wild Bunch*, dir. Sam Peckinpah. *Films in Review*. 20.7 (1969): 446-447.

Clark, Suzanne. "*Fight Club*: Historicizing the Rhetoric of Masculinity, Violence, and Sentimentality." *JAC: A Journal of Composition Theory*. 21.2 (2001): 411-420.

Clarkson, Wensley. *Quentin Tarantino: Shooting From the Hip*. London: Judy Piatkus, 1995.

Coates, Paul. *Film at the Intersection of High and Mass Culture*. Cambridge: Cambridge UP, 1994.

Coleman, Francis J. "Is Aesthetic Pleasure a Myth?" *Journal of Aesthetics and Art Criticism*. 29.3 (1971): 319-332.

Coleman, John. "Thudding Home." Wake and Hayden. 216.

Collingwood, R.G. *The Principles of Art*. 1938. Oxford: Clarendon P, 1964.

Combs, James. "Introduction. Understanding The Politics of Movies." Combs 3-25.

— (ed.) *Movies and Politics: The Dynamic Relationship*. New York: Garland Publishing, 1993.

Combs, Richard. "Shadowing the Hero." *Sight and Sound*. 2.6. (1992): 12-16.

Cook, Bernard Joseph. "Let it Bleed: Production of the Meanings of Violence in American Film, 1962-1976." Diss. University of California, Los Angeles, 1999.

Cook, Bernie. "Censorship." Gottesman and Brown 543-548.

Cook, David A. "Ballistic Balletics: Styles of Violent Representation in *TheWild Bunch* and After." Prince, *Sam Peckinpah's* The Wild Bunch 130-154.

— "*The Wild Bunch*, Fifteen Years After." *North Dakota Quarterly*. 51.3 (1983): 123-130.

Cook, Jim. "*Bonnie and Clyde*." *Screen: The Journal of the Society for Education in Film and Television*. 10.4-5 (1969): 101-114.

Corliss, Richard. "A Blast to the Heart." Rev. of *Pulp Fiction*, dir. Quentin Tarantino. *Time*. 10 Oct. 1994: 76.

Corrigan, Timothy. *A Cinema Without Walls: Movies and Culture after Vietnam*. London: Routledge, 1991.

Cott, Nancy F. "*Bonnie and Clyde*." *Past Imperfect: History According to the Movies*. Ed. Mark C. Carnes. New York: Henry Holt and Company, 1995. 220-223.

Coursodon, Jean-Pierre, with Pierre Savvage. *American Directors Vol. 2*. New York: McGraw-Hill Book Company, 1983.

Courtwright, David. T. "Way Cooler than Manson: *Natural Born Killers*." *Oliver Stone's USA: Film, History, and Controversy*. Ed. Robert Brent Toplin. Lawrence: UP of Kansas, 2000.

Coyne, Michael. *The Crowded Prairie: American National Identity in the Hollywood Western*. London: L.B. Tauris P, 1997.

Crane, Jonathan Lake. *Terror and Everyday Life: Singular Moments in the History of the Horror Film*. Thousand Oaks, California: Sage, 1994.

Creed, Barbara. "Horror and the Carnivalesque: The Body-Monstrous." *Fields of Vision: Essays in Film Studies, Visual Anthropology, and Photography*. Eds. Leslie Devereaux and Roger Hillman. Berkeley: U of California P, 1995. 127-159.

Crist, Judith. "The Legend of Bonnie and Clyde." Wake and Hayden 219.

— "Sam Peckinpah: *Straw Dogs*." Rainer 263-265.

Croce, Benedetto. *Æsthetic: A Science of Expression and General Linguistic*. 1909. Trans. Douglas Ainslie. Farrar, Straus & Giroux. 1972.

Crowther, Bosley. Rev. of *Bonnie and Clyde*, dir. Arthur Penn. Wake and Hayden 221.

Culp, Robert. "Sam Peckinpah, the Storyteller and *The Wild Bunch*: An Appreciation." Bliss 3-13.

Currie, Gregory. *Image and Mind: Film, Philosophy, and Cognitive Science*. Cambridge: Cambridge UP, 1995.

—"The Moral Psychology of Fiction." *Australasian Journal of Philosophy*. 73.2 (1995): 250-259.

Dale, Edgar. *The Content of Motion Pictures*. 1935. New York: Arno P, 1970.

Darey, Serge. "Vieillesse du Même (*Rio Lobo*)." *Cahiers du Cinéma*. 230 (1971): 22-27.

Dariels, Don. Rev. of *A Clockwork Orange*, dir. Stanley Kubrick. *Sight and Sound*. 42.1 (1972-73): 44-46.

Darto, Arthur C. *After the End of Art: Contemporary Art and the Pale of History*. Princeton: Princeton UP, 1997.

— *The Transfiguration of the Commonplace: A Philosophy of Art*. Cambridge, Mass.: Harvard UP, 1981.

Dargis, Manohla. "Pulp Instincts." *Sight and Sound*. 4.5 (1994): 6-11.

— "Sleeping With Guns." *Sight and Sound*. 7.5 (1997): 18-21.

Darke, Chris. "The Kubrick Connection." *Sight and Sound*. 5.11 (1995): 22-27.

Davis, Natalie Zemon. *Society and Culture in Early Modern France*. 1965. Oxford: Polity P, 1987.

Davis, Robert Murray. *Playing Cowboys: Low Culture and High Art in the Western*. Norman: U of Oklahoma P, 1992.

Davis, Todd F. "Shepherding the Weak: The Ethics of Redemption in Quentin Tarantino's *Pulp Fiction*." *Literature/Film Quarterly*. 26.1 (1998): 60-66.

Dawson, Jeff. *Quentin Tarantino: The Cinema of Cool*. New York: Applause, 1995.

Debord, Guy. *The Society of the Spectacle*. 1967. New York: Zone Books, 1994.

De Duve, Thierry. *Kant After Duchamp*. Cambridge, Mass.: The MIT P, 1996.

DeFleur, Melvin L., and Everette E. Dennis. *Understanding Mass Communication: A Liberal Arts Perspective*. Boston: Houghton Mifflin Company, 1994.

DeGenaro, William. "Post-Nostalgia in the Films of Quentin Tarantino and Robert Rodriguez."*Journal of American Studies of Turkey*. 6 (1997): 57-63.

Degli-Esposti, Cristina. "Postmodernism(s)." *Postmodernism in the Cinema*. Ed. Cristina Degli-Esposti. New York: Berghahn Books, 1998. 3-18.

De Lauretis, Teresa. *Technology of Gender: Essays on Theory, Film and Fiction*. Bloomington: Indiana UP, 1987.

De Laurot, Yves. "From Logos to Lens." *Movies and Methods*. Ed. Bill Nichols. 1976. Berkeley: U of California P, 1985. 578-582.

De Man, Paul. "Autobiography as De-Facement." *The Rhetoric of Romanticism*. New York: Columbia UP, 1984. 67-81.

— *The Resistance to Theory*. Foreword Wlad Godzich. Minneapolis: U of Minnesota P, 1986.

De Onís, Federico: *Antologia de la poesia española e hispanoamericana*. Madrid: Hernando, 1934.

De Quincey, Thomas. "On Murder Considered as One of the Fine Arts." *Tales and Prose Phantasies*. Ed. David Mason. Edinburgh: Adam and Charles Black, 1890. Vol. 13 of *The Collected Writings of Thomas De Quincey*. 9-124.

De Tarde, Gabriel. *The Laws of Imitation*. Trans. Elsie Clews Parson. New York: H. Holt & Company, 1903

Deleuze, Gilles. *Cinema 1: The Movement-Image*. Trans. Hugh Tomlinson and Barbara Habberjam. London: The Athlone Press, 1986.

— *Cinema 2: The Time-Image*. Trans. Hugh Tomlinson and Robert Galeta. Minneapolis: U of Minnesota P, 1989.

Deleuze, Gilles, and Felix Guattari. *A Thousand Plateaus: Capitalism and Schizophrenia*. 1980. Trans. B. Massumi. Minneapolis: U of Minnesota P, 1987.

DeLillo, Don. *Libra*. New York: Penguin Books, 1988.

Denby, David. "Violence Enshrined." *Atlantic Monthly*. 229.4 (1972): 118-122.

Denitto, Dennis. *Film: Form and Feeling*. New York: Harper and Row, 1985.

Derrida, Jacques. *Aporias*. Trans. Thomas Dutoit. Stanford: Stanford UP, 1993.

— "The Double Session." *Dissemination*. Trans. Barbara Johnson. London: The Athlone P, 1981. 172-285.

De Vries, Daniel. *The Films of Stanley Kubrick*. Grand Rapids, Mich.: William B. Eerdmans Publishing Company, 1973.

De Vries, Hent, and Samuel Weber. Introduction. de Vries and Weber 1-13.

— (eds.) *Violence, Identity and Self-Determination*. Stanford: Stanford UP, 1997.

Dewey, John. *Art as Experience*. 1934. New York: Capricorn Books, 1958.

Diamond, Stephen A. *Anger, Madness and the Daimonic: The Psychological Genesis of Violence, Evil and Creativity*. New York: State U of New York P, 1996.

Dickie, George. "The New Institutional Theory of Art." Neill and Ridley 213- 223.

Dickos, Andrew. *Street With No Name: A History of the Classic American Film Noir*. Lexington: UP of Kentucky, 2002.

Die Hard. Dir. John McTiernan. 20th Century Fox Film Corporation, 1988.

Dixon, Robert. *The Baumgarten Corruption: From Sense to Nonsense in Art and Philosophy*. London: Pluto P, 1995.

Dixon, Wheeler Winston. *Disaster and Memory: Celebrity Culture and the Crisis of Hollywood Cinema*. New York: Columbia UP, 1999.

— "Re-Visioning the Western: Code, Myth, and Genre in Peckinpah's *The Wild Bunch*." Prince, *Sam Peckinpah's* The Wild Bunch 155-174.

— *The Transparency of Spectacle: Meditations on the Moving Image*. Albany: State U of New York P, 1998.

— "Twenty-five Reasons Why it's All Over." Lewis, *The End of Cinema* 356- 366.

D'Lugo, Marvin. *The Films of Carlos Saura: The Practice of Seeing*. Princeton: Princeton UP, 1991.

Doherty, Thomas. *Pre-Code Hollywood: Sex, Immorality, and Insurrection in American Cinema, 1930-1934*. New York: Columbia UP, 1999.

Donald, Ralph R. "Masculinity and Machismo in Hollywood's War Films." *Men, Masculinity and the Media*. Ed. Steve Craig. Newbury Park, Cal.: Sage Publications, 1992. 124-136.

Dooley, Roger Burke. *From Scarface to Scarlett: American Films of the 1930s*. New York: Harcourt Brace Jovanovich, 1979.

Doty, Alexander. *Flaming Classics: Queering the Film Canon*. New York: Routledge, 2000.

Dowell, Pat. "Pulp Friction: Two Shots at Quentin Tarantino's *Pulp Fiction*." *Cineaste*. 21.3 (1995): 4-5.

Drake, Chris. "The Kubrick Connection." *Sight and Sound*. 5.11 (1995): 22- 27.

Dr. Strangelove or: How I Learned to Stop Worrying and Love the Bomb. Dir. Stanley Kubrick. Columbia Pictures, 1964.

Dubbert, Joe L. *A Man's Place: Masculinity in Transition*. Englewood Cliffs, N.J.: Prentice-Hall, 1979.

Dubois, Philippe. *L'acte photographique*. Paris: Nathan, 1983.

— *L'acte photographique et autres essais*. Paris: Nathan, 1990.

Duclos, Denis. *The Werewolf Complex: America's Fascination with Violence*. Trans. Amanda Pingree. Oxford: Berg, 1998.

Dukore, Bernard F. *Sam Peckinpah's Feature Films*. Urbana: U of Illinois P, 1999.

Durgnat, Raymond. "Hawks isn't Good Enough." *Film Comment*. 4 (1977): 8-19.

— 'Paint it Black: The Family Tree of Film Noir." *Cinema*. 6-7 (1970): 49-56. Rpt. in *Film Noir: A Reader*. Eds. Alain Silver and James Ursini. New York: Limelight Editions, 1996. 37-51.

Dyer, Richard, ed. *Gays and Film*. London: British Film Institute, 1977.

— *Now You See It: Studies on Lesbian and Gay Film*. London: Routledge, 1990. Eagleton, Terry. *The Ideology of the Aesthetic*. Oxford: Blackwell, 1990.

— *Sweet Violence: The Idea of the Tragic*. Malden, Mass.: Blackwell, 2003.

Eaton, Marcia Muelder. "Aesthetics: The Mother of Ethics?" *Journal of Aesthetics and Art Criticism*. 55.4 (1997): 355-364.

Ebert, Robert. "On Violence." Rainer 150-152.

— Rev. of *The Wild Bunch*, dir. Sam Peckinaph. *Filmfacts: A Publication of the American Film Institute*. 12.10 (1969): 218-219.

Edgar, Patricia May. *Children and Screen Violence*. St. Lucia: U of Queensland P, 1977.

Eikhenbaum, Boris. "Problems of Film Stylistics." *Screen: The Journal of the Society for Education in Film and Television*. 15.3 (1974): 7-32.

Eisenstein, Sergei. "Collision of Ideas." MacCann 34-37.

Elkins, James. *The Object Stares Back: On the Nature of Seeing*. New York: Simon and Schuster, 1996.
— *Pictures of the Body: Pain and Metamorphosis*. Stanford: Stanford UP, 1999.
Elsaesser, Thomas. "Screen Violence: Emotional Structure and Ideological Function in *A Clockwork Orange*." *Approaches to Popular Culture*. Ed. C.W.E. Bigsby. London: E. Arnold, 1976. 171-200.
Elster, Jon. *Sour Grapes: Studies in the Subversion of Rationality*. Cambridge: Cambridge UP, 1983.
Engel, Leonard. "Sam Peckinpah's Heroes: Natty Bumppo and the Myth of the Rugged Individual Still Reign." *Literature/Film Quarterly*. 16.1 (1988): 22-30.
— "Space and Enclosure in Cooper and Peckinpah: Regeneration in the Open Spaces." *Journal of American Culture*. 14.2 (1991): 86-93.
Esselman, Kathryn C. "From Camelot to Monument Valley: Dramatic Origins of the Western Film." Nachbar 9-18.
Estey, George F., and Doris A. Hunter, eds. *Violence: A Reader in the Ethics of Action*. Waltham, Mass.: Xerox College Publishing, 1971.
Etulain, Richard W. "Cultural Origins of the Western". Nachbar 19-24.
Evensmo, Sigurd. *Vold i Filmene: Ett års Kinoprogrammer i Norge og Noen Perspektiver*. Oslo: Gyldendal, 1969.
Eves, Vicki. "The Effects of Violence in the Mass Media." *Screen: The Journal of the Society for Education in Film and Television*. 11.3 (1970): 31-42.
The Exorcist. Dir. William Friedkin. Warner Brothers, 1973.

Falcon, Richard. "Reality is too Shocking." *Sight and Sound*. 9.1 (1999): 10-13.
Falsetto, Mario. "Patterns of Filmic Narration in *The Killing* and *Lolita*." *Perspectives on Stanley Kubrick*. Ed. Mario Falsetto. New York: G.K. Hall & Co, 1996. 100-108.
— *Stanley Kubrick: A Narrative and Stylistic Analysis*. Westport, Conn.: Greenwood P, 1994.
Faludi, Susan. *Stiffed: The Betrayal of the American Man*. New York: William Morrow and Company, 1999.
Fanon, Frantz. *The Wretched of the Earth*. 1959. Trans. Constance Farrington. New York: Grove P, 1963.
Farber, Stephen. "Peckinpah's Return." *Film Quarterly*. 23.1 (1969): 2-11.
— Farber, Stephen. Rev. of *Straw Dogs*, dir. Sam Peckinpah. *Cinema*. 7.2 (1972): 2-7.
Faure, William. *Images of Violence*. London: Studio Vista, 1973.
Fear and Desire. Dir. Stanley Kubrick. Joseph Burstyn Inc., 1953.
Fearnow, Mark. "Theater." Gottesman and Brown 291-296.
Fenin, George N, and William K. Everson. *The Western: From Silents to the Seventies*. New York: Grossman Publishers, 1973.
Fenton, Frances. *The Influence of Newspaper Presentations upon the Growth of Crime and other Anti-Social Activity*. Chicago: U of Chicago P, 1911
Ferro, Marc. *Cinema and History*. Trans. Naomi Greene. Detroit: Wayne State UP, 1988.
Fiedler, Leslie A. *Love and Death in the American Novel*. 1960. New York: Stein and Day, 1966.
Fight Club. Dir. David Fincher. 20th Century Fox Film Corporation, 1999.
Fine, Marshall. *Bloody Sam: The Life and Films of Sam Peckinpah*. New York: D.I. Fine, 1991.

Finkelstein, Sidney. *Existentialism and Alienation in American Literature*. 1965. New York: International Publishers, 1968.

Fish, Stanley. "Interpreting the *Variorum*." Lodge 311-329.

Five Easy Pieces. Dir. Bob Rafelson. Columbia Pictures, 1970.

Flusser, Vilém. *Towards a Philosophy of Photography*. Gottingen, West Germany: European Photography, 1984.

Foakes, R. A. *Shakespeare and Violence*. Cambridge: Cambridge UP, 2003.

Focillon, H. *The Life of Forms in Art*. New Haven: Yale UP, 1942.

Folsom, James K. *The American Western Novel*. New Haven, Conn.: College & University Press Publishers, 1966.

— "Westerns as Social and Political Alternatives." Nachbar 81-83.

Ford, Andrew. "*Katharsis*: The Ancient Problem." *Performativity and Performance*. Eds. Andrew Parker and Eve Kosofsky Sedgwick. New York: Routledge, 1995. 109-132.

Forman, Henry James. *Our Movie Made Children*. New York: Macmillan, 1933.

Foucault, Michel. *Discipline and Punish: The Birth of the Prison*. 1975. Trans. Alan Sheridan. New York: Vintage Books, 1979.

— (ed.) *I, Pierre Rivière, Having Slaughtered My Mother, My Sister, and My Brother...: A Case of Parricide in the Nineteenth Century*. Trans. Frank Jellinek. New York: Pantheon, 1975.

Fox, Robin. *The Violent Imagination*. New Brunswick: Rutgers UP, 1989.

Frappier-Mazur, Lucienne. "Sadean Libertinage and the Esthetics of Violence." *Yale French Studies*. 94 (1999): 184-198.

Fraser, John. *Violence in the Arts*. London: Cambridge UP, 1974.

Frazer, James. *The Golden Bough*. London: Macmillan, 1890.

French, Karl. Introduction. French 1-11.

— (ed.) *Screen Violence*. London: Bloomsbury, 1996.

French, Peter A. *Cowboy Metaphysics: Ethics and Death in Westerns*. Lanham: Rowman & Littlefield Publishers, 1997.

French, Philip. "Violence in the Cinema." *Sight, Sound and Society: Motion Pictures and Television in America*. Eds. David Manning White and Richard Averson. Boston: Beacon P, 1968. 320-334.

Freud, Sigmund. *Civilization and Its Discontents*. 1930. Trans. James Strachey. New York: W.W. Norton & Company, 1961.

— "Instincts and Their Vicissitudes." *General Psychological Theory: Papers on Metapsychology*. Ed. Philip Rieff. New York: Macmillan/Collier Books, 1963. 91-94.

Fried, John. "Pulp Friction: Two Shots at Quentin Tarantino's *Pulp Fiction*." *Cineaste*. 21.3 (1995): 6-7.

Friedman, Alan W. "D. H. Lawrence: Pleasure and Death." *Studies in the Novel*. 32.2 (2000): 207-228.

Friedman, Lester D. Ed. *Arthur Penn's* Bonnie and Clyde. Cambridge: Cambridge UP, 2000.

— "Introduction. Arthur Penn's Enduring Gangsters." Friedman 1-10.

Frohock, W.M. *The Novel of Violence in America*. Dallas: UP of Dallas, 1950.

Fry, Roger. *Vision and Design*. London: Chatto & Windus, 1957.

Fuery, Patrick. *New Developments in Film Theory*. Basingstoke: Macmillan P, 2000.

Fulton, Valerie. "The Meaning of Violence in Quentin Tarantino's *Pulp Fiction*: Annotated Version." Wright and Kaplan 178-182.

Fulwood, Neil. *The Films of Sam Peckinpah*. London: B T Batsford, 2002.

Funny Games. Dir. Michael Haneke. Attitude Films, 1997.

Fussell, Edwin. *Lucifer in Harness: American Meter, Metaphor, and Diction*. Princeton, N.J.: Princeton UP, 1973.

Gabler, Neal. *Life the Movie: How Entertainment Conquered Reality*. New York: Alfred A. Knopf, 1998.

Gallafent, Edward. Rev. of *Back in the Saddle Again: New Essays on the Western*, by Eds. Edward Buscombe and Roberta E. Pearson, and *Savage Cinema: Sam Peckinpah and the Rise of Ultraviolent Movies*, by Stephen Prince. *Screen*. 40.3. (1999): 354-357.

Gallagher, Mark. Rev. of *Action/Spectacle Cinema: A Sight and Sound Reader*, by Ed. José Arroyo, and *Screening Violence*, by Ed. Stephen Prince. *Scope: An Online Journal of Film Studies*. November 2001. 24 Oct. 2001 .

Galperin, William. "History into Allegory." *Western Humanities Review*. 2 (1981): 166-172.

Garbner, Marjorie, Jann Matlock, and Rebecca L. Walkowitz, eds. *Media Spectacles*. New York: Routledge, 1993.

Garver, Newton. "What Violence is." *Moral Problems: A Collection of Philosophical Essays*. Ed. James Rachels. New York: Harper and Row Publishers, 1971. 242-249.

Gaut, Berys. "The Ethical Criticism of Art." Levinson 182-203.

Genette, Gérard. *The Aesthetic Relation*. Trans. G.M. Goshgarian. Ithaca: Cornell UP, 1999.

— *The Architext: An Introduction*. Trans. Jane E. Lewin. Berkeley: U of California P, 1992.

— *Narrative Discourse: An Essay in Method*. Ithaca: Cornell UP, 1980.

Genova, Judith. "The Significance of Style." *Journal of Aesthetics and Art Criticism*. 37.3 (1979): 315-324.

Gentner, Richard & Diane Birdsall. "Midsection: Sam Peckinpah." *Film Comment*. 17.1 (1981): 33-48.

Gerbner, George. "Death in Prime Time: Notes on the Symbolic Functions of Dying in the Mass Media." *The Annals of the American Academy of Political and Social Science*. Ed. Renée C. Fox. Philadelphia, 1980. 64-70.

Gibson, James William. *Warrior Dreams: Violence and Manhood in Post-Vietnam America*. New York: Hill & Wang, 1994.

Gilliatt, Penelope. "A Western for Villon." Morgenstern and Kanfer 148-150.

Gilmore, David D. *Manhood in the Making: Cultural Concepts of Masculinity*. New Haven: Yale UP, 1990.

Girard, René. "Mimesis and Violence." *The Girard Reader*. Ed. James G. Williams. New York: The Crossroad Publishing Company, 1996.

— *Things Hidden Since the Foundation of the World*. 1978. Trans. Stephen Bann and Michael Metteer. Stanford: Stanford UP, 1987.

— "Violence and Biblical Narrative." *Philosophy and Literature*. 23.2 (1999): 387-392.

Giroux, Henry A. "Private Satisfactions and Public Disorders: *Fight Club*, Patriarchy, and the Politics of Masculine Violence." *JAC: A Journal of Composition Theory*. 21.1 (2001): 1-31.

— "*Pulp Fiction* and the Culture of Violence." *Harvard Educational Review*. 65.2 (1995): 299-314.

— "Racism and the Aesthetics of Hyper-real Violence: *Pulp Fiction* and Other Visual Tragedies." *Breaking In To the Movies: Film and the Culture of Politics*. Malden, Mass.: Blackwell, 2002. 195-235.

Giroux, Henry A., and Imre Szeman. "Ikea Boy Fights Back: *Fight Club*, Consumerism, and the Political Limits of Nineties Cinema." Lewis, *The End of Cinema* 95-104.

Glucksmann, André. *Violence on the Screen: A Report on Research into the Effects on Young People of Scenes of Violence in Films and Television*. Trans. Susan Bennett. London: The British Film Institute Education Department, 1971.

Glushanok, Paul. Rev. of *Bonnie and Clyde*, dir. Arthur Penn. *Cineaste*. 1.2 (1967): 14-17.

Godard, Jean-Luc. *Godard on Godard*. Eds. Jean Narboni and Tom Milne. Introduction. Richard Roud. New York: The Viking P, 1972.

Goldberg, Vicki. "Death Takes a Holiday, Sort Of." Goldstein 27-52.

Goldstein, Jeffrey. Introduction. Goldstein 1-6.

— 'Why We Watch." Goldstein 212-226.

— (ed.) *Why We Watch: The Attractions of Violent Entertainment*. New York: Oxford UP, 1998.

Gombrich, E.H. *Norm and Form: Studies in the Art of the Renaissance*. 1966. London: Phaidon, 1971.

Gombrich, E.H, Julian Hochberg, and Max Black. *Art, Perception, and Reality*. 1972. Baltimore: Johns Hopkins UP, 1984.

The Good, the Bad, and the Ugly. Dir. Sergio Leone. United Artists, 1966.

Goodfellas. Dir. Martin Scorsese. Warner Brothers, 1990.

Goodman, Steve. "Nihilism and the Philosophy of Virtue." Sumner 159-188.

Gorer, Geoffrey. "The Pornography of Death." *Identity and Anxiety: Survival of the Person in Mass Society*. Eds. Maurice R. Stein, Arthur J. Vidich, and David Manning White. New York: The Free P, 1960. 402-405.

Gottesman, Ronald and Richard Maxwell Brown, eds. *Violence in America: An Encyclopedia*. 3 vols. New York: Scribner, 1999.

Graham, Allison. "The Final Go-Around: Peckinpah's Wild Bunch at the End of the Frontier."*Mosaic: A Journal For the Interdisciplinary Study of Literature*. 16.1-2 (1983): 55-70.

Graham, Hugh Davis. "The Paradox of American Violence." Graham and Gurr 475-490.

Graham, Hugh Davis, and Ted Robert Gurr, eds. *Violence in America: Historical and Comparative Perspectives*. Beverly Hills: Sage Publications, 1979.

Grant, Barry Keith. "American Psycho/sis: The Pure Products of America Go Crazy." Sharrett, *Mythologies* 23-40.

— "Landmark Films." Gottesman and Brown 518-525.

— (ed.) *Planks of Reason: Essays on the Horror Film*. Metuchen, N.J: The Scarecrow P, 1984.

Grayson, Charles. *Stories For Men: An Anthology*. 1936. New York: Garden City Publishing, 1938.

The Great Train Robbery. Dir. Edwin S. Porter. Edison Manufacturing Company, 1903.

Green, Daniel. "*Natural Born Killers* and American Decline." *The Films of Oliver Stone*. Ed. Don Kunz. Lanham, Maryland: The Scarecrow P, 1997.

Greenberg, Harvey. "The Shows of Violence." *Journal of Popular Film and Television*. 26.2 (1998): 50-51.

Gripsrud, Jostein. "Skräck och fasa i kropp og själ: Om en historisk förflyttning i skräckfiktionens fokus." *Våld Från Alla Håll: Forskningsperspektiv På Våld i Rörliga Bilder*. Eds. Cecilia von Feilitzen, Michael Forsman, and Keith Roe. Stockholm/Stehag: Brutus Östlings Bokförlag, 1993. 227-248.

Grodal, Torben. *Moving Pictures: A New Theory of Film Genres, Feelings, and Cognition*. Oxford: Clarendon, 1997.

— *Cognition, Emotion and Visual Fiction: Theory and Typology of Affective Patterns and Genres in Film and Television*. Copenhagen: University of Copenhagen, 1994.

Gross, Larry. "Exploding Hollywood." *Sight and Sound*. 5.3 (1995): 8-9.

— "Hawks and the Angels." *Sight and Sound*. 7.2 (1997): 12-15.

Gross, Theodore L. *The Heroic Ideal in American Literature*. New York: The Free Press, 1971.

Grossman, Morris. "Art and Morality: On the Ambiguity of a Distinction." *Journal of Aesthetics and Art Criticism*. 32.1 (1973): 103-106.

Grønstad, Asbjørn. "The Lying Game? Historical Films and the Re-Invention of the 'Past'." *Film and History: An Interdisciplinary Journal of Film and Television Studies*. 2001 CD-ROM Annual. Cleveland: Historians Film Committee, 2002.

— "Peckinpah's *Walden*: The Violent Indictment of 'Civilization' in *The Wild Bunch*. From *Virgin Land to Disney World: Nature and Its Discontents in the USA of Yesterday and Today*. Ed. Bernd Herzogenrath. Amsterdam: Editions Rodopi, 2001. 167-186.

— "Straitjacketing the Image: Illocutionary Writing and the Obstruction of Cine-Semiosis in Hawks' *Scarface*." *Redoubt*. 29 (2001): 109-116.

— "Topographies of Defeat: Masculinity and Desolation in *Fat City* and *Junior Bonner*." *Kinema: A Journal for Film and Audiovisual Media*. 16 (2001): 33-48.

— "Violence as Form and Rhetoric: Peckinpah's *The Wild Bunch*." *American, British, and Canadian Studies*. 4 (2001): 212-227.

Gunning, Tom. "Film History and Film Analysis: The Individual Film in the Course of Time." *Wide Angle*. 12.3 (1990): 4-19.

Gunter, Barrie, Jackie Harrison, and Maggie Wykes. *Violence on Television: Distribution, Form, Context, and Themes*. London: Lawrence Erlbaum Associates, 2003.

Gunzenhäuser, Randi. "'All Plots Lead Toward Death:' Memory, History, and the Assassination of John. F. Kennedy." *Amerikastudien*. 43.1 (1998): 75-91.

Hagemann, E. R. "*Scarface*: The Art of Hollywood, Not 'The Shame of the Nation'." *Journal of Popular Culture*. 18.1 (1984): 30-42.

Hagenauer, Fedor, and James W. Hamilton. "*Straw Dogs*: Aggression and Violence in Modern Film." *American Imago*. 3 (1973): 221-248.

Hall, Stuart, and Paddy Whannel. *The Popular Arts*. 1964. London: Hutchinson Educational, 1969.

Hana-Bi. Dir. Takeshi Kitano. Milestone, 1997.

Hansen, Miriam. "Benjamin, Cinema and Experience: 'The Blue Flower in the Land of Technology." *New German Critique*. 40 (1987): 179-224.

Hanson, Curtis Lee. "Arthur Penn as Director." Wake and Hayden 182-194.

Hanson, Peter. *The Cinema of Generation X: A Critical Study of Films and Directors*. Jefferson, North Carolina: McFarland & Company, 2002.

Hantke, Steffen. "Violence Incorporated: John McNaughton's *Henry: Portrait of a Serial Killer* and the Uses of Gratuitous Violence in Popular Narrative." *College Literature*. 28.2 (2001): 29-47.

Harbord, Victoria. "Natural Born Killers: Violence, Film, and Anxiety." Sumner 137-156.

Harmetz, Aljean. "Man Was a Killer Long Before He Served a God." Bliss 169- 174.

Hausken, Liv. "Om det Utidige. Medieanalytiske Undersøkelser av Fotografi, Fortelling og Stillbildefilm." Diss. University of Bergen, 1998.

Hedges, Inez. *Breaking the Frame: Film Language and the Experience of Limits.* Bloomington: Indiana UP, 1991.

Hedling, Erik. "Regissören som kritikens hjältefigur. Om Kanoniseringen av Sam Peckinpah." *Filmhäftet: Tidskrift om Film och TV.* 3-4 (1992): 45-58.

Hegel, Georg Wilhelm Friedrich. *Hegel's Introduction to Aesthetics, Being The Introduction to the Berlin Aesthetics Lectures of the 1820s.* Trans. T.M. Knox. Oxford: Clarendon P, 1979.

Henry: Portrait of a Serial Killer. Dir. John McNaughton. Greycat Films, 1986.

Heredero, Carlos F. *Sam Peckinpah.* Madrid: Ediciones JC, 1982.

Hersh, Kristin. *Murder, Misery and Then Goodnight.* 4AD, 1998.

Herzog, Todd. "Scapegoat." Gottesman and Brown 96.

Hill, Annette. "Risky Business: Film Violence as an Interactive Penomenon." Stokes and Maltby 175-186.

— *Shocking Entertainment: Viewer Response to Violent Movies.* Luton: U of Luton P, 1997.

Hillier, Jim. "Arthur Penn." *Screen: The Journal of the Society for Education in Film and Television.* 10.1 (1969): 5-13.

— (ed.) *Cahiers du Cinéma. Volume 2. 1960-1968. New Wave, New Cinema, Re-evaluating Hollywood: An Anthology From* Cahiers du Cinéma *Nos. 103-207, January 1960-December 1968.* London: Routledge & Kegan Paul, 1986.

Hillier, Jim, and Peter Wollen, eds. *Howard Hawks: American Artist.* London: British Film Institute, 1996.

Hine, Robert V. *The American West: An Interpretive History.* Boston: Little, Brown and Company, 1973.

Hinman, Wilbur F. *Corporal Si Klegg and His 'Pard:' How They Lived and Talked, and What They did and Suffered, while Fighting for the Flag.* 1877. Cleveland: The N.G. Hamilton Publishing Co., 1892.

Hirsch, Foster. *The Dark Side of the Screen: Film Noir.* San Diego: A. S. Barnes, 1981.

Hitt, Jim. *The American West From Fiction (1823-1976) Into Film (1909-1986).* Jefferson, N. C.: McFarland and Company, 1990.

Hoberman, J. 'A Test for the Individual Viewer': *Bonnie and Clyde's* Violent Reception." Goldstein 116- 143.

Hofstadter, Richard. Introduction. Hofstadter and Lipset 3-8.

Hofstadter, Richard, and Seymour Martin Lipset, eds. *Turner and the Sociology of the Frontier.* New York: Basic Books, 1968

Hofstadter, Richard, and Michael Wallace, eds. *American Violence: A Documentary History.* New York: Vintage Books, 1971.

Hollingsworth, Keith. *The Newgate Novel, 1830-1847: Bulwer, Ainsworth, Dickens, and Thackeray.* Detroit: Wayne State UP, 1963.

Hollon, Eugene. W. *Frontier Violence: Another Look.* New York: Oxford UP, 1974.

Holm, Claus Krohn, Mette Weisberg, and Niels Weisberg. *Westerns: Theory and Analysis.* Copenhagen: Gjellerup 6 Gad, 1986.

Holoday, Perry W. *Getting Ideas From the Movies.* New York: Macmillan, 1933.

Horrocks, Roger. *Male Myths and Icons: Masculinity in Popular Culture.* New York: St. Martin's P, 1995.

Horsley, Jake. *The Blood Poets. A Cinema of Savagery 1958-1999: American Chaos. From* Touch of Evil *to* The Terminator. Lanham, Maryland: The Scarecrow P, 1999.

— *The Blood Poets. A Cinema of Savagery 1958-1999: Millennial Blues. From* Apocalypse Now *to* The Matrix. Lanham, Maryland: The Scarecrow P, 1999.

Howlett, Jana, and Rod Mengham, eds. *The Violent Muse: Violence and the Artistic Imagination in Europe 1910-1939.* Manchester: Manchester UP, 1994.

Hughes, Robert. *Culture of Complaint: The Fraying of America.* Oxford: Oxford UP, 1993.

Huhn, Thomas. "The Kantian Sublime and the Nostalgia for Violence." *Journal of Aesthetics and Art Criticism.* 53.3 (1995): 269-275.

Hulme, T.E. *Selected Writings.* Ed. Patrick McGuinness. Manchester: Fyfield Books, 1998.

Hume, David. "Of the Standard of Taste." *Four Dissertations.* 1757. Introduction John Immerwahr. Bristol: Thoemmes P, 1995. 203-240.

Hutcheon, Linda. *A Poetics of Postmodernism: History, Theory, Fiction.* New York: Routledge, 1988.

Huyssen, Andreas. *After the Great Divide: Modernism, Mass Culture, Postmodernism.* Bloomington: Indiana UP, 1986.

Hyams, Jay. *The Life and Times of the Western Movie.* New York: Gallery Books, 1983.

Iampolski, Mikhail. *The Memory of Tiresias: Intertextuality and Film.* Trans. Harsha Ram. Berkeley: U of California P, 1998.

Infante, Guillermo Cabrera. "Cowboy Cop." Hillier and Wollen 48-49.

Inglis, Ruth A. *Freedom of the Movies: A Report on Self-Regulation from the Commission on Freedom of the Press.* Chicago: The U of Chicago P, 1947.

Irwin, Mark. "Pulp and the Pulpit: The Films of Quentin Tarantino and Robert Rodriguez." *Literature and Theology: An International Journal of Religion, Theory and Culture.* 12.1 (1998): 70-81.

Jackie Brown. Dir. Quentin Tarantino. Miramax Films, 1997.

Jacobs, Jason. "Gunfire." *Sight and Sound.* 5.10 (1995): 38-41.

James. David E. *Allegories of Cinema: American Film in the Sixties.* Princeton, N.J.: Princeton UP, 1989.

Jameson, Fredric. *The Political Unconscious: Narrative as a Socially Symbolic Act.* London: Methuen, 1981.

— *Postmodernism, or, the Cultural Logic of Late Capitalism.* London: Verso, 1991. Jameson, Richard T. "Midsection: Sam Preckinpah." *Film Comment.* 17.1 (1981): 33-48.

Jauss, Hans Robert. *Toward an Aesthetic of Reception.* Trans. Timothy Bahti. Minneapolis: U of Minnesota P, 1982.

Jay, Martin. "Mimesis and Mimetology: Adorno and Lacoue-Labarthe." *Cultural Semantics: Keywords of Our Time.* Amherst: U of Massachusetts P, 1998. 120-137.

— *The Dialectical Imagination: A History of the Frankfurt School and the Institute of Social Research 1923-50.* London: Heinemann, 1973.

Jed, Stephanie. "The Scene of Tyranny. Violence and the Humanistic Tradition." Armstrong and Tennenhouse 29-44.

Jeffords, Susan. "The Big Switch: Hollywood Masculinity in the Nineties." *Film Theory Goes to the Movies.* Eds. Jim Collins, Hilary Radner, and Ava Preacher Collins. New York: Routledge, 1993. 196-208.

— "Can Masculinity be Terminated?" Graeme Turner 344-354.

— *The Remasculinization of America*. Bloomington: Indiana UP, 1989. Jerslev, Anne. "Violence and the Body in Contemporary Action and Horror Films." *Young: Nordic Journal of Youth Research*. 4.4 (1996): 39-53.

Jenkins, Steve. Rev. of *The Killing*, dir. Stanley Kubrick. *Monthly Film Bulletin*. 51 (1984). http://www.visualmemory.co.uk/sk/films/thekilling.html

Jewett, Richard, and John Shelton Lawrence. *The American Monomyth*. Garden City, N.Y.: Anchor P, 1977.

Johnson, Albert. Rev. of *Bonnie and Clyde*, dir. Arthur Penn. *Film Quarterly*. 21.3 (1967-68): 45-48.

Johnson, Denis. *Angels*. New York: Alfred A. Knopf, 1983.

Johnson, William. Rev. of *Straw Dogs*, dir. Sam Peckinpah. *Film Quarterly*. 26.1 (1972): 61-63.

Jowett, Garth S. "'A Significant Medium for the Communication of Ideas:' The Miracle Decision and the Decline of Motion Picture Censorship, 1952-1968. *Movie Censorship and American Culture*. Ed. Francis G. Couvares. Washington: Smithsonian Institution Press, 1996. 258-276.

Jowett, Garth S, Ian C. Jarvie, and Kathryn H. Fuller. *Children and the Movies: Media Influence and the Payne Fund Controversy*. Cambridge: Cambridge UP, 1996.

Juhasz, Alexandra. "The Phallus Unfetished: The End of Masculinity As We Know It In Late-1990s 'Feminist' Cinema." Lewis, *The End of Cinema* 210-221.

Kael, Pauline. "Crime and Poetry." Schickel and Simon 38-58.

— "Notes on the Nihilist-Poetry of Sam Peckinpah." *The New Yorker*. 12 January 1976: 70-75.

— Rev. of *A Clockwork Orange*, dir. Stanley Kubrick. *Filmfacts: A Publication of the American Film Institute*. 14.24 (1971): 653-655.

Kagan, Norman. *The Cinema of Oliver Stone*. New York: Continuum, 1995.

— *The Cinema of Stanley Kubrick*. 1972. Oxford: Roundhouse, 2000.

Kant, Immanuel. *The Critique of Judgement*. 1790. Trans. James Creed Meredith. Oxford: Clarendon P, 1991.

Kaplan, Ann E., ed. *Women in Film Noir*. London: BFI, 1978.

Karimi, Amir Massoud. *Toward a Definition of the American Film Noir, 1941- 1949*. New York: Arno P, 1976.

Karpf, Stephen Louis. *The Gangster Film: Emergence, Variation and Decay of a Genre*. New York: Arno P, 1973.

Kastenbaum, Robert. "Thanatology." Gottesman and Brown 290-291.

Kastenbaum, Robert, and Ruth Aisenberg. *The Psychology of Death*. New York: Springer Publishing Company, 1972.

Kauffmann, Stanley. *Before my Eyes: Film Criticism and Comment*. New York: Da Capo, 1980.

— *Living Images. Film Criticism and Comment*. New York: Harper and Row, 1975.

— "Made to Order." Schickel and Simon 33-38.

Kawin, Bruce F. *Telling it Again and Again: Repetition in Literature and Film*. Ithaca: Cornell UP, 1972.

Keen, Sam. *Fire in the Belly: On Being a Man*. New York: Bantam, 1991.

Keller, James R. *Queer (Un)Friendly Film and Television*. Jefferson, North Carolina: McFarland and Company, 2002.

Keniston, Kenneth. *Young Radicals*. New York: Harvest, 1968.

Keough, Peter, ed. *Flesh and Blood: The National Society of Film Critics on Sex, Violence, and Censorship*. San Francisco: Mercury House, 1995.

Kermode, Frank. *The Sense of an Ending: Studies in the Theory of Fiction*. London: Oxford UP, 1966.

Killer's Kiss. Dir. Stanley Kubrick. United Artists, 1955.

The Killing. Dir. Stanley Kubrick. United Artists, 1956.

Killing Zoe. Dir. Roger Avary. October Films, 1994.

Kimmel, Michael S. "The Contemporary 'Crisis' of Masculinity in Historical Perspective." *The Making of Masculinities: The New Men's Studies*. Ed. Harry Brod. Boston: Allen and Unwin, 1987. 121-153.

Kinder, Marsha. *Blood Cinema: The Reconstruction of National Identity in Spain*. Berkeley: U of California P, 1993.

— "Violence American Style: The Narrative Orchestration of Violent Attractions." Slocum 63-100.

Kinder, Marsha, and Beverle Houston. *Close-Up: A Critical Perspective on Film*. New York: Harcourt Brace Jovanovich, 1972.

King, Geoff. *New Hollywood Cinema: An Introduction*. London: I.B.Tauris, 2002.

Kirkham, Pat, and Janet Thumim, eds. *You Tarzan: Masculinity, Movies and Men*. London: Lawrence and Wishart, 1993.

Kitar̄o [sic], Nishida. *Art and Morality*. 1923. Trans. David A. Dilwort and Valdo H. Viglielmo. Honolulu: The UP of Hawaii, 1973.

Kitses, Jim. *Horizons West: Anthony Mann, Budd Boetticher, Sam Peckinpah: Studies of Authorship Within the Western*. 1969. Bloomington: Indiana UP, 1970.

Knight, Arthur. Rev. of *The Wild Bunch*, dir. Sam Peckinpah. *Filmfacts: A Publication of the American Film Institute*. 12.10 (1969): 219-220.

Kohtes, Martin Maria. *Guerilla Theater: Theorie und Praxis des Politischen Straßentheaters in den USA (1965-1970)*. Tybingen: Forum Modernes Theater, 1990.

Kolker, Robert. "Oranges, Dogs, and Ultra-Violence." *Journal of Popular Film*. 1.3 (1972): 159-172.

Krieger, Murray. "My Travels With the Aesthetic." *Revenge of the Aesthetic: The Place of Literature in Theory Today*. Ed. Michael P. Clark. Berkeley: U of California P, 2000. 208-236.

Kriegsman, Alan M. Rev. of *A Clockwork Orange*, dir. Stanley Kubrick. *Filmfacts: A Publication of the American Film Institute*. 14.24 (1971): 655.

Kristeva, Julia. *Powers of Horror: An Essay on Abjection*. Trans. Leon S. Roudiez. New York: Columbia UP, 1982.

Kristiansen, Claus K. "Voldens Virkelighet." *Z Filmtidsskrift*. 48 (1994): 18-20.

Kroker, Arthur, and Michael Dorland. "Panic Cinema: Sex in the Age of the Hyperreal." Sharrett, *Crisis Cinema* 11-16.

Krutnik, Frank. *In a Lonely Street : Film Noir, Genre, Masculinity*. London: Routledge, 1991.

Kübler-Ross, Elisabeth. *On Death and Dying*. New York : Macmillan, 1969.

Kuntzel, Thierry. "The Film-Work, 2." *Camera Obscura*. 5 (1980): 7-69.

Labarthe, André, and Jean-Louis Comolli. "The Arthur Penn Interview." Wake and Hayden 165-173.

Lane, Anthony. "Degrees of Cool." *New Yorker* 10 Oct. 1994: 95-97.

Lang, Berel. "The Form of Aesthetics." *Journal of Aesthetics and Art Criticism*. 27.1 (1968): 35-47.

Lang, Robert. *Masculine Interests: Homoerotics in Hollywood Film*. New York: Columbia UP, 2002.

Langer, Lawrence L. *The Age of Atrocity: Death in Modern Literature*. Boston: Beacon P, 1978.

Langfeld, Herbert Sidney. *The Æsthetic Attitude*. 1920. Port Washington, N.Y.: Kennikat P, 1967.

Larsen, Otto N., ed. *Violence and the Mass Media*. New York: Harper and Row, 1968.

Lasch, Christopher. *The Culture of Narcissism: American Life in an Age of Diminishing Expectations*. New York: Warner Books, 1979.

Lawrence, D. H. *Women in Love*. 1920. Hertfordshire: Wordsworth Classics, 1992.

Leach, Michael. *I Know it When I see it: Pornography, Violence, and Public Sensitivity*. Philadelphia: The Westminster Press, 1975.

Ledbetter, Mark. *Victims and the Postmodern Narrative or Doing Violence to the Body: An Ethic of Reading and Writing*. New York: St. Martin's P, 1996.

Lee. Everett S. "The Turner Thesis Re-Examined." Hofstadter and Lipset 65- 72.

Legman, Gershon. *Love and Death: A Study in Censorship*. New York: Hacker Art Books, 1963.

Leitch, Thomas. *Crime Films*. Cambridge: Cambridge UP, 2002.

Lenihan, John H. *Showdown: Confronting Modern America in the Western Film*. Urbana: U of Illinois P, 1980.

Leutrat, J.-L. *Le Western: Archéologie d'un genre*. Lyon: Presses Universitaires de Lyon, 1987.

Levinas, Emmanuel. *Ethics and Infinity*. Trans. Richard A. Cohen. Pittsburgh, Pa.: Duquesne UP, 1995.

— "Time and the Other." *The Levinas Reader*. Ed. Seán Hand. Oxford: Basil Blackwell, 1989. 37-58.

— *Totality and Infinity: An Essay on Exteriority*. Trans. Alphonso Lingis. The Hague: Nijhoff, 1969.

Levinson, Jerrold, ed. *Aesthetics and Ethics: Essays at the Intersection*. Cambridge: Cambridge UP, 1998.

Levy, Shawn. "Jock of Gold." *Sight and Sound*. 9.12 (1999): 16-19.

Lewis, Jon, ed. *The End of Cinema As We Know It*. New York: New York UP, 2001.

— "Money Matters: Hollywood in the Corporate Era." *The New American Cinema*. Ed. Jon Lewis. Durham: Duke UP, 1998. 87-121.

Lewis, Patricia Scheiern. "Fine Arts." Gottesman and Brown 555-559.

Lewis, R. W. B. *The Picaresque Saint: Representative Figures in Contemporary Fiction*. Philadelphia: Keystone Books, 1961.

Lindenberger, Herbert. "The Mimetic Bias in Modern Anglo-American Criticism." Spariosu 1-26.

Lipman, Amanda. Rev. of *Pulp Fiction*, dir. Quentin Tarantino. *Sight and Sound*. 4.11 (1994): 50-51.

Lippard, Chris. "Directors." Gottesman and Brown 526-529.

Liszka, James Jakób. "Mythic Violence: Hierarchy and Transvaluation." *Semiotica*. 54.1-2 (1985): 223-249.

Litch, Mary M. *Philosophy Through Film*. New York: Routledge, 2002.

Little Caesar. Dir. Mervyn LeRoy. Warner Brothers, 1931.

Livingston, Paisley. *Literature and Rationality: Ideas of Agency in Theory and Fiction*. Cambridge: Cambridge UP, 1991.

Lloyd, Ronald. *American Film Directors: The World As They See It*. New York: F. Watts, 1976.

LoBrutto, Vincent. *Stanley Kubrick: A Biography*. New York: Donald I. Fine Books, 1997.

Lodge, David, ed. *Modern Criticism and Theory. A Reader*. London: Longman, 1988.

The Long Goodbye. Dir. Robert Altman. Lions Gate Films, 1973.

Longinus. *On the Sublime*. Trans. James A. Arieti and John M. Crossett. Toronto: Edwin Mellen P, 1985.

Lorand, Ruth. "Beauty and Its Opposites." *Journal of Aesthetics and Art Criticism*. 53.4 (1994): 399-406.

Lorenz, Konrad. *On Aggression*. 1963. Trans. Marjorie Latzke. London: Methuen and Co., 1966.

Lotman, Jurij. *Semiotics of Cinema*. Trans. Mark E. Suino. Ann Arbor: U of Michigan, 1976.

Luck, Richard. *Sam Peckinpah*. Herts: Pocket Essentials, 2000.

Lukacs, John. "America's Malady is not Violence but Savagery." Rose 349-358.

Lynn, Kenneth. "Violence in American Literature and Folklore." Graham and Gurr 133-143.

Lyons, Charles H. *The New Censors: Movies and the Culture Wars*. Philadelphia: Temple UP, 1997.

Lyotard, Jean-François. *Discours, figure*. Paris : Klincksieck, 1971.

— "On the Strength of the Weak. " Trans. A. K. M. Adam. *Critical Theology*. 1 (1991): 27-35.

— *The Postmodern Condition: A Report on Knowledge*. 1979. Trans. Geoff Bennington and Brian Massumi. Manchester: Manchester UP, 1997.

M, J. C. Rev. of *Scarface*. *The New Yorker*. 28 May 1932: 51-52.

Maalouf, Amin. *In the Name of Identity: Violence and the Need to Belong*. 1996. Trans. Barbara Bray. New York: Arcade Publishing, 2000.

MacCabe, Colin, ed. *High Theory/Low Culture: Analysing Popular Television and Film*. Manchester: Manchester UP, 1986.

MacCann, Richard Dyer, ed. *Film: A Montage of Theories*. New York: E.P. Dutton & Co, 1966.

Mack, Burton. "Introduction: Religion and Ritual." *Violent Origins: Walter Burkert, René Girard, and Jonathan Z. Smith on Ritual Killing and Cultural Formation*. Ed. Robert G. Hamerton-Kelly. Stanford: Stanford UP, 1987. 1-32.

Macnab, Geoffrey. Rev. of *The Way of the Gun*, dir. Christopher McQuarrie. *Sight and Sound*. 10.12 (2000): 57.

Mainar, Luis M. Garcia. *Narrative and Stylistic Patterns in the Films of Stanley Kubrick*. Rochester, New York: Camden House, 1999.

Maltby, Richard. "'D' for Disgusting: American Culture and English criticism." *Hollywood and Europe: Economics, Culture, National Identity 1945-95*. Eds. Geoffrey Nowell-Smith and Steven Ricci. London: British Film Institute, 1998. 104-115.

— "Grief in the Limelight." Al Capone, Howard Hughes, the Hays Code and the Politics of the Unstable Text." Combs 133-182.

— *Harmless Entertainment: Hollywood and the Ideology of Consensus*. Metuchen, N.J.: Scarecrow P, 1983.

— Introduction. Stokes and Maltby 1-20.

— "The Spectacle of Criminality." Slocum 117-152.

Mamber, Stephen. "Simultaneity and Overlap in Stanley Kubrick's *The Killing*." *Postmodern Culture*. 8.2 (1998). 19 Apr. 2002 .

Man, Glenn. *Radical Visions: American Film Renaissance 1967-1976*. Westport, Conn.: Greenwood P, 1994.

Man Bites Dog. Dirs. Rémy Belvaux, André Bonzel, and Benoît Poelvoorde. Roxie Releasing, 1992.

The Man Who Shot Liberty Valence. Dir. John Ford. Paramount Pictures, 1962.

Marc, David. "Popular Culture." Gottesman and Brown 562-567.

Marcuse, Herbert. *The Aesthetic Dimension: Toward a Critique of Marxist Aesthetics*. 1977. Boston: Beacon P, 1978.

— *One-Dimensional Man: Studies in the Ideology of Advanced Industrial Society*. 1964. Boston: Beacon P, 1967.

Marsh, Peter. *Aggro: The Illusion of Violence*. London: J.M. Dent & Sons, 1978.

Marshall, Cynthia. *The Shattering of the Self: Violence, Subjectivity, and Early Modern Texts*. Baltimore: The Johns Hopkins UP, 2002.

Marshall, Henry Rutgers. *Pain, Pleasure, and Æsthetics: An Essay Concerning the Psychology of Pain and Pleasure, With Special Reference to Æsthetics*. London: Macmillan, 1894.

Marshall, Susan Elaine. "Within the Moral Eye – Peckinpah's Art of Visual Narration." Diss. University of Florida, 1984.

Mason, Fran. *American Gangster Cinema: From* Little Caesar *to* Pulp Ficion. Basingstoke: Palgrave, 2002.

Mast, Gerald. *Film. Cinema. Movie: A Theory of Experience*. 1977. Chicago: U of Chicago P, 1983.

— *Howard Hawks, Storyteller*. New York: Oxford UP, 1982.

Maxfield, James F. *The Fatal Woman: Sources of Male Anxiety in American Film Noir, 1941-1991*. Madison, N.J.: Fairleigh Dickinson UP, 1996.

Maynard, Richard A., ed. *The American West on Film: Myth and Reality*. Rochelle Park, N.J. : Hayden Book Company, 1974.

Mayne, Judith. *Cinema and Spectatorship*. London: Routledge, 1993. 1-9.

McArthur, Colin. "Sam Peckinpah's West." *Sight and Sound*. 36.4. (1967): 180- 81.

McBride, Joseph, ed. *Hawks on Hawks*. Berkeley: U of California P, 1982.

McCarthy, Todd. *Howard Hawks: The Grey Fox of Hollywood*. New York: Grove P, 1997.

McCarty, John. *Hollywood Gangland: The Movies' Love Affair with the Mob*. New York: St. Martin's P. 1993.

McCarty, John Alan. "Sam Peckinpah and *The Wild Bunch*. *Film Heritage*. 5.2 (1969-70): 1-10.

McCaughey, Martha, and Neal King, eds. *Reel Knockouts: Violent Women in the Movies*. Austin: U of Texas P, 2001.

McCauley, Clark. "When Screen Violence Is Not Attractive." Goldstein 144- 162.

McConnell, Frank D. *The Spoken Seen: Film and the Romantic Imagination*. Baltimore: The Johns Hopkins UP, 1975.

McKenna, Andrew J. *Violence and Difference: Girard, Derrida and Deconstruction*. Urbana: U of Illinois P, 1992.

McKinney, Devin. "Violence: The Strong and the Weak." Prince, *Screening Violence* 99-109.

— *"The Wild Bunch*: Innovation and Retreat." Prince, *Sam Peckinpah's* The Wild Bunch 175-199.

McKinney, Doug. *Sam Peckinpah*. Boston: Twayne Publishers, 1979.

McReynolds, Douglas J. "Alive and Well: Western Myth in Western Movies*." Literature/ Film Quarterly.* 26.1 (1998): 46-52.

Mead, Margaret, and Rhoda Métraux, eds. *The Study of Culture at a Distance.* 1953. New York: Berghahn Books, 2000.

Medved, Michael. *Hollywood vs. America.* 1992. New York: HarperPerennial, 1993.

Meehan, Eileen R. "'Holy Commodity Fetish, Batman!': The Political Economy of a Commercial Intertext." *The Many Lives of the Batman.* Eds. Roberta E. Pearson, and William Uricchio. New York: BFI-Routledge, 1991. 47-65.

Mekas, Jonas. "Notes on the New American Cinema." MacCann 333-340.

Mellen, Joan. *Big Bad Wolves: Masculinity in the American Film.* London: Elm Tree Books, 1978.

Merleau-Ponty, Maurice. *Sense and Non-Sense.* Trans. Hubert L. Dreyfus and Patricia Allen Dreyfus. Evanston, Ill.: Northwestern UP, 1964.

Merrill, Robert, ed. *Ethics/Aesthetics: Post-Modern Positions.* Washington DC: Maisonneuve P, 1988.

Mesce, Bill. *Peckinpah's Women: A Reappraisal of the Portrayal of Women in the Period Westerns of Sam Peckinpah.* Lanham, M.D.: Scarecrow, 2001.

Metcalfe, Stanley J. *Evolutionary Economics and Creative Destruction.* London: Routledge, 1998.

Metz, Christian. *Language and Cinema.* Trans. Donna Jean Umiker-Sebeok. The Hague: Mouton Publishers, 1974.

— "Methodological Propositions for the Analysis of Film." Trans. Diana Matias. *Screen Reader 2: Cinema and Semiotics.* London: Society for Education in Film and Television, 1981. 86-98.

— "On the Impression of Reality in the Cinema." *Film Language: A Semiotics of the Cinema.* Trans. Michael Taylor. New York: Oxford UP, 1974. 3-15.

Meyer, William J. "Structural Violence, Peace, and the Good Life." *Insights from Film into Violence and Oppression: Shattered Dreams of the Good Life.* Ed. John P. Lowell. Westport: Praeger, 1998. 3-21.

Middleton, Peter. *The Inward Gaze: Masculinity and Subjectivity in Modern Culture.* London: Routledge, 1992.

Miles, Josephine. "Toward a Theory of Style and Change." *Journal of Aesthetics and Art Criticism.* 22.1 (1963): 63-67.

Miller, J. Hillis. *The Ethics of Reading: Kant, de Man, Eliot, Trollope, James and Benjamin.* New York: Columbia UP, 1987.

— "Is There an Ethics of Reading?" Phelan 79-101.

— *Tropes, Parables, Performatives : Essays on Twentieth-Century Literature.* New York: Harvester Wheatsheaf, 1990.

Miller, Mark Crispin. "In Defense of Sam Peckinpah." *Film Quarterly.* 28.3 (1975): 2-17.

Miller, William Ian. *Humiliation and Other Essays on Honor, Social Discomfort, and Violence.* Ithaca: Cornell UP, 1993.

Milne, Tom. "Brushing up the Gangster Film." Wake and Hayden 220.

— Rev. of *Bonnie and Clyde*, dir. Arthur Penn. *Sight and Sound*. 36.4 (1967): 203-204.

— Rev. of *The Wild Bunch*, dir. Sam Peckinpah. *Sight and* Sound. 38.4 (1969): 208-209.

— Rev. of *Straw Dogs*, dir. Sam Peckinpah. *Sight and Sound*. 41.1 (1971/72): 50.

Mintz, Steven & Randy Roberts, eds. *Hollywood's America: United States History Through Its Films*. St. James, New York: Brandywine Press, 1993.

Mitchell, Lee Clarke. "Violence in the Film Western." Slocum 176-191.

— *Westerns: Making the Man in Fiction and Film*. Chicago: U of Chicago P, 1996.

Mitchell, W.J.T. "The Commitment to Form; or, Still Crazy After All These Years." *PMLA*. 118.2 (2003): 321-325.

— *Iconology: Image, Text, Ideology*. Chicago: U of Chicago P, 1986.

— *Picture Theory: Essays on Verbal and Visual Representation*. Chicago: U of Chicago P, 1994.

— "Representation of Violence." Gottesman and Brown 39-48.

Mitford, Jessica. *The American Way of Death*. New York: Simon and Schuster, 1963.

Mitry, Jean. *Semiotics and the Analysis of Film*. 1987. Trans. Christopher King. London: The Athlone P, 2000.

Modleski, Tania. "The Context of Violence in Popular Culture." *Chronicle of Higher Education*. 47.33 (2001): B15-B16.

Moeran, Brian. "The Beauty of Violence: *Jidaigeki, Yakuza* and the 'Eroduction' Films in Japanese Cinema." *The Anthropology of Violence*. Ed. David Riches. New York: Basil Blackwell, 1986. 103-117.

Moravia, Alberto. *The Voyeur*. 1985. Trans. Tim Parks. London: Futura, 1989.

Morgenstern, Joseph. Rev. of *Bonnie and Clyde*. Wake and Hayden 218.

— "Ugly," and "A Thin, Red Line." Schickel and Simon 25-29.

Morgenstern, Joseph, and Stefan Kanfer, eds. *Film 69/70: An Anthology by the National Society of Film Critics*. New York: Simon & Schuster, 1970.

Moriel, Liora. "Erasure and Taboo. A Queer Reading of *Bonnie and Clyde*." Friedman 148-176.

Morrison, Ken. "The Technology of Homicide: Constructions of Evidence and Truth in the American Murder Film." Sharrett, *Mythologies* 301-316.

Mottram, James. "Daddy Cool." *Sight and Sound*. 12.3 (2002): 24-26.

Mourlet, Michael. "In Defense of Violence." Jim Hillier 132-134.

Mozina, Andrew Thomas. "The Art of Sacrifice: The Evolution of the Scapegoat Theme in Joseph Conrad's Fiction." Diss. Washington University, 1998.

Mukařovský, Jan. *Aesthetic Function, Norm and Value as Social Facts*. Trans.

Mark E. Suino. Ann Arbor: Michigan Slavic Contributions, 1979.

Muller, Eddie. *Dark City Dames: The Wicked Women of Film Noir*. New York: Regan Books, 2001.

Mumby, Dennis K, ed. *Narrative and Social Control: Critical Perspectives*. Newbury Park: Sage Publications, 1993.

Munby, Jonathan. *Public Enemies, Public Heroes: Screening the Gangster From Little Caesar to Touch of Evil*. Chicago: U of Chicago P, 1999.

Munro, Thomas. "Art and Violence." *Journal of Aesthetics and Art Criticism*. 27.3 (1969): 317-322.

— *Form and Style in the Arts: An Introduction to Aesthetic Morphology*. Cleveland: The P of Case Western Reserve U in collaboration with The Cleveland Museum of Art, 1970.

Murch, Walter. *In the Blink of an Eye: A Perspective on Film Editing*. Sydney: AFTRS, 1992.

Murdock, Graham. "Reservoirs of Dogma." *Ill Effects: The Media/Violence Debate*. Eds. Martin Barker and Julian Petley. London: Routledge, 1997. 78-83.

Murray, Edward. *Ten Film Classics: A Re-Viewing*. New York: Frederick Ungar Publishing Co, 1978.

Nachbar, Jack, ed. *Focus on the Western*. Englewood Cliffs, N.J.: Prentice-Hall, 1974.

Naremore, James. *More Than Night: Film Noir in its Contexts*. Berkeley: U of California P, 1998.

Naremore, James, and Patrick Brantlinger. "Introduction: Six Artistic Cultures." Naremore and Brantlinger 1-23.

— (eds.) *Modernity and Mass Culture*. Bloomington: Indiana UP, 1991.

Nashville. Dir. Robert Altman. Paramount Pictures, 1975.

Natoli, Joseph. *Speeding to the Millennium: Film and Culture 1993-1995*. New York: State U of NY P, 1998.

Natural Born Killers. Dir. Oliver Stone. Warner Brothers, 1994.

Neale, Steve. *Genre and Hollywood*. London: Routledge, 2000.

— "Masculinity as Spectacle. Reflections on Men and Mainstream Cinema." *Screening the Male: Exploring Masculinities in Hollywood Cinema*. 1983. Eds. Steven Cohan and Ina Rae Hark. London: Routledge, 1993. 9-20.

— "Sam Peckinpah, Robert Ardrey and the Notion of Ideology." *Film Form*. 1 (1976): 107-111.

— "Westerns and Gangster Films Since the 1970s." *Genre and Contemporary Hollywood*. Ed. Steve Neale. London: BFI Publishing, 2002. 27-47.

Neibaur, James L. *Tough Guy: The American Movie Macho*. Jefferson, North Carolina: McFarland and Company, 1989.

Neill, Alex and Aaron Ridley, eds. *The Philosophy of Art: Readings Ancient and Modern*. New York: McGraw-Hill, 1995.

Nelson, Thomas Allen. *Kubrick: Inside a Film Artist's Maze*. Bloomington: Indiana UP, 1982. 29-37.

Nesbet, Anne. "The Aesthetics of Violence in Russian and East German Literature." Diss. University of California, Berkeley, 1992.

Neupert, Richard. *The End: Narration and Closure in the Cinema*. Detroit: Wayne State UP, 1995.

Newman, David. "What's it Really All About? Pictures at an Execution." Friedman 32-41.

Newman, Kim. Rev. of *Reservoir Dogs*, dir. Quentin Tarantino. *Sight and Sound*. 3.1 (1993): 51-52.

— *Wild West Movies, or How the West was Found, Won, Lost, Lied About, Filmed and Forgotten*. London: Bloomsbury, 1990.

Newton, Adam Zachary. *Narrative Ethics*. Cambridge, Mass.: Harvard UP, 1995.

Nichols, Jill. "Violent Believing." Wright and Kaplan 391-395.

Nietzsche, Friedrich. *On the Genealogy of Morals*. 1887. Trans. Walter Kaufman and R.J. Hollingdale. New York: Vintage, 1967.

The Night of the Hunter. Dir. Charles Laughton. United Artists, 1955.

Nochimson, Martha P. "Waddaya Lookin' At? Re-reading the Gangster Genre Through 'The Sopranos'." *Film Quarterly*. 56.2 (2002-2003): 2-13.

Nochlin, Linda. *The Body in Pieces: The Fragment as a Metaphor of Modernity*. London: Thames & Hudson, 1994.

Nuttall, A.D. *Why Does Tragedy Give Pleasure?* Oxford: Clarendon P, 1996.
Nyman, Jopi. *Men Alone: Masculinity, Individualism, and Hard-Boiled Fiction.* Amsterdam: Costerus, 1997.

October. Dirs. Sergei Eisenstein and Grigori Aleksandrov. Amkino Corporation, 1927.
Oliver, Kelly, and Benigno Trigo. *Noir Anxiety.* Minneapolis: U of Minnesota P, 2002.
Olsen, Mark. "Fist in the Face." *Sight and Sound.* 10.11 (2000): 24-26.
Orr, John. *The Art and Politics of Film.* Edinburgh: Edinburgh UP, 2000.
Ostertag, Isa. "'I got them all:' (De-)Constructing Masculinity through Violence in Sam Peckinpah's *Straw Dogs. Amerikastudien–American Studies.* 43.4 (1998): 657-670.
Oudart, Jean-Pierre. "L'Idéologie moderniste dans quelques films récents: Un Discours en défaut." *Cahiers du Cinéma.* 232 (1971): 4-12.

Palahniuk, Chuck. *Fight Club.* 1996. London: Vintage, 1997.
Palmer, R. Barton. *Hollywood's Dark Cinema: The American Film Noir.* New York: Twayne Publishers, 1994.
— (ed.) *Perspectives on Film Noir.* New York: G. K. Hall, 1996.
Palmieri, Rory. "*Straw Dogs*: Sam Peckinpah and the Classical Western Narrative." *Studies in the Literary Imagination.* 16.1 (1983): 29-42.
Panhoff, Trygve. "Underholdningsvoldens Mekanikk." *Z Filmtidsskrift.* 64 (1998): 6-7.
Pareto, Vilfredo. *Sociological Writings.* Trans. Derick Mirfin. New York: Frederick A. Praeger, 1966.
Parish, James Robert, and Michael R. Pitts. *The Great Western Pictures.* Metuchen: The Scarecrow Press, 1976.
Parker, Dewitt H. *The Principles of Aesthetics.* 1920. Westport, Conn.: Greenwood P, 1946.
Parks, Rita. *The Western Hero in Film and Television: Mass Media Mythology.* Ann Arbor: UMI Research P, 1982.
Parrill, William. *Heroes' Twilight: The Films of Sam Peckinpah.* Minneapolis: Alpha Editions, 1980.
Partridge, Eric. *Dictionary of Slang and Unconventional English.* London: Routledge and Kegan Paul, 1961.
Paskow, Alan. "What is Aesthetic Catharsis?" *Journal of Aesthetics and Art Criticism.* 42.1 (1983): 59-68.
Pasolini, Pier Paolo. *Selected Poems.* 1982. Trans. Norman MacAfee and Luciano Martinengo. London: John Calder, 1984.
Pat Garrett and Billy the Kid. Dir. Sam Peckinpah. Metro-Goldwyn-Mayer, 1973.
Paths of Glory. Dir. Stanley Kubrick. United Artists, 1957.
Pawelczak, Andy. Rev. of *Natural Born Killers,* dir. Oliver Stone. *Films in Review.* 45.11-12 (1994): 57-58.
Peary, Gerald, ed. *Quentin Tarantino: Interviews.* Jackson: UP of Mississippi, 1998.
Pechter, William S. *Twenty-Four Times a Second: Films and Filmmakers.* New York: Harper & Row, 1971.
Penley, Constance, and Sharon Willis, eds. "Editorial: Male Trouble." *Camera Obscura: A Journal of Feminism and Film Theory.* 17 (1988): 4-5.
— *Male Trouble.* Minneapolis: U of Minnesota P, 1993.
Penn, Arthur. "Making Waves. The Directing of *Bonnie and Clyde*." Friedman 11-31.
— ' Private Integrity and Public Violence." Wake and Hayden 7-11.

Péret, Benjamin. *Mort aux vaches et au champ d'honneur.* Paris: Eric Losfeld, 1967.

Perrine, Toni A. *Film and the Nuclear Age: Representing Cultural Anxiety.* New York: Garland Publishing Inc., 1998.

Pettit, Arthur G. "The Polluted Garden: Sam Peckinpah's Double Vision of Mexico." *Southwest Review.* 62.3 (1977): 280-294.

Peucker, Brigitte. *Incorporating Images: Film and the Rival Arts.* Princeton: Princeton UP, 1995.

Phelan, James, ed. *Reading Narrative: Form, Ethics, Ideology.* Columbus: Ohio State UP, 1989.

Phillips, Gene D. *Stanley Kubrick: A Film Odyssey.* New York: Popular Library, 1975.

Phillipson, Michael. "Managing 'Tradition:' The Plight of Aesthetic Practices and Their Analysis in a Technoscientific Culture." *Visual Culture.* Ed. Chris Jenks. London: Routledge, 1995. 202-217.

Pierrot le Fou. Dir. Jean-Luc Godard. Pathé Contemporary Films, 1965. Pilkington, William T, and Don Graham, eds. *Western Movies.* Albuquerque: U of New Mexico P, 1979.

Pizzato, Mark. "Jeffrey Dahmer and Media Cannibalism: The Lure and Failure of Sacrifice." Sharrett, *Mythologies* 85-118.

Pizzello, Steven. "*Natural Born Killers* Blasts Big Screen with both Barrels." *Oliver Stone. Interviews.* Ed. Charles L.P. Silet. Jackson: UP of Mississippi, 2001. 137-157.

Plantinga, Carl. "Spectacles of Death: Clint Eastwood and Violence in *Unforgiven.*" *Cinema Journal.* 37.2 (1998): 65-80.

Plantinga, Carl, and Greg M. Smith, eds. *Passionate Views: Film, Cognition and Emotion.* Baltimore, Md.: Johns Hopkins UP, 1999.

Plato. *Republic.* Trans. Robin Waterfield. Oxford: Oxford UP, 1994.

Poague, Leland A. *Howard Hawks.* Boston: Twayne Publishers, 1982.

Polan, Dana. *Power and Paranoia: History, Narrative, and the American Cinema, 1940-1950.* New York: Columbia UP, 1986.

Ponga, Paula. "*Tango* According to Saura." *Carlos Saura: Interviews.* Ed. Linda M. Willem. Jackson: U of Mississippi, 2003. 150-155.

Poole, Roger. *Towards Deep Subjectivity.* London: Allen Lane the Penguin P, 1972.

Porfirio, Robert G. "No Way Out: Existential Motifs in the Film Noir." Silver and Ursini 77-94.

Porter, Vincent. *On Cinema.* London: Pluto Press, 1985.

Potter, W. James. *On Media Violence.* Thousand Oaks: Sage Publications, 1999.

Powdermaker, Hortense. *Hollywood: The Dream Factory. An Anthropologist Looks at the Movie-Makers.* Boston: Little, Brown & Company, 1950.

Powers, Stephen, David J. Rothman, and Stanley Rothman. *Hollywood's America: Social and Political Themes in Motion Pictures.* Boulder: Westview P, 1996.

Prendergast, Christopher. *The Order of Mimesis: Balzac, Stendhal, Nerval, Flaubert.* Cambridge: Cambridge UP, 1986.

— *The Triangle of Representation.* New York: Columbia UP, 2000.

Prince, Stephen. "Graphic Violence in the Cinema: Origins, Aesthetic Design, and Social Affects." Prince, *Screening Violence* 1-44.

— "The Hemorrhaging of American Cinema. *Bonnie and Clyde*'s Legacy of Cinematic Violence." Friedman 127-147.

— "Introduction: Sam Peckinpah, Savage Poet of American Cinema." Prince, *Sam Peckinpah's* The Wild Bunch 1-36.

— (ed.) *Sam Peckinpah's* The Wild Bunch. Cambridge: Cambridge UP, 1999.
— *Savage Cinema: Sam Peckinpah and the Rise of Ultraviolent Movies.* Austin: U of Texas P, 1998.
— (ed.) *Screening Violence.* New Brunswick, N.J.: Rutgers UP, 2000.
— *Visions of Empire: Political Imagery in Contemporary American Film.* New York: Praeger, 1992.
— "Why Do Film Scholars Ignore Movie Violence?" *The Chronicle of Higher Education.* 10 Aug. 2001: B18-B19.
Psycho. Dir. Alfred Hitchcock. Paramount Pictures, 1960.
The Public Enemy. Dir. William A. Wellman. Warner Brothers, 1931.
Pu p Fiction. Dir. Quentin Tarantino. Miramax Films, 1994.
Pye, Douglas. "Genre and Movies [The Western]." *Film Genre: Theory and Criticism.* Ed. Barry K. Grant. Metuchen, N.J.: The Scarecrow P, 1977. 195-211.

The Quiet Man. Dir. John Ford. Republic Pictures Corporation, 1952.

Rabinowitz, Paula. *Black and White and Noir: America's Pulp Modernism.* New York: Columbia UP, 2002.
Ratter, Nicole, ed. *Shots in the Mirror: Crime Films and Society.* New York: Oxford UP, 2000.
Raging Bull. Dir. Martin Scorsese. United Artists, 1980.
Rainer, Peter, ed. *Love and Hisses: The National Society of Film Critics Sound off on the Hottest Movie Controversies.* San Francisco: Mercury House, 1992.
Rashomon. Dir. Akira Kurosawa. RKO Radio Pictures, 1950.
Rausschenberg, Robert. "Hollywood – The Shock of Freedom in Films." *Time International: The Weekly Newsmagazine.* 8 Dec. 1967: 52-56.
Ray, Robert B. *A Certain Tendency of the Hollywood Cinema 1930-1980.* Princeton, N.J.: Princeton UP, 1985.
— *The Avant-Garde Finds Andy Hardy.* Cambridge, Mass.: Harvard UP, 1995.
— *How a Film Theory Got Lost and Other Mysteries in Cultural Studies.* Bloomington: Indiana UP, 2001.
Read, Herbert. "Towards a Film Aesthetic." MacCann 165-170.
Reed, Joseph W. *American Scenarios: The Uses of Film Genre.* Middletown: Wesleyan UP, 1989.
Regan, Stephen. "Introduction: The Return of the Aesthetic." *The Politics of Pleasure: Aesthetics and Cultural Theory.* Ed. Stephen Regan. Buckingham: Open UP, 1992. 1-16.
Renek, Morris. "Reflections on Violence as a Literary Tool." Estey and Hunter 285-291.
"The Report on Violence." *Film Bulletin.* 41.1 (1972): 4-6.
Reservoir Dogs. Dir. Quentin Tarantino. Miramax Films, 1992.
Rev. of *The Killing,* dir. Stanley Kubrick. *Time: The Weekly Newsmagazine.* 4 June 1956: 106.
Rev. of *Scarface,* dir. Howard Hawks. *Time: The Weekly Newsmagazine.* 18 Apr. 1932: 17.
Rev. of *Straw Dogs,* dir. Sam Peckinpah. *Time: The Weekly Newsmagazine.* 20 Dec. 1971: 85-87.
Reynolds, Joshua. *Discourses on Art.* 1797. Ed. Robert R. Wark. New Haven: Yale UP, 1988.
Rich, B. Ruby. "Art House Killers." *Sight and Sound.* 2.8 (1992): 5-6.

Ricouer, Paul. *The Symbolism of Evil*. Trans. Emerson Buchanan. New York: Harper & Row, 1967.

Ride the High Country. Dir. Sam Peckinpah. Metro-Goldwyn-Mayer, 1962.

Rieser, Max. "Problems of Artistic Form: The Concept of Art." *Journal of Aesthetics and Art Criticism*. 27.3 (1969): 261-269.

Riffaterre, Michael. *Fictional Truth*. Baltimore: The Johns Hopkins UP, 1990.

— *Semiotics of Poetry*. Bloomington: Indiana UP, 1978.

Riordan, James. *Stone: The Controversies, Excesses, and Exploits of a Radical Filmmaker*. New York: Hyperion, 1995.

Rittger, Guy C. "The Regime of the Exploding Body and the Erotics of Film Violence: Penn, Peckinpah, Tarantino, and Beyond... " Wright and Kaplan 357-362.

Rivette, Jacques. "Notes on a Revolution." Hillier 95.

Robinson, David. "Violence." *Sight and Sound*. 46.2 (1977): 74-78.

— *World Cinema: A Short History*. 1973. London: Eyre Methuen, 1981.

Robinson, Sally. "'Emotional Constipation' and the Power of Dammed Masculinity. *Deliverance* and the Paradoxes of Male Liberation." *Masculinity: Bodies, Movies, Culture*. Ed. Peter Lehman. New York: Routledge, 2001. 133-147.

Rodowick, D.N. "The Enemy Within: The Economy of Violence in *The Hills Have Eyes*." Grant 321-330.

— "Reading the Figural." *Camera Obscura: A Journal of Feminism and Film Theory*. 24 (1990): 11-46.

— *Reading the Figural, or, Philosophy after the New Media*. Durham: Duke UP, 2001.

Romney, Jonathan. *Short Orders: Film writing*. London: Serpent's Tail, 1997.

Root, Deborah. *Cannibal Culture: Art, Appropriation, and the Commodification of Difference*. Boulder: Westview P, 1996.

Ropars-Wuilleumier, Marie-Claire. "The Graphic in Filmic Writing: *À bout de souffle*, or The Erratic Alphabet." *Enclitic*. 5.2-6.1 (1982): 147-161.

Rose, Thomas. "How Violence Occurs: A Theory and Review of the Literature." Rose 26-53.

— (ed.) *Violence in America: A Historical and Contemporary Reader*. New York: Random House, 1969.

Ross, T.J. "Straw Dogs, Chessmen, and War Games." *Film Heritage*. 8.1 (1972): 1-6.

— "Western Approaches: A Note on Dialogue." Nachbar 78-80.

Rossellini, Roberto. "Seeing with our own eyes (1972)." *Roberto Rossellini: Magician of the Real*. Eds. David Forgacs, Sarah Lutton, and Geoffrey Nowell-Smith. London: BFI Publishing, 2000. 165-166.

Rothman, William. *The "I" of the Camera: Essays in Film Criticism, History and Aesthetics*. Cambridge: Cambridge UP, 1988.

— "Violence and Film." Slocum 37-46.

Russell, Catherine. *Narrative Mortality: Death, Closure, and New Wave Cinemas*. Minneapolis: U of Minnesota P, 1995.

Russo, Vito. *The Celluloid Closet: Homosexuality in the Movies*. New York: Harper and Row, 1981.

Ruth, David E. *Inventing the Public Enemy: The Gangster in American Culture, 1918-1934*. Chicago: U of Chicago P, 1996.

Ryan, Michael, and Douglas Kellner. "Films of the Late Sixties and Early

Seventies. From Counterculture to Counterrevolution, 1967-1971." Mintz and Roberts 265-274.

Salewicz, Chris. *Oliver Stone*. London: Orion Media, 1997.

Salt, Barry. "Cut and Shuffle." *Cinema: The Beginnings and the Future. Essays Marking the Centenary of the First Film Show Projected to a Paying Audience in Britain*. Ed. Christopher Williams. London: U of Westminster P, 1996. 171-183.

— 'Let a Hundred Flowers Bloom. Film Form, Style and Aesthetics." *Sight and Sound*. 43.2 (1974): 108-109.

Samuels, Charles Thomas. "Doing Violence." *The American Scholar*. 40.4 (1971): 695-699.

Santner, Eric L. *Stranded Objects: Mourning, Memory, and Film in Postwar Germany*. Ithaca: Cornell UP, 1990.

Sarris, Andrew. *The American Cinema: Directors and Directions 1929-1968*. New York: E.P. Dutton, 1968.

— Rev. of *Bonnie and Clyde*, dir. Arthur Penn. Wake and Hayden 222.

— Rev. of *The Wild Bunch*, dir. Sam Peckinpah. *Filmfacts: A Publication of the American Film Institute*. 12.10 (1969): 220-221.

— "The World of Howard Hawks." *Focus on Howard Hawks*. Ed. Joseph McBride. Englewood Cliffs, N.J.: Prentice-Hall, 1972. 35-47.

Sartre, Jean-Paul. No Exit *and Three Other Plays*. New York: Vintage Books, 1955.

Sarup, Madan. *An Introductory Guide to Post-Structuralism and Postmodernism*. 1988. Athens: The U of Georgia P, 1993.

Saving Private Ryan. Dir. Steven Spielberg. Paramount Pictures, 1998.

Savran, David. *Taking It Like A Man: White Masculinity, Masochism, and Contemporary American Culture*. Princeton, N.J.: Princeton UP, 1998.

Sayre, Gordon M., ed. *American Captivity Narratives*. Boston: Houghton Mifflin, 2000.

Scarface, Shame of the Nation. Dir. Howard Hawks. United Artists, 1932.

Scarry, Elaine. *The Body in Pain: The Making and Unmaking of the World*. New York: Oxford UP, 1985.

Schaff, Adam. Foreword. *The Fallacy of Social Science Research: A Critical Examination and New Qualitative Model*. By Pablo Gonzáles Casanova. Trans. Susan Beth Kapilian and Georganne Weller. New York: Pergamon P, 1981. ix-xiii.

Schatz, Thomas. *Hollywood Genres: Formulas, Filmmaking, and the Studio System*. Philadelphia: Temple UP, 1981.

— "The New Hollywood." Graeme Turner 184-205.

Schechter, Harold, and Jonna Gormely Semeiks. "Leatherstocking in 'Nam. Rambo, *Platoon*, and the American Frontier Myth." Combs 115-127.

Schickel, Richard. "Mastery of the 'Dirty Western.'" Morgenstern and Kanfer 150-152.

— *Second Sight: Notes on Some Movies 1965-1970*. New York: Simon & Schuster, 1972.

Schickel, Richard, and John Simon, eds. *Film 67/68: An Anthology by the National Society of Film Critics*. New York: Simon & Schuster, 1968.

Schlesinger, Arthur M. Jr. *The Crisis of Confidence: Ideas, Power and Violence in America*. London: Andre Deutsch, 1969.

Schneider, Steven Jay. "Killing in Style: The Aestheticization of Violence in Donald Cammell's *White of the Eye*." *Scope: An Online Journal of Film Studies*. June 2001. 24 Oct. 2001 .

Schrader, Paul. "Notes on Film Noir." *Film Comment*. 8 (1972): 8-13.

— "Sam Peckinpah Going to Mexico." Bliss 17-30.

Schubart, Rikke. "Passion and Acceleration: Generic Change in the Action Film." Slocum 192-207.

The Searchers. Dir. John Ford. Warner Brothers, 1956.

Segal, Naomi. "Who whom? Violence, Politics and the Aesthetic." Howlett and Mengham 141-149.

Segaloff, Nat. "Greenland." *Film Comment*. 29.1 (1993): 40-49.

Self, Will. "The American Vice." Karl French 71-81.

Selincourt, O. de. *Art and Morality*. London: Methuen, 1935.

Seltzer, Mark. *Serial Killers: Death and Life in America's Wound Culture*. New York: Routledge, 1998.

Senelick, Laurence. *The Prestige of Evil: The Murderer as Romantic Hero from Sade to Lacenaire*. New York: Garland Publishing, 1987.

Seul conre tous. Dir. Gaspar Noé. Strand Releasing, 1998.

Seven Samurai. Dir. Akira Kurosawa. Columbia Pictures, 1954.

Seydor, Paul. *Peckinpah: The Western Films*. Urbana: U of Illinois P, 1980.

— *Peckinpah: The Western Films. A Reconsideration*. Urbana: U of Illinois P, 1997.

— "Sam Peckinpah." *Sight and Sound*. 5.10 (1995): 18-23.

— "*The Wild Bunch* as Epic." Bliss 113-157.

— "*The Wild Bunch*: The Screenplay." Prince, *Sam Peckinpah's* The Wild Bunch 37-78.

Seyhan, Azade. "Visual Citations: Walter Benjamin's Dialectic of Text and Image." *Languages of Visuality: Crossings Between Science, Art, Politics, and Literature*. Ed. Beate Allert. Detroit: Wayne State UP, 1996. 229-241.

Shadoian, Jack. *Dreams and Dead Ends: The American Gangster/Crime Film*. Cambridge, Massachusetts: The MIT P, 1977.

Shaffer, Lawrence. "*The Wild Bunch* versus *Straw Dogs*." *Sight and Sound*. 41.3 (1972): 132-133.

Sharrett, Christopher. "Afterword. Sacrificial Violence and Postmodern Ideology." Sharrett, *Mythologies* 413-434.

— (ed.) *Crisis Cinema: The Apocalyptic Idea in Postmodern Narrative Film*. Washington D.C.: Maisonneuve P, 1993.

— "End of Story: The Collapse of Myth in Postmodern Narrative Film." Lewis, *The End of Cinema* 319-331.

— "The Idea of Apocalypse in *The Texas Chainsaw Massacre*." Grant 255-276.

— Introduction. Sharrett, *Mythologies of Violence in Postmodern Media* 9-20.

— "Introduction. Crisis Cinema." Sharrett, *Crisis Cinema* 1-10.

— (ed.) *Mythologies of Violence in Postmodern Media*. Detroit: Wayne State UP, 1999.

— "Peckinpah the Radical: The Politics of *The Wild Bunch*." Prince, *Sam Peckinpah's* The Wild Bunch 79-104.

— Rev. of *Gunfighter Nation: The Myth of the Frontier in Twentieth-Century America*, by Richard Slotkin. *Film Quarterly*. 47.1 (1993): 50-52.

Shaviro, Steven. *The Cinematic Body*. Minneapolis: U of Minnesota P, 1993.

Shelley, Jim. "The Boys are Back in Town." *Guardian*. 7 Jan. 1993: 7.

— "Down These Mean Streets Many Men Have Gone." *Times: Saturday Review*. 20 Feb. 1993: 12.

Sheppard, Anne. *Aesthetics: An Introduction to the Philosophy of Art*. Oxford: Oxford UP, 1987.

Shklovsky, Victor. "Art as Technique." Lodge 16-30.

Shulman, Robert. "Fiction." Gottesman and Brown 262-266.

Signorielli, Nancy, and George Gerbner. *Violence and Terror in the Mass Media: An Annotated Bibliography.* New York: Greenwood P, 1988.

Silver, Alain, and James Ursini, eds. *Film Noir: A Reader.* New York: Limelight Editions, 1996.

Silver, Alain, and Elizabeth Ward, eds. *Film Noir.* New York: Overlook P, 1979.

Silverado. Dir. Lawrence Kasdan. Columbia Pictures, 1985.

Silverman, Kaja. *Male Subjectivity at the Margins.* New York: Routledge, 1992.

— *The Threshold of the Visible World.* New York: Routledge, 1996.

— *World Spectators.* Stanford: Stanford UP, 2000.

Simmons, Garner. *Peckinpah: A Portrait in Montage.* Austin: U of Texas P, 1982.

Simon, John. "The Case for Inhumanity." Schickel and Simon 29-33.

— "Violent Idyll." Morgenstern and Kanfer 152-156.

Simmons, John L. "The Tragedy of Love in *The Wild Bunch.*" Bliss 90-106.

Sinclair, Alison. "Disasters of War: Image and Experience in Spain." Howlett and Mengham 77-87.

Sklar, Robert. "When Looks Could Kill: American Cinema of the Sixties." *Cineaste.* 16.1-2 (1987-88): 50-53.

Slocum, J. David, chair. "Do Film Scholars Ignore Movie Violence?" 2002.

— Society For Cinema Studies Conference. Westin Tabor Center, Denver. 25 May 2002.

— Rev. of *Mythologies of Violence in Postmodern Media,* by Christopher
Sharrett. *Film Quarterly.* 54.4 (2001): 58-59.

— (ed.) *Violence and American Cinema.* New York: Routledge, 2001.

— "Violence and American Cinema: Notes For an Investigation." Slocum 1-34.

Slotkin, Richard. "Dreams and Genocide: The American Myth of Regeneration Through Violence." *The Popular Culture Reader.* Eds. Jack Nachbar, Deborah Weiser, and John L. Wright. Bowling Green: Bowling Green U Popular P, 1978. 51-63.

— *The Fatal Environment: The Myth of the Frontier in the Age of Industrialization 1800-1890.* 1985. Norman: U of Oklahoma P, 1998.

— *Gunfighter Nation: The Myth of the Frontier in Twentieth-Century America.* 1992. Norman: U of Oklahoma P, 1998.

— *Regeneration Through Violence: The Mythology of the American Frontier, 1600-1860.* 1973. Norman: U of Oklahoma P, 2000.

Smith, Gavin. "Inside Out." *Film Comment.* 35.5 (1999): 58-68.

— "When You Know You're in Good Hands." Peary 97-114.

Smith, Henry Nash. *Virgin Land: The American West as Symbol and Myth.* Cambridge, Mass.: Harvard UP, 1950.

Smith, Joan. "Speaking Up For Corpses." Karl French 196-204.

Smith, Murray. *Engaging Characters: Fiction, Emotion and the Cinema.* Oxford: Clarendon Press, 1995.

Smith, Paul. "Eastwood Bound." Berger, Wallis, and Watson 77-97.

Sobchack, Vivian C. *The Address of the Eye: A Phenomenology of Film Experience.* Princeton: Princeton UP, 1992.

— "Inscribing Ethical Space: Ten Propositions on Death, Representation, and Documentary." *Quarterly Review of Film Studies.* 9.4 (1984): 283-300.

— "The Violent Dance: A Personal Memoir of Death in the Movies." *Graphic Violence on the Screen*. Ed. Thomas R. Atkins. New York: Monarch P, 1976. 79-96. Rpt. in Prince, *Screening Violence* 110-124.

Soldier Blue. Dir. Ralph Nelson. Avco Embassy Pictures, 1970.

Sontag, Susan. *Against Interpretation and Other Essays*. New York: Delta, 1966.

— *Illness as Metaphor*. 1978. New York: Penguin Books, 1983.

— "The Pornographic Imagination." *Styles of Radical Will*. London: Secker & Warburg, 1966. 44-47.

— *Regarding the Pain of Others*. New York: Farrar, Straus & Giroux, 2003. Sorel, Georges. *Reflections on Violence*. 1915. Trans. T.E. Hulme. New York: Peter Smith, 1941.

Sova, Dawn B. *Forbidden Films: Censorship Histories of 125 Motion Pictures*. New York: Facts on File, Inc., 2001.

Spariosu, Mihai. Introduction. Spariosu 1-12.

— (ed.) *Mimesis in Contemporary Theory: An Interdisciplinary Approach*. 2 vols. Philadelphia: John Benjamins, 1984.

— "Murder as Play: Conrad Aiken's *King Coffin*." Bogue and Cornis-Pope 165-180.

Sparshott, F.E. *The Structure of Aesthetics*. Toronto: U of Toronto P, 1963.

Sragow, Michael. "The Homeric Power of Peckinpah's Violence." *Atlantic Monthly*. 273.6 (1994): 116-122.

— Rev. of *The Wild Bunch*, dir. Sam Peckinpah. *Film Society Review*. 5.3 (1969): 31-37.

— "Sam Peckinpah: *The Wild Bunch*." Rainer 260-263.

Stagecoach. Dir. John Ford. United Artists, 1939.

Staiger, Janet. "Cinematic Shots: The Narration of Violence." *The Persistence of History: Cinema, Television and the Modern Event*. Ed. Vivian Sobchack. New York: Routledge, 1996. 39-54.

Stam, Robert. *Film Theory: An Introduction*. Malden, Mass.: Blackwell, 2000.

Stanley, Lisa. "Digital Domain uses Houdini to get inside Jack's Head." *Digital Animators*. 15 Mar. 2003

Starobinski, Jean. "The Natural and Literary History of Bodily Sensation." Trans. Lydia Davis. *Zone: Fragments For a History of the human Body*. Ed. Michel Feher et al. Vol. 2. New York: Urzone, 1989. 351-394.

Starrs, Roy. *Deadly Dialectics: Sex, Violence amd Nihilism in the World of Yukio Mishima*. Honolulu: U of Hawaii P, 1994.

Stein, Michael Eric. "The New Violence or Twenty Years of Violence in Films: An Appreciation." *Films in Review*. 46.1-2 (1995): 40-48; 46.3-4 (1995): 14-21.

Stephens, Chuck. "Both Barrels." *Film Comment*. 36.5 (2000): 16-17.

Stern, Lesley. "Meditation on Violence." *Kiss Me Deadly: Feminism and Cinema for the Moment*. Ed. Laleen Jayamanne. Sydney: Power Publications, 1995. 252-285.

Sternberg, Meir. *Expositional Modes and Temporal Ordering in Fiction*. Baltimore: Johns Hopkins UP, 1978.

Stevens, Brad. "All Cut Up." *Sight and Sound*. 3.7 (1993): 59.

Stewart, Garrett. *Between Film and Screen: Modernism's Photo Synthesis*. Chicago: U of Chicago P, 1999.

— *Death Sentences: Styles of Dying in British Fiction*. Cambridge, Mass.: Harvard UP, 1984.

— "Photo-gravure: Death, Photography, and Film Narrative." *Wide Angle: A Quarterly Journal of Film History, Theory and Criticism*. 9.1 (1987): 11- 31.

— ʿThresholds of the Visible: The Death Scene of Film." *Mosaic: A Journal for the Interdisciplinary Study of Literature*. 16.1-2 (1983): 33-54.

Stoddart, Helen. "'I Don't Know Whether To Look At Him or Read Him:' *Cape Fear* and Male Scarification." *Me Jane : Masculinity, Movies and Women*. Eds. Pat Kirkham and Janet Thumim. London: Lawrence & Wishart, 1995. 194-202. Stoehr, Kevin L, ed. *Film and Knowledge: Essays on the Integration of Images and Ideas*. Jefferson, North Carolina: McFarland and Company, 2002.

Stokes, Melvyn, and Richard Maltby, eds. *Identifying Hollywood's Audiences: Cultural Identity and the Movies*. London: British Film Institute, 1999.

Stone, Bryan P. "Religion and Violence in Popular Film." *The Journal of Religion and Film*. 3 1 (1999). 15 Dec. 1999 .

Strange Days. Dir. Kathryn Bigelow. 20th Century Fox Film Corporation, 1995.

Straw Dogs. Dir. Sam Peckinpah. Cinerama, 1971.

Striniati, Dominic, and Stephen Wagg, eds. *Come on Down? Popular Media Culture in Post-War Britain*. London: Routledge, 1992.

Strug, Cordell. "*The Wild Bunch* and the Problem of Idealist Aesthetics, or, How Long Would Peckinpah Last in Plato's Republic?" Bliss 80- 89.

Studlar, Gaylyn. *In the Realm of Pleasure: Von Sternberg, Dietrich, and the Masochistic Aesthetic*. Urbana: U of Illinois P, 1988.

— ʿShadowboxing: *Fat City* and the Malaise of Masculinity." *Reflections in a Male Eye: John Huston and the American Experience*. Eds. Gaylyn Studlar and David Desser. Eds. Washington: Smithsonian Institute P, 1993. 177-198.

Sumner, Colin. "Introduction: The Violence of Censure and the Censure of Violence." Sumner 1-6.

— (ed.) *Violence, Culture, and Censure*. London: Taylor & Francis, 1997.

Tan, Ed S. *Emotion and the Structure of Narrative Film: Film as an Emotion Machine*. Trans. Barbara Fasting. Mahwah, N.J.: Lawrence Erlbaum, 1996.

Tango. Dir. Carlos Saura. Adela Pictures, 1998.

Tarantino, Quentin. "*Pulp Fiction*." *Sight and Sound*. 4.11 (1994): 16-19.

Tasker, Yvonne. *Spectacular Bodies: Gender, Genre and the Action Cinema*. London: A Comedia Book Published by Routledge, 1993.

Taubin, Amy. Interview with Tim Roth. *Sight and Sound*. 2.8 (1992): 4.

— ʿThe Men's Room." *Sight and Sound*. 2.8 (1992): 2-4.

— ʿSo Good It Hurts." *Sight and Sound*. 9.11 (1999): 16-18.

Taxi Driver. Dir. Martin Scorsese. Columbia Pictures, 1976.

Taylor, Clyde R. *The Mask of Art: Breaking the Aesthetic Contract - Film and Literature*. Bloomington: Indiana UP, 1998.

Taylor, Ella. "Quentin Tarantino's *Reservoir Dogs* and the Thrill of Excess." Peary 41-48.

Taylor, Julie. *Paper Tangos*. Durham, N.C.: Duke UP, 1998.

Telotte, J. P. *Voices in the Dark: The Narrative Patterns of Film Noir*. Urbana: U of Illinois P, 1989.

The Terminator. Dir. James Cameron. Metro-Goldwyn-Mayer, 1984.

Tester, Keith. *Media, Culture and Morality*. London: Routledge, 1994.

Thomas, Brook. "Turner's 'Frontier Thesis' as a Narrative of Reconstruction." *Centuries' Ends, Narrative Means*. Ed. Robert Newman. Stanford: Stanford UP, 1996. 117-137.

Thomas, Dylan. *The Collected Letters*. London: Paladin, 1987.

Thomas, Tony. *The West That Never Was: Hollywood's Vision of the Cowboys and Gunfighters*. New York: A Citadel Press Book, 1989.

Thompson, Kristin. *Breaking the Glass Armour: Neoformalist Film Analysis*. Princeton: Princeton UP, 1988.

— *Eisenstein's Ivan the Terrible: A Neoformalist Analysis*. Princeton: Princeton UP, 1981.

— *Storytelling in the New Hollywood: Understanding Classical Narrative Technique*. Cambridge, Mass.: Harvard UP, 1999.

Thomson, David. *America in the Dark: The Impact of Hollywood Films on American Culture*. New York: William Morrow, 1977.

— "Death and its Details." *Film Comment*. 29.5 (1993): 12-18.

Tilghman, B. R. *But is it Art? The Value of Art and the Temptation of Theory*. Oxford: Basil Blackwell, 1984.

Todd, Drew. "The History of Crime Films." Rafter 15-45.

Todorov, Tzvetan. *Symbolism and Interpretation*. Trans. Catherine Porter. Ithaca: Cornell UP, 1982.

Tolstóy, Leo Nikolaevic. *What Is Art? and Essays on Art*. 1930. Trans. Aylmer Maude. London: Oxford UP, 1975.

Tompkins, Jane. *West of Everything: The Inner Life of Westerns*. Oxford: Oxford UP, 1992.

Toplin, Robert Brent. *History by Hollywood: The Use and Abuse of the American Past*. Urbana: U of Illinois P, 1996.

— *Unchallenged Violence: An American Ordeal*. Westport, Conn.: Greenwood P, 1975.

Torry, Robert. "Therapeutic Narrative: *The Wild Bunch, Jaws*, and Vietnam." *The Velvet Light Trap*. 31 (1993): 27-38.

Toynbee, Arnold. *A Study of History*. London: Oxford UP, 1934.

Trail, Armitage. *Scarface*. 1930. London: Bloomsbury, 1997.

The Treasure of the Sierra Madre. Dir. John Huston. Warner Brothers, 1948.

True Romance. Dir. Tony Scott. Warner Brothers, 1993.

Tsao, Leonardo Garcâia. *Sam Peckinpah*. Guadalajara: Universidad de Guadalajara, 1990.

Tudor, Andrew. *Image and Influence: Studies in the Psychology of Film*. New York: St. Martin's P, 1974.

Turner, Frederick Jackson. "The Significance of the Frontier in American History." *Frontier and Section*. Englewood Cliffs, N.J.: Prentice-Hall, 1961. 37-62.

Turner, Graeme. *Film as Social Practice*. 1988. London: Routledge, 1993.

— (ed.) Graeme Turner. *The Film Cultures Reader*. London: Routledge, 2002.

Turner, Mark. *Death is the Mother of Beauty: Mind, Metaphor, Criticism*. Chicago: U of Chicago P, 1987.

Turner, Ralph Lamar and Robert J. Higgs. *The Cowboy Way: The Western Leader in Film, 1945-1995*. Westport, Conn.: Greenwood P, 1999.

Turner, Victor. *From Ritual to Theatre: The Human Seriousness of Play*. New York City: Performing Arts Journal Publications, 1982.

Tuska, Jon. *Dark Cinema: American Film Noir in Cultural Perspective*. Westport: Greenwood P, 1984.

— *Encounters With Filmmakers: Eight Career Studies*. New York: Greenwood P, 1991.

Twain, Mark. *The Adventures of Huckleberry Finn*. 1884. Introduction. T.S. Eliot. London: The Cresset P, 1950.

Twitchell, James B. *Preposterous Violence: Fables of Aggression in Modern Culture*. New York: Oxford UP, 1989.

Tyler, Parker. *Screening the Sexes: Homosexuality in the Movies*. New York: Holt, Reinhart, Winston, 1972.

The UNESCO International Clearinghouse on Children and Violence on the Screen. Nordicom. Oct. 2002. Gøteborg University. 29 Oct. 2002. .

Unforgiven. Dir. Clint Eastwood. Warner Brothers, 1992.

Usai, Paolo Cherchi. *The Death of Cinema: History, Cultural Memory and the Digital Dark Age*. London: BFI Publishing, 2001.

Vacche, Angela Dalle. *Cinema and Painting: How Art is Used in Film*. Austin: U of Texas P, 1996.

Valenti, Jack. Statement by Jack Valenti, MPAA President, before The National Commission on the Causes and Prevention of Violence. Prince, Screening Violence 62-75.

Vera Cruz. Dir. Robert Aldrich. United Artists, 1954.

Virilio, Paul. *War and Cinema: The Logistics of Perception*. 1984. Trans. Patrick Camiller. London: Verso, 1989.

Vizzard, Jack. *See no Evil: Life Inside a Hollywood Censor*. New York: Simon & Schuster, 1970.

Vygotsky, Lev Semenovich. *The Psychology of Art*. Cambridge, Mass.: The M.I.T. P, 1971.

Wake, Sandra, and Nicola Hayden, eds. *The* Bonnie and Clyde *Book*. New York: Simon & Schuster, 1972.

Walker, Alexander. *National Heroes: British Cinema in the Seventies and Eighties*. London: Harrap, 1985.

— *Stanley Kubrick Directs*. New York: Harcourt Brace Jovanovich, 1971.

Walker, Janet. "Introduction. Westerns Through History." *Westerns: Films Through History*. Ed. Janet Walker. New York: Routledge, 2001. 1-24.

Walker, Michael. "Film Noir. Introduction." *The Movie Book of Film Noir*. Ed. Ian Cameron. London: Studio Vista, 1992. 8-38.

Walton, Kendall L. "How Remote are Fictional Worlds from the Real World?" *Journal of Aesthetics and Art Criticism*. 37.1 (1978): 11-23.

Warshow, Robert. "The Gangster as Tragic hero." Abel 83-88.

— "Movie Chronicle: The Westerner." Abel 89-106.

Watson, Paul. "There's no Accounting for Taste: Exploitation Cinema and the Limits of Film Theory." Cartmell 66-83.

Watt, Stephen. "Baudrillard's America (and Ours?): Image, Virus, Catastrophe." Naremore and Brantlinger 135-141.

Wead, George, and George Lellis. *Film: Form and Function*. Boston: Houghton Mifflin Company, 1981.

Weddle, David. *If they Move... Kill 'Em! The Life and Times of Sam Peckinpah*. New York: Grove P, 1994.

— "The Making of *The Wild Bunch*." *Film Comment*. 30.3 (1994): 44-57.

— "They Want To See Brains Flying Out?" *Sight and Sound*. 5.2 (1995): 20- 25.

— "Wild Things." *Sight and Sound*. 5.10 (1995): 24-32.

Week End. Dir. Jean-Luc Godard. Athos Films, 1967.

Weir, Robert F, ed. *Death in Literature*. New York: Columbia UP, 1980.

Wertham, Frederic. "The Goddess of Violence." Estey and Hunter 230-243.

— *Seduction of the Innocent*. New York: Rinehart & Company, 1954.

Wesley, Marilyn C. "The Paradox of Virility: Narrative Violence in a Modern Anthology." *Journal of the Short Story in English*. 33 (1999): 75-87.

Whalen, Tom. "Film Noir: Killer Style." *Literature/Film Quarterly*. 23.1 (1995): 2-5.

Whitaker, Sheila. Introduction. *Film and Censorship: The Index Reader*. Ed. Ruth Petrie. London: Cassell, 1997. 1-3.

White, Hayden. *The Context of the Form: Narrative Discourse and Historical Representation*. Baltimore: The Johns Hopkins UP, 1990.

White, Lionel. *Clean Break*. New York: Dutton, 1955.

Whitehall, Richard. "Talking with Peckinpah." *Sight and Sound*. 38.4 (1969): 172-175.

Whitehouse, Charles. Rev. of *Fight Club*, dir. David Fincher. *Sight and Sound*. 9.12 (1999): 45-46.

Whitehouse, Mary. "Time to Face Responsibility." Karl French 52-61.

Whitmer, Barbara. *The Violence Mythos*. Albany: State U of New York P, 1997.

Whittock, Trevor. *Metaphor and Film*. Cambridge: Cambridge UP, 1990.

Wiesenthal, Christine, and Brad Bucknell. "Essays into the Imagetext: An Interview with W.J.T. Mitchell." *Mosaic: a Journal for the Interdisciplinary Study of Literature*. 33.2 (2000): 1-23.

Wild, David. "Quentin Tarantino, Violence and Twisted Wit." Peary 124-135.

The Wild Bunch. Dir. Sam Peckinpah. Warner Brothers, 1969.

Williams, James G. *The Bible, Violence, and the Sacred: Liberation from the Myth of Sanctioned Violence*. San Francisco: Harper, 1991.

Williams, Linda Ruth. "Women Can Only Misbehave." *Sight and Sound*. 5.2 (1995): 26-27.

Williams, Tony. "Narrative Patterns and Mythic Trajectories in Mid-1980s Vietnam Movies." *Inventing Vietnam: The War in Film and Television*. Ed. Michael Anderegg. Philadelphia: Temple UP, 1991. 129-130.

— Rev. of *Justified Lives: Morality and Narrative in the Films of Sam Peckinpah*, by Michael Bliss. *Film Quarterly*. 48.2 (1994-95): 62-63.

— Rev. of *Savage Cinema: Sam Peckinpah and the Rise of Ultraviolent Movies*, by Stephen Prince. *Film Quarterly*. 53.2 (1999-2000): 55-56.

Williams, William Carlos. *In the American Grain*. 1925. New York: New Directions, 1956.

Willis, Donald C. *The Films of Howard Hawks*. Metuchen: The Scarecrow P, 1975.

Wiloquet-Maricondi, Paula. "Full-Metal-Jacketing, or Masculinity in the Making." *Cinema Journal*. 33.2 (1994): 5-21.

Wilson, Ronald W. "'Then the Timetable Breaks Down:' The Function of the Voice-Over Narrator in Stanley Kubrick's *The Killing*." *Creative Screenwriting*. 7.5 (2000): 76-78.

Wind, Edgar. *Art and Anarchy*. 1964. Evanston, Illinois: Northwestern UP, 1985.

Wolf, William. "Wasn't That Just Lovely, the Way His Head Exploded?." Maynard 110-113.

Wolfe, Charles. "Film: Overview." Gottesman and Brown 512-518.

Wollen, Peter. "Cinema's Conquistadors." *Sight and Sound*. 2.7 (1992): 20-23.

— *Paris Hollywood: Writings on Film*. London: Verso, 2002.

Wood, Robin. *Howard Hawks*. 1968. London: The British Film Institute, 1981.

Worringer, Wilhelm. *Abstraction and Empathy: A Contribution to the Psychology of Style*. 1908. Trans. Michael Bullock. Chicago: Elephant Paperbacks, 1997.

Wright, Will. *Sixguns and Society: A Structural Study of the Western*. 1975. Berkeley: U of California P, 1977.

Wright, Will, and Steven Kaplan, eds. *The Image of Violence in Literature, the Media, and Society.* Proc. of Society for the Interdisciplinary Study of Social Imagery, March 1995, U of Southern Colorado. Pueblo: Society for the Interdisciplinary Study of Social Imagery, 1995.

Wölfflin, Heinrich. *Principles of Art History: The Problem of the Development of Style in Later Art.* 1915. Trans. M.D. Hottinger. New York: Dover Publications, 1932.

Yeats, William Butler. *On the Boiler.* Dublin: The Cuala P, 1938.

— *Stories of Michael Robartes and His Friends: An Extract Made From a Record by His Pupils.* Dublin: The Cuala P, 1931.

Yoos, George E. "A Work of Art as a Standard of Itself." *Journal of Aesthetics and Art Criticism.* 26.1 (1967): 81-89.

Young, Lola. *Fear of the Dark: 'Race,' Gender and Sexuality in the Cinema.* London: Routledge, 1996.

Zillmann, Dolf. "The Psychology of the Appeal of Portrayals of Violence." Goldstein 179-211.

Zimmerman, Paul D. Rev. of *A Clockwork Orange,* dir. Stanley Kubrick. *Filmfacts: A Publication of the American Film Institute.* 14.24 (1971): 652-653.

Ziolkowski, Theodore. *Dimensions of the Modern Novel: German Texts and European Contexts.* Princeton, N.J.: Princeton UP, 1969.

Index of Names

Index of Film Titles

Index of Subjects

Film Culture in Transition

General Editor: *Thomas Elsaesser*

Thomas Elsaesser, Robert Kievit and Jan Simons (eds.)
Double Trouble: Chiem van Houweninge on Writing and Filming, 1994
ISBN paperback 978 90 5356 025 9

Thomas Elsaesser, Jan Simons and Lucette Bronk (eds.)
Writing for the Medium: Television in Transition, 1994
ISBN paperback 978 90 5356 054 9

Karel Dibbets and Bert Hogenkamp (eds.)
Film and the First World War, 1994
ISBN paperback 978 90 5356 064 8

Warren Buckland (ed.)
The Film Spectator: From Sign to Mind, 1995
ISBN paperback 978 90 5356 131 7; ISBN hardcover 978 90 5356 170 6

Egil Törnqvist
Between Stage and Screen: Ingmar Bergman Directs, 1996
ISBN paperback 978 90 5356 137 9; ISBN hardcover 978 90 5356 171 3

Thomas Elsaesser (ed.)
A Second Life: German Cinema's First Decades, 1996
ISBN paperback 978 90 5356 172 0; ISBN hardcover 978 90 5356 183 6

Thomas Elsaesser
Fassbinder's Germany: History Identity Subject, 1996
ISBN paperback 978 90 5356 059 4; ISBN hardcover 978 90 5356 184 3

Thomas Elsaesser and Kay Hoffmann (eds.)
Cinema Futures: Cain, Abel or Cable? The Screen Arts in the Digital Age, 1998
ISBN paperback 978 90 5356 282 6; ISBN hardcover 978 90 5356 312 0

Siegfried Zielinski
Audiovisions: Cinema and Television as Entr'Actes in History, 1999
ISBN paperback 978 90 5356 313 7; ISBN hardcover 978 90 5356 303 8

Kees Bakker (ed.)
Joris Ivens and the Documentary Context, 1999
ISBN paperback 978 90 5356 389 2; ISBN hardcover 978 90 5356 425 7

Egil Törnqvist
Ibsen, Strindberg and the Intimate Theatre: Studies in TV Presentation, 1999
ISBN paperback 978 90 5356 350 2; ISBN hardcover 978 90 5356 371 7

Michael Temple and James S. Williams (eds.)
The Cinema Alone: Essays on the Work of Jean-Luc Godard 1985-2000, 2000
ISBN paperback 978 90 5356 455 4; ISBN hardcover 978 90 5356 456 1

Patricia Pisters and Catherine M. Lord (eds.)
Micropolitics of Media Culture: Reading the Rhizomes of Deleuze and Guattari, 2001
ISBN paperback 978 90 5356 472 1; ISBN hardcover 978 90 5356 473 8

William van der Heide
Malaysian Cinema, Asian Film: Border Crossings and National Cultures, 2002
ISBN paperback 978 90 5356 519 3; ISBN hardcover 978 90 5356 580 3

Bernadette Kester
Film Front Weimar: Representations of the First World War in German Films of the Weimar Period (1919-1933), 2002
ISBN *paperback 978 90 5356 597 1;* ISBN *hardcover 978 90 5356 598 8*

Richard Allen and Malcolm Turvey (eds.)
Camera Obscura, Camera Lucida: Essays in Honor of Annette Michelson, 2003
ISBN paperback 978 90 5356 494 3

Ivo Blom
Jean Desmet and the Early Dutch Film Trade, 2003
ISBN paperback 978 90 5356 463 9; ISBN hardcover 978 90 5356 570 4

Alastair Phillips
City of Darkness, City of Light: Émigré Filmmakers in Paris 1929-1939, 2003
ISBN paperback 978 90 5356 634 3; ISBN hardcover 978 90 5356 633 6

Thomas Elsaesser, Alexander Horwath and Noel King (eds.)
The Last Great American Picture Show: New Hollywood Cinema in the 1970s, 2004
ISBN paperback 978 90 5356 631 2; ISBN hardcover 978 905356 493 6

Thomas Elsaesser (ed.)
Harun Farocki: Working on the Sight-Lines, 2004
ISBN paperback 978 90 5356 635 0; ISBN hardcover 978 90 5356 636 7

Kristin Thompson
Herr Lubitsch Goes to Hollywood: German and American Film after World War I, 2005
ISBN paperback 978 90 5356 708 1; ISBN hardcover 978 90 5356 709 8

Marijke de Valck and Malte Hagener (eds.)
Cinephilia: Movies, Love and Memory, 2005
ISBN paperback 978 90 5356 768 5; ISBN hardcover 978 90 5356 769 2

Thomas Elsaesser
European Cinema: Face to Face with Hollywood, 2005
ISBN paperback 978 90 5356 594 0; ISBN hardcover 978 90 5356 602 2

Michael Walker
Hitchcock's Motifs, 2005
ISBN paperback 978 90 5356 772 2; ISBN hardcover 978 90 5356 773 9

Nanna Verhoeff
The West in Early Cinema: After the Beginning, 2006
ISBN paperback 978 90 5356 831 6; ISBN hardcover 978 90 5356 832 3

Anat Zanger
Film Remakes as Ritual and Disguise: From Carmen to Ripley, 2006
ISBN paperback 978 90 5356 784 5; ISBN hardcover 978 90 5356 785 2

Wanda Strauven
The Cinema of Attractions Reloaded, 2006
ISBN paperback 978 90 5356 944 3; ISBN hardcover 978 90 5356 945 0

Malte Hagener
*Moving Forward, Looking Back: The European Avant-garde and the Invention of Film
    Culture, 1919-1939,* 2007
ISBN paperback 978 90 5356 960 3; ISBN hardcover 978 90 5356 961 0

Tim Bergfelder, Sue Harris and Sarah Street
*Film Architecture and the Transnational Imagination: Set Design in 1930s European
    Cinema,* 2007
ISBN paperback 978 90 5356 984 9; ISBN hardcover 978 90 5356 980 1

Jan Simons
Playing the Waves: Lars von Trier's Game Cinema, 2007
ISBN paperback 978 90 5356 991 7; ISBN hardcover 978 90 5356 979 5

Marijke de Valck
Film Festivals: From European Geopolitics to Global Cinephilia, 2007
ISBN paperback 978 90 5356 192 8; ISBN hardcover 978 90 5356 216 1